Verse by Verse Commentary on

EZEKIEL

Enduring Word Commentary Series
By David Guzik

The grass withers, the flower fades,
but the word of our God stands forever.
Isaiah 40:8

Commentary on Ezekiel

Copyright ©2021 by David Guzik

Printed in the United States of America or in the United Kingdom

Print Edition ISBN: 978-1-939466-67-9

Enduring Word

5662 Calle Real #184

Goleta, CA 93117

Electronic Mail: ewm@enduringword.com

Internet Home Page: www.enduringword.com

Contents

Ezekiel 1 – Ezekiel's Vision of God and His Throne

A. Introduction to the vision.

1. (1) Ezekiel among the captives.

Now it came to pass in the thirtieth year, in the fourth *month*, on the fifth *day* of the month, as I *was* among the captives by the River Chebar, *that* the heavens were opened and I saw visions of God.

a. **In the thirtieth year, in the fourth month, on the fifth day**: Ezekiel's account of his prophecy isn't a fairy tale from an unknown time and place. He was a real man who lived in a real place and on a real day had remarkable **visions of God**.

i. The **thirtieth year** was likely the age of the prophet Ezekiel. According to Numbers 4:3, priests normally began their temple service in their **thirtieth year**. This date also means that Ezekiel grew up during the reform years of King Josiah (640-690 B.C.).

ii. Ezekiel's prophetic ministry "was in a sense a compensation for the priestly ministry which the misfortune of exile had snatched away from him. When his moment of ministry was due to begin, God summoned him to another sphere of work. The priest was commissioned as a prophet." (Taylor)

iii. "If Ezekiel were thirty years old in 593, therefore, he would have been born about 622, during the reign of the pious King Josiah. About 600, when he was some twenty-three years of age, the prophet married. With his wife he went to Babylonia as an exile in 597 at the age of twenty-six. The last dated prophecy of his book (Ezekiel 29:17) is that of the year 571, when he would have been fifty-one. Meanwhile he would have lost his wife when he was thirty-seven (24:18)." (Vawter and Hoppe)

7

b. **I was among the captives by the River Chebar**: In a series of attacks, the Babylonian Empire overwhelmed the Kingdom of Judah and they carried away captives in three waves:

- 605 B.C. – Jerusalem was attacked, and Daniel and other captives were taken to Babylon.

- 597 B.C. – Jerusalem was attacked, treasure taken from the temple, and more captives taken to Babylon.

- 587 B.C. – Jerusalem falls and almost everyone remaining in the kingdom was exiled.

i. Ezekiel was taken captive in the second phase, in 597 B.C. 2 Kings 24:12-16 describes the conquest that led to Ezekiel's captivity. There is no indication that he ever returned to Judah.

ii. Ezekiel's prophetic ministry began when Judah still stood as an independent kingdom (though under Babylon's powerful domination) and the temple still stood and functioned in Jerusalem. During this time, before Judah's complete conquest, there were many false prophets in Jerusalem and Babylonia who claimed God would rescue Judah and those already taken captive (like Ezekiel) would soon return (Jeremiah 28:1-4; 29:15-28). Ezekiel's message was a rebuke because of the sinful wish to escape the deserved judgment the Babylonians would soon bring, and to give God's people *real* hope, instead of the empty hope of the false prophets.

iii. **Among the captives**: "The arresting fact at the outset of our reading is that to a man in exile, and at a time when the national outlook was of the darkest, God granted these unveilings of Himself in a mystic and marvellous imagery." (Morgan)

iv. **Among the captives**: "He was a victim of a common ancient Near Eastern policy toward conquered peoples: the mass deportation of entire populations designed to break down national resistance at home by removing political and spiritual leadership, and to bolster the economy and military machine of the conqueror's homeland." (Block)

v. **The River Chebar**: "The river Kebar, a navigable canal, flowed southeast from the city of Babylon." (Alexander)

c. **The heavens were opened and I saw visions of God**: Ezekiel experienced these amazing visions by the river. Apparently, they came before him as **visions**, mental images like dreams while awake.

i. **Heavens were opened**: "There was a supreme, sovereign, and Divine power and authority by which this was done; it is not said the heavens

did open, but they were opened. It was no meteor, chasm, or yawning."
(Poole)

2. (2-3) The word of the LORD and the hand of the LORD upon Ezekiel.

On the fifth *day* of the month, which *was* in the fifth year of King Jehoiachin's captivity, the word of the LORD came expressly to Ezekiel the priest, the son of Buzi, in the land of the Chaldeans by the River Chebar; and the hand of the LORD was upon him there.

a. **Which was in the fifth year of King Jehoiachin's captivity**: By many reckonings, the captivity of King Jehoiachin (2 Kings 24) happened in 597 B.C., ten years before the complete fall of the Kingdom of Judah. The **fifth year** of his captivity would have been five years before the complete fall of Jerusalem and Judah.

i. "The specific date of his call is fixed at the fifth day of the fourth month. Assuming a spring New Year, the call came to him on the fifth day of Tammuz, which for the year 593 B.C. translates as July 31." (Block)

b. **The word of the LORD came expressly to Ezekiel the priest**: Not only did God's word come to **Ezekiel the priest**, but it came in a remarkable way – **expressly**.

i. The name **Ezekiel** "Signifies either, the strength of God, or, strengthened by God." (Poole)

ii. Feinberg listed what we know of **Ezekiel** the man. We know:

- The meaning of his name.
- He was probably born in 627 B.C. (if Ezekiel 1:1 refers to his age).
- He was a priest (Ezekiel 1:3).
- He was taken captive with King Jehoiachin in 597 B.C. (Ezekiel 1:2, 33:21).
- He was at Chebar, likely a royal canal of Nebuchadnezzar (Ezekiel 1:3).
- He was married and had his own home (Ezekiel 8:1, 24:18).
- His wife died during his ministry and God commanded him to not remarry (Ezekiel 24:16-18).
- He served during the same time as Jeremiah and Daniel, making no mention of Jeremiah but three mentions of Daniel (Ezekiel 14:14, 14:20, 28:3).

• He prophesied for about 20 years (Ezekiel 1:2 and 29:17).

iii. **Ezekiel the priest**: "No other prophet, not even the professional priest Jeremiah (Jeremiah 1:1), displays such an intense interest in priestly matters (sacrifices…regulations concerning ceremonial purity, the temple, precision in description and dating)." (Block)

c. **In the land of the Chaldeans by the River Chebar**: Ezekiel likely lived with other Jewish captives in this city or town on the river.

d. **The hand of the LORD was upon him there**: Ezekiel received God's word in a special way (**expressly**). He also was God's agent or representative in a special way because **the hand of the LORD was upon him**.

i. "'The hand of the Lord was upon him' connotes the idea of God's strength on behalf of the person involved (3:14; cf. Isaiah 25:10; 41:10, 20), a concept inherent in the name 'Ezekiel' (*yehezqel*), which means 'God strengthens.'" (Alexander)

B. Ezekiel's vision of God and the living creatures.

1. (4) The whirlwind out of the north.

Then I looked, and behold, a whirlwind was coming out of the north, a great cloud with raging fire engulfing itself; and brightness *was* all around it and radiating out of its midst like the color of amber, out of the midst of the fire.

a. **A whirlwind was coming out of the north**: Ezekiel saw a **whirlwind** – something like a tornado – coming from **the north**. The **north** is often associated with God's judgment through Israel's powerful enemies (Jeremiah 1:14-15) and Israel's captivity (Jeremiah 3:18).

i. This begins Ezekiel's description of what might be the most unusual and detailed vision of God in the Scriptures.

ii. Taking Ezekiel 1-3 as a unit, it is also the longest and most in-depth description of a prophet's calling in the Scriptures. "The vision Ezekiel had at the time of his call never left him but influenced his thought continually. It was the knowledge of God: holy, glorious and sovereign. The prophet does not show a struggle with his feelings such as is so evident in Jeremiah's life and service." (Feinberg)

iii. It was significant that this vision of God and the living creatures came from the direction of captivity and conquest imposed upon Israel. It was a way of saying that those calamities were from God.

b. **A great cloud with raging fire engulfing itself**: The **whirlwind** Ezekiel saw was associated with the great images of God's presence. The **cloud** by day and **fire** by night was the expression of God's presence with Israel through the wilderness (Exodus 13:21-22). A **raging fire engulfing itself** is a reminder of the burning bush that Moses saw, which burned but did not consume itself (Exodus 3:2).

i. One great effect of this vision was to assure Ezekiel that Yahweh was in fact the sovereign God of all creation – no matter how great Babylon and her gods seemed to be. "The multiplicity of temples, the incredible prosperity of the city, the hive of industry and culture, all this would have made any Hebrew captive feel how small his home country was and how great were the all-conquering gods of Nebuchadrezzar." (Taylor)

c. **Brightness was all around it and radiating out of its midst**: This radiating **brightness** is an expression of the glory of God.

i. "If the message of Isaiah centers about the salvation of the Lord, that of Jeremiah about the judgment of the Lord, and that of Daniel about the kingdom of the Lord, then that of Ezekiel is concerned with the glory of the Lord." (Feinberg)

2. (5-9) The four living creatures.

Also from within it *came* **the likeness of four living creatures. And this** *was* **their appearance: they had the likeness of a man. Each one had four faces, and each one had four wings. Their legs** *were* **straight, and the soles of their feet** *were* **like the soles of calves' feet. They sparkled like the color of burnished bronze. The hands of a man** *were* **under their wings on their four sides; and each of the four had faces and wings. Their wings touched one another.** *The creatures* **did not turn when they went, but each one went straight forward.**

a. **From within it came the likeness of four living creatures**: Four remarkable beings were notable from **within** this whirlwind of God's presence. Ezekiel later identified these remarkable **creatures** as *cherubim* (Ezekiel 10:8-15), angels of unique power and glory surrounding God.

i. Some try to emphasize the connection between what Ezekiel described and the artistic images of half-beast, half-human monsters of ancient cultures. Yet the Biblical idea of *cherubim* goes back much further.

- Cherubim first appear in the garden of Eden, those who guarded the way to the tree of life with a flaming sword (Genesis 3:24).
- Artistic designs of cherubim were prominent on the lid to the ark of the covenant, the mercy seat (Exodus 25:18-20).

- Since the ark of the covenant represented the presence of God among Israel, Yahweh was sometimes called He *who dwells between the cherubim* (1 Samuel 4:4, 2 Samuel 6:2; 1 Chronicles 13:6; Psalm 80:1, 99:1; Isaiah 37:16). This was an earthly artistic expression of a heavenly reality (Hebrews 8:5). Sometimes the phrase speaks of the earthly picture, and sometimes the heavenly reality.

- The interior of the tabernacle was decorated with designs of cherubim, giving the impression to anyone in the tabernacle that they were surrounded by cherubim (Exodus 26:1).

- The veil separating the most holy place of the tabernacle was decorated with cherubim, adding to the sense of their presence (Exodus 26:31).

- The designs of cherubim were prominent in Solomon's temple (1 Kings 6:23-35).

- The four creatures mentioned by John surrounding the throne of God are rightly thought to be cherubim (Revelation 4:6-8).

- Before his fall, Satan was among the cherubim covering God's throne (Ezekiel 28:14-16).

ii. "Certainly Ezekiel was acquainted with cherubim from his training in the temple, with its many representations of these creatures (Exodus 25–26; 36–37; 1 Kings 6; 2 Chronicles 3)." (Alexander)

b. **They had the likeness of a man**: Ezekiel noted that they were *not* men; they were angelic beings, not human beings. Yet they had **the likeness of a man** – in general form and structure, they looked like men.

i. As the description following will show, they were unlike any person on earth – men don't have **four faces** and **four wings**! Yet they were generally more like men than dragons or whales or other forms.

ii. When angelic beings appear to men and women in the Bible, they often have *the likeness of a man*. Perhaps the general form and appearance of angels is something like the general form and appearance of human beings.

c. **Each one had four faces**: Ezekiel will describe their faces in the following lines. The fact that *one* being had *four* faces perhaps indicates that some beings can comprise more than one *person*. In a way beyond our total comprehension, there is one God in three persons; perhaps the **four faces** indicate that these cherubim comprise one being in four persons.

d. **Each one had four wings**: Cherubim are a very special class of angelic beings, and this is one of the few places in Scripture that tells us that **wings** are associated with angelic beings at all.

i. The artistic designs of cherubim commanded to be made with the tabernacle, temple, and the ark of the covenant emphasized their wings (Exodus 25:20 and 37:9; 1 Kings 6:24-27 and 8:7).

ii. In Isaiah 6:1-4, the prophet described his heavenly vision where he saw beings he called *seraphim* who had six wings. It is likely that *cherubim* and *seraphim* are the same beings described from slightly different perspectives or noting different details. The name *seraphim* means *burning ones*, which seems to fit with these cherubim as described in Ezekiel 1:13.

e. **Their legs were straight**: Being in **the likeness of a man**, they had something like human legs – but with very different feet, **like the soles of calves' feet**.

f. **They sparkled like the color of burnished bronze**: These beings had a shiny, radiant appearance. They **sparkled** and gave off something of a **bronze** color.

i. "There is scarcely any thing that gives a higher lustre than highly *polished* or *burnished brass*. Our blessed Lord is represented with legs like *burnished brass*, Revelation 1:15." (Clarke)

g. **The hands of a man were under their wings**: This is another example of the ways in which they resembled **a man**.

h. **Their wings touched one another**: The four cherubim were close together, not spread-out at large distances.

i. **Each one went straight forward**: They did not turn to the left or the right but kept **straight** ahead in their course. There was nothing erratic or chaotic about their movements.

3. (10-14) The appearance and movement of the living creatures.

As for the likeness of their faces, *each* had the face of a man; each of the four had the face of a lion on the right side, each of the four had the face of an ox on the left side, and each of the four had the face of an eagle. Thus *were* their faces. Their wings stretched upward; two *wings* of each one touched one another, and two covered their bodies. And each one went straight forward; they went wherever the spirit wanted to go, and they did not turn when they went. As for the likeness of the living creatures, their appearance *was* like burning coals of fire, like the appearance of torches going back and forth among the living creatures.

The fire was bright, and out of the fire went lightning. And the living creatures ran back and forth, in appearance like a flash of lightning.

a. **As for the likeness of their faces**: Each of the cherubim had the face of **a man**, a **lion**, an **ox**, and an **eagle**. In John's vision of heaven, he seems to describe four creatures with each one having one of these four faces (Revelation 4:6-8). Most think that John simply described the particular face that was turned towards his line of sight.

i. These four **faces** have stirred the imagination of Bible scholars, students, and artists throughout history. These four faces or figures are a common motif in Christian art, especially in medieval Europe, with the association of a figure with a gospel writer. In the sculpture work on European cathedrals one may often see a figure of a man with a book, a lion with a book, and also an ox and an eagle.

ii. The problem is that there has been no absolute agreement on which figure represents which gospel writer.

	Victorinus	Irenaeus	Augustine	Clarke	Suggested
Matthew	Man	Man	Lion	Man	Lion
Mark	Lion	Eagle	Man	Lion	Ox
Luke	Ox	Ox	Ox	Ox	Man
John	Eagle	Lion	Eagle	Eagle	Eagle

iii. Some commentators say these four creatures speak of the ensigns of the head tribes as Israel camped in four groups around the tabernacle in the wilderness. Numbers 2:3, 2:10, 2:18, and 2:25 mention this organization of the tribes under these four heads but do not assign "mascots" to tribal banners. Seiss, Clarke, and Poole each mention this approach, and cite "Jewish writers" (Seiss), "The Talmudists" (Clarke), and "the learned Mede...from the Rabbins" (Poole). Poole explains: "That these were the four creatures whose portraitures were in the four ensigns of the Israelites as they were marshalled into four companies, allotting the men of three tribes to each company. Judah's standard had a lion in its colours, according to Jacob's prophecy of that tribe, Genesis 49:9, Ephraim had an ox, Reuben had a man, Dan an eagle. This the learned Mede proves from the Rabbins, who, though fabulous enough, yet in such a thing may be credited."

iv. Perhaps it is safest to say that the four faces are important because they represent all of animate creation, in its utmost excellence. The lion is the mightiest of wild animals, the ox strongest of domesticated animals, the eagle king of all birds, and man is highest of all creation.

"Man is exalted among creatures; the eagle is exalted among birds; the ox is exalted among domestic animals; the lion is exalted among wild beasts; and all of them have received dominion, and greatness has been given them, yet they are stationed below the chariot of the Holy One." (*Midrash R. Shemoth*, cited in Feinberg)

v. "The four represent all sentient creation. Man is the highest creature God made. Lion, eagle and ox dominate the wild animal kingdom, the skies, and the domesticated animals respectively. Since God sits on a throne above the cherubim, the thought is that all sentient creation is subordinate to him." (Smith)

vi. There are many examples of paintings and sculptures from the Middle East that combine animal and human forms – for example, a winged bull with a human head. But there is nothing like this, beings that have four faces.

b. **Two wings of each one touched one another, and two covered their bodies**: This is different, though not contradictory, to what Isaiah recorded in Isaiah 6:2. There he saw seraphim (burning ones) with six wings: two for flight, two to cover the face, and two for covering the feet. Ezekiel seems to record the two used for flight and the two used to cover the feet. We have no explanation as to why the faces were covered in Isaiah's vision but not in Ezekiel's.

c. **Each one went straight forward**: The idea from Ezekiel 1:9 is repeated for emphasis. These beings **did not turn when they went**, not moving to the right or the left.

i. "God is moving forward undeviatingly, unhesitatingly toward the accomplishment of His purpose in this world today. Nothing will deter Him—nothing can sidetrack Him at all." (McGee)

d. **They went wherever the spirit wanted to go**: It's hard to know if this refers to the *spirit* of the cherub or the Holy *Spirit*. If the former, it means there is no battle between the flesh and the spirit for these beings; their "flesh" does exactly what their spirit desires (unlike men, as in Mark 14:38). If the latter, then they are perfectly responsive to the leading of the Holy Spirit.

e. **Their appearance was like burning coals of fire**: There was something radiant, **bright**, and even "warm" about the appearance of these cherubim. Isaiah described them as *burning ones* (seraphim, Isaiah 6:2), and so did Ezekiel. **Out of the fire went lightning** shows the power and awe associated with these creatures.

i. "Angels are all on a light fire, as it were, with zeal for God and indignation against sin; let us be similarly affected." (Trapp)

f. **The living creatures ran back and forth**: The cherubim were *active*, seeming to not stand still for a moment. Their movements were as quick as **a flash of lightning**.

4. (15-21) Looking below: the wheels associated with the living creatures.

Now as I looked at the living creatures, behold, a wheel *was* on the earth beside each living creature with its four faces. The appearance of the wheels and their workings *was* like the color of beryl, and all four had the same likeness. The appearance of their workings *was*, as it were, a wheel in the middle of a wheel. When they moved, they went toward any one of four directions; they did not turn aside when they went. As for their rims, they were so high they were awesome; and their rims *were* full of eyes, all around the four of them. When the living creatures went, the wheels went beside them; and when the living creatures were lifted up from the earth, the wheels were lifted up. Wherever the spirit wanted to go, they went, *because* there the spirit went; and the wheels were lifted together with them, for the spirit of the living creatures *was* in the wheels. When those went, *these* went; when those stood, *these* stood; and when those were lifted up from the earth, the wheels were lifted up together with them, for the spirit of the living creatures *was* in the wheels.

a. **A wheel was on the earth beside each living creature**: It isn't easy to picture exactly what Ezekiel saw or described here. It is probably the idea of a grand four-wheeled chariot bringing the throne of God. The general impression is of constant activity and motion, not only by the living creatures themselves (Ezekiel 1:14), but also by the throne of God (specifically mentioned in Ezekiel 1:26).

i. "Ezekiel saw a throne-chariot, a supernatural chariot giving the effect of great motion and irresistible progress." (Feinberg)

ii. "Ancient Jewish writers found in this passage what they called the *merkabhah*, the divine throne chariot." (Smith)

b. **The color of beryl**: The mineral **beryl** can come in many different colors, but one of the more notable and precious is the emerald. This may mean that **the wheels and their workings** gave off a green color.

i. **A wheel in the middle of a wheel**: "Each wheel is composed of two wheels apparently at right angles to each other. This is impossible in reality, but in the vision in enables the chariot to run instantly in any direction without turning." (Wright)

c. **When they moved, they went toward any one of four directions; they did not turn aside when they went**: The sense seems to be that the wheels and their workings could move in any direction, but there was no sense of chaos or disorder to their movements.

> i. "Like a ball-bearing they could move in any direction without any steering mechanism." (Smith)

> ii. "They lost no time in a difficult or tedious turning, as we see in other chariots, for which way soever they were to go, thither they had faces directed, and so readily moved forward on their way, whether east or west, north or south." (Poole)

d. **As for their rims, they were so high they were awesome; and their rims were full of eyes**: Again, it isn't easy to picture exactly what Ezekiel saw or described here. The description of **full of eyes** was how John described the cherubim themselves (Revelation 4:6). The sense is of great knowledge and intelligence.

> i. "They are not dead metal; their livingness is shown by their eyes with which they can see the way, and by their life-link with the living creatures above them." (Wright)

> ii. "The wheels symbolize the omnipresence of God, while the eyes on their rims suggest the omniscience of God, seeing and knowing everything." (Wiersbe)

e. **When the living creatures went, the wheels went beside them**: As the four cherubim moved, so did the four wheels and their workings. They were so closely connected that Ezekiel could write, **the spirit of the living creatures was in the wheels**.

> i. In thirteen months the cherubim and this heavenly chariot will return to remove the glory of the Lord from the temple and Jerusalem (Ezekiel 9-10). Yet, graciously, God also gave Ezekiel a vision of the return of God's glory to the temple, along with these cherubim and the heavenly chariot (Ezekiel 43:1-5).

5. (22-25) Looking above: the firmament and the wings of the living creatures.

The likeness of the firmament above the heads of the living creatures *was* like the color of an awesome crystal, stretched out over their heads. And under the firmament their wings *spread out* straight, one toward another. Each one had two which covered one side, and each one had two which covered the other side of the body. When they went, I heard the noise of their wings, like the noise of many waters, like the voice of the Almighty, a tumult like the noise of an army; and when they stood still, they let down their wings. A voice came from above the firmament

that *was* over their heads; whenever they stood, they let down their wings.

a. **The likeness of the firmament above the heads of the living creatures**: As Ezekiel looked above the cherubim, he saw space **like the color of an awesome crystal**. There was something spectacular about the "sky" above the cherubim.

> i. Taylor regarding the Hebrew word *raqia* translated **firmament**: "The Hebrew meaning of something 'made firm' by beating or stamping, e.g. a hammered piece of metalwork. It usually refers to the curve of the heavens, which to an observer on the ground appears like a vast inverted bowl of blue. In passages like Genesis 1:6; Psalms 19:1; 150:1; Daniel 12:3, it clearly has this meaning, but in Ezekiel it has the sense of a firm, level surface or platform. In the book of Revelation this same phrase becomes 'a sea of glass, like crystal' before the throne of God (Revelation 4:6)."

b. **I heard the noise of their wings, like the noise of many waters, like the voice of the Almighty**: This seems to describe the loud and majestic noise of a great waterfall. John used this phrase to describe the voice of the ascended Jesus (Revelation 1:15), the voice of God (Revelation 14:2), and the voice of a great multitude (Revelation 19:6).

c. **A voice came from above the firmament**: The living creatures responded to this voice that **came from** above all.

6. (26-28) Above all things: the throne and He who sat upon the throne.

And above the firmament over their heads *was* the likeness of a throne, in appearance like a sapphire stone; on the likeness of the throne *was* a likeness with the appearance of a man high above it. Also from the appearance of His waist and upward I saw, as it were, the color of amber with the appearance of fire all around within it; and from the appearance of His waist and downward I saw, as it were, the appearance of fire with brightness all around. Like the appearance of a rainbow in a cloud on a rainy day, so *was* the appearance of the brightness all around it. This *was* the appearance of the likeness of the glory of the LORD. So when I saw *it*, I fell on my face, and I heard a voice of One speaking.

a. **Above the firmament over their heads was the likeness of a throne**: Since the wheels and their working seemed to be on the earth beside each living creature (Ezekiel 1:15) and the voice and the throne came from above the firmament (Ezekiel 1:25-26), the presence of God was *above* the cherubim and the wheels and their workings.

i. "In the Book of Isaiah we have the *principles* of the throne of God; in Jeremiah we have the *practice* of that throne; but in Ezekiel we have the *Person* who is on the throne." (McGee)

b. **In appearance like a sapphire stone**: Moses described parts of his heavenly vision with the blue color and brilliance of a sapphire stone (Exodus 24:10).

i. "He observes the most majestic throne one could imagine, made entirely of lapis lazuli, one of the most precious stones known to the ancients." (Block)

ii. "The pure oriental sapphire, a large well cut specimen of which is now before me, is one of the most beautiful and resplendent blues that can be conceived." (Clarke)

c. **On the likeness of the throne was a likeness with the appearance of a man high above it**: The repetition of the word **likeness** means that Ezekiel was concerned to emphasize that what he saw were representations of the real. Ezekiel might very well deny that he saw the *actual* throne of God or God Himself; he saw their **likeness**.

i. **With the appearance of a man**: "It was a deeply held tenet of Israelite religion from Moses onwards that God could not be visibly expressed, and for that very reason idolatry was out. But given the possibility of a theophany, no form but the human form could conceivably have been used to represent the Deity." (Taylor)

ii. "If God is to be portrayed in concrete form, the highest symbol man can use is the human form. When God wanted to reveal Himself in the supreme revelation of His person, He did so in the form of the Man Christ Jesus." (Feinberg)

iii. "The description suggests that Ezekiel did not see a face and a body that he could have drawn, but rather a fiery brightness that had a human shape and that he knew to be living and personal." (Wright)

d. **A likeness with the appearance of a man**: The representation Ezekiel saw of God was *something* like a man. This is consistent with the other descriptions of God in heavenly visions (such as Isaiah 6:1-4 and Revelation 4-5) and the general idea that God made man in His image (Genesis 1:26-27). Again, Ezekiel did not say that God was a man, merely that His **appearance** was something like a man.

i. "Unlike the gods of the nations depicted on ancient seals and carvings, the glory of Yahweh defies human description, verbally or visually. And unlike the images of the heathen, which require constant attention and polishing, Yahweh's radiance emanates from his very being." (Block)

e. **The color of amber**: This is the fourth association of color. First beryl or emerald green (Ezekiel 1:16), then clear crystal (Ezekiel 1:22), then sapphire blue (Ezekiel 1:26), and now golden-brown **amber**.

i. Alexander says the word translated **amber** (*hasmal*) is more literally "glowing metal," and has the idea of something that shines, such as a shining metal.

f. **From the appearance of His waist and downward I saw, as it were, the appearance of fire with brightness all around**: Flashing red and yellow light came downward from this representation of God. The suggestion is of His power and radiance going from heaven down to earth.

i. "The symbolism points to God as high and lifted up above the heavens, far removed from this world. Yet he still gives direction and order to his creation from his heavenly throne." (Smith)

g. **Like the appearance of a rainbow in a cloud on a rainy day, so was the appearance of the brightness all around it**: The whole picture is of colorful, bright, happy radiance – like **a rainbow in a cloud**.

i. In John's heavenly vision, he saw the throne of God surrounded by a rainbow (Revelation 4:3). **All around** this setting of all sovereignty, power, authority and glory – this setting of the throne of God – God set a *reminder* of His promise to never destroy the earth again with water (Genesis 9:13-16), a promise that *directs* His sovereignty, so that it is not capricious or against His promises.

ii. A throne says, "I can do whatever I want because I rule." A promise says, "I will fulfill this word to you, and I cannot do otherwise." **A rainbow** over the throne of God is a remarkable thing, showing that God will always limit Himself by His own promises.

h. **This was the appearance of the likeness of the glory of the LORD**: Ezekiel artfully built up to this declaration, revealing that the radiant being he described was in fact Yahweh, the God of Israel Himself. Ezekiel did not claim to see God directly, but only the **appearance of the likeness of the glory** of Yahweh.

i. "Many believe that such visions were pre-incarnation appearances of Jesus Christ, as John 12:41 suggests in the context which refers to Isaiah 6. Such appearances could illuminate, but could not redeem: for redemption full Incarnation was necessary, and not simply an appearance as a Man." (Wright)

ii. "All that was suggested to Ezekiel by the fire, the living ones, the wheels, the spirit of life, has been more clearly revealed to us in the Son of His love." (Morgan)

iii. "This was the man Christ Jesus, and this is the last and best part of the vision – viz., Christ set by his Father in super celestial places, far above all principality and power." (Trapp)

iv. "No matter what message God gave him to preach, or what opposition arose from the people, Ezekiel would be encouraged and strengthened because he had seen the mighty throne of God in the midst of the fiery trial. He had seen the glory of God." (Wiersbe)

v. **Glory**: "The term *kabod* derives from a root meaning 'to be heavy,' but when applied to royalty and divinity it denotes the sheer weight of that person's majesty, that quality which evokes a response of awe in the observer." (Block)

i. **I fell on my face, and I heard a voice of One speaking**: Ezekiel's response was one of humble surrender before such a God of glory. God's response was to reveal Himself through His word. One might think that the mere revelation of God in a vision was enough, but it was not enough for God. Something in His nature demands that He reveal Himself through His word, making this vision valuable not only for Ezekiel the prophet but for all who will read and consider His word.

i. If Ezekiel didn't know it before, now he clearly understood that the glory of God is *not* restricted to Jerusalem and the temple.

ii. "There is no doubt that through all his ministry, whether Ezekiel listened to the voice, or spoke the messages entrusted to him, he did so in the consciousness of the glory of Jehovah as he had seen it in those visions." (Morgan)

Ezekiel 2 – Ezekiel's Call as a Prophet

A. The calling of the prophet.

1. (1-2) Ezekiel commanded and enabled to stand to receive his call.

And He said to me, "Son of man, stand on your feet, and I will speak to you." Then the Spirit entered me when He spoke to me, and set me on my feet; and I heard Him who spoke to me.

a. **And He said to me**: There were no chapter divisions in the original writing of Ezekiel, so we should not miss the fact that Ezekiel's call to prophetic work came from the overwhelming vision of God, His chariot throne, and the cherubim described in Ezekiel 1.

b. **Son of man**: This is the first of 93 times God used this phrase to address Ezekiel. It is a title that emphasizes that he is a man among men and something of a representative of humanity.

   i. "The phrase *son of man* is a Hebraism which emphasizes Ezekiel's insignificance or mere humanity. 'Son of' indicates 'partaking of the nature of' and so when combined with *adam*, 'man', it means nothing more than 'human being'." (Taylor)

   ii. *Son of Man* was also a phrase Jesus used to refer to Himself, recorded some 80 times in the Gospels. Yet Jesus' use of the phrase is more connected with the idea from Daniel 7:13, where *Son of Man* describes the divine Messiah.

   iii. "By the time the *Similitudes of Enoch* were written (46:1, 2) the Son of man had come to mean specifically the Messiah. Our Lord's use of the title seems to have taken advantage of the ambiguity between the simple and the technical meanings." (Taylor)

c. **Stand on your feet**: Ezekiel 1:28 tells us that the prophet fell on his face at the sight of the *likeness of the glory of the LORD* in the vision of Ezekiel 1. Now he is told to **stand**, to hear God's message and to receive his call.

i. "That prostrate soul was called to a new attitude, for which it had been prepared by a vision and the prostration. It was that of standing erect before God in order that face to face he might receive the word of God." (Morgan)

ii. "Oracles are for standers, not prostrate ones. They require utmost attention of body, intention of mind, and retention of memory." (Trapp)

iii. "Service, not servility, was what God desired from this man. In those days servants always stood in the presence of their Master." (Smith)

d. **The Spirit entered me when He spoke to me**: For Ezekiel, God's word became the way the Holy Spirit **entered** and worked in him. The Holy Spirit still works and enters His people through the Word of God.

i. "On many occasions, the Spirit would lift him up (Ezekiel 2:2, 3:14; 8:3; 11:1, 24; 37:1; 43:5) and give him special power for his tasks (3:24; 11:5). The important thing was that Ezekiel stand obediently before the Lord and listen to His Word." (Wiersbe)

ii. "He who is sent by the God of all grace to convert sinners must be influenced by the Holy Ghost; otherwise he can neither be saved himself, nor become the instrument of salvation to others." (Clarke)

e. **Set me on my feet**: At first, Ezekiel could not stand before the glory of the LORD but was then commanded to stand. As he heard the word of God's command, the Spirit entered him and worked in him to do what God commanded. This same pattern of the work of the Spirit and God's word is evident in believers today.

i. "If God has called you to do a certain thing, He'll give you the power to do it. The best position you can come to is to recognize that you are not able in your own strength to do the job the Lord has given to you." (McGee)

2. (3-5) The call: speaking to the rebellious house of Israel.

And He said to me: "Son of man, I am sending you to the children of Israel, to a rebellious nation that has rebelled against Me; they and their fathers have transgressed against Me to this very day. For *they are* impudent and stubborn children. I am sending you to them, and you shall say to them, 'Thus says the Lord GOD.' As for them, whether they hear or whether they refuse—for they *are* a rebellious house—yet they will know that a prophet has been among them.

a. **I am sending you to the children of Israel**: At this time the children of Israel still had something of a kingdom in Judah and a temple in Jerusalem. Yet many of them were also scattered across the Middle East, by the forced exiles under the Assyrians and the Babylonians. Ezekiel's word was for all of them.

i. **I am sending you**: "Prophets functioned primarily as messengers of God, and the critical issue in the conflict between true and false prophets was which persons had actually been commissioned (*salah*) by Yahweh. Accordingly, the most serious charge that could be leveled against a true prophet was 'Yahweh has not sent you' (cf. Jeremiah 43:2)." (Block)

b. **To a rebellious nation that has rebelled against Me**: God sent Ezekiel to speak to a difficult audience. They were **rebellious** by nature, and their rebellion was even worse because it was **against** Yahweh, the God who had loved them and done so much for them. Truly, they were **impudent and stubborn children**.

i. **Rebellious nation** is literally *rebellious nations*, in the plural. The word is the familiar term *goyim*, most often referring to heathen nations. "The plural noun (*goyim*, 'nations'; NIV, 'nation') refers to the two separate nations of Israel and Judah, which made up the entire nation of Israel in Ezekiel's day." (Alexander)

ii. Block on the use of *goyim* (**nation**) here: "When the word is used of this nation, it tends to carry a pejorative sense, highlighting Israel's indistinguishability from other nations, and Yahweh's rejection of Israel. Apart from faith in and fidelity to Yahweh, Israel is just another 'heathen' nation."

iii. "The people are further described as *impudent and stubborn* (4, RSV; lit. 'hard of face and firm of heart'). The first phrase suggests the shameless attitude of the man who will not lower his gaze but prefers to brazen it out; the second describes the stubborn, unyielding will that refuses point-blank to give way even when found guilty." (Taylor)

iv. Collectively, it is a remarkably negative picture:

- They are the **children of Israel**, yet often fleshly and grasping like their father Jacob.
- They are a **rebellious nation**, often more like the Gentiles(*goyim*) than God's own people.
- They have **rebelled against** God and are traitors and rebels.

- They are **impudent and stubborn children**, like insubordinate teens.

v. "It is a characteristic of Ezekiel's message that he saw nothing good in Israel's past history (cf. chapters 16 and 23), and so to describe the people as both 'heathen' and 'rebellious' (i.e. idolatrous) at the very outset of God's word of commissioning is quite in keeping with the outworking of the prophet's message in the rest of the book." (Taylor)

c. **You shall say to them, "Thus says the Lord GOD"**: Ezekiel was sent to Israel to speak *God's* words, not his own. This was not about what Ezekiel liked or did not like; it was about being God's messenger. So it should be true for every pastor, preacher, and Bible teacher today.

i. **They are a rebellious house**: "Over a dozen times in Ezekiel the phrase 'rebellious house' (literally, 'house of rebellion') is employed; instead of the 'house of Israel' they had become the 'house of rebellion.' The greater the position of privilege, the greater the extent of disobedience." (Feinberg)

d. **Yet they will know that a prophet has been among them**: God told Ezekiel that whether Israel would **hear or refuse**, it would never change the prophet's fundamental message. Being the messenger, he was not ultimately responsible for how the message was received – only to demonstrate **that a prophet has been among them**. If Ezekiel did demonstrate that he was indeed a **prophet** of God, truly **among them** with God's word, then he could leave the results up to God.

i. "This vindication will obviously not come through masses of repentant converts, and probably not through the commendation of other prophets. All that remains is the traditional sign of a true prophet—the fulfillment of his predictions." (Block)

ii. "By this they shall be assured of *two* things: 1. That God in his mercy had given them due warning. 2. That themselves were inexcusable, for not taking it." (Clarke)

B. Instructions for the prophet called by God.

1. (6-8) Do not fear but speak boldly.

"And you, son of man, do not be afraid of them nor be afraid of their words, though briers and thorns *are* with you and you dwell among scorpions; do not be afraid of their words or dismayed by their looks, though they *are* a rebellious house. You shall speak My words to them, whether they hear or whether they refuse, for they *are* rebellious. But

you, son of man, hear what I say to you. Do not be rebellious like that rebellious house; open your mouth and eat what I give you."

a. **Do not be afraid of them nor be afraid of their words**: God warned Ezekiel that many would reject his message. Their rejection would sting like **briars**, like **thorns**, and like **scorpions** – yet it should not drive the prophet to fear and despair.

i. "Note how Isaiah (6.9-12), Jeremiah (1.17-19) and Ezekiel, here (3-7), were all given a depressing call. They were needed in a desperate situation, and had to be prepared for a large measure of rejection and even threats on their life." (Wright)

ii. This difficult call was easier for Ezekiel to embrace because it came from a genuinely awesome encounter with God. Because he was absolutely convinced of the power, majesty, and glory of God it gave him strength and courage to stand against the stinging rejection of men.

iii. "**Be not afraid;** the admonition against sinful fear is repeated; lest Ezekiel should forget, or we in like case should fail of our duty, it is four times given in charge." (Poole)

b. **Or dismayed by their looks**: Sometimes the rejection of a message is seen in a look of disdain or proud defiance.

i. **Dismayed by their looks**: "The verb here is a very strong word, meaning 'to be shattered'." (Taylor)

c. **Whether they hear or whether they refuse**: Ezekiel was not to allow the acceptance or the rejection of the message to determine his work. Like Paul exhorted Timothy, he was to preach the word in season and out of season (2 Timothy 4:2).

d. **Hear what I say to you**: Though the house of Israel may rebel against God's word, it was essential that Ezekiel the prophet surrender and submit to it. God then gave Ezekiel an acted-out illustration of this acceptance of every word of God – to **eat** the words of God.

e. **Do not be rebellious like that rebellious house**: The people were rebellious, but Ezekiel could not be. He had to be surrendered to the LORD even if they were not, indeed especially if they were not.

f. **Open your mouth and eat what I give to you**: God immediately challenged Ezekiel's obedience, telling him to do something unusual. If the people of Israel rejected God's word, Ezekiel had to accept it completely, taking it into the innermost core of his being.

i. "Jeremiah had God's words put into his mouth (Jeremiah 1.9), and Ezekiel here is given a written scroll to digest. It is the objective Word of God which becomes part of himself." (Wright)

ii. God's servants should receive God's word as if they actually *eat* it. Actually eating the material pages of a Bible would do one no spiritual good, but using the figure of eating the scroll as a picture of how we should receive God's word can do us great good. Eating the scroll speaks of many things that should mark our reception of God's revealed word:

- Deliberate action.
- Readiness to receive.
- Internal reception.
- Repetitious chewing.
- Complete reception.
- The process of digestion.
- Necessity.
- Sweetness.
- Strength, nourishment.

2. (9-10) The written-out words of judgment against Israel.

Now when I looked, there was a hand stretched out to me; and behold, a scroll of a book *was* in it. Then He spread it before me; and *there was* writing on the inside and on the outside, and written on it *were* lamentations and mourning and woe.

a. **There was a hand stretched out to me**: In the vision of Ezekiel 1, the only hands mentioned were that of the cherubim surrounding God's throne. It isn't clear if this was the hand of God or an angelic hand.

i. "Whether it is actually the hand of the Lord or simply a figure made necessary by the visionary symbolism is not important. The scroll, of course, represents the word which Ezekiel is to proclaim." (Vawter and Hoppe)

b. **A scroll of a book was in it**: This emphasizes that God's word was not only the spontaneous word spoken to His appointed prophets. God had a plan, a purpose, and authority for His *written* word.

i. "This scroll was probably made from papyrus rather than skin, since the former was the more common scroll material in biblical times." (Block)

c. **There was writing on the inside and on the outside**: As God (or the angel) spread the scroll out for Ezekiel, he could see that it was *full* of God's message. It was complete.

i. "Usually parchments were written on one side only, but here the message of the Lord was so full of threatenings and woes that both sides had to be utilized." (Feinberg)

ii. "Implying not only a well-defined but also a complete message. Ezekiel may not modify it with his own comments, nor does God allow himself any room for adjustments." (Block)

d. **On it were lamentations and mourning and woe**: This was the most important message for the house of Israel to hear, and it was the message that would be sharply rejected.

i. Under the New Covenant, we can be happy that in general we have a much better message to bring. "What a mercy to have that which is emphatically called, the *glad tidings*, the *good news*! *Christ Jesus is come into the world to save sinners*; and he wills that *all men should be saved and come to the knowledge of the truth*. Here are *rejoicings, thanksgivings*, and *exultation*." (Clarke)

Ezekiel 3 – The Messenger and the Watchman

A. Receiving the call.

1. (1-3) Eating the scroll.

Moreover He said to me, "Son of man, eat what you find; eat this scroll, and go, speak to the house of Israel." So I opened my mouth, and He caused me to eat that scroll. And He said to me, "Son of man, feed your belly, and fill your stomach with this scroll that I give you." So I ate, and it was in my mouth like honey in sweetness.

a. **Son of man, eat what you find**: Ezekiel 2 ended with God giving Ezekiel a scroll full of writing on both sides. Earlier in chapter 2 the prophet was told that he must eat the scroll (Ezekiel 2:8). Now, with the scroll in front of him the command is repeated.

> i. "It is specially incumbent on those who have to go forth and speak, to open their mouths and eat the roll. There is no greater mistake than to suppose that, because we are constantly handling God's Word for the purpose of teaching and exhorting others, we are therefore feeding on it for ourselves. It is possible to acquire an intellectual knowledge of the truth, while the heart is entirely unaffected." (Meyer)

b. **And go, speak to the house of Israel**: The eating of the scroll was not just a spiritual experience for Ezekiel. It acted out a spiritual truth: Ezekiel must *receive* and *internalize* and *digest* the word of God before he could be a messenger of that word to **the house of Israel**.

c. **So I opened my mouth, and He caused me to eat that scroll**: The context is almost certainly a vision God gave the prophet. He didn't actually eat a physical scroll, but experienced the happening of it in a vision, sort of a spiritual and divine virtual reality. It was real, but in a vision.

> i. "It was in vision doubtless that the prophet did eat the roll, and not in very deed, as the foolish patient did the physician's recipe." (Trapp)

ii. "The reader will observe a blurring of boundaries between visions and reality in all Ezekiel's visions. In any case, the experience is real—so real that the power of the divine word will propel the prophet for more than half a decade as he delivers his relentless messages of judgment to a hardened audience." (Block)

d. **Fill your stomach with this scroll that I give you**: Ezekiel wasn't to merely "taste" or "sample" God's written revelation. He was to **fill** himself with it, especially because it was received from God (**that I give you**).

e. **It was in my mouth like honey in sweetness**: Ezekiel obeyed, and God **caused** this unusual food to be eaten. When he did, he experienced it as not only sweet but as sweet as the sweetest thing he could imagine.

i. In a sense, Ezekiel experienced what Psalm 119:103 says: *How sweet are Your words to my taste, sweeter than honey to my mouth!* The Bible is filled with passage after passage that anyone with spiritual sensitivity would find sweet **like honey**. Passages like Psalm 23:1-3, Psalm 8:1, John 3:16, Romans 8:28, or Revelation 22:20 are just a beginning. If one can't find something sweet and satisfying in such verses, their spiritual taste buds are dulled and defective.

ii. "If the word of God be not very sweet to me, have I an appetite? Solomon says, 'The full soul loatheth an honeycomb; but to the hungry soul every bitter thing is sweet.' Ah, when a soul is full of itself, and of the world, and of the pleasures of sin, I do not wonder that it sees no sweetness in Christ, for it has no appetite!" (Spurgeon on Psalm 119:103)

iii. "The prophet declared that having eaten the roll, he found it in his mouth 'as honey for sweetness,' and by this declaration reveals that whereas the ministry he was about to exercise would be difficult, yet he himself was in perfect accord with the purpose of God and found delight in His will." (Morgan)

2. (4-9) Strength for a difficult calling.

Then He said to me: "Son of man, go to the house of Israel and speak with My words to them. For you *are* not sent to a people of unfamiliar speech and of hard language, *but* to the house of Israel, not to many people of unfamiliar speech and of hard language, whose words you cannot understand. Surely, had I sent you to them, they would have listened to you. But the house of Israel will not listen to you, because they will not listen to Me; for all the house of Israel *are* impudent and hard-hearted. Behold, I have made your face strong against their faces, and your forehead strong against their foreheads. Like adamant stone,

harder than flint, I have made your forehead; do not be afraid of them, nor be dismayed at their looks, though they *are* a rebellious house."

a. **Go to the house of Israel and speak with My words to them**: Ezekiel's call as a prophet is once again stated, as in Ezekiel 2:3-5 and 2:7. As a prophet he could not be silent; he had to **speak**. Yet he could not speak his words, but God's **words to them**.

b. **You are not sent to a people of unfamiliar speech and of hard language, but to the house of Israel**: Ezekiel's calling was not primarily to the Gentile nations, but to Israel. Jesus would also say that He was *not sent except to the lost sheep of the house of Israel* (Matthew 15:24).

c. **Had I sent you to them, they would have listened to you**: Ezekiel's focus on his own people made his ministry *harder*. The Gentiles would have been more receptive to his message, even as Nineveh responded to the preaching of Jonah.

> i. "People with prophetic or pseudo-prophetic gifts were regarded with awe in countries beyond their own, e.g. Elisha (2 Kings 5 and 8.7-9}, Jeremiah (39.11-14) and Jonah (3.6-10)." (Wright)

> ii. "The words are used to point the contrast between the excusable inability of people of a foreign language to understand and the quite inexcusable stubbornness of Ezekiel's Israelite hearers." (Taylor)

> iii. **They will not listen to Me**: "A man's will is his hell, saith Bernard. And it is easier, saith another, to deal with twenty men's reasons, than with one man's will. What hope is there of those that will not hear; or, if they do, yet have made their conclusion beforehand, and will stir no more than a stake in the midst of a stream?" (Trapp)

> iv. "Verse 7 is one of the most dangerous verses in Scripture, though the Bible does not hesitate to include it…. It is a call to intense humility, for fear that we comfort ourselves concerning our off-putting presentation of the truth by calling our rejection the rejection of Christ. Off-putting presentation can lie in our own character as well as in inept words out of season." (Wright)

d. **For all the house of Israel are impudent and hard-hearted**: God repeated the description first used in Ezekiel 2:4. Ezekiel needed and received special strength from God for this difficult calling (**I have made your face strong against their faces**).

e. **Like adamant stone, harder than flint, I have made your forehead**: Israel was committed to their rebellion and rejection of God. Strengthened by God, Ezekiel answered their commitment with a *greater* commitment on his part. If they were hard in their rebellion, God would make him **harder than flint** in his courage and integrity.

> i. **I have made your face strong**: "God promised to equip Ezekiel emotionally and intellectually to deal with the anticipated rejection. God had made the prophet's face and forehead just as hard as theirs. He would be able to 'butt heads' with his antagonists." (Smith)

> ii. "Make your face like adamant if their hearts are like adamant; if they are not ashamed to sin do not you be ashamed to warn them; if they are not ashamed of their unbelief, be not you ashamed of your faith in the divine testimony." (Spurgeon)

> iii. "It was certainly a characteristic mark of his ministry that he was able to outlast his opponents and not to be worn down by their apparent intransigence." (Taylor)

> iv. "God didn't make Jeremiah's head hard. Jeremiah had a soft heart, and he couldn't stand up against all the trouble he faced. At one time he even went to the Lord and resigned. Ezekiel is not about to resign. God says, 'The children of Israel are hardheaded, and I am going to make your head harder than theirs.'" (McGee)

3. (10-11) Receiving the message and going to those who must hear.

Moreover He said to me: "Son of man, receive into your heart all My words that I speak to you, and hear with your ears. And go, get to the captives, to the children of your people, and speak to them and tell them, 'Thus says the Lord GOD,' whether they hear, or whether they refuse."

> a. **Receive into your heart all My words that I speak to you**: The prophet's work began with *receiving*. He had to listen and **receive** everything God said. In the later words of Paul, he needed to receive the whole counsel of God (Acts 20:27).

> b. **Go, get to the captives, to the children of your people**: Having received God's word, Ezekiel then needed to **get** among his people, those to whom he would speak. He needed to know them and be among them.

> > i. "It's a good thing for the servant of God to be among his people, to weep with those who weep and rejoice with those who rejoice, for he can better minister to them when he knows their hearts and feels their pain." (Wiersbe)

> c. **Speak to them, and tell them, "Thus says the Lord GOD"**: Once he was among his people, Ezekiel then had to actually speak to them God's word. His job was to deliver God's message and not one from himself or any other.

d. **Whether they hear, or whether they refuse**: Ezekiel had to faithfully deliver this message no matter how it was received. His proclamation of it didn't depend on their reception. Among all the prophets Ezekiel probably spoke in the most unusual and innovative ways, yet it was always to deliver *God's* message.

4. (12-15) The conclusion of the vision of the LORD and the living creatures.

Then the Spirit lifted me up, and I heard behind me a great thunderous voice: "Blessed *is* the glory of the LORD from His place!" *I* also *heard* **the noise of the wings of the living creatures that touched one another, and the noise of the wheels beside them, and a great thunderous noise. So the Spirit lifted me up and took me away, and I went in bitterness, in the heat of my spirit; but the hand of the LORD was strong upon me. Then I came to the captives at Tel Abib, who dwelt by the River Chebar; and I sat where they sat, and remained there astonished among them seven days.**

a. **Blessed is the glory of the LORD from His place**: Ezekiel heard a **great thunderous voice** behind him say these words, probably from one of the **living creatures** (cherubim) that came again to his attention. Having been given such a difficult commission, it was important for Ezekiel to remain impressed by and confident in **the glory of the LORD**.

i. **Blessed is the glory of the LORD from His place**: "The expression has been retained in Jewish devotions and is to be found in the morning service of the Jewish Prayer Book." (Taylor)

b. **I also heard the noise of the wings of the living creatures**: The strange and amazing vision of Ezekiel chapter 1 once again came into view. The sense is that the **living creatures** and the **wheels** and all associated with them remained present all the time, but Ezekiel was so focused on God and his own experience of calling that he paid them little attention.

c. **So the Spirit lifted me up and took me away**: We don't completely understand what happened to Ezekiel *physically* or *spiritually*. He spoke of being taken away, yet he began at the River Chebar (Ezekiel 1:3) and was still there at the end of the vision (**I came to the captives at Tel Abib, who dwelt by the River Chebar**).

i. We know what the vision was *not*. "Ezekiel's transportation was not a case of hypnotism, autosuggestion, or the parapsychic phenomena of bodily levitation." (Alexander)

ii. "The prophet was reluctant to leave the scene of his dramatic encounter with God. He was not anxious to undertake the hard service to which he had been assigned. So God took matters into his own hands. Ezekiel felt himself being "lifted up" and taken away by the Spirit of God." (Smith)

iii. **Tel Abib**: "This is Hebrew for 'the hill of ears [of corn].'" (Vawter and Hoppe)

d. **I went in bitterness, in the heat of my spirit**: Perhaps Ezekiel was bitter at his lot as a captive, while others still lived and served in Jerusalem at the temple. Perhaps he was bitter at the difficulty of his call. Perhaps he was bitter at the sin and rebellion of the people of Israel. Whatever the exact cause, Ezekiel was bitter, angry, and stunned (**astonished**).

i. God's word was sweet to Ezekiel (Ezekiel 3:3), but he soon experienced some **bitterness** in carrying out his call.

ii. "Hebrew *mar*, 'bitter', can express fierce temper or anger, as of a bear robbed of her cubs (2 Samuel 17:8); discontentment, as of the Adullamites (1 Samuel 22:2); or wretchedness, as of Job (Job 3:20) and Hezekiah (Isaiah 38:15). Of these possible meanings the associated phrase 'heat of spirit' points to anger as the dominant emotion in Ezekiel's heart." (Taylor)

e. **I sat where they sat, and remained there astonished**: Ezekiel did what God told him to do. He said, *go, get to the captives* (Ezekiel 3:11) and he did. Once among them, he spent **seven days** stunned by the amazing vision and call of God upon his life.

i. "Perhaps it is not without significance that seven days was the period for the consecration of a priest (Lev. 8:33) and Ezekiel may have regarded this as the preparation for his ordination to a prophetic priesthood." (Taylor)

ii. "This was a time of reflection and observation such as many great men of God experienced prior to launching their ministries. Those days of silence changed his attitude about his mission. He learned patience; he came to accept responsibility." (Smith)

B. The responsibility of a watchman.

1. (16-19) The responsibility to warn the wicked.

Now it came to pass at the end of seven days that the word of the LORD came to me, saying, "Son of man, I have made you a watchman for the house of Israel; therefore hear a word from My mouth, and give them warning from Me: When I say to the wicked, 'You shall surely die,' and you give him no warning, nor speak to warn the wicked from his wicked way, to save his life, that same wicked *man* shall die in his iniquity; but his blood I will require at your hand. Yet, if you warn the wicked, and

he does not turn from his wickedness, nor from his wicked way, he shall die in his iniquity; but you have delivered your soul.

a. **I have made you a watchman for the house of Israel**: God used the figure of the **watchman** to describe Ezekiel's responsibility, here and in Ezekiel 33. He fulfilled his role as a **watchman** not primarily by observing others, but by faithfully proclaiming God's word and bringing God's **warning** to the people. God was gracious to provide a **watchman** at all.

i. "**A watchman**: "See therefore that thou be *Episcopus,* not *Aposcopus;* an overseer, not a byseer; a watcher, not a sleeper." (Trapp)

ii. "Ezekiel was not the first to define the prophetic office in terms of a sentry. The 8th-century prophet Hosea makes the identification in 9:8, and alludes to it in 5:8 and 8:1, where he calls for the blowing of the horn. Isaiah 56:10 refers to blind sentries, visionaries who are asleep, presumably false or negligent prophets." (Block)

iii. There are many who consider themselves watchmen to the people of God today. They watch carefully and look for signs of error or apostasy. There is always a place for those to do what Ezekiel was called to do as a watchman – to **hear a word** from God's word and to **give them a warning**. Yet many who do this focus on the examination of supposed error more than the proclamation of God's truth. This is a distortion of Ezekiel's calling as a **watchman**.

iv. Another way this modern office of watchman may distort the Biblical idea is by untruthful or unfair examination of others in search of error or apostasy. If a watchman alerts people to dangers but does not give an honest and fair report, then he will not be believed when he warns of a genuine danger.

v. "Herodotus telleth of one Euenius, a city shepherd, who for sleeping and allowed the wolf to enter the fold and kill sixty sheep, had his eyes pulled out. God threateneth the like punishment upon sleepy watchmen, idol shepherds. [Zechariah 11:17]." (Trapp)

b. **When I say to the wicked, "You shall surely die," and you give him no warning**: God explained the sin and the penalty for failing to be a faithful watchman. If God's message was not delivered, then **his blood I will require at your hand**. Again, the focus of the watchman's work is not on the examination of the **wicked**, but on the faithful declaration of God's message.

i. **His blood I will require at your hand**: "Hear it, *ye priests,* ye *preachers,* ye *ministers* of the Gospel; ye, especially, who have entered into the ministry *for a living,* ye who *gather a congregation* to yourselves that ye may feed upon their fat, and clothe yourselves with their wool; in whose parishes and in whose congregations souls are dying unconverted from day to day, who have never been solemnly warned by you, and to whom you have never shown the way of salvation, probably because ye know nothing of it yourselves! O what a perdition awaits *you*! To have the blood of every soul that has died in your parishes or in your congregations unconverted laid at your door! To suffer a common damnation for *every* soul that perishes through your neglect! How *many loads* of endless woe must such have to bear! Ye take your *tithes*, your *stipends*, or your *rents*, to the last *grain*, and the last *penny;* while the souls over whom you made yourselves watchmen have perished, and are perishing, through *your* neglect. O worthless and hapless men! better for you had ye never been born! Vain is your boast of *apostolical authority*, while ye do not the *work of apostles*! Vain your boast of *orthodoxy*, while ye neither *show* nor *know* the *way of salvation*! Vain your pretensions to a *Divine call*, when ye do not the work of *evangelists*! The state of the most wretched of the human race is enviable to that of such ministers, pastors, teachers, and preachers." (Clarke)

c. **Yet, if you warn the wicked**: If Ezekiel did faithfully deliver God's message, then he would bear no guilt if the message was rejected. The one who rejected the message would **die in his iniquity**, under the judgment of God. Yet of Ezekiel, faithfully delivering God's message, it would be said, **you have delivered your soul**.

i. "A phrase which our fathers often used, is not heard to-day frequently, about the work of the prophet. I refer to the phrase, 'blood-guiltiness.' Yet that phrase finds its warrant in this paragraph. There is such a thing. If the wicked die in wickedness for lack of the prophetic word, the prophet is guilty of his blood." (Morgan)

d. **Shall die in his wickedness**: This probably has the sense of death in this life, not eternal death – though, of course, most all who would be specifically judged with death in this life would be judged with death in the age to come. Death was part of God's promised curse for disobedience to the Mosaic covenant.

i. The judgment of death had special relevance in the days of Ezekiel and Jeremiah. False prophets gave false hope to the people and told them to resist the Babylonians and put their trust in the Egyptians to save them. Those who did this would die either in conquest or exile. The path of safety was an obedient trust in the judgments of God.

ii. "'Life' and 'death' in this context are to be understood as physical, not eternal, life and death. The concept of life and death in the Mosaic covenant is primarily physical." (Alexander)

2. (20-21) The responsibility to warn the righteous.

"Again, when a righteous *man* **turns from his righteousness and commits iniquity, and I lay a stumbling block before him, he shall die; because you did not give him warning, he shall die in his sin, and his righteousness which he has done shall not be remembered; but his blood I will require at your hand. Nevertheless if you warn the righteous** *man* **that the righteous should not sin, and he does not sin, he shall surely live because he took warning; also you will have delivered your soul."**

a. **When a righteous man turns from his righteousness**: The previous verses told of Ezekiel's responsibility to warn the wicked. Then God told him he also had a responsibility to warn the **righteous** who may stray from God's path. If Ezekiel **did not give him warning**, he would share in the responsibility for the sin (**his blood I will require at your hand**).

i. "The *righteous* (Heb. *saddiq*) was essentially the man who showed by his good living his adherence to the covenant. It went without saying that he was dutiful in carrying out the requisite religious observances." (Taylor)

ii. "Ezekiel admonished the righteous man not to turn from his righteous ways—loyalty to the Mosaic code—and disobey God's commands; for if he did, he would surely die." (Alexander)

iii. **A stumbling block**: "It does not here indicate that God deliberately sets out to trip up the righteous and bring him crashing to the ground, but that he leaves opportunities for sin in the paths of men, so that if their heart is bent on sin they may do so and thus earn their condemnation." (Taylor)

iv. "The idea that God tests the fidelity of the righteous is a well-worn biblical theme, most graphically presented in the prose story of the book of Job. In the Lord's Prayer there is a petition that God preserve the believer in the midst of such a test. Elsewhere Ezekiel speaks of stumbling blocks that God has laid in Israel's path in the form of silver and gold (7:19) and idolatry (14:3; 44:12)." (Vawter and Hoppe)

b. **His righteousness which he has done shall not be remembered**: This is the tragic price paid by many **righteous** men and women who fail to finish well. The real good they have **done shall not be remembered**. One sin or a short season of sin can easily wipe out an otherwise good reputation.

c. **If you warn the righteous man**: If Ezekiel were faithful to bring the message and the righteous were appropriately warned and kept from their sin, it would be good for the one who kept the warning (**he shall surely live because he took warning**), and good for the prophet (**you will have delivered your soul**).

3. (22-23) Another vision of the glory of the LORD.

Then the hand of the LORD was upon me there, and He said to me, "Arise, go out into the plain, and there I shall talk with you." So I arose and went out into the plain, and behold, the glory of the LORD stood there, like the glory which I saw by the River Chebar; and I fell on my face.

a. **The hand of the LORD was upon me there**: For the third time (Ezekiel 1:3 and 3:14) Ezekiel experienced this. Once again Ezekiel had to prepare himself to hear and receive God's word.

b. **Behold, the glory of the LORD stood there**: Once again, Ezekiel had a vision similar to that which he experienced in chapter 1.

i. "Although this is the third time he sees the *kabod*, the sight still catches him by surprise and overwhelms him with awe. His relationship with God never becomes familiar or casual—even a commissioned and authorized spokesman must prostrate himself in the presence of God." (Block)

ii. "First he has a renewed vision of the glory of the Lord (22,23). Already, perhaps, he had begun to tum in on himself under the strain that he could foresee was coming. A wise man once said something to the effect that we should take ten looks at Christ to one at ourselves." (Wright)

4. (24-27) The difficulty of the call restated.

Then the Spirit entered me and set me on my feet, and spoke with me and said to me: "Go, shut yourself inside your house. And you, O son of man, surely they will put ropes on you and bind you with them, so that you cannot go out among them. I will make your tongue cling to the roof of your mouth, so that you shall be mute and not be one to rebuke them, for they *are* a rebellious house. But when I speak with you, I will open your mouth, and you shall say to them, 'Thus says the Lord GOD.' He who hears, let him hear; and he who refuses, let him refuse; for they *are* a rebellious house.

a. **The Spirit entered me and set me on my feet and spoke with me**: As in Ezekiel 2:1-2, God made Ezekiel stand before speaking His word to him.

b. **Go, shut yourself inside your house**: God told Ezekiel to symbolically act out a message through isolation, inactivity, and silence. There are several different ways this action has been interpreted.

- An acted-out prophecy of what would happen to Ezekiel from the people of Israel as they rejected his message and punished him (Trapp).

- An acted-out prophecy of the doom and helplessness to come upon Israel (Vawter and Hoppe).

- God's restriction upon Ezekiel, keeping him inactive and silent until the appointed time (Wright, Taylor).

- An illustration of God's silence toward Israel (Clarke).

c. **I will make your tongue cling to the roof of your mouth**: To illustrate that Israel had no regard for the word of God, the LORD told Ezekiel not to speak. Possibly, God afflicted Ezekiel with a temporary muteness to illustrate God's silence to those who will not listen.

d. **But when I speak with you, I will open your mouth**: God would not stay silent forever, and neither would Ezekiel. God would restore his ability to speak and he would fulfill his role as God's messenger.

i. Ezekiel's call came over time. "It seems therefore preferable to regard 3:22–27 as the final episode in a protracted period of commissioning which lasted some days and in which there were these various high-point experiences, when God spoke to Ezekiel and the course and pattern of his ministry were gradually unfolded." (Taylor)

e. **He who hears, let him hear; and he who refuses, let him refuse**: With Ezekiel speaking as he should, delivering God's message, the responsibility would be on those he spoke to and not upon himself. Israel as **a rebellious house** would have to answer for their own sin and could not claim they never heard.

i. **He who hears, let him hear**: "The two Hebrew words, *hassomea yisma*, lit. 'let the hearer hear', or 'he who hears will hear' (27), are the prototype for our Lord's favourite formula: 'He who has ears to hear, let him hear'…. The hearer's response is dictated by his inner being." (Taylor)

Ezekiel 4 – Signs of Siege and Exile

A. The sign of Jerusalem's siege.

1. (1-3) A model of the siege of Jerusalem.

"You also, son of man, take a clay tablet and lay it before you, and portray on it a city, Jerusalem. Lay siege against it, build a siege wall against it, and heap up a mound against it; set camps against it also, and place battering rams against it all around. Moreover take for yourself an iron plate, and set it *as* an iron wall between you and the city. Set your face against it, and it shall be besieged, and you shall lay siege against it. This *will be* a sign to the house of Israel.

a. **Take a clay tablet and lay it before you, and portray on it a city, Jerusalem**: Living in Babylon, exiled by force from Jerusalem many years before, Ezekiel received God's command to depict Jerusalem on a clay tablet.

i. "The tile mentioned in the text was a tablet of soft clay, baked to make it durable, such as the Babylonians used for writing purposes." (Feinberg)

ii. "The practice of sketching a city plan on a clay brick is confirmed by several exemplars discovered by archeologists. One of these represents a 2nd-millennium plan of the city of Nippur, the predecessor of the very city in the vicinity of which the exiles were settled." (Block)

b. **Lay a siege against it**: Like a child playing with toy soldiers, Ezekiel arranged a **siege wall** against his clay Jerusalem, along with the **camps** of siege armies and their **battering rams**.

i. "Prophets were often told to drive home their message by strange acted parables (e.g. Isaiah 20.2,3; Jeremiah 13.1-7)." (Wright)

ii. "We must imagine that the strange actions which Ezekiel was now told to perform were to be carried out either just inside his house or, more likely, on the open space in front of his doorway. The actions were pointless unless they could be watched by a large number of people." (Taylor)

iii. "This, of course, was what would happen at Jerusalem in 588 B.C. when the Babylonian army began the siege of the city." (Wiersbe)

c. **Take for yourself an iron plate, and set it as an iron wall between you and the city**: Finally, Ezekiel made an unbreakable barrier between himself and the scene *he* constructed. This symbolized the barrier between God and Jerusalem, meaning that God would *not* intervene and rescue Jerusalem in the coming siege.

i. "It was the kind of utensil that the priests used in the temple for preparing some of the offerings (Lev. 2:5; 6:21; 7:9). The iron griddle symbolized the wall that stood between God and the sinful Jewish nation so that He could no longer look on them with approval and blessing." (Wiersbe)

d. **This will be a sign to the house of Israel**: There were some among the Israelite captives in Babylon (and also in Jerusalem) who thought that God would defend Jerusalem and rescue her when the Babylonians came again against her. This was a sure **sign** that it would not be so.

2. (4-6) Acting out the years of iniquity.

"Lie also on your left side, and lay the iniquity of the house of Israel upon it. *According* to the number of the days that you lie on it, you shall bear their iniquity. For I have laid on you the years of their iniquity, according to the number of the days, three hundred and ninety days; so you shall bear the iniquity of the house of Israel. And when you have completed them, lie again on your right side; then you shall bear the iniquity of the house of Judah forty days. I have laid on you a day for each year.

a. **Lie also on your left side, and lay the iniquity of the house of Israel upon it**: God commanded Ezekiel to enact another sign related to judgment against Israel. Presumably lying on his bed in his house, Ezekiel was to lie on his **left side** and in some unknown symbolic way **lay the iniquity of the house of Israel** upon himself.

i. "The symbolism of *upon your left side* was probably helped out by the prophet's lying on the ground in an east-west direction, with his head towards Jerusalem, and facing northwards as if towards Israel while on his left side and southwards towards Judah while on his right." (Taylor)

ii. "He now plays the role of the priest, carrying the burden of his people's sins on his shoulder." (Block)

b. **According to the number of days that you lie on it, you shall bear their iniquity**: Ezekiel was to act out this ritual for **three hundred and ninety days**. Perhaps he did it at night when he slept, or at some regular time of the day. After the 390 days for the **house of Israel**, he was then to do it for 40 days to symbolically **bear the iniquity of the house of Judah**.

> i. "We should probably envision him adopting his prone position for several hours each day, and then, while the audience watched, eat one small bite of the loaf." (Block)

c. **I have laid on you a day for each year**: Ezekiel acted out 390 years of iniquity for the kingdom of Israel and 40 years for Judah.

> i. Many different explanations have been given for these 390 and 40 years. Probably the best one was stated by Wiersbe: "When you add the years of the reigns of the kings of Judah from Rehoboam to Zedekiah, as recorded in 1 and 2 Kings, you have a total of 394 years. Since during three of the years of his reign Rehoboam walked with God (2 Chronicles 11:16–17), we end up with a number very close to Ezekiel's 390 years."

> ii. "Verse 4 makes it plain that the period must not represent the time of Israel's sinning, but the period during which the nation bears its iniquity and is punished." (Feinberg)

3. (7-8) Restrained according to the years of the siege.

"Therefore you shall set your face toward the siege of Jerusalem; your arm *shall be* uncovered, and you shall prophesy against it. And surely I will restrain you so that you cannot turn from one side to another till you have ended the days of your siege.

a. **You shall set your face toward the siege of Jerusalem; your arm shall be uncovered**: In this acted-out prophecy, Ezekiel demonstrated that the strong arm of God's judgment against Jerusalem would be active and unrestrained.

> i. "**Thine arm,** thy right arm, the stronger and more ready to act, shall be uncovered, naked and stretched out, as being ready to strike and slay." (Poole)

b. **I will restrain you so that you cannot turn from one side to another**: After symbolically standing in the place of God, Ezekiel then stood in the place of Jerusalem, restrained and helpless before God and His coming judgment.

i. "It is not necessary to assume that Ezekiel was in the prone position day and night. It was doubtless part of each day, if he were to prepare his food as stated later in the chapter." (Feinberg)

B. The sign of defiled bread.

1. (9-13) Preparing bread defiled according to the rules of kosher food.

"Also take for yourself wheat, barley, beans, lentils, millet, and spelt; put them into one vessel, and make bread of them for yourself. *During* **the number of days that you lie on your side, three hundred and ninety days, you shall eat it. And your food which you eat** *shall be* **by weight, twenty shekels a day; from time to time you shall eat it. You shall also drink water by measure, one-sixth of a hin; from time to time you shall drink. And you shall eat it** *as* **barley cakes; and bake it using fuel of human waste in their sight." Then the LORD said, "So shall the children of Israel eat their defiled bread among the Gentiles, where I will drive them."**

a. **Make bread of them for yourself**: During the 390 days of lying on his side, Ezekiel was commanded to make bread of many different grains and **eat it** during those days. This shows that during those days, Ezekiel was not *completely* inactive and laying on his side continually.

b. **Wheat, barley, beans, lentils, millet, and spelt**: The unusual bread was an acted-out prediction of life during a siege, when anything and everything that could be eaten was. It was also carefully measured out (**by weight, twenty shekels a day**) as bread (and water) would be carefully weighed and rationed during a siege.

i. "In times of *scarcity*, it is customary in all countries to mix several kinds of coarser grain with the finer, to make it last the longer." (Clarke)

ii. "With a *shekel* calculated at about 11.4 grammes, this would amount to almost exactly 8 ounces of bread per day. The water measurement of one-sixth of a *hin* would be equal to a fraction over a pint, or 0.61 litres." (Taylor)

iii. "Scarce enough to keep the man alive. Such proportions of bread and water rather fed death than the man." (Poole)

c. **Bake it using fuel of human waste**: In this Ezekiel demonstrated not only the desperation of a siege but also the misery of exile **among the Gentiles**, where care for keeping kosher food and its preparation were impossible.

i. "Some have wholly misunderstood the command of verse 12 which relates only to the fuel to prepare the food and not to the making of the food itself." (Feinberg)

ii. God did not tell Ezekiel to disobey the Law of Moses. "There is no recorded prohibition in the *kashrut* ('kosher') laws of the Torah regarding the use of human excrement for fuel." (Vawter and Hoppe)

iii. "Dried animal dung was used as fuel in the east, and still is, and it was not regarded as ritually, unclean. However, in the siege all cattle would be killed for food, so only human excrement would be available for fuel." (Wright)

d. **In their sight**: Ezekiel acted out these long, daily prophesies before the people of his community. No doubt, he would explain them as he did them daily.

2. (14-17) God's accommodation to Ezekiel's objection.

So I said, "Ah, Lord God! Indeed I have never defiled myself from my youth till now; I have never eaten what died of itself or was torn by beasts, nor has abominable flesh ever come into my mouth." Then He said to me, "See, I am giving you cow dung instead of human waste, and you shall prepare your bread over it." Moreover He said to me, "Son of man, surely I will cut off the supply of bread in Jerusalem; they shall eat bread by weight and with anxiety, and shall drink water by measure and with dread, that they may lack bread and water, and be dismayed with one another, and waste away because of their iniquity.

a. **I have never defiled myself from my youth till now**: Ezekiel objected to the command to prepare bread from a fire fueled by burning human waste. It was both disgusting and against kosher customs. Ezekiel's objection was based on the fact that he had never so offensively broken Jewish dietary laws.

i. "Let us be as careful of spiritual uncleanness; sin is the devil's excrement, the corruption of a dead soul." (Trapp)

b. **See, I am giving you cow dung instead of human waste**: God accommodated the appeal of the prophet. The lesson could be made without actually using **human waste** to bake the bread.

i. Ancients (and some in today's world) would use dung to fuel a fire, but according to Feinberg, normally dung would not be used for a fire to bake bread. It was considered unclean whether it was animal dung or human dung. God allowed Ezekiel to *lessen* the offense, but not take it away.

ii. Meyer saw a lesson in God's response to Ezekiel's appeal. "We may be feeling that certain trials are insupportable, or certain demands beyond our power to meet. At such hours of bitter anguish it is quite permissible for us to go into the secret place of the Most High and gasp out our complaint, saying, 'Ah, Lord God!'"

c. **Surely I will cut off the supply of bread in Jerusalem**: Yet God emphasized His point. A terrible siege was coming to Jerusalem and both bread and water would be **cut off**. The siege would bring **anxiety** and **dread** to Jerusalem, and they would **waste away because of their iniquity**.

i. "The purpose of all the acts in symbolic form was to impress the people with the coming famine during the siege of Jerusalem and the people's subsequent pollution in exile among the heathen." (Feinberg)

ii. "Thus their sins would bring them to extremest want and shame." (Poole)

Ezekiel 5 – The Sword of God's Judgment

A. Acting out the prophecy of the thirds.

1. (1-4) The prophecy of the thirds illustrated by cutting Ezekiel's hair.

"And you, son of man, take a sharp sword, take it as a barber's razor, and pass *it* over your head and your beard; then take scales to weigh and divide the hair. You shall burn with fire one-third in the midst of the city, when the days of the siege are finished; then you shall take one-third and strike around *it* with the sword, and one-third you shall scatter in the wind: I will draw out a sword after them. You shall also take a small number of them and bind them in the edge of your *garment.* Then take some of them again and throw them into the midst of the fire, and burn them in the fire. From there a fire will go out into all the house of Israel.

a. **Take a sharp sword, take it as a barber's razor**: In Ezekiel 4, God gave the prophet three prophetic demonstrations of coming judgment. Ezekiel 5 begins with a fourth, using **a sharp sword** as **a barber's razor** to cut Ezekiel's **head** and **beard**.

i. "It takes little imagination to see Ezekiel in action. First, whetting the sword-blade to a sharp cutting-edge while the crowd gathered to see what new act was going to be performed. Then the horrified gasp from the bystanders as he went to work with his crude razor, followed by the meticulous weighing of the hair in the balances." (Taylor)

ii. A **sword** isn't usually used to cut hair – swords are used in battle. Because this acted-out prophecy concerned the judgment the army of Nebuchadnezzar would bring upon Jerusalem, a **sword** was appropriate.

iii. **Sword**: "Although the word was used for various kinds of cutting instruments, in Ezekiel it always refers to a military weapon, which, with one possible exception, is the sword." (Block)

iv. "*Cutting off the hair* was a sign of *mourning*; see on Jeremiah 41:5; 48:37; and also a sign of great *disgrace*; see 2 Samuel 10:4. 5." (Clarke)

v. "Such shaving was forbidden to a priest like Ezekiel and ordinarily meant the loss of priestly status and position. The hair of the priest was a mark of his consecration to God's service (see Lev. 21:5; 19:27)." (Feinberg)

b. **Take scales to weigh and divide the hair**: God wanted Ezekiel to divide the hair into thirds, using a scale to divide it accurately.

i. "The balances showed that the judgment was a discriminating one. God's justice is accurate (Jeremiah 15:2)." (Feinberg)

ii. "This showeth that God's judgments are just to a hair's weight." (Trapp)

c. **Burn with fire one-third in the midst of the city**: Using the divided groups of hair, God told Ezekiel to act out another prophecy. This message powerfully contradicted the false promises of deliverance spoken by false prophets.

- One third was burned **in the midst of the city** of Jerusalem.
- One third was struck **with the sword**.
- One third was scattered **in the wind**.

i. Several commentators (such as Smith and Alexander) believe **the midst of the city** was actually the clay tablet Ezekiel made with the drawing of Jerusalem on it (Ezekiel 4:1).

d. **Also take a small number of them and bind them in the edge of your garment**: Ezekiel was also to attach a few hairs to the hem of his clothing and burn a few more in a fire. This spoke of the small remnant left behind and the suffering they would face.

i. "The *few hairs* which he was to take in his skirts, Ezekiel 5:3, was intended to represent those few Jews that should be left in the land under *Gedaliah*, after the taking of the city. The throwing a part of these last into the fire, Ezekiel 5:4, was intended to show the miseries that these suffered." (Clarke)

2. (5-10) The promise of severe judgment against Jerusalem.

"Thus says the Lord GOD: 'This *is* Jerusalem; I have set her in the midst of the nations and the countries all around her. She has rebelled against My judgments by doing wickedness more than the nations, and against My statutes more than the countries that *are* all around her; for they have refused My judgments, and they have not walked

in My statutes.' Therefore thus says the Lord GOD: 'Because you have multiplied *disobedience* more than the nations that *are* all around you, have not walked in My statutes nor kept My judgments, nor even done according to the judgments of the nations that *are* all around you'— therefore thus says the Lord GOD: 'Indeed I, even I, *am* against you and will execute judgments in your midst in the sight of the nations. And I will do among you what I have never done, and the like of which I will never do again, because of all your abominations. Therefore fathers shall eat *their* sons in your midst, and sons shall eat their fathers; and I will execute judgments among you, and all of you who remain I will scatter to all the winds.

a. **I have set her in the midst of the nations**: This is true in many ways. In both a historical and redemptive sense, Israel has been at the center of God's plan and work in the world. In some sense, it is also true geographically, as Israel stands at the meeting point of continents and empires.

i. "As far as His eternal purposes were concerned, Jerusalem was His city and the center of the nations (38:12). 'Salvation is of the Jews' (John 4:22). Israel was a privileged people, but privilege involves responsibility and accountability." (Wiersbe)

ii. "Jerusalem, the chosen city, was the spiritual centre of the earth and, indeed, of the universe, since Jesus Christ died there (Colossians 1.20)." (Wright)

b. **She has rebelled against My judgments by doing wickedness more than the nations**: Speaking of His holy city, God said "This is Jerusalem." Jerusalem should have honored and submitted to Him but was more rebellious and wicked than the pagan **nations**.

i. To these exiles, it would have felt that the city of Babylon was a more appropriate target of God's judgment. Nevertheless, God said: **this is Jerusalem**.

ii. "Given Jerusalem's clear knowledge of the will of her God and the uniquely just nature of his ordinances, Ezekiel's characterization of his people as more wicked than the nations is justified." (Block)

iii. "But instead of being a witness to the heathen nations about her, Israel excelled them in idolatrous practices. It has been denied that God's people were actually worse than the pagans about them, but reckoning must be in proportion to spiritual knowledge and privileges enjoyed." (Feinberg)

iv. "Let us not count on the privilege of relationship as a safeguard against reprobation, if we fail to fulfill the responsibilities of that relationship. That is what Israel did, and for the doing of which the judgments of God overtook her." (Morgan)

c. **I, am against you and will execute judgments in your midst**: Because of their great sin, God promised to *personally* bring judgment against them. Even though it would come largely through the instrument of the Babylonian army, it was *God's* judgment upon them.

    i. **Indeed I, even I, am against you**: What a terrible declaration! This phrase "may originally have constituted the cry by which one person would challenge another in man-to-man combat." (Block)

d. **I will do among you what I have never done**: Never before had God brought such a severe judgment upon His people as He did in the fall and conquest of Jerusalem under the Babylonians. One may say that *since* then such judgments have equaled or surpassed them (as in the fall of Jerusalem under the Romans), but not *before* then.

    i. "It is an awful thing when those who have sinned against conspicuous privilege and opportunity come under the rod. Their punishment is infinitely heavier than that of such as have never known." (Meyer)

    ii. "Though the old world perished by water, and the judgment was greater in its extent, and Sodom was destroyed by fire, yet neither one or other was so lingering a death. These poor Jews were long dying, and felt themselves dying." (Poole)

    iii. "Israel, suffering for her sins under God's righteous wrath, would be an object lesson to the nations. The heathen would be amazed because they had not seen a national deity so deal with a people who professed his worship." (Feinberg)

e. **Therefore fathers shall eat their sons**: God promised to do a terrible and unique work of judgment. Those remaining in Jerusalem would be reduced to the most terrible suffering (such as cannibalism); those who survived, God would **scatter to all the winds**.

    i. **Shall eat their sons**: "Though we have not this fact so particularly stated in *history*, yet we cannot doubt of it, considering the extremities to which they were reduced during the siege. The same is referred to by Jeremiah, Lamentations 4:10. Even the *women*, who were remarkable for *kindness* and *humanity*, *boiled* their own children, and ate them during the siege." (Clarke)

    ii. Leviticus 26:29 and Deuteronomy 28:53-57 warned Israel of such horrific judgments if they persistently rejected and rebelled against God's covenant with them. "He would execute the judgments pronounced in the Mosaic covenant on Jerusalem in the sight of the nations." (Alexander)

B. The application of the prophecy of the thirds.

1. (11-12) Judgment on Jerusalem by thirds.

'Therefore, *as* I live,' says the Lord GOD, 'surely, because you have defiled My sanctuary with all your detestable things and with all your abominations, therefore I will also diminish *you;* My eye will not spare, nor will I have any pity. One-third of you shall die of the pestilence, and be consumed with famine in your midst; and one-third shall fall by the sword all around you; and I will scatter another third to all the winds, and I will draw out a sword after them.

a. **Therefore, as I live**: This was an appropriate declaration, contrasting Yahweh, the living God, with the idols of surrounding nations.

b. **Because you have defiled My sanctuary with all your detestable things**: Earlier God said that Israel's sins against Him were worse than the pagan nations (Ezekiel 5:6). Here is one significant example of this. The pagans did not have God's **sanctuary** in their midst; yet when Israel did, they **defiled** it with **detestable things** and **abominations**.

c. **Therefore I will also diminish you**: They **defiled** God's sanctuary; He would **diminish** them. He promised to do it in the proportion of thirds suggested by Ezekiel's prophetic demonstration with the sword-cut hair (Ezekiel 5:2).

- One third **shall die of the pestilence** and **famine**.
- One third shall be killed **by the sword all around**.
- One third shall be scattered **to all the winds**, with a **sword** following them.

2. (13-14) The spending out of God's anger.

'Thus shall My anger be spent, and I will cause My fury to rest upon them, and I will be avenged; and they shall know that I, the LORD, have spoken *it* in My zeal, when I have spent My fury upon them. Moreover I will make you a waste and a reproach among the nations that *are* all around you, in the sight of all who pass by.

a. **Thus shall My anger be spent**: The idea is that God's **fury** had built up for a long time against His wicked and rebellious people. When the time was right, in the near future, it would **be spent** and it would **rest upon them**.

i. "Above all, this highly anthropopathic passage features the 'fury' and the 'jealousy' of God (v. 13). 'Jealousy makes a man furious,' wrote the sage, 'and he will not spare when he takes revenge' (Prov. 6:34). So the text depicts Yahweh, in one of the most somber of all the prophetic rejections of Israel." (Vawter and Hoppe)

ii. **In My zeal**: "The Hebrew word *gina* suggests 'ardour', 'passionate feeling' (the root meaning is 'to grow purple in the face'), and therefore covers both zeal and jealousy, as well as resentment and indignation at an insult done to the honour of oneself or of another." (Taylor)

iii. Adam Clarke, writing around 1800, had an interesting comment on the phrase, **I will cause My fury to rest upon them**: "My displeasure, and the evidences of it, shall not be *transient*; they shall be *permanent* upon you, and among you. And is not this dreadfully true to the present day?" That was an accurate observation of the Jewish people of his time; yet one cannot deny the remarkable work of restoration that has brought the Jewish people to prosperity and prominence.

b. **They shall know that I, the LORD, have spoken it**: When it came to pass, it would witness to Israel as a vindication of the repeated announcements and warnings of judgment. It would witness to the surrounding nations as a demonstration of God's righteousness (**I will make you a waste and a reproach among the nations**).

3. (15-17) The great destruction of God's judgment.

'So it shall be a reproach, a taunt, a lesson, and an astonishment to the nations that *are* all around you, when I execute judgments among you in anger and in fury and in furious rebukes. I, the LORD, have spoken. When I send against them the terrible arrows of famine which shall be for destruction, which I will send to destroy you, I will increase the famine upon you and cut off your supply of bread. So I will send against you famine and wild beasts, and they will bereave you. Pestilence and blood shall pass through you, and I will bring the sword against you. I, the LORD, have spoken.'"

a. **So it shall be a reproach, a taunt, a lesson, and an astonishment to the nations**: God *would* accomplish His purpose of teaching the nations through Israel. If they had obeyed the covenant He would have taught them through the blessings given (as in the days of Solomon). For the covenant breakers, God would teach the nations through His judgment upon His people.

i. **Terrible arrows**: "Famine and pestilence are represented as *poisoned arrows*, inflicting death wherever they *wound*." (Clarke) "Not to warn you, as Jonathan's arrows did David, but to wound you to the heart, and to lay you heaps upon heaps." (Trapp)

b. **So I will send against you famine and wild beasts.... pestilence and blood**: The judgment would come as promised, and would come in many different ways.

> i. "Heb. *evil beast*: either the king of Babylon, which, like a ravenous and insatiable beast, tore and devoured all. Or, literally, lions, bears, &c., which are one of his four sore judgments, Ezekiel 14:21." (Poole)

> ii. "In 593 B.C. Ezekiel pronounced this word of judgment; in 586 his prophetic status was confirmed." (Block)

Ezekiel 6 – Judgment and Restoration from Idolatry

A. The prophecy against the mountains of Israel.

1. (1-3) A word against the high places.

Now the word of the LORD came to me, saying: "Son of man, set your face toward the mountains of Israel, and prophesy against them, and say, 'O mountains of Israel, hear the word of the Lord GOD! Thus says the Lord GOD to the mountains, to the hills, to the ravines, and to the valleys: "Indeed I, *even* I, will bring a sword against you, and I will destroy your high places.

a. **Set your face toward the mountains of Israel**: This prophecy was directed against the **mountains** because they helped define the geography of Israel, and more importantly, they were centers of idol worship – the infamous **high places** mentioned many times in the Old Testament.

i. "Probably in any part of Palestine at this time you would have found some mountain or hill crowned with an altar, one or two standing stones, a wooden pillar, and a clump of evergreen trees (Jeremiah 3.6-9); They were flourishing centres of the old Canaanite religion which should have been destroyed (Deuteronomy 7.5)." (Wright)

ii. "Each high place would have its altar for sacrifice, and perhaps a pillar (Heb. *masseba*), which may well have been regarded as a phallic symbol, and an image of the Canaanite goddesses, Asherah or Ashtoreth." (Taylor)

iii. "Because hilltops often served as sites on which cultic rituals were performed, *bama* could serve as a designation for any open cultic installation, regardless of location." (Block)

iv. **To the ravines, and to the valleys**: "There must have been some similar worship in the ravines and valleys (Isaiah 57.5,6; Jeremiah

2.23; 7.31), perhaps sometimes cave worship of an earth-mother, or, as Isaiah and Jeremiah suggest, child sacrifice." (Wright)

b. **A sword against you, and I will destroy your high places**: Altars to pagan gods were often set on the tops of hills and mountains in ancient Israel and the broader region. This idolatry on the **high places** was inherited from the Canaanites and often practiced by the Israelites. God promised the judgment of the **sword against** these places and their idolatries.

> i. "Ezekiel the watchman was warning the people that an invasion was coming because God had seen their sins and was about to punish them." (Wiersbe)

2. (4-7) The complete destruction to come.

Then your altars shall be desolate, your incense altars shall be broken, and I will cast down your slain *men* before your idols. And I will lay the corpses of the children of Israel before their idols, and I will scatter your bones all around your altars. In all your dwelling places the cities shall be laid waste, and the high places shall be desolate, so that your altars may be laid waste and made desolate, your idols may be broken and made to cease, your incense altars may be cut down, and your works may be abolished. The slain shall fall in your midst, and you shall know that I *am* the LORD.

a. **I will cast down your slain men before your idols**: God promised to bring His strong judgment against the **altars** of idolatry and those who worshipped there. God would desecrate those places set aside to pagan gods with the **bones** of unfaithful Israel.

> i. Matthew Poole noted that God called them **your altars;** "God's altar was only at Jerusalem, these were their altars."
>
> ii. "This oracle announces that the time has come for Yahweh to clean house, to rid the land of its pagan worship once and for all." (Block)
>
> iii. "The 'scattering of bones' is a phrase used for judgment in which uncleanness and shame are conveyed (cf. Pss 53:5; 141:7). The bones would be those of the Israelites who had become engrossed in these pagan practices." (Alexander)
>
> iv. **I will scatter your bones**: "This was literally fulfilled by the Chaldeans. According to *Baruch*, Bar 2:24, 25, they opened the sepulchres of the principal people, and threw the bones about on every side." (Clarke)

b. **The cities shall be laid waste, and the high places shall be desolate**: The armies of Babylon would destroy both the **cities** and the country regions.

i. "**Desolate**; no priest to attend, no sacrifice offered, nor a votary come to them." (Poole)

c. **Your idols may be broken and made to cease**: This promise was fulfilled. The devastating judgment did come, and when Israel came again into the land, they never had the same problem with idolatry as before.

i. "Because the land had been defiled by idols, the idols themselves would now be defiled by the corpses of the worshipers, a retribution in kind. This would be the height of desecration, replacing the fragrance of incense with the odor of putrefaction." (Feinberg)

d. **You shall know that I am the LORD**: This is the first use of a phrase repeated many times in Ezekiel. It shows that God worked in His judgments and His restorations to reveal Himself to Israel and the world.

i. **You shall know that I am the LORD**: "This so-called recognition formula, which occurs some sixty times in the book, captures the theme of this prophet. God's motive in all that he does is that he might be recognized as the only God." (Smith)

B. The promise of a remnant.

1. (8) A remnant who escapes the sword.

"Yet I will leave a remnant, so that you may have *some* who escape the sword among the nations, when you are scattered through the countries.

a. **Yet I will leave a remnant**: The remnant was illustrated in the acted-out parable of the cut hair (Ezekiel 5:3-4). Here God specifically promised to **leave a remnant** that would be the basis of a later restoration.

b. **When you are scattered**: Some of the remnant would be among those **scattered**, and some would remain in the land.

2. (9-10) The spiritual renewal of the remnant.

Then those of you who escape will remember Me among the nations where they are carried captive, because I was crushed by their adulterous heart which has departed from Me, and by their eyes which play the harlot after their idols; they will loathe themselves for the evils which they committed in all their abominations. And they shall know that I *am* the LORD; I have not said in vain that I would bring this calamity upon them."

a. **Those of you who escape will remember Me**: God promised that one day some of those who had been exiled out of the land of Israel would **remember** their covenant God and call upon His name.

i. **Will remember Me**: "My precepts which they violated, my mercies which they abused, my threats which they despised, my promises which they refused, my prophets whom they persecuted, my judgments which have executed; and shall consider and return, and seek me in their affliction." (Poole)

b. **Because I was crushed by their adulterous heart**: This is a startling statement. Using a human analogy, God expressed the depth of the grief He felt over Israel's idolatry by likening Himself to a husband with a constantly unfaithful wife.

i. "The strongest figure possible is used to portray the Divine suffering. God is represented as broken." (Morgan)

ii. "The amazing truth is most vividly brought out in the prophecy of Hosea, a man who was brought into an understanding of the suffering of God, by his own domestic tragedy. That is the force of these words." (Morgan)

iii. "Our sin can give God the heartbreak, because He loves us so. Indeed, on the Cross the Lord died of a broken heart; of this the issuing stream of blood and water was the sign. O heart of stone, thou too must break and loathe thyself, when thou seest thy Lord broken by thy sin!" (Meyer)

c. **After their idols**: Israel's unfaithfulness to Yahweh was all the worse because of whom they forsook Yahweh for – empty, filthy, disgusting **idols**. Ezekiel's choice of word for **idols** reflects that.

i. **After their idols**: "The word for *idols* (Heb. *gullulim*) is a favourite with Ezekiel, occurring no less than thirty-eight times, as against nine times in the rest of the Old Testament. Its derivation is uncertain but it is quite likely that it is a home-made word consisting of the vowels of Hebrew *siqqus*, for which the dictionaries give the polite translation of 'detested thing', and the consonants of a noun meaning 'a pellet of dung'. The final combination carries about as much disdain and revulsion as any word could do." (Taylor)

d. **They will loathe themselves for the evils which they committed**: First they would remember the Lord; then they would be deeply ashamed of their sin. It was a terrible but necessary step in their restoration.

i. Understanding the grief expressed by "**I was crushed by their adulterous heart**" is connected to **they will loathe themselves**. On both a divine and human level, it could be said, one day you will realize how your sin broke the heart of those who loved you the most and you will hate yourself for it.

ii. **They will loathe themselves**: "They shall bleed inwardly, and blush outwardly, deeply detesting their former abominations, and not waiting till others condemn them, they shall condemn themselves." (Trapp)

iii. They would **loathe themselves** for **all their abominations**, not merely *some* of them. "It is a hypocrite's repentance which is but for some; this of the reserved remnant shall be sound, it is for all abominations, for all kinds of their abominations." (Poole)

e. **They shall know that I am the LORD**: After their repentance, they would be restored to a relationship with Yahweh again. The **calamity** God brought upon them, as severe as it was, would fulfill its corrective purpose in the people.

i. We can see a progression that is often still evident:

- Remembrance of God.
- Repentance from sin.
- Relationship restored.

ii. "Those that escape the sword, the pestilence, and the famine, and shall be led into captivity, shall plainly see that it is God who has done this, and shall humble themselves on account of their abominations, leave their idolatry, and worship me alone. And this they have done from the Babylonish captivity to the present day." (Clarke)

iii. "The escapees will emerge from their dispersal among the nations a transformed people. The process of transformation is not without its ironies. First, the spiritual renewal will occur on foreign soil, which most Israelites considered unclean or defiled. Second, to many Israelites, contact with Yahweh depended on residence in his land. Now they would learn that the very opposite was the case—continued presence in the land signified God's rejection. The future lay with the exiles." (Block)

C. God revealed to Israel through His judgment upon them.

1. (11-12) A call to anger and mourning over Israel's great sins.

'**Thus says the Lord GOD: "Pound your fists and stamp your feet, and say, 'Alas, for all the evil abominations of the house of Israel! For they shall fall by the sword, by famine, and by pestilence. He who is far off** shall die by the pestilence, he who is near shall fall by the sword, and he who remains and is besieged shall die by the famine. Thus will I spend My fury upon them.

a. **Pound your fists and stamp your feet**: God told Ezekiel to say the following words with these strong gestures. He needed to arrest the attention of Israel because they regarded their idolatry as a light thing; God saw them as **evil abominations**.

i. "'Clap your hands, and stamp your foot' are instructions that intend both to draw attention and to convey a premonition of threat and defiance." (Vawter and Hoppe)

b. **They shall fall by the sword, by famine, and by pestilence**: The coming judgment would be complete and devastating. As Ezekiel had said in the previous chapter, God would **spend** His **fury upon** them.

i. "Emphatic warning was directed to them in the light of the three dread calamities predicted: sword, famine and pestilence. There would be no escape when these somber horsemen began their ride of death." (Feinberg)

2. (13-14) God revealed in His judgment against Israel for their idolatry.

Then you shall know that I *am* the LORD**, when their slain are among their idols all around their altars, on every high hill, on all the mountaintops, under every green tree, and under every thick oak, wherever they offered sweet incense to all their idols. So I will stretch out My hand against them and make the land desolate, yes, more desolate than the wilderness toward Diblah, in all their dwelling places. Then they shall know that I *am* the L**ORD**.'"''**

a. **Then you shall know that I am the L**ORD**, when their slain are among their idols**: The fulfillment of these prophecies would demonstrate to Israel that Yahweh was their God, and worthy of their repentance. They would (and did) reject their idols after these severe judgments.

i. **Stretch out My hand:** "This noteth the greatness of the blow, God striketh hard when he stretcheth out his hand, and therefore you find a mighty hand joined with outstretched arm." (Poole)

b. **More desolate than the wilderness toward Diblah**: There are some ancient texts that read *Riblah* instead of **Diblah**. This may be due to an error in copying the text. We know *Riblah* as a place in Syria; the exact meaning or place of **Diblah** is unknown.

i. "In Ezekiel 6:14 the received Hebrew text reads not 'Riblah' but 'Diblah.' This is undoubtedly due to a scribal confusion of the Hebrew letters 'd' and 'r,' a thing that has occurred several times over in the transmission of the biblical text." (Vawter and Hoppe)

ii. "Some Hebrew manuscripts read 'Riblah,' a city in Syria, and this seems to fit. God promised to devastate the land 'from the desert to Riblah [Diblah]' (NIV), that is, from the south to the north. It's like saying 'from Dan to Beersheba,' from the north to the south." (Wiersbe)

iii. "Riblah was to be the fateful site where Nebuchadnezzer would seal the doom of Jerusalem and Judah after the debacle of 587/6, which Ezekiel is here prophesying (2 Kgs. 25:20–21). It was already a site fraught with significance for Ezekiel's fellow exiles." (Vawter and Hoppe)

c. **Then they shall know that I am the LORD**: This declares the corrective purpose God had even in this terrible judgment. God would do good for His people even in the midst of the coming desolation.

i. **Then they shall know that I am the LORD**: "The words typify Ezekiel's message and longing, that Yahweh may be known by all men, Israelite and non-Israelite, for what he is—the one true God, the God of the world, the God of history, the God who speaks and does not speak *in vain*." (Taylor)

Ezekiel 7 – Then You Shall Know That I Am the LORD

A. The end reveals Yahweh to His people.

1. (1-2) Introduction.

Moreover the word of the LORD came to me, saying, "And you, son of man, thus says the Lord GOD to the land of Israel:

a. **The word of the LORD came to me**: The repetition of this phrase reminds us that fundamentally, Ezekiel was a *prophet*. He was a man to whom the **word of the LORD** came, and who then had to deliver that word.

b. **To the land of Israel**: Ezekiel was in Babylon, and his most immediate hearers were fellow exiles. Yet at the time he spoke this, Jerusalem had not yet been destroyed and Judah had not yet been completely conquered. This was a message **to the land of Israel**, to announce coming judgment upon them.

2. (3-4) Announcement of the end.

'An end! The end has come upon the four corners of the land.
Now the end *has come* upon you,
And I will send My anger against you;
I will judge you according to your ways,
And I will repay you for all your abominations.
My eye will not spare you,
Nor will I have pity;
But I will repay your ways,
And your abominations will be in your midst;
Then you shall know that I *am* the LORD!'

a. **The end has come upon the four corners of the land**: Prophetically, Ezekiel could see **the end** for the entire land of Israel. No place would be spared. There would remain no land under the control of the tribes of

60

Israel. Their "party" of rebellion and idolatry was over – **now the end has come upon you**.

> i. "The words here 'An end' are exclamatory. That is the message in its entirety – 'An end!' The time of patience was over, there was to be no more waiting." (Morgan)

> ii. It has been said, *if something can't go on forever, it won't*. It is wise to consider **the end** *before* it actually comes upon you. Ezekiel hoped to bring this wisdom to rebellious Israel.

> iii. "Ezekiel's accent on immanency and the urgency of his tone represent his reaction to public indifference and the refusal to take the divine threats seriously." (Block) ⟶ Conduct

b. **I will judge you according to your ways**: God promised to bring simple justice to the people of Judah and Jerusalem. As a kingdom, their **ways** would determine their judgment, and the judgment would be severe: **My eye will not spare you, nor will I have pity**.

c. **Then you shall know that I am the LORD**: This great judgment had a purpose, and a *good* purpose. It would be the way that God's people would return to a true relationship with, and knowledge of, their covenant God.

B. Repayment for their abominations reveals Yahweh to His people.

1. (5-7) The day of disaster.

**"Thus says the Lord GOD:
'A disaster, a singular disaster;
Behold, it has come!
An end has come,
The end has come;
It has dawned for you;
Behold, it has come!
Doom has come to you, you who dwell in the land;
The time has come,
A day of trouble *is* near,
And not of rejoicing in the mountains.**

a. **A disaster, a singular disaster; behold, it has come**: The future **disaster** brought by the Babylonian armies was revealed to Ezekiel. The short, excited phrases were spoken as if they were in the mouth of someone watching this overwhelming army do its damage.

b. **Doom has come to you**: The people would face a dawn (**it has dawned for you**), but it would be a dawn of doom. The time of Israel's **rejoicing**

in the mountains over their pagan altars and perverted worship would be over.

i. **It has dawned for you**: "In a beautiful play on words, impossible to reproduce in English, Ezekiel pictured the end as though it had been quiescent or asleep, but would be awakened and aroused to come against the people of the land of Israel." (Feinberg)

ii. "God's vengeance seems to slumber, and sinners dream it will never awake, but here the prophet assureth the sinners of Jerusalem, and its people, that God hath awakened his vengeance, which now watcheth to take the first opportunity, or rather to hasten it." (Poole)

iii. "Thus the prophet told the exiles in Babylon, what Jeremiah was telling them in Jerusalem, that the opportunity for recovery was past, that the nation had overstepped the boundaries of the forbearance and waiting of God." (Morgan)

2. (8-9) Repayment for their abominations.

Now upon you I will soon pour out My fury,
And spend My anger upon you;
I will judge you according to your ways,
And I will repay you for all your abominations.
'My eye will not spare,
Nor will I have pity;
I will repay you according to your ways,
And your abominations will be in your midst.
Then you shall know that I *am* the Lord who strikes.

a. **I will repay you for all your abominations**: As in other places, the word **abominations** mainly has the sense of terrible, even disgusting idolatry. God's **fury** and **anger** would come upon them for this idolatry.

b. **Then you shall know that I am the Lord who strikes**: Once again, ultimate restoration is in mind. The severe judgment for their idolatry would show that their idols were powerless to save them. In destroying their reliance on idols, they could come back to a true relationship with Yahweh.

i. "The message closed by stunning the exiles with a new name for God: 'The Lord who strikes the blow' (*YHWH makkeh*), the one who would now judge Judah." (Alexander)

C. The coming day of Yahweh's revelation to His people.

1. (10-13) In that day, judgment will come upon everyone.

'Behold, the day!
Behold, it has come!
Doom has gone out;
The rod has blossomed,
Pride has budded.
Violence has risen up into a rod of wickedness;
None of them *shall remain,*
None of their multitude,
None of them;
Nor *shall there be* wailing for them.
The time has come,
The day draws near.
'Let not the buyer rejoice,
Nor the seller mourn,
For wrath *is* on their whole multitude.
For the seller shall not return to what has been sold,
Though he may still be alive;
For the vision concerns the whole multitude,
And it shall not turn back;
No one will strengthen himself
Who lives in iniquity.

a. **Behold the day! Behold, it has come**: In Ezekiel's time, there were many false prophets who said God would rescue Judah and Jerusalem. These hopeful lies made it hard to believe that the **day** of great judgment would actually come, but it did. Ezekiel tried to prepare them for this.

b. **The rod has blossomed, pride has budded**: This is an interesting reference to Aaron's rod that budded (Numbers 17). That miraculous blossoming was a supernatural demonstration of God's favor and His approval of Moses and Aaron. The judgment to come upon Jerusalem would also be supernatural, but it would demonstrate God's anger and the **pride** of His disobedient people.

i. "Ezekiel has hereby twisted what was originally a positive symbol of election and legitimate authority into an emblematic cudgel of oppression and wickedness." (Block)

ii. Smith is an example of those who identify the **rod** with Babylon: "The day of Jerusalem's judgment would begin with the blossoming of the arrogant superpower Babylon, God's judgment 'rod.' The wickedness and violent deeds of the citizens of Judah created the need for this rod of correction."

c. **None...none...none of them**: With poetic power and repetition, Ezekiel assured them that none would escape the coming calamity. Both the **buyer** and the **seller** would have reasons to mourn, **for wrath is on their whole multitude**.

> i. **The buyer...the seller**: "The point is, of course, that buying and selling will have lost their significance in the face of the total disaster that will come on buyer and seller alike." (Vawter and Hoppe)

> ii. **The seller shall not return**: "In a grim parody of the ancient laws of Jubilee, the prophet declares that patrimonial property that has been lost to the family will not return; the year of Jubilee will be canceled." (Block)

d. **It shall not turn back**: Most of the time in the Scriptures, when God announces judgment it is an implied invitation for repentance, whereupon God will relent from the announced judgment. With this prophecy of Ezekiel, this was not the case. The judgment was coming; **it shall not turn back**.

> i. **No one will strengthen himself who lives in iniquity**: "Ezekiel indicated the foolishness of the man who thought he could strengthen himself in the very iniquity which called down the wrath of God. Hardening oneself in sin would not accomplish immunity from punishment. On the contrary, it would assure it all the more." (Feinberg)

2. (14-18) In that day, shame and horror will be upon all.

'They have blown the trumpet and made everyone ready,
But no one goes to battle;
For My wrath *is* on all their multitude.
The sword *is* outside,
And the pestilence and famine within.
Whoever *is* in the field
Will die by the sword;
And whoever *is* in the city,
Famine and pestilence will devour him.
'Those who survive will escape and be on the mountains
Like doves of the valleys,
All of them mourning,
Each for his iniquity.
Every hand will be feeble,
And every knee will be *as* weak *as* water.
They will also be girded with sackcloth;
Horror will cover them;

Shame *will be* on every face,
Baldness on all their heads.

a. **No one goes to battle**: There would be very little resistance to the coming Babylonian conquest. Perhaps the people took comfort in the idea, "Our soldiers will fight bravely to save our land from the Babylonians." Ezekiel told them they would not fight at all, much less bravely.

i. "Its first manifestation would be the paralysis of the people, so that when the trumpet was blown for the battle, and all was ready, none would move forward, being overcome by terror and grief." (Morgan)

b. **Whoever is in the field will die by the sword**: Ezekiel methodically described the fate of those **in the field**, those **in the city**, and those **who survive**. Each would experience the coming calamity in their own way, but none would escape it.

i. **Like doves of the valleys**: "What the prophet seems to be envisaging is the total destruction of the towns and cities of Judah, forcing those who survive to seek refuge in the mountains. The sound of their mourning would resemble the plaintive cooing of ordinary pigeons." (Block)

ii. **Every knee will be as weak as water**: "There is a vivid account of the panic that will follow. The RSV's 'all knees [are] weak as water' means 'all knees will run water': a euphemism for the loss of bladder control in moments of terror." (Vawter and Hoppe)

iii. "However, the LXX translators have captured its sense: 'and all their knees will run with urine.' The prophet is hereby referring to the loss of bladder control that occurs in a moment of extreme crisis." (Block)

c. **Horror will cover them; shame will be on every face**: When the calamity came, it would not be light. This was far beyond an inconvenience. In their own way, all would share in the **horror** and **shame**.

3. (19-22) In that day, material things will be of no help.

'They will throw their silver into the streets,
And their gold will be like refuse;
Their silver and their gold will not be able to deliver them
In the day of the wrath of the LORD;
They will not satisfy their souls,
Nor fill their stomachs,
Because it became their stumbling block of iniquity.
'As for the beauty of his ornaments,
He set it in majesty;
But they made from it

The images of their abominations—
Their detestable things;
Therefore I have made it
Like refuse to them.
I will give it as plunder
Into the hands of strangers,
And to the wicked of the earth as spoil;
And they shall defile it.
I will turn My face from them,
And they will defile My secret place;
For robbers shall enter it and defile it.

a. **Their silver and their gold will not be able to deliver them in the day of the wrath of the Lord**: The completeness of the coming judgment meant that it would also affect both rich and poor. The wealth of the rich would give them no advantage.

i. **They will throw their silver into the streets**: "As burdensome, and not beneficial to them. Thus Judas threw away his wages of wickedness; and many, on their deathbeds, detest their cursed hoards of ill gotten goods, saying unto them, as once Charles V did, *Abite hinc, abite longe,* – Away from me, away, away." (Trapp)

ii. "Generally silver and gold stand for much among the children of men; they are the keys to the unlocking of the treasures of life. But when the supreme crises come; when all hands are feeble, and all knees weak as water; when the day of the wrath of the Lord breaks—there is no help in silver and gold; they cannot satisfy or save." (Meyer)

b. **Because it became their stumbling block of iniquity**: Their riches *got* them into trouble; they could not *rescue* them from trouble.

c. **Therefore I have made it like refuse to them**: The word here and in verse 19 translated **refuse** refers to sexual impurity, such as the ritual uncleanness associated with menstruation.

i. **Refuse**: "This word, *nidda*, belongs to the language of female impurity and expresses the revulsion that will be felt not only towards their wealth, but also towards *their beautiful ornament* (20, RSV), i.e. their expensively decked idols. " (Taylor)

ii. "Money would be thrown away like something sexually unclean (Lev 20–21)." (Alexander)

d. **He set it in majesty; but they made from it the images of their abominations**: God blessed Israel with wealth and resources, but they used those things to further and promote idolatry. Fittingly, all that wealth would be given **as plunder into the hands of strangers**.

e. **They will defile My secret place**: God even announced that **robbers** would sack His temple, including the **secret place** (the holy of holies). This coming judgment would be complete, not sparing even the temple.

4. (23-27) In that day, all human help will fail.

'**Make a chain,**
For the land is filled with crimes of blood,
And the city is full of violence.
Therefore I will bring the worst of the Gentiles,
And they will possess their houses;
I will cause the pomp of the strong to cease,
And their holy places shall be defiled.
Destruction comes;
They will seek peace, but *there shall be* **none.**
Disaster will come upon disaster,
And rumor will be upon rumor.
Then they will seek a vision from a prophet;
But the law will perish from the priest,
And counsel from the elders.
'**The king will mourn,**
The prince will be clothed with desolation,
And the hands of the common people will tremble.
I will do to them according to their way,
And according to what they deserve I will judge them;
Then they shall know that I *am* **the LORD!**'"

a. **Make a chain, for the land is filled with crimes of blood**: This was likely a **chain** to restrain violent criminals, those guilty of **crimes of blood**. God would allow great judgment to be a punishment and restraint to His violent, wicked people.

i. "Ezekiel was commanded to perform a symbolic act by making a chain which was emblematic of the captivity awaiting them (see Jeremiah 27:2; Nahum 3:10)." (Feinberg)

ii. "In Nah. 3:10 this word describes the treatment of prisoners of war, in this instance consisting of persons from the upper class. The 'chain' would have been used to tie the captives together to form a long train headed for exile." (Block)

iii. **Crimes of blood**: "*Judicial murders*, occurs only here…. the phrase is best understood as 'murderous judicial decisions,' rather than 'crimes of violence.'" (Block)

b. **Therefore I will bring the worst of the Gentiles**: God made no claim that the invaders would be good or righteous. They were instruments of His severe correction against His people, but they were not good – they were **the worst of the Gentiles**.

i. "The Jews were bad enough, but the Chaldees were worse, if worse might be; malignants above measure, Poneropolitans, breathing devils. A hard knot must have a harder wedge, as the proverb is." (Trapp)

ii. "How he may use a more wicked population to punish a less wicked one may create theological problems for mortal minds, but it is consistent with his sovereignty over all." (Block)

c. **They will seek peace, but there shall be none**: There would be no quickly made peace treaty or tribute paid to prevent the disaster. It would surely come.

d. **Then they will seek a vision from a prophet**: Frightened by the **disaster** and confused by the **rumor**, some would finally seek a word from God. In that day of judgment, there would be none. **The law will perish from the priest, and counsel from the elders**.

i. Ezekiel 7:26 seems to be an answer to what was said in Jerusalem at the time, as recorded by Jeremiah 18:18: *Then they said, "Come and let us devise plans against Jeremiah; for the law shall not perish from the priest, nor counsel from the wise, nor the word from the prophet. Come and let us attack him with the tongue, and let us not give heed to any of his words."*

ii. **The king will mourn**: "In the eyes of Ezekiel, the king was Jehoiachin (1:2) and the prince was Zedekiah. Though Zedekiah was the last king of Judah, the prophet didn't recognize his reign but considered him only a prince (12:10, 12)." (Wiersbe)

e. **According to what they deserve I will judge them**: This was a terrible promise. Israel had sinned greatly, so a great judgment was coming upon them.

f. **Then they shall know that I am the LORD**: The triple repetition in this chapter makes the point strongly. God's purpose was not Israel's pain, but their restoration to a true relationship with Him.

Ezekiel 8 – Abominations at the Temple

A. Ezekiel goes to Jerusalem in a vision.

1. (1) Ezekiel, the elders, and the hand of the LORD.

And it came to pass in the sixth year, in the sixth *month,* on the fifth *day* of the month, as I sat in my house with the elders of Judah sitting before me, that the hand of the Lord GOD fell upon me there.

> a. **In the sixth year, in the sixth month**: Ezekiel 1:2 began a series of visions beginning with *in the fifth year of King Jehoiachin's captivity.* This is a new time marker describing visions that happened about a year and a half later. This series of visions is in Ezekiel 8-11.

> > i. Ezekiel 8-11 is the record of one long vision. In the beginning of the vision Ezekiel sees the glory of the LORD at the temple in Jerusalem. By the end of the vision (chapters 10 and 11), this glory will depart.

> > ii. "They also supply us with a date corresponding to 17 September 592 B.C.E., therefore something more than a year after Ezekiel had received his prophetic call." (Vawter and Hoppe)

> b. **I sat in my house with the elders of Judah sitting before me**: This reminds us that Ezekiel had his own **house**, and that he was respected enough as God's prophet to receive the **elders of Judah** for an audience in his home.

> > i. "The reason for their presence in Ezekiel's house is not given, though 14:1–3 and 20:1 suggest that they came to him customarily to seek a word from Yahweh." (Block)

> c. **The hand of the Lord GOD fell upon me there**: As before in Ezekiel 1:3, 3:14, and 3:22, Ezekiel felt the presence and strength of Yahweh upon him.

2. (2-4) In a vision, Ezekiel is transported to Jerusalem.

Then I looked, and there was a likeness, like the appearance of fire— from the appearance of His waist and downward, fire; and from His

waist and upward, like the appearance of brightness, like the color of amber. He stretched out the form of a hand, and took me by a lock of my hair; and the Spirit lifted me up between earth and heaven, and brought me in visions of God to Jerusalem, to the door of the north gate of the inner *court,* where the seat of the image of jealousy *was,* which provokes to jealousy. And behold, the glory of the God of Israel *was* there, like the vision that I saw in the plain.

a. **There was a likeness, like the appearance of fire**: Ezekiel saw something similar to the **likeness** he saw in the vision of God and His glory in the first chapter (Ezekiel 1:27). That was a representation of God in some human **likeness**, and we see the same here.

b. **He stretched out the form of a hand**: In his vision, something like a hand grabbed Ezekiel by the hair, and the **Spirit** carried him **between heaven and earth**, bringing him to Jerusalem in a vision.

i. Ezekiel had this spiritual vision of Jerusalem in the days when Jeremiah served as a prophet, in that period between the second invasion of the Babylonians and their final conquest of Jerusalem.

ii. "That he did not actually leave Babylon is clear from 11:24. He was carried back in spirit to Babylon after the visions were completed (11:22-25)." (Feinberg)

iii. In this vision Ezekiel saw four abominations at the temple. They were probably not literal in the sense that they were happening all at the same time at the temple and Ezekiel saw this in real time. God showed Ezekiel what was literally happening, in both an outward and in a spiritual sense.

- The outrageous idol, associated with the king (Ezekiel 8:5-6).
- The images and censers, associated with the city leaders (Ezekiel 8:7-13).
- The weeping over Tammuz, associated with the women (Ezekiel 8:14-15).
- The worship of the sun, associated with the priests (Ezekiel 8:16-18).

c. **To…the north gate of the inner court**: Specifically, Ezekiel came to the temple. As a priest, he had a special interest not only in the temple but also in all that happened there.

d. **Where the seat of the image of jealousy was**: In his vision, Ezekiel apparently saw an idolatrous image – **the image of jealousy** – standing in the **inner court**. This was likely right outside the temple building itself.

i. "It was called *the image of jealousy* because it *provokes to jealousy*, i.e. it was an insult both to God and to his temple and to his people." (Taylor)

ii. Hezekiah removed idolatry from Judah (2 Kings 18:1-5), but his son Manasseh restored it and made it worse than ever, even putting an idol into the temple (2 Kings 21:1-7). Manasseh's son Amon continued the state-sponsored idolatry of his father. King Josiah cleansed Judah of idolatry and burned the idol Manasseh had put in the temple (2 Kings 23:4-20). Now we see that the idol in the temple was back.

iii. "The word 'image' is *semel,* which occurs elsewhere only in Deuteronomy 4.16 (where it is translated 'figure') and in 2 Chronicles 33.7,15, of a special 'idol' set up by King Manasseh in the Temple. Although this idol was later removed, Ezekiel's use of the word may mean that a replica, if not the original, was put back. The word also occurs in Phoenician writings." (Wright)

e. **Behold, the glory of the God of Israel was there**: In his vision, Ezekiel saw the same **glory** of God that he **saw in the plain**. The glory of God was present at the temple of God in Jerusalem. There is a strong contrast between this **glory** and the debased idols and idolatry Ezekiel will see in the rest of this vision.

i. God's glory filled the tabernacle (Exodus 40:34-35) and later the temple (1 Kings 8:11). By the end of this vision (Ezekiel 10-11) the glory of the LORD will no longer dwell in the temple.

3. (5) Ezekiel looks to the north.

Then He said to me, "Son of man, lift your eyes now toward the north." So I lifted my eyes toward the north, and there, north of the altar gate, was this image of jealousy in the entrance.

a. **Lift your eyes now toward the north**: If one stood facing the entrance to the temple, the **north** would be on the right side. We don't know which way Ezekiel had to turn, but he was directed to face **toward the north**.

b. **North of the altar gate, was this image of jealousy in the entrance**: There again, Ezekiel saw this idol in the temple court. It was called **the image of jealousy** because it provoked God to holy jealousy.

i. The connection of this image with the **north gate** (Ezekiel 8:3) was significant, connecting this **image of jealousy** with royalty and the king. "This was the most honourable of the three gateways because, the royal palace being on the north side of the temple, the king would have used it whenever he went in to worship." (Taylor)

4. (6-8) Great and greater abominations.

Furthermore He said to me, "Son of man, do you see what they are doing, the great abominations that the house of Israel commits here, to make Me go far away from My sanctuary? Now turn again, you will see greater abominations." So He brought me to the door of the court; and when I looked, there was a hole in the wall. Then He said to me, "Son of man, dig into the wall"; and when I dug into the wall, there was a door.

a. **The great abominations that the house of Israel commits here**: Ezekiel saw the *image of jealousy*, and God told him that it represented **the great abominations** of Israel.

b. **To make Me go far away from My sanctuary**: The idolatry was so persistent and offensive to God that it made Him determined to **go far away**. It was His **sanctuary**, belonging to God Himself, but He would leave it because of their **great abominations**.

c. **Now turn again, you will see greater abominations**: What Ezekiel saw was bad enough; God now promised to show him worse things, **greater abominations**.

d. **Son of man, dig into the wall**: To see those **greater abominations**, Ezekiel had to dig through a wall to see in his vision what was inside the temple itself.

i. "While we may puzzle over how he is able to dig a hole in the wall or why he does not use the existing entrance to this room, the visionary nature of this entire unit removes the necessity for realism or logical consistency." (Block)

ii. In spiritual application, this shows that it may take some effort and energy to truly see the interior. If only an easy or surface observation is allowed, the true state of things may not be seen.

B. What Ezekiel saw behind the wall.

1. (9-12) Wicked things and blind men.

And He said to me, "Go in, and see the wicked abominations which they are doing there." So I went in and saw, and there—every sort of creeping thing, abominable beasts, and all the idols of the house of Israel, portrayed all around on the walls. And there stood before them seventy men of the elders of the house of Israel, and in their midst stood Jaazaniah the son of Shaphan. Each man had a censer in his hand, and a thick cloud of incense went up. Then He said to me, "Son of man, have you seen what the elders of the house of Israel do in the dark, every man

in the room of his idols? For they say, 'The LORD does not see us, the LORD has forsaken the land.'"

a. **Every sort of creeping thing, the abominable beasts, and all the idols**: In his vision, Ezekiel saw the inside of the temple with all sorts of unclean and idolatrous things **portrayed all around on the walls**. The interior of the temple was supposed to have cherubim surrounding God's throne portrayed on the walls, and instead had filthy idols.

i. God called these **wicked abominations**; "the most abominable wickednesses; these are loathsome in their nature, and multiplied in number before me." (Poole)

ii. "The consensus of interpreters is that these were the animal cults of Egypt (see Rom. 1:23). In Egypt such worship had perhaps its highest and most extensive development in ancient times." (Feinberg)

iii. "This piece of idolatry the Jews had learned of the Egyptians, who madly worshipped oxen, asses, goats, dogs, cats, serpents, crocodiles, the bird ibis, &c." (Trapp)

b. **There stood before them seventy men of the elders of the house of Israel**: In front of these foul and idolatrous images were the leaders of Israel, each with **a censer** giving out a **thick cloud of incense**. They offered priestly service and incense associated with prayers, in the midst of the idolatry and impurity.

i. **Elders** "refers to the lay leaders who had risen to prominence in Jerusalem after the deportation of Jehoiachin and his officials (2 Kings 24:12-16). These were obviously important men in the city." (Block)

ii. **Jaazaniah the son of Shaphan**: "*Shaphan* is probably to be identified with Josiah's secretary of state (2 Kings 22:3), and Ahikam, another of Shaphan's sons, was an influential supporter of Jeremiah (Jereremiah 26:24). Clearly Jaazaniah was the black sheep of a worthy family." (Taylor)

c. **Have you seen what the elders of the house of Israel do in the dark, every man in the room of his idols?** God showed Ezekiel that the vision was about what the leaders of Israel did **in the dark**, and **in the room of his idols**. It wasn't about what the leaders did in the temple, but the hidden place of their heart was filled with dark deeds and idolatry – yet they carried on their service as if all was right.

i. Ezekiel was probably shocked to see that all these city leaders were secret idolaters.

ii. "They had carried the idolatry of the temple into their private homes. Public and private worship was permeated with the God-dishonoring idolatry. And they were smugly complacent in it all." (Feinberg)

iii. "While the external rites of the Temple of Jehovah were being observed, these very observances were made a cloak for the thoughts, desires, activities of the heart. This is the most hopeless stage and stale of pollution." (Morgan)

iv. "Is it quite certain that evil thoughts and imaginations have not imprinted themselves on the walls of the heart? Ah, it may be so. What seems fair and beautiful in the eye of man may be concealing terrible secrets, open only to that of God." (Meyer)

d. **The LORD does not see us, the LORD has forsaken the land**: They excused their sin because they did not think Yahweh saw them, either in their minds or their actions. They also excused their sin because they believed God had **forsaken** Israel, when in fact they had forsaken God.

i. "With this kind of rationalization they permitted themselves to do anything they desired. If God did not exist then no one need care about him. It is tragic that the same attitude exists today among so many people." (Alexander)

ii. "What the men in this dark room are saying about Yahweh is in fact false about *him,* but it is true of the images before which they stand." (Block)

2. (13-14) Women weeping for Tammuz.

And He said to me, "Turn again, *and* you will see greater abominations that they are doing." So He brought me to the door of the north gate of the LORD's house; and to my dismay, women were sitting there weeping for Tammuz.

a. **You will see greater abominations**: Ezekiel saw idolatry outside the temple and corruption among the leaders within. Yet there were **greater abominations** to see.

i. "We need not then perplex our reader with a long discourse, to show wherein these latter sins are greater than the former mentioned; they are all very great." (Poole)

b. **To my dismay, women were sitting there weeping for Tammuz**: This is the only mention of **Tammuz** in Ezekiel and the Old Testament. This was another example of pagan worship, and **Tammuz** was a deity worshiped by many in neighboring nations, often with immoral or impure rites. Ezekiel was dismayed because women were **there**, in the holy place reserved only for priests, and because of their immoral idolatry.

> i. "It is likely that the prophet would have viewed the presence of women in the inner court as a profanation." (Vawter and Hoppe)

> ii. "The worship of Tammuz came from Babylon through the Phoenicians (Canaanites) and then the Greeks. Tammuz, mentioned nowhere else in the Scriptures, was the Babylonian Dumuzi, beloved of Ishtar, and is to be identified with the Greek Adonis." (Feinberg)

> iii. "In the seasonal mythological cycle, he died early in the fall when vegetation withered. His revival by the wailing of Ishtar was marked by the buds of spring and the fertility of the land. Such renewal was encouraged and celebrated by licentious fertility festivals." (Alexander)

> iv. "With the worship of this god in ancient times were connected the basest immoralities. With the greatest of abandon women gave themselves up to most shameful practices." (Feinberg)

3. (15-16) Priests worshipping the sun.

Then He said to me, "Have you seen *this*, O son of man? Turn again, you will see greater abominations than these." So He brought me into the inner court of the LORD's house; and there, at the door of the temple of the LORD, between the porch and the altar, *were* about twenty-five men with their backs toward the temple of the LORD and their faces toward the east, and they were worshiping the sun toward the east.

> a. **You will see greater abominations than these**: God continually promised Ezekiel that he would see greater and **greater abominations**. This time, his vision would display them in **the inner court of the LORD's house**.

> > i. "The idolatry of the seventy elders was hidden in the temple, but these men practiced their idolatry openly!" (Wiersbe)

> b. **About twenty-five men with their backs toward the temple…and they were worshipping the sun toward the east**: These men stood where the priests would normally stand to bless the people. Yet, with the temple behind them and the altar before them (**their faces toward the east**), **they were worshipping the sun toward the east**. They didn't worship Yahweh, *even at His own temple* – they worshipped the sun, as the other pagan nations did.

> > i. The *number* and the *location* of these men make it likely (though not certain) they were priests. "If they were priests perhaps the number is twenty-five because there was a representative of each of the twenty-

four courses of the priests plus the high priest (cf. 1 Chron 23)." (Alexander)

ii. "These worshippers showed their contempt for God by standing in such a way that they had their backs to the Temple while they reverenced the sun (cf. 2 Kings 23.5,11), worshipping the creature rather than the Creator (Rom. 1.25)." (Wright)

iii. Block on the **sun** cult in Israel: "According to 2 K. 21:5 it appears to have gained royal sponsorship during the reign of Manasseh, who built altars for the entire host of heaven in the courts of the temple. From 2 K. 23:11–12 one may also infer that the horses and chariots of the sun at the entrance of the temple that Josiah demolished had also been erected by Manasseh."

4. (17-18) A promise of judgment upon all these abominations.

And He said to me, "Have you seen *this*, O son of man? Is it a trivial thing to the house of Judah to commit the abominations which they commit here? For they have filled the land with violence; then they have returned to provoke Me to anger. Indeed they put the branch to their nose. Therefore I also will act in fury. My eye will not spare nor will I have pity; and though they cry in My ears with a loud voice, I will not hear them."

a. **Is it a trivial thing to the house of Judah to commit the abominations**: In his vision of the temple, Ezekiel saw a terrible variety of idolatries and **abominations**. The leaders and people of Jerusalem regarded it all as **a trivial thing**; God did not.

b. **For they have filled the land with violence**: These were not only religious or spiritual sins. Their rejection of Yahweh and His true worship led to a breakdown in the social order.

i. "The inhabitants of Judah were not content to provoke the Lord with their abominations. They had also filled the land with 'violence,' i.e., social chaos and injustice." (Smith)

c. **Indeed they put the branch to their nose**: This is an unusual statement, used only here in the Old Testament. It was some obscure expression of contempt for God.

i. "The phrase 'put the branch to their nose' is obscure. Jewish commentators understood it to refer to some revolting and wicked rite. If it was a ritual act in an idolatrous cult, then it is grave indeed. But no such ritual act is known among Semitic peoples. Some take it to be a gesture of contempt toward God." (Feinberg)

ii. "'Sticking the branch to the nose' may simply describe an insulting physical gesture, here employed euphemistically to express how Yahweh feels about the way his subjects have treated him." (Block)

iii. Wright had another idea: "The branch held to the nose may have been in imitation of the Egyptian *ankh*, a symbol of life, which is shown in carvings as held to the nose, or it may have been connected with plants sacred to Tammuz or some other god."

iv. Vawter and Hoppe argue that the text has been corrupted and *should* read, "A branch in My nose." "All that the Lord is saying is that in place of the pleasing odor of honest sacrificial worship (Leviticus 1:9, etc.), what God is receiving from the Israelites comes as a stench in God's nostrils."

d. **My eye will not spare nor will I have pity**: Because of the great idolatries and sins of Jerusalem, and that the people regarded it all as **a trivial thing**, God's judgment was assured, and could not be turned back.

i. "Because of this utter corruption of the people, Jehovah would proceed in judgment, in spite of all the loud crying of the people." (Morgan)

ii. "Yahweh hereby affirms that from now on his ears are closed to all pleas for mercy…. He will not allow his heart to overrule his head." (Block)

Ezekiel 9 – Marked for Preservation, Marked for Judgment

A. Angelic judgment upon Jerusalem.

1. (1-2) The men beside the bronze altar.

Then He called out in my hearing with a loud voice, saying, "Let those who have charge over the city draw near, each *with* a deadly weapon in his hand." And suddenly six men came from the direction of the upper gate, which faces north, each with his battle-ax in his hand. One man among them *was* clothed with linen and had a writer's inkhorn at his side. They went in and stood beside the bronze altar.

a. **Let those who have charge over the city draw near**: In his vision of Jerusalem and the corruptions at the temple (Ezekiel 8), Ezekiel heard God speaking with a **loud voice**, calling forward **six men** who, in some sense, had **charge over the city**.

i. "Those who had charge over the city were those whom God set to watch over the welfare of the city. They were not earthly agents, but heavenly. Angels are frequently called men because of their outward appearance." (Feinberg)

b. **Each with a deadly weapon in his hand**: The **six men** of Ezekiel's vision were armed, each with a **battle-ax in his hand**. It's best to understand these **six men** as angelic beings with responsibility over Jerusalem.

i. "For all Ezekiel's outward appearance of severity, beneath the hard shell there was a heart that felt deeply for and with his people. He did not relish the message of judgment that he had to give, still less the reality that followed when the message was rejected." (Wiersbe)

ii. In ways we don't completely understand, sometimes angelic beings have or desire assignments related to places, to geography. This is true of both faithful and fallen angelic beings.

- In Daniel's day, a demonic spirit was assigned to Persia (Daniel 10:13, 10:20) and to Greece (Daniel 10:20).
- Daniel 12:1 says that Michael had some responsibility regarding Israel.
- Satan himself was connected with the king of Babylon (Isaiah 14).
- Mark 5:10 indicates that demons wanted to stay in one place and not be sent to another by Jesus.

iii. **Which faces north**: "The angelic executioners came from the way of the upper gate which was built by Jotham (II Kings 15:35), called the upper Benjamin gate (Jeremiah 20:2) or the new gate (Jeremiah 26:10; 36:10). The gate was toward the north of the city, the direction from which the Babylonian invaders came, as well as the area where the idolatries had taken place." (Feinberg)

c. **One man among them was clothed with linen and had a writer's inkhorn at his side**: In addition to these **six men**, there was another dressed differently and who also carried an **inkhorn**, ready to write.

i. There is some debate among commentators as to if this **one man among them** is an additional person or included in the number of the **six men**. Keil and Delitzsch are among those who think there were a total of seven: "In the midst of the six men furnished with smashing-tools there was one clothed in white byssus, with writing materials at his side. The dress and equipment, as well as the instructions which he afterwards receives and executes, show him to be the prince or leader of the others."

ii. "*Linen* was the fabric used for the dress of priests (Exod. 28:29–42) and angelic beings (Dan. 10:5; 12:6–7), two classes of beings directly involved in divine service." (Block)

iii. "At his side was *a writing case* (RSV; AV, RV *inkhorn*): the word is peculiar to this chapter and may be a loan-word from Egyptian, where it refers to the scribe's writing equipment, incorporating pen, ink-horn and wax writing-tablet." (Taylor)

d. **They went in and stood beside the bronze altar**: The seven men – who actually seem to be angels – were ready for service.

i. "They march in past the image of jealousy and the mourners for Tammuz, and take their stand near the sun-worshippers, invisible to all except Ezekiel." (Wright)

ii. **Stood beside the bronze altar**: "To signify that the people against whom they had their commission were, for their crimes, to be sacrificed to the demands of Divine justice." (Clarke)

2. (3-4) The command to mark the foreheads of godly men in Jerusalem.

Now the glory of the God of Israel had gone up from the cherub, where it had been, to the threshold of the temple. And He called to the man clothed with linen, who *had* the writer's inkhorn at his side; and the LORD said to him, "Go through the midst of the city, through the midst of Jerusalem, and put a mark on the foreheads of the men who sigh and cry over all the abominations that are done within it."

a. **The glory of the God of Israel had gone up from the cherub**: The visible representation of God's **glory** rose up higher than where the cherub stood.

i. "The Lord vividly demonstrated his readiness to judge by withdrawing his glory from his people. God's glory moved from the Most Holy Place to the entry of the temple to assign the tasks of judgment." (Alexander)

ii. **Had gone up**: "The departure of the glory of the Lord from Israel is one of the basic disclosures of this prophetic book, so Ezekiel traces it very carefully in its different stages (cf. 9:3; 10:18-19; 43:2-5)." (Feinberg)

iii. **From the cherub**: "For the first time, in this and the following chapters, the 'living creatures' that were the support of the LORD's throne in Ezekiel's inaugural vision of ch. 1 receive the name that properly applies to them: *cherub* in the singular and collective, and in the plural *cherubim*." (Vawter and Hoppe)

iv. "Being of priestly descent, Ezekiel was undoubtedly familiar with the images of the cherubim in the temple. Apparently this vision offered him an opportunity that was impossible in real life—a look into the inner sanctum of the divine palace, the holy of holies." (Block)

b. **Go through the midst of the city...put a mark on the foreheads**: God commanded the one with the inkwell to **mark** the righteous men of the city. Ezekiel 9:6 shows this was a *protective* identification, to protect them in the coming invasion and also to protect them spiritually for the age to come. It shows that even when judgment comes upon an entire nation, God still knows how to mark and identify the righteous.

i. "Like the blood on the doorposts of the Israelites' houses on the night of the Passover (Exod. 12) and the scarlet cord in Rahab's window (Josh. 2:18–21; 6:22–25), it was a sign of hope." (Block)

ii. "There is a prophetic significance in the Hebrew word for the mark. It is the Hebrew letter T (Tau), which at that time was written as a cross. Without being superstitious we can rejoice in this anticipation of salvation through the death of Christ on the cross." (Wright)

iii. Revelation 7:3 later describes God's servants again being sealed on their foreheads. Revelation 13:16 (and several other passages) also describe a later Satanic counterfeit of this mark, identifying allegiance to Satan and his false messiah.

iv. "This is in allusion to the ancient every-where-used custom of setting marks on servants and slaves, to distinguish them from others. It was also common for the worshippers of particular idols to have their idol's *mark* upon their *foreheads, arms,* &c." (Clarke)

c. **Of the men who sigh and cry over all the abominations**: The remnant God would spare had nothing to do with age or perceived innocence. The remnant was those who had broken hearts over the idolatry and wickedness of the city, men like Jeremiah.

i. **The men who sigh**: "[Sigh] will resurface in 21:6–7, where the moaning will be a symptom of a broken heart and intense grief over impending doom. In 24:17 [**sigh**] describes the grief that Ezekiel expresses over the death of his wife. Here the scribe is to search for individuals who will display a similar emotion over all the abominations being perpetrated in Jerusalem." (Block)

ii. "Let us mourn in time of sinning: so shall we be marked in times of punishing." (Trapp)

iii. "Amid scenes of judgment, whether in the Church or the world, there is always a remnant, upon whom is the mark; on Lot in Sodom; on Israel amid the plagues of Egypt; on Rahab in the fall of Jericho; on the 144,000 at the Great Tribulation. They are safe amid the fiery indignation which devours the adversaries." (Meyer)

3. (5-7) The command to kill in judgment.

To the others He said in my hearing, "Go after him through the city and kill; do not let your eye spare, nor have any pity. Utterly slay old *and* young men, maidens and little children and women; but do not come near anyone on whom *is* the mark; and begin at My sanctuary." So they began with the elders who *were* before the temple. Then He said to them, "Defile the temple, and fill the courts with the slain. Go out!" And they went out and killed in the city.

a. **Go after him through the city and kill**: God commanded the other of the six men to use their weapons of judgment against the city as a whole, sparing none except **anyone on whom is the mark**.

> i. "Regard no state or sex, neither the loveliness of the virgin, nor the prettiness of the infant, nor the comeliness and gravity of the matron; spare none." (Poole)

> ii. 2 Chronicles 36:17 described the fulfillment of this: *Therefore He brought against them the king of the Chaldeans, who killed their young men with the sword in the house of their sanctuary, and had no compassion on young man or virgin, on the aged or the weak; He gave them all into his hand.*

b. **And begin at My sanctuary**: God decrees that judgment should begin at His house. Peter later applied this principle to the people of God under the New Covenant (1 Peter 4:17). Therefore, these judging angels **began with the elders who were before the temple**.

> i. "In the sanctuary God should have been most honored, but there He was most dishonored and provoked, and there His holiness would most fully and certainly be vindicated." (Feinberg)

c. **Defile the temple, and fill the courts with the slain**: In Ezekiel 6:4-5 and 6:13, God promised that He would defile and desecrate the pagan altars on the high places because of Israel's idolatry. Here He promised the same desecration at His own house.

> i. "These people had defiled God's house by their wicked lives, and now they would defile it further in their terrible deaths." (Wiersbe)

B. Ezekiel's reaction.

1. (8) Ezekiel's grief.

So it was, that while they were killing them, I was left *alone;* and I fell on my face and cried out, and said, "Ah, Lord God! Will You destroy all the remnant of Israel in pouring out Your fury on Jerusalem?"

a. **I fell on my face and cried out**: Though Ezekiel had many times announced such a severe judgment when he actually saw it carried out in his vision, it made him completely undone.

> i. "For all Ezekiel's outward appearance of severity, beneath the hard shell there was a heart that felt deeply for and with his people. He did not relish the message of judgment that he had to give, still less the reality that followed when the message was rejected." (Taylor)

b. **Will You destroy all the remnant of Israel**: In desperation (**Ah, Lord God!**), Ezekiel begged God to not destroy the **remnant** as He poured out His **fury on Jerusalem**.

2. (9-10) God's explanation.

Then He said to me, "The iniquity of the house of Israel and Judah *is* exceedingly great, and the land is full of bloodshed, and the city full of perversity; for they say, 'The LORD has forsaken the land, and the LORD does not see!' And as for Me also, My eye will neither spare, nor will I have pity, *but* I will recompense their deeds on their own head."

a. **The iniquity of the house of Israel and Judah is exceedingly great**: God reminded Ezekiel of what he had been preaching – that as terrible as the judgment was, it was fully deserved and a long time in coming.

b. **The LORD has forsaken the land, and the LORD does not see**: This is what the leaders of the city said earlier in Ezekiel's vision (Ezekiel 8:12). Because of their persistent, offensive rejection of God, Yahweh vowed, **My eye will neither spare, nor will I have pity**.

i. "Since the righteous are marked, the fate of the wicked is sealed. For them there is no hope of escape." (Block)

3. (11) The report of the man with the inkhorn.

Just then, the man clothed with linen, who *had* the inkhorn at his side, reported back and said, "I have done as You commanded me."

a. **Reported back**: Angels are diligent and accountable in their service.

i. "Angels and men must all give account of their conduct to God; for although he is every where, and his eye sees all things, yet they must personally account for all that they have done." (Clarke)

b. **I have done as You commanded me**: The angel could report that he had marked the faithful remnant in Jerusalem.

i. This was "an encouragement to Ezekiel that all Judah had not strayed from God, the man with the writing kit reported, 'I have done as you commanded.' In other words, the righteous ones had been marked." (Alexander)

ii. "These grand words are reminiscent of the declaration of the Lord Jesus Christ in John 17:4. How worthwhile and fruitful was that life!" (Feinberg)

Ezekiel 10 – The Glory and the Cherubim

A. The vision of God's glory at the temple.

1. (1-2) The likeness of a throne.

And I looked, and there in the firmament that was above the head of the cherubim, there appeared something like a sapphire stone, having the appearance of the likeness of a throne. Then He spoke to the man clothed with linen, and said, "Go in among the wheels, under the cherub, fill your hands with coals of fire from among the cherubim, and scatter *them* **over the city." And he went in as I watched.**

a. **There in the firmament that was above the head of the cherubim, there appeared something like a sapphire stone**: Ezekiel 8-11 is an extended description of the prophet's vision of corruption and judgment at the temple in Jerusalem. Another important part of this vision is the glory of God, described in the same terms as what Ezekiel saw in the vision of his calling in Ezekiel 1-3. Here is the description of a **firmament** that was **above the head of the cherubim**.

i. From the association with other passages, we understood that the *living creatures* of Ezekiel 1 were cherubim, but they were not given that specific name in Ezekiel 1. Now at the temple they are more properly titled **cherubim**, because there were artistic depictions of **cherubim** all over the temple, including the large statues set up by Solomon (1 Kings 6:23).

ii. "These cherubim are the living heavenly realities that the static sculptures in the inner sanctum symbolize! They have come to earth from the heavenly throne room to transport the *kabod*, the visible sign of God's presence, out of his earthly dwelling place." (Block)

b. **The firmament**: As with the vision in Ezekiel 1, Ezekiel saw something above the **cherubim** surrounding God's throne, something like a sky or space. The **cherubim** are the mighty angels associated with God's presence and throne.

c. **The likeness of a throne**: Ezekiel describes the throne just as in Ezekiel 1:26, but here he did not mention *the appearance of a man high above it*. Yet the person on the throne is *implied*, from the **He** who **spoke to the man clothed with linen.**

d. **Fill your hands with coals of fire from among the cherubim**: This was the command directed to **the man clothed with linen**, who was the one who marked the few faithful in Jerusalem (Ezekiel 8). God commanded this angel to take the burning coals **and scatter them over the city**.

> i. Previously we read that Jerusalem would be judged by siege, slaughter, famine, and disease. Now we learn that Jerusalem will also be burnt, and the fire comes *from the throne and glory of God itself*; the **coals of fire** come **from among the cherubim.**

> ii. "Emphasis on fire in this chapter is noteworthy, because it looked forward to the fire which destroyed Jerusalem in 586 B.C. (II Kings 25:9)." (Feinberg)

> iii. "In Isaiah 6 the coals were for the purification of the prophet; here they were for the destruction of the wicked. Where evil is concerned, it is true that 'our God is a consuming fire' as stated in Hebrews 12:29." (Feinberg)

> iv. "In Ezekiel's mind, Jerusalem was going to be treated in the same way as Sodom and Gomorrah (Genesis 19:24)." (Taylor)

e. **He went in as I watched**: The angel was quick to obey, even as he was in Ezekiel 9:11.

2. (3-5) The cloud of God's glory.

Now the cherubim were standing on the south side of the temple when the man went in, and the cloud filled the inner court. Then the glory of the Lord went up from the cherub, *and paused* over the threshold of the temple; and the house was filled with the cloud, and the court was full of the brightness of the Lord's glory. And the sound of the wings of the cherubim was heard *even* in the outer court, like the voice of Almighty God when He speaks.

a. **The cherubim were standing on the south side of the temple**: This was the opposite side from where the angels of judgment started their work (Ezekiel 9:1-2).

b. **The cloud filled the inner court**: This was the cloud of glory, seen often in the Old and New Testaments, sometimes called the cloud of *Shekinah* glory. It is hard to *define* the glory of God; we could call it the radiant outshining of His character and presence. Here it was given some visible representation in **the cloud**.

- This is the cloud that stood by Israel in the wilderness (Exodus 13:21-22).

- This is the cloud of glory that God spoke to Israel from (Exodus 16:10).

- This is the cloud from which God met with Moses and others (Exodus 19:9, 24:15-18, Numbers 11:25, 12:5, 16:42).

- This is the cloud that stood by the door of the Tabernacle (Exodus 33:9-10).

- This is the cloud from which God appeared to the High Priest in the Holy Place inside the veil (Leviticus 16:2).

- This is the cloud that so filled the temple when Solomon dedicated it that the priests could not continue to serve (1 Kings 8:1-11).

- This is the cloud of Ezekiel's vision, filling the temple of God with the brightness of His glory (Ezekiel 10:4).

- This is the cloud of glory that overshadowed Mary when she conceived Jesus by the power of the Holy Spirit (Luke 1:35).

- This is the cloud present at the transfiguration of Jesus (Luke 9:34-35).

- This is the cloud of glory that received Jesus into heaven at His ascension (Acts 1:9).

- This is the cloud that will display the glory of Jesus Christ when He returns in triumph to this earth (Luke 21:27, Revelation 1:7).

   i. Ezekiel saw this in a vision, and in what he saw there is a strange tragedy. Ezekiel saw many people at the temple (Ezekiel 8), but only he saw the glory of God. "The sad thing was that Ezekiel was evidently the only person who saw the glory of God. The rest had eyes only for images, pictures, and the lesser glory of the sun." (Wright)

c. **The glory of the LORD went up from the cherub, and paused over the threshold of the temple**: In Ezekiel's vision, the glory of the LORD shined brightly and the **cloud** of His glory filled the temple. Yet, it was on the move (as also seen in Ezekiel 9:3), pausing as it was about to leave **the temple**.

   i. **Paused over the threshold**: "Showing both his unwillingness to leave, and giving them time to bethink themselves, and return by repentance; and he stands where he might be seen both by priests and people, that both might be moved to repentance." (Poole)

d. **The sound of the wings of the cherubim was heard**: As this visible representation of God's glory was moving, the **wings of the cherubim** were active and noisy, with a sound as loud and as striking as **the voice of Almighty God when He speaks**.

> i. "The sound of the cherubim's wings reverberates throughout the temple complex and creates an impression of restlessness, an eagerness to be off." (Block)

3. (6-8) The fire from among the wheels.

Then it happened, when He commanded the man clothed in linen, saying, "Take fire from among the wheels, from among the cherubim," that he went in and stood beside the wheels. And the cherub stretched out his hand from among the cherubim to the fire that *was* among the cherubim, and took *some of it* and put *it* into the hands of the *man* clothed with linen, who took *it* and went out. The cherubim appeared to have the form of a man's hand under their wings.

a. **Take fire from among the wheels, from among the cherubim**: Again, we note the emphasis that the fire of judgment upon Jerusalem comes *from the throne and glory of God itself*.

> i. "In addition to bringing the *kabod* of Yahweh down to him, the heavenly chariot now arrives with the coals of divine judgment for Jerusalem, and will depart bearing the glory out of the temple and away from the city." (Block)

> ii. "The stage was now set for the fiery destruction of Jerusalem which here is symbolically represented as coming from the Lord himself." (Smith)

> iii. "Fire that proceeds from Him will be absolutely just in its activity. It will harm nothing save that which is evil. The wrath of God is terrible, but it is never passion overleaping the boundaries of righteous action. It is always restrained by the strictest justice." (Morgan)

b. **He went in and stood beside the wheels**: The **man clothed in linen** promptly obeyed the command of God.

c. **The cherub stretched out his hand**: The man clothed in linen did not take the fire directly, but received it from a cherub. Ezekiel explained that the cherub was able to do this because he **appeared to have the form of a man's hand under** his **wings**.

i. "Possibly it was meant to show that even an angelic messenger like the man clothed in linen had to keep his distance from the aweful throne of God." (Taylor)

d. **Put it into the hands of the man clothed with linen**: Now this angel (angels are sometimes described as men in the Bible) could fulfill the command to scatter the coals of fire over the city (Ezekiel 10:2).

B. The appearance of the cherubim.

1. (9-13) The wheels associated with the cherubim.

And when I looked, there were four wheels by the cherubim, one wheel by one cherub and another wheel by each other cherub; the wheels appeared *to have* the color of a beryl stone. *As for* their appearance, all four looked alike—as it were, a wheel in the middle of a wheel. When they went, they went toward *any of* their four directions; they did not turn aside when they went, but followed in the direction the head was facing. They did not turn aside when they went. And their whole body, with their back, their hands, their wings, and the wheels that the four had, *were* full of eyes all around. As for the wheels, they were called in my hearing, "Wheel."

a. **There were four wheels by the cherubim**: Ezekiel 1:15-21 described these wheels in some detail. The general impression is of constant activity and motion, and free movement with no chaos or disorder (**they did not turn aside when they went, but followed in the direction the head was facing**).

i. "These wheels are in ceaseless activity and speak of the fact that God is busy." (McGee)

ii. If the wheels and the cherubim represent God's chariot or chariot-throne, then it is clear that Ezekiel was to understand that it was *on the move*. It was in Babylon, now it is in Jerusalem at the temple.

b. **The color of a beryl stone**: The mineral **beryl** can come in many different colors, but one of the more notable and precious is the emerald. This may mean that the wheels and their workings gave off a green color.

c. **Their whole body, with their back, their hands, their wings, and the wheels that the four had, were full of eyes all around**: Ezekiel 1:18 described **eyes** in connection with the **wheels**. Here we learn that the cherubim themselves were **full of eyes all around**. This matches the later description of cherubim found in Revelation 4:6.

i. "The image seems bizarre to the modern reader, but one must remember that this is a visionary experience, and surrealistic features may overwhelm realism." (Block)

ii. Adam Clarke spoke for many who are mystified at the nature and complexity of these descriptions: "And perhaps from the whole of this vision and its difficulties, he will see the propriety of the council of rabbins ordering Rabbi Ananias *three hundred* barrels of oil to light his lamp during the time it would be necessary for him to employ in explaining this one vision."

2. (14-17) The faces and the movement of the cherubim.

Each one had four faces: the first face *was* the face of a cherub, the second face the face of a man, the third the face of a lion, and the fourth the face of an eagle. And the cherubim were lifted up. This *was* the living creature I saw by the River Chebar. When the cherubim went, the wheels went beside them; and when the cherubim lifted their wings to mount up from the earth, the same wheels also did not turn from beside them. When the cherubim stood still, *the wheels* stood still, and when one was lifted up, the other lifted itself up, for the spirit of the living creature *was* in them.

a. **Each one had four faces**: This is almost the same description of the cherubim found in Ezekiel 1:10-14. Here Ezekiel didn't describe four faces on each cherub, just the one face turned toward him. Another difference lies in that in the previous passage the faces were listed as *a man*, a *lion*, an *ox*, and an *eagle*. Here they are listed as **a cherub**, a **man**, a **lion**, and an **eagle**. For some reason Ezekiel chose to use the word **cherub** to describe the face associated with the *ox*.

- Some explain this by saying that since these beings are cherubim and each face is actually **the face of a cherub**, there was simply some unknown reason why the substitute word was used (Wright, Wiersbe).

- Some explain this by saying that **the face of a cherub** *is* something like the face of an ox (Alexander, Smith).

- Some explain this by the error of a scribe who copied the text (Taylor).

b. **This was the living creature I saw by the River Chebar**: This is a direct reference to the vision of Ezekiel 1 (Ezekiel 1:1).

c. **The same wheels also did not turn**: This is the same description of the wheels and their association with the cherubim as described in Ezekiel 1:17, 1:20-21. The idea is that the cherubim and the wheels are perfectly coordinated in their motions together. They were so closely connected that Ezekiel could write, **the spirit of the living creature was in them**.

3. (18-19) The glory of the LORD and the cherubim at the door of the temple.

Then the glory of the LORD departed from the threshold of the temple and stood over the cherubim. And the cherubim lifted their wings and mounted up from the earth in my sight. When they went out, the wheels *were* beside them; and they stood at the door of the east gate of the LORD's house, and the glory of the God of Israel *was* above them.

a. **Then the glory of the LORD departed from the threshold of the temple and stood over the cherubim**: Earlier in Ezekiel 10 the glory of the Lord was described as moving to the threshold of the temple (Ezekiel 10:4). Here it continued to move and **departed from the threshold of the temple**.

> i. "The Jews dreamed that God could not depart from his temple; indeed, whilst it was his, and used as his, he did not, nor would he depart, but he will abandon it when profaned, and thereby made not his." (Poole)

b. **The cherubim lifted their wings and mounted up from the earth**: The cherubim were something like guardians or attendants to this visible representation of the glory of God. Ezekiel noted in his vision that as the glory moved, so did the cherubim.

> i. "The chariot not only serves as a vehicle to proclaim Yahweh's glory and his sovereignty (ch. 1) but also provides the means whereby he will abandon his temple, by which he declares the termination of his special relationship with Jerusalem and with his covenant people." (Block)

c. **They stood at the door of the east gate of the LORD's house**: The sense seems to be that the glory of God traveled from the holy of holies to the threshold of the temple building, then across the court of the temple, and now **stood at the door of the east gate**. It was moving *away* from the temple and about to leave the temple courts.

> i. The last mention of the east in this vision goes back to Ezekiel 8:16, where 25 priestly men faced east and worshipped the sun. "But the men who faced east worshipping the sun must have looked through the vision at the gate: their eyes were so dazzled by the created ball of light that they could not see the True Light." (Wright)

> ii. It is a striking and shocking thought that the glory of God was about to leave the temple altogether. Yet, Ezekiel also will later tell us (Ezekiel 43:2-4) that it will come back. "But turn to xliii. 2-4. The glory of the Lord returned to the renovated temple. Like the dawn of a

new day; like the sound of many waters, it came, it came. 'This,' God said, 'is the place of My throne…and the house of Israel shall no more defile.'" (Meyer)

iii. "Note that when the Lord does finally return, He is seen coming back through the East Gate (Ezekiel 43.4)." (Wright)

d. **The glory of the God of Israel was above them**: Ezekiel phrased this with a bit of irony, or perhaps tragedy. The **God of Israel** should have His glory rest in Israel, but now that glory was about to depart.

i. "The departure of the glory signals the end of a relationship that had existed for almost four centuries. The divine king has abandoned his residence." (Block)

4. (20-22) The connection with the vision of the cherubim in Ezekiel 1.

This *is* the living creature I saw under the God of Israel by the River Chebar, and I knew they *were* cherubim. Each one had four faces and each one four wings, and the likeness of the hands of a man *was* under their wings. And the likeness of their faces *was* the same *as* the faces which I had seen by the River Chebar, their appearance and their persons. They each went straight forward.

a. **I knew they were cherubim**: Ezekiel again connected what he saw in this vision with what he saw in a vision at the **River Chebar**, recorded in Ezekiel 1.

b. **They each went straight forward**: "The final word is that every cherub went straight forward, thus proclaiming the impossibility of thwarting or frustrating the plans of God. They kept their object and mission undeviatingly before them at all times." (Feinberg)

Ezekiel 11 – The Departure of God's Glory, the Promise of a New Covenant

A. Judgment on Jerusalem and beyond.

1. (1-4) Prophesy against the princes of the people.

Then the Spirit lifted me up and brought me to the East Gate of the LORD's house, which faces eastward; and there at the door of the gate were twenty-five men, among whom I saw Jaazaniah the son of Azzur, and Pelatiah the son of Benaiah, princes of the people. And He said to me: "Son of man, these *are* the men who devise iniquity and give wicked counsel in this city, who say, '*The time is* not near to build houses; this city is the caldron, and we *are* the meat.' Therefore prophesy against them, prophesy, O son of man!"

> a. **The Spirit lifted me up**: This is the continuation of Ezekiel's vision that began in chapter 8. He physically remained in Babylon, but God gave him a vision of the spiritual corruption of Jerusalem and God's response to it, both of judgment and the departing of God's glory from the temple and the city.

> b. **To the East Gate of the LORD's house**: The last mention of this **East Gate** in Ezekiel's vision described how the visible representation of God's glory hovered there on its way away from the holy of holies (Ezekiel 10:19).

> c. **There at the door of the gate were twenty-five men**: A group of this many men is previously mentioned in Ezekiel 8:16, who stood with their backs to the temple and worshipped the sun as they faced the east gate. Now Ezekiel saw **Jaazaniah** and **Pelatiah** among them.

>> i. The **Jaazaniah** named here seems to be different than the one mentioned in (Ezekiel 8:9-11), having a different father.

> d. **These are the men who devise iniquity and give wicked counsel in this city**: God meant this of the entire group of **twenty-five men**, though

Jaazaniah and **Pelatiah** were notable among the group. These were the wicked leaders of a wicked city.

e. The time is not near to build houses; this city is the caldron, and we are the meat: This seems to be the content of their **wicked counsel**. This phrasing is obscure and may refer to figures of speech that were well known in Ezekiel's day but mysterious to us. The sense *seems* to be that they were defiantly confident that they would be safe in Jerusalem, despite what prophets such as Jeremiah (as in Jeremiah 29:5) and Ezekiel had told them.

i. It seems better to regard **the time is not near to build houses** as a *question*, not a statement. *Isn't it time to build houses?* This was a statement of confidence that Jerusalem would be safe and delivered from the Babylonian threat. Just as pieces of meat are safe in a covered **caldron**, so they claimed to be safe.

ii. "This sentiment expresses confidence that all will be well and, if building houses is taken as a symbol of peaceful activity (cf. 28:26), it advocates a policy of ignoring the threat of a further Babylonian invasion." (Taylor)

iii. "The city would be a shield about them as the caldron is to seething flesh. Thus they were scorning the message of God's prophet, and relying on a false confidence in Jerusalem and its power to withstand siege and ultimate exile." (Feinberg)

iv. "The innuendo in this metaphor was that the people in Jerusalem were choice cuts of meat while the exiles in Babylon were just the scraps and rejected pieces." (Wiersbe)

2. (5-6) The cause of the devastating judgment on Jerusalem.

Then the Spirit of the LORD fell upon me, and said to me, "Speak! 'Thus says the LORD: "Thus you have said, O house of Israel; for I know the things that come into your mind. You have multiplied your slain in this city, and you have filled its streets with the slain."

a. **For I know the things that come into your mind**: God knew not only the actions but also the *thinking* of the leaders and people of Jerusalem.

b. **You have multiplied your slain in this city**: God reminded the leaders and the people of *their* responsibility in the great judgment coming upon them. God's judgment was the response to their persistent, deep rebellion.

3. (7-10) God's dealing with Israel will not end when Jerusalem falls.

Therefore thus says the Lord GOD: "Your slain whom you have laid in its midst, they *are* the meat, and this *city is* the caldron; but I shall bring you out of the midst of it. You have feared the sword; and I will

bring a sword upon you," says the Lord God. "And I will bring you out of its midst, and deliver you into the hands of strangers, and execute judgments on you. You shall fall by the sword. I will judge you at the border of Israel. Then you shall know that I *am* the Lord.

a. **They are the meat, and this city is the caldron**: Ezekiel turned their defiant claim of confidence into a predication of doom. They wouldn't be *protected* in the **caldron**, they would be cooked – and then devoured!

i. "Thus their own words, spoken in mockery, are wittily retorted upon them, and driven back again down their throats as it were." (Trapp)

ii. "No longer is Jerusalem a crock in which food is securely stored; she is a pot over the fire in which the meat is cooked." (Block)

b. **But I shall bring you out of the midst of it**: God promised that though the devastation to come upon Jerusalem would be terrible, it would not be the *last* word. The story of Israel and Jerusalem would not end with the Babylonian conquest.

c. **I will bring you out of its midst, and deliver you into the hands of strangers**: Not everyone would perish in Jerusalem. God would send many into exile. When Jerusalem was destroyed the judgments upon them would not end; God would continue to deal with His people **at the border of Israel** and beyond.

i. **I will judge you at the border of Israel**: "In the northern border, even at Riblah. [2 Kings 25:6; 2 Kings 25:21 Jeremiah 52:10; Jeremiah 52:26; Jeremiah 52:27]." (Trapp)

4. (11-12) God's judgment will extend beyond the city of Jerusalem.

This *city* shall not be your caldron, nor shall you be the meat in its midst. I will judge you at the border of Israel. And you shall know that I *am* the Lord; for you have not walked in My statutes nor executed My judgments, but have done according to the customs of the Gentiles which *are* all around you.""

a. **This city shall not be your caldron, nor shall you be the meat in its midst**: Ezekiel quoted their defiant claim to them one last time. Jerusalem would be no protection for them at all.

b. **And you shall know that I am the Lord**: God's dealing with His people *after* the fall of Jerusalem would be another way He revealed Himself to His people. He would not give up on them, either ending His discipline or His promises.

c. **Have done according to the customs of the Gentiles which are all around you**: Since Israel imitated the idolatry and wickedness of the surrounding pagan nations, it was appropriate for God to exile them among those nations.

B. Renewal promised as the glory departs.

1. (13) The question after the death of one of the princes of Jerusalem.

Now it happened, while I was prophesying, that Pelatiah the son of Benaiah died. Then I fell on my face and cried with a loud voice, and said, "Ah, Lord God! Will You make a complete end of the remnant of Israel?"

a. **Pelatiah the son of Benaiah died**: In Ezekiel's vision, he saw one of the leaders of Jerusalem (mentioned earlier in the chapter) die, no doubt under the promised judgments of God.

i. "Pelatiah may have been the leader of those who scoffed at God's word (vv. 1-3). His death was a foretaste of what awaited the rest whom Ezekiel had warned." (Feinberg)

ii. Vawter and Hoppe say the name **Pelatiah** means *Yahweh preserves a remnant*. Block gives the meaning as *Yahweh has rescued*.

b. **Will You make a complete end of the remnant of Israel?** Ezekiel asked God the same question he asked earlier in the vision (Ezekiel 9:8). Stunned by the depth and the breadth of God's judgments, he wondered if *any* would remain.

2. (14-16) God's promise to sustain His people in exile.

Again the word of the LORD came to me, saying, "Son of man, your brethren, your relatives, your countrymen, and all the house of Israel in its entirety, *are* those about whom the inhabitants of Jerusalem have said, 'Get far away from the LORD; this land has been given to us as a possession.' Therefore say, 'Thus says the Lord GOD: "Although I have cast them far off among the Gentiles, and although I have scattered them among the countries, yet I shall be a little sanctuary for them in the countries where they have gone."'

a. **Get far away from the LORD; this land has been given to us as a possession**: This seems to be the cry of those who ignored the warning of Jeremiah and Ezekiel, telling those who believed Jerusalem would be conquered to leave, because *they* would possess the land.

i. **Get far away from the LORD**: "These are the words of the inhabitants of Jerusalem, against those of Israel who had been carried away to Babylon with Jeconiah. *Go ye far from the Lord*: but as for us, the land of Israel is given to us for a possession, we shall never be removed from it, and *they* shall never return to it." (Clarke)

ii. "The scornful *Get you far from the Lord* (av, rv) is reminiscent of David's lament in 1 Samuel 26:19, "They have driven me out this day that I should have no share in the heritage of the Lord, saying, "Go, serve other gods.""" (Taylor)

b. **Although I have cast them far off among the Gentiles**: We know from Jeremiah (Jeremiah 24:1-7) that Jews who remained in Jerusalem and who had not yet been carried off to exile considered themselves superior to those who had been taken. Here God spoke well of those already exiled, saying though He had **cast them far off** He had not forsaken them.

c. **Yet I shall be a little sanctuary for them in the countries where they have gone**: God promised to sustain His people in exile. One of the reasons the leaders and people clung to the hope of possessing the land, even in opposition to God, was because they could not understand that God could be with them in exile. They thought opposing God was their best chance for survival as a people, but the opposite was true.

i. The tone of Ezekiel's recorded prophecies up to this point in the book has been dark and filled with judgment. There have been few examples of hope and light. Here is one; God *promised* – with the same faithfulness as His promises of judgment – that He would care for and sustain His people even in exile. The Babylonian conquest would not be the end of Israel, as it was for several other nations and peoples.

ii. "For the period of their absence from their land and the earthly temple, He would be their Sanctuary." (Morgan)

iii. "This statement is without parallel in the OT. The sanctuary was normally conceived of as a cult site or building rendered sacred by the presence of the deity. Here Yahweh promises to be for the exiles what the temple has heretofore been for them in Jerusalem." (Block)

iv. "Away from the outward ordinances and the material edifice, the exiles would find more than the equivalent in God Himself. He would give them the reality, of which there had been the outward and visible emblems." (Meyer)

v. **A little sanctuary**: The sense of **little** is not *small*, but *of short season*. "It is not a 'little sanctuary' (v. 16, AV, which could never be true of God), but 'for a little while' (ASV)." (Feinberg)

3. (17-21) God's promise to restore Israel to the land and renew them spiritually.

Therefore say, 'Thus says the Lord God: "I will gather you from the peoples, assemble you from the countries where you have been scattered, and I will give you the land of Israel."' And they will go there, and they will take away all its detestable things and all its abominations from

there. Then I will give them one heart, and I will put a new spirit within them, and take the stony heart out of their flesh, and give them a heart of flesh, that they may walk in My statutes and keep My judgments and do them; and they shall be My people, and I will be their God. But *as for those* whose hearts follow the desire for their detestable things and their abominations, I will recompense their deeds on their own heads," says the Lord God.

a. **Thus says the Lord God**: The declared message from *Adonai Yahweh* is commonly used in Ezekiel (more than 200 times). It gives special attention to Yahweh's status as Master and Lord over His covenant people.

b. **I will gather you from the peoples**: God first promised to sustain His people in exile (Ezekiel 11:14-16). Then He promised to **gather** and **assemble** them from their places of exile and to **give you the land of Israel**. Judgment was assured, but so was restoration.

i. **I will give you the land of Israel** is a remarkable promise to make to *post-exilic* Israel. "The gathering is to be by divine direction and from all lands and countries of their dispersion. And the promise is unequivocal: 'I will give you the land of Israel' (v. 17). Is it not pointless then to speak now as though the land of promise may belong to the Arabs or Israel? When did God reverse His land grant?" (Feinberg)

c. **They will take away all its detestable things and all its abominations**: God promised that Israel's time of exile would be a *cleansing* time, a time to **take away** their previous devotion to idols. This was fulfilled in history; the people of Israel did not have the same problem with the idols of the nations *after* the exile as they did before.

d. **Then I will give them one heart, and I will put a new spirit within them**: As God promised His work of restoration, He began to speak in terms associated with His greater work of restoration in the new covenant (Jeremiah 31:31-34). These promises are later repeated by Ezekiel and spoken of specifically as a *covenant* (Ezekiel 37:21-28). Here in Ezekiel 11 we see several features of the new covenant.

- Israel gathered together again (**one heart**).

- Spiritual transformation (**a new spirit…and give them a heart of flesh**).

- The law written on the heart (**that they may walk in My statutes**).

- Special relationship with God (**they shall be My people, and I will be their God**).

i. Throughout the Bible, God reveals His plan of redemption through a series of covenants. After the extended story of the fall and ruin of humanity in Genesis 1-11, the story of the covenants begins.

- The Abrahamic Covenant promised to Abraham and His covenant descendants a *land*, a *nation*, and a *blessing* to extend to all nations (Genesis 12:1-3).

- The Mosaic or Sinai Covenant gave Israel the *law*, the *sacrifices*, and the *choice* of blessing or curse (Exodus 19).

- The Davidic Covenant that promised an *everlasting dynasty*, a *perfect ruler*, and the *Promised Messiah* (2 Samuel 7).

- God's plan of redemption through the covenants is completed and perfected in the New Covenant. Over the span of Old Testament passages that announce the new covenant (especially Ezekiel 11:16-20, 36:16-28, and 37:21-28), we see the promises of a *gathered Israel* [**one heart**], of *cleansing and spiritual transformation* [**new spirit...heart of flesh**], of a *new and real relationship with God* [**they shall be My people, and I will be their God**] and the *reign of the Messiah*.

ii. "The term *berit* [covenant] is absent, but in the declaration *They will become my people, and I will become their God,* the reader is introduced for the first time to what is generally known as 'the covenant formula.'" (Block)

iii. The promise of **one heart** may speak of a singularly devoted heart, or of a unified, gathered Israel. "If MT is followed, with EVV, the gift is of *one heart*, implying the reunion of the old northern and southern kingdoms, as in 37:15–22." (Taylor)

e. **I will recompense their deeds on their own heads**: The promise of coming restoration (especially as seen in the new covenant) is not the message of universalism, saying that all will be restored, even if they persist in their rejection of God. Those who **follow the desire for their detestable things and their abominations** will be judged for their sins.

4. (22-23) The departure of the glory of the LORD.

So the cherubim lifted up their wings, with the wheels beside them, and the glory of the God of Israel *was* high above them. And the glory of the LORD went up from the midst of the city and stood on the mountain, which *is* on the east side of the city.

a. **So the cherubim lifted up their wings, with the wheels beside them**: As seen in the previous chapter, the cloud of God's glory was being carried by or with God's chariot throne, attended by the **cherubim**. As the **cherubim** moved, so did the **glory of the God of Israel**.

b. **The glory of the LORD went up from the midst of the city and stood on the mountain**: After progressing from the holy of holies to the threshold of the temple, to the east gate, the **glory of the LORD** then *left* the temple and even the city of Jerusalem, pausing then at the Mount of Olives **on the east side of the city**. We can imagine this as a pause to regret and sorrow over the departure, even as Jesus later looked over Jerusalem with regret and sorrow.

> i. Ezekiel left the description with the **glory of the LORD** hovering over the Mount of Olives. If it departed further, Ezekiel did not describe it. "The vision's present ending reflects its primary concern: the departure of Yahweh from the temple. In any case, to a person inside the city, the Mount of Olives represents the eastern horizon." (Block)

> ii. "No further movement is described, as if the prophet is saying that though the Lord has left his temple and the holy city he is still standing by in case there should be a repentance on the part of the people." (Taylor)

> iii. "The rabbis have enumerated ten stages whereby the Shekinah withdrew. These stages unmistakably reveal the loving and longing reluctance of God to leave His sanctuary where He dwelt in the midst of His beloved and erring people. Before He departed, however, He set forth the consoling promise of restoration for the remnant which we have been considering." (Feinberg)

5. (24-25) The end of the vision.

Then the Spirit took me up and brought me in a vision by the Spirit of God into Chaldea, to those in captivity. And the vision that I had seen went up from me. So I spoke to those in captivity of all the things the LORD had shown me.

a. **Then the Spirit took me up and brought me in a vision**: In his vision, Ezekiel returned to **Chaldea** (Babylon), and then the vision ended.

b. **So I spoke to those in captivity all the things the LORD had shown me**: Ezekiel wasn't given this message for his own amazement, but to instruct and warn the people and elders of Israel. They were perhaps shocked at the depths of Jerusalem's depravity, the severity of the coming judgment, and the promised departure of God's glory.

> i. **I spoke to those**: "Either the elders who came to him, Ezekiel 8:1, or to the body of the people, who were in those parts where Ezekiel was; for many were scattered into other parts of Chaldea." (Poole)

Ezekiel 12 – Two Signs Warning of Judgment

John B. Taylor wrote of Ezekiel chapters 12-24: "The section could, in today's idiom, be entitled 'Objections to Judgment', as long as it is understood that the objections are raised only to be demolished." These are some of the objections that are answered in this extended section:

- We have heard this all before, but it hasn't happened.
- Those who say we will be delivered are right.
- God will never do this to His people.

A. The sign of coming captivity.

1. (1-2) Speaking to a rebellious house.

Now the word of the LORD came to me, saying: "Son of man, you dwell in the midst of a rebellious house, which has eyes to see but does not see, and ears to hear but does not hear; for they *are* a rebellious house.

a. **Now the word of the LORD came to me**: This begins another section of Ezekiel's prophetic work, mainly a series of announcements of judgment coming against the kingdom of Judah.

b. **You dwell in the midst of a rebellious house**: Ezekiel was *among* a rebellious people, those who had been carried into exile under the Babylonians. Ezekiel was also part of the larger community of Israel, including those still living in the yet-to-be judged and conquered kingdom of Judah.

c. **Which has eyes to see but does not see**: This was part of the great tragedy for the children of Israel. Because they had the word of God, the institution of the priesthood, the sacrifices, and the temple, and because they had the prophets of Yahweh among them they *could have* seen and heard – but they would not.

2. (3-6) The command to act out captivity.

"Therefore, son of man, prepare your belongings for captivity, and go into captivity by day in their sight. You shall go from your place into captivity to another place in their sight. It may be that they will consider, though they *are* a rebellious house. By day you shall bring out your belongings in their sight, as though going into captivity; and at evening you shall go in their sight, like those who go into captivity. Dig through the wall in their sight, and carry your belongings out through it. In their sight you shall bear *them* on *your* shoulders *and* carry *them* out at twilight; you shall cover your face, so that you cannot see the ground, for I have made you a sign to the house of Israel."

a. **Prepare your belongings for captivity**: God commanded Ezekiel to act as if he were going into captivity or exile. He *already was* an exile in Babylon, but God wanted him to act this out among the exiles to make a message from God clear: all those remaining in Judah and Jerusalem would **go into captivity**.

i. It is important to remember that there were many false prophets in Judah, Jerusalem, and likely among the exiles in Babylon who promised that God would *rescue* His people from the Babylonians. These false prophets spoke smooth words of certain deliverance. The prophets Jeremiah and Ezekiel strongly warned them that this deliverance would not come and that God had appointed them to be conquered.

ii. "Rival prophets were foretelling a speedy return to a flourishing Jerusalem (Ezekiel 12:24; 13.16; Jeremiah 28.1-4; 29.8,9,15,21)." (Wright)

iii. "Ezekiel was to play the part of an exile, reenacting a scene all the exiles had painfully experienced when led from their land. He dramatized the fate of the inhabitants of Jerusalem." (Feinberg)

iv. **Your belongings**: "The article in question is illustrated in a series of neo-Assyrian monumental reliefs that portray captives being led away in procession with large bags slung over their shoulders. The packs were made either of durable cloth or skin, and loaded with such bare necessities for survival during the long trek as could be salvaged from the ruins of a conquered city." (Block)

v. "Part of his activity occurred in the daytime and part at twilight, and the curious but perplexed Jewish exiles watched his strange actions." (Wiersbe)

b. **Dig through the wall in their sight**: Ezekiel was also to act out a person desperately escaping from a city under siege. These also could end up as exiles, leaving with their face covered in shame (**cover your face, so that you cannot see the ground**).

> i. "Digging through the wall pictured the desperation with which they would seek to escape." (Feinberg)

> ii. "In particular King Zedekiah will creep out of the city walls by night (Ezekiel 12:12; 2 Kings 25.4), but the Lord plans for him to be caught and brought to Babylon." (Wright)

3. (7) Ezekiel acts out what God commanded.

So I did as I was commanded. I brought out my belongings by day, as though going into captivity, and at evening I dug through the wall with my hand. I brought *them* out at twilight, *and* I bore *them* on *my* shoulder in their sight.

a. **So I did as I was commanded**: God asked Ezekiel to act out many prophetic messages, so that both his words and his actions would communicate God's warning. Each time, Ezekiel did as he **was commanded**.

> i. "Ezekiel was a very brilliant man, but I think he also had a real sense of humor. I would love to have seen his face when he went through some of these mechanics! I think he might have been somewhat of a ham actor and been greatly amused as he did these things." (McGee)

b. **As though going into captivity**: Ezekiel became a living lesson to his fellow exiles in Babylon, and perhaps to those in Judah who would hear of his strange actions and what those actions meant.

> i. "Since all the exiles had participated in a deportation themselves (either in 605 B.C. or 597 B.C.), they should have understood clearly Ezekiel's picture of deportation." (Alexander)

> ii. "Perhaps this action would make this rebellious people realize that those left in Jerusalem would shortly be joining those who had been deported to Babylon." (Smith)

4. (8-14) The message to the princes and people of Jerusalem.

And in the morning the word of the Lord came to me, saying, "Son of man, has not the house of Israel, the rebellious house, said to you, 'What are you doing?' Say to them, 'Thus says the Lord God: "This burden *concerns* the prince in Jerusalem and all the house of Israel who are among them."' Say, 'I *am* a sign to you. As I have done, so shall it be done to them; they shall be carried away into captivity.' And the prince who *is* among them shall bear *his belongings* on *his* shoulder at twilight and go out. They shall dig through the wall to carry *them* out through it. He shall cover his face, so that he cannot see the ground with *his* eyes.

I will also spread My net over him, and he shall be caught in My snare. I will bring him to Babylon, *to* the land of the Chaldeans; yet he shall not see it, though he shall die there. I will scatter to every wind all who *are* around him to help him, and all his troops; and I will draw out the sword after them.

a. **What are you doing?** Ezekiel's strange actions invited this question. That was the whole purpose for an exiled man acting as if he were going into exile all over again.

i. **What are you doing?** "Is more than a demand to know what he was doing; their eyes had seen plainly enough what he had done. At issue is the significance of his actions." (Block)

b. **This burden concerns the prince in Jerusalem and all the house of Israel who are among them**: The prophet clearly explained that those who were about to go into exile were not those already in Babylon, but those still in Jerusalem and Judah. The warning was for both **the prince** and **all the house of Israel**.

i. **The prince**, specifically, was Zedekiah. "The subject of the message was King Zedekiah, who was always spoken of by Ezekiel as prince, never king. Jehoiachin was regarded as the true king (Ezekiel 17:13)…. In ration tablets found by archaeologists in Babylon, Jehoiachin was still referred to as the king of Judah." (Feinberg)

ii. "He was called 'the prince' (v.12) because he was not the legitimate king. That right belonged to Jehoiachin who was in Babylonia." (Alexander)

c. **The prince who is among them shall bear his belongings on his shoulder**: Even the mighty and prominent men among them would be brought low and have to bear their own burdens – something princes are not used to doing.

i. **Shall bear his belongings**: "Disguised no doubt as a common ordinary servant, in hope so to escape; but to conceal himself he flees in a disguise, and chooseth the twilight as the time that would best favour his design; so 2 Kings 25:4." (Poole)

d. **He shall cover his face**: Some think the prince would do this out of shame, others to disguise himself. Either way, it spoke of defeat and not deliverance.

i. "Shame, grief, humiliation, the instinctive furtiveness with which the defeated flee the scene of their disaster—doubtless all these combine

in the gesture of covering the face and refusing to look on the land."
(Vawter and Hoppe)

e. **I will also spread My net over him**: This refers to king Zedekiah of
Judah, who tried to escape but was caught, captured, and made captive
to Babylon (Jeremiah 39:2-4 and 2 Kings 25:4). His soldiers would be
powerless to help him; God promised to **scatter to every wind all who are
around him to help him, and all his troops**.

i. "The destruction of the king was like the dropping of a net over a
snarling wild beast that the hunter then drags away to an inevitable
slaughter." (Vawter and Hoppe)

f. **Yet he shall not see it, though he shall die there**: This was fulfilled in
Jeremiah 39:6-7. The Babylonians were not known to be as cruel as the
Assyrians who conquered the northern kingdom of Israel some 130 years
earlier, but they were still experts in cruelty in their own right. They made
certain that the last sight King Zedekiah saw was the murder of his own
sons, and that he spent the rest of his life in darkness.

i. "All the prophecies from this to the *twentieth* chapter are supposed
to have been delivered in the *sixth* year of Zedekiah, *five* years before
the taking of Jerusalem. How accurate the prediction! and how exactly
fulfilled!" (Clarke)

5. (15-16) Yahweh revealed in His judgments.

**"Then they shall know that I *am* the LORD, when I scatter them among
the nations and disperse them throughout the countries. But I will spare
a few of their men from the sword, from famine, and from pestilence,
that they may declare all their abominations among the Gentiles
wherever they go. Then they shall know that I *am* the LORD."**

a. **Then they shall know that I am the LORD**: Ezekiel often used this
phrase to explain *why* God allowed such great and devastating judgment to
come against His people. In the end, it was to reveal Himself to them, even
if it were in His judgments.

b. **I will spare a few of their men from the sword, from famine, and
from pestilence**: God promised to **spare** a remnant, so they could **declare**
the sins of God's people among the Gentiles, and so that God would be
revealed.

B. The sign of the bread.

1. (17-20) Eating bread and drinking water with great worry.

**Moreover the word of the LORD came to me, saying, "Son of man, eat
your bread with quaking, and drink your water with trembling and**

anxiety. And say to the people of the land, 'Thus says the Lord God to the inhabitants of Jerusalem *and* to the land of Israel: "They shall eat their bread with anxiety, and drink their water with dread, so that her land may be emptied of all who are in it, because of the violence of all those who dwell in it. Then the cities that are inhabited shall be laid waste, and the land shall become desolate; and you shall know that I *am* the Lord."'"

a. **Eat your bread with quaking, and drink your water with trembling and anxiety**: God told Ezekiel to act out another sign speaking of the coming conquest and captivity of Jerusalem and Judah. Those under siege would be so traumatized by their experience that they could not even **eat** or **drink** without **quaking** and **trembling**.

i. "By themselves, eating and drinking represent life at its most basic level, carrying on as if all is well. But the accompanying trembling announces the opposite." (Block)

ii. "He was illustrating the tragic condition of the people in Jerusalem during the Babylonian siege. They would have very little food and would eat it with fear and trembling because it might well be their last meal." (Wiersbe)

iii. **Say to the people of the land**: "This phrase is used consistently to refer to the peasant population of Judah, as distinct from the ruling classes, and particularly to those left there during the exile." (Taylor)

b. **Then the cities that are inhabited shall be laid waste**: When the siege was over, the **cities** would be conquered and all carried off into captivity (**the land shall become desolate**).

i. "The land would be emptied of its fruitfulness because of the violence that had been done in it (v.19). The violence they had done to others would return on their own heads, reflecting the principle of lex talionis [law of retaliation]." (Alexander)

2. (21-25) Answering a false proverb.

And the word of the Lord came to me, saying, "Son of man, what *is* this proverb *that* you *people* have about the land of Israel, which says, 'The days are prolonged, and every vision fails'? Tell them therefore, 'Thus says the Lord God: "I will lay this proverb to rest, and they shall no more use it as a proverb in Israel."' But say to them, "The days are at hand, and the fulfillment of every vision. For no more shall there be any false vision or flattering divination within the house of Israel. For I *am* the Lord. I speak, and the word which I speak will come to pass; it will no more be postponed; for in your days, O rebellious house, I will say the word and perform it," says the Lord God.'"

a. **The days are prolonged, and every vision fails**: This was a **proverb** in use among the people of Israel in Ezekiel's day. By it they meant that things would continue on as before (**the days are prolonged**) and that the visions and prophecies of doom would never come to pass (**every vision fails**).

i. "The captives asserted that they believed all the previous judgments proclaimed by Isaiah, Micah et al. were not true, for they had not come to pass. Why should they now accept Ezekiel's prophecies as valid?" (Alexander)

ii. **The days are prolonged** was actually an act of God's *mercy*. "A saying had become current among them because God's long-suffering, which should have led *to* repentance, was made an argument against His word." (Feinberg)

b. **I will lay this proverb to rest, and they shall no more use it as a proverb in Israel**: God promised to permanently answer this proverb, forever proving it wrong. Things would *not* continue on as before, and the visions of judgment would not fail and would come to pass.

c. **The days are at hand, and the fulfillment of every vision**: The sad and terrible things prophesied by Ezekiel, Jeremiah, and many others *would* come to pass. God promised, **the word which I speak will come to pass**.

i. "By skillfully recasting the proverb, Ezekiel announces that 'every vision' has not failed; on the contrary, 'every vision' is about to be fulfilled." (Block)

ii. **Flattering divination**: "*Divination* suggests that the false prophets used mechanical means of obtaining their oracles, either by the use of lots or by throwing arrows into the air and studying the way they fell, or by other methods of augury. The term clearly carries overtones of opprobrium." (Taylor)

3. (26-28) No more postponement.

Again the word of the Lord came to me, saying, "Son of man, look, the house of Israel is saying, 'The vision that he sees *is* for many days *from now*, and he prophesies of times far off.' Therefore say to them, 'Thus says the Lord God: "None of My words will be postponed any more, but the word which I speak will be done," says the Lord God.'"

a. **The vision that he sees is for many days from now**: This was one way the people of Israel explained away Ezekiel and his warnings. Whatever danger he might announce was for a distant future, and **he prophesies of times far off**.

> i. "They did not deny that he spoke the word of God; but comforted themselves with the reflection that it was not likely to be fulfilled for some time yet." (Meyer)

> ii. "The heart of man, set upon evil courses, constantly adopts one of these two expedients to comfort itself. Either it mocks at the prophetic word, or says that fulfillment is postponed." (Morgan)

> iii. "'These predictions either will not come in our days, or will wholly fail; why then should *we* disquiet ourselves about them?' Strange, that the very means used by the most gracious God to bring sinners to repentance, should be made by them the very instruments of their own destruction!" (Clarke)

> iv. Spurgeon saw in this an excuse that many make to *delay* their trust in and surrender to God, especially many young people. "God knows the frivolity of your plea for delay, he knows that you yourself are doubtful about it, and dare not stand to it so as to give it anything like a solemn consideration. Very hard do you try to deceive yourself into an easy state of conscience concerning it, but in your inmost soul you are ashamed of your own falsehoods." (Spurgeon)

b. **None of My words will be postponed any more**: God promised there would be no more delay in the carrying out of the terrible things He had warned of for so long.

Ezekiel 13 – Against False and Foolish Prophets

A. God's word against false prophets.

1. (1-2) The command to speak against the false prophets.

And the word of the LORD came to me, saying, "Son of man, prophesy against the prophets of Israel who prophesy, and say to those who prophesy out of their own heart, 'Hear the word of the LORD!'"

a. **Prophesy against the prophets of Israel who prophesy**: Among the Jewish people of Ezekiel's time there were many false prophets, both in Israel and in the Babylonian exile. These false **prophets of Israel** mostly had an optimistic, positive message: *God will deliver Jerusalem and Judah from the Babylonians, and those already in exile will come home soon.*

i. Block sees the phrase **the prophets of Israel who prophesy** as a deliberate repetition, meant to be sarcastic. The sense is that they were always blabbing on and on with their pretended words from God.

b. **Who prophesy out of their own heart**: The source of their false prophecy wasn't necessarily directly demonic. There was simply a large element of **their own heart** in what they said. Their own desires, their own hopes, their own wisdom, their own need for acceptance prompted their words.

i. "They were misled by their own desires, which is the scriptural method of asserting they were not inspired of God. The wish was father to the thought, and they spoke accordingly." (Feinberg)

c. **Hear the word of the LORD**: This was the fundamental message these false prophets needed to hear. They needed to stop listening to the message of their own heart and start paying close attention to **the word of the LORD**.

2. (3-7) The prophets Yahweh did not send.

Thus says the Lord God: "Woe to the foolish prophets, who follow their own spirit and have seen nothing! O Israel, your prophets are like foxes in the deserts. You have not gone up into the gaps to build a wall for the house of Israel to stand in battle on the day of the Lord. They have envisioned futility and false divination, saying, 'Thus says the Lord!' But the Lord has not sent them; yet they hope that the word may be confirmed. Have you not seen a futile vision, and have you not spoken false divination? You say, 'The Lord says,' but I have not spoken."

a. **Woe to the foolish prophets**: These self-proclaimed prophets were not only *false* they were also **foolish**. One reason they were **foolish** was because they regarded what came from *their own heart* and **their own spirit** to be more important than what God has said.

i. "The word 'foolish' (*nabal*) implied more than our concept of stupidity. It was a broad term that encompassed spiritual and moral insensitivity contrary to the nature of a wise man." (Alexander)

ii. "These prophets, whether in good faith but self-deluded or in bad faith and deliberately deceiving, have professed to speak the mind of the Lord when in reality no spirit other than their own moved them." (Vawter and Hoppe)

b. **Who follow their own spirit and have seen nothing**: Their message was not based on a *true* relationship with God. In that regard, they had **seen nothing**. Their message followed **their own spirit**, not God's Holy Spirit.

c. **Your prophets are like foxes in the deserts**: This probably means *jackals* more than **foxes** and *ruins* more than **deserts**. The idea is of animals that burrow among the ruins, helping nothing, adding nothing, and delighting in the destruction.

i. "These prophets of falsehood were likened to foxes in waste places, preying on the desolation around them and under-mining foundations and causing havoc everywhere. As foxes they were crafty, mischievous and destructive (cf. Matthew 7:15; Acts 20:29)." (Feinberg)

ii. **Like foxes**: "Cowardly, crafty, cruel, greedy.... Heretics are such, and false prophets; Arius, for instance." (Trapp)

d. **You have not gone up into the gaps to build a wall for the house of Israel to stand in battle on the day of the Lord**: These self-proclaimed prophets also lacked courage. Trained and courageous soldiers rush **into the gaps** along the line of battle. The false prophets did not have the courage to stand and strengthen Israel in the time of crisis.

i. If the false prophets had received and delivered a message from God Himself, it would have given the **house of Israel** a secure place to stand when judgment came (here in this context called **the day of the** LORD).

ii. "The prophets had shown no courage in battle. In time of war a brave soldier would rush to any break in the defensive perimeter and defend it until the position could be secured. These prophets, however, had not 'gone up into the breaches' in the moral and spiritual walls of the nation." (Alexander)

iii. "*The day of the Lord* in Ezekiel refers to the day of judgment which the Lord has decreed upon his people and particularly upon Jerusalem. It is to be identified here with the sack of Jerusalem in 587 BC, a day in which the storm of judgment eventually broke." (Taylor)

e. **But the** LORD **has not sent them**: This was a strong condemnation of the self-appointed prophets. To claim a calling when there is none is a significant sin. They claimed to speak in the name of the Lord, but it was an empty claim.

3. (8-9) The nonsense spoken by false prophets.

Therefore thus says the Lord GOD: **"Because you have spoken nonsense and envisioned lies, therefore I *am* indeed against you," says the Lord** GOD. **"My hand will be against the prophets who envision futility and who divine lies; they shall not be in the assembly of My people, nor be written in the record of the house of Israel, nor shall they enter into the land of Israel. Then you shall know that I *am* the Lord** GOD.

a. **Because you have spoken nonsense and envisioned lies**: The self-proclaimed prophets actually spoke **nonsense**. It probably wasn't immediately perceived to be **nonsense** because it sounded spiritual or at least mysterious. Yet God looked at it and said, "**nonsense**" and "**lies**."

b. **Therefore I am indeed against you**: Of all people, prophets should be the ones whom God works *for*. Here He promised to be **against** these self-proclaimed prophets.

c. **They shall not be in the assembly of My people**: One aspect of God's judgment upon these false prophets was for the Lord to regard them as not among His covenant people. They had no share in Israel's **assembly**, in Israel's **house**, or in Israel's **land**. This exclusion would declare that Yahweh is God (**you shall know that I am the Lord** GOD).

i. "These three punishments strike at the heart of what it meant to be an Israelite." (Block)

ii. "When it was affirmed that they would not come into the council of God's people, the sense is that they would lose the place of authority and respect they held among the people by virtue of their alleged calling." (Feinberg)

B. The weak wall and the storm.

1. (10-12) The wall that falls in the storm.

"Because, indeed, because they have seduced My people, saying, 'Peace!' when *there is* no peace—and one builds a wall, and they plaster it with untempered *mortar*— say to those who plaster *it* with untempered *mortar,* that it will fall. There will be flooding rain, and you, O great hailstones, shall fall; and a stormy wind shall tear *it* down. Surely, when the wall has fallen, will it not be said to you, 'Where *is* the mortar with which you plastered *it?*'"

a. **They have seduced My people**: The message of the false prophets was attractive and even seductive. Their message was essentially to say **peace** even **when there is no peace**. Their message was filled with hope and inspiration, packed with optimism and confidence – *don't despair, God will deliver us and we will win against the Babylonians!*

> i. **Seduced My people**: "Made my people to err, both in their apprehension of their sin and danger, and of my displeasure and threats, as if all were less than it was, and there needed no repentance, or submission to the Babylonish king." (Poole)
>
> ii. **My people**: "The expression 'my people' is found seven times in the chapter, a constant reminder to the culprits of those whom they have misled." (Feinberg)
>
> iii. **"Peace!" when there is no peace**: "They never spoke of repentance, but guaranteed that the blessings of God were just around the corner." (Wright)
>
> iv. "That is the essence of false prophesying. Men, who have no Divine message, but pose as though they had, seek to find favour with those to whom they speak, and so agree with them in their desires and policies." (Morgan)

b. **One builds a wall, and they plaster it with untempered mortar**: Their seductive message looked great on the outside, but it had no true strength. It was like a **wall** built with poor materials.

> i. "The false prophets were compared to those who build an unsafe wall and cover up its defects. The untempered mortar was actually

whitewash, which is useless for strengthening insecure walls." (Feinberg)

ii. "Just as an ill-built wall—of stone or brick poorly joined, not mortared, and held together only by precarious tension—can still give the impression of stability when a thin layer of plaster covers it (RSV 'whitewash'), such has been the effect of these prophets who have produced a façade of impregnability that is totally illusory." (Vawter and Hoppe)

c. **A stormy wind shall tear it down**: God promised that a storm would come against this weakly built wall, and it would knock it over. When the Babylonians did come and quickly overwhelm Jerusalem, then everyone would know how false the self-appointed prophets were, that their **wall** was built with terrible materials.

i. To use the figures of building and walls: the problem with the false prophets was that their work was not *inspected* before the great storm or test came. When the storm came, and the wall fell, everyone knew the message was false. The key was to do a proper inspection of the "wall" before the storm came.

ii. "The daubing makes the wall look as strong as possible, but it cannot save it from collapsing before the overflowing shower of God's judgment and the great hailstones of His wrath." (Meyer)

iii. "As fall it will, and with a force, because made of ill mortar; and they that stand under it for shelter shall perish." (Trapp)

2. (13-14) The coming storm.

Therefore thus says the Lord God: "I will cause a stormy wind to break forth in My fury; and there shall be a flooding rain in My anger, and great hailstones in fury to consume *it*. So I will break down the wall you have plastered with untempered *mortar*, and bring it down to the ground, so that its foundation will be uncovered; it will fall, and you shall be consumed in the midst of it. Then you shall know that I *am* the Lord.

a. **Will cause a stormy wind to break forth in My fury**: The power of a storm is greater than anything man-made, even in the modern world. God promised that a tremendous **stormy wind** of judgment would come to Jerusalem and Judah, and that God Himself would send it.

b. **So I will break down the wall you have plastered with untempered mortar**: God promised to **break down** the self-appointed prophets together with their man-made message.

c. **It will fall, and you shall be consumed**: The fall of their weak wall would not only mean the loss of a structure. It would take many lives with it; symbolically speaking, the wall would fall upon many people.

3. (15-16) God's purpose in the storm.

"Thus will I accomplish My wrath on the wall and on those who have plastered it with untempered *mortar;* and I will say to you, 'The wall *is* no *more,* nor those who plastered it, *that is,* the prophets of Israel who prophesy concerning Jerusalem, and who see visions of peace for her when *there is* no peace,'" says the Lord GOD**.**

a. **Thus will I accomplish My wrath on the wall and on those who have plastered it**: God hated the work of the false prophets and promised to destroy it. The false prophets themselves would also be judged and destroyed.

i. "The counterfeit prophets gave the people a false hope, so God gave them no hope at all." (Wiersbe)

b. **Who see visions of peace for her when there is no peace**: The essential message of Jeremiah and Ezekiel was that judgment was on the way, and they should accept it as God's chastening and cleansing. The false prophets had **visions of peace**, leaving God's people completely unprepared for the judgment that was on the way.

C. Against the false prophetesses.

1. (17-19) Against the female false prophets.

"Likewise, son of man, set your face against the daughters of your people, who prophesy out of their own heart; prophesy against them, and say, 'Thus says the Lord GOD**: "Woe to the *women* who sew *magic* charms on their sleeves and make veils for the heads of people of every height to hunt souls! Will you hunt the souls of My people, and keep yourselves alive? And will you profane Me among My people for handfuls of barley and for pieces of bread, killing people who should not die, and keeping people alive who should not live, by your lying to My people who listen to lies?"**

a. **Set your face against the daughters of your people**: After speaking against false prophets in general, Ezekiel then specifically addressed *women* who were false prophets. This was not mere repetition. A female false prophet may have special appeal to other women as well as men.

i. "Women held a higher place in Israel than among most other nations. While there were no priestesses in Israel, the nation knew the prophetic ministry of women." (Feinberg) There are several examples:

- Miriam, the sister of Moses (Exodus 15:20, Numbers 12:2).
- Deborah (Judges 4:4).
- Huldah (2 Kings 22:14).
- The wife of Isaiah (Isaiah 8:3).
- Noadiah, a false prophetess (Nehemiah 6:14).
- Anna, the daughter of Phanuel (Luke 2:36).
- The four daughters of Philip (Acts 21:9).

ii. "While the expression *nebia*, 'prophetess,' is applied to at least five women in the OT, Ezekiel refuses to dignify his target audience with the title. At best, he allows that they 'acted like prophets,' but like the false prophets in the previous oracle, these women are frauds." (Block)

iii. "There are only a handful of passages in the Old Testament which are critical of a class of women, and this section keeps company with Isaiah 3:16–4:1; 32:9–13 and Amos 4:1–3." (Taylor)

iv. "Women are delicate; yet the prophet must set his face against them as stout agents for the devil, who hath ever made great use of them. Such were Noadiah; [Nehemiah 6:14] that apocalyptical Jezebel, Bridget Matild…[and] our recent most impudent preacheresses in London and elsewhere." (Trapp)

b. **Who prophesy out of their own heart**: One basic failing of the female false prophets was the same as false prophets in general (Ezekiel 13:2). They spoke **out of their own heart**, not from God and His word. It is common for people to trust their own hearts instead of God's revelation.

c. **Woe to the women who sew magic charms on their sleeves**: As part of their false prophecy, these **women** used symbols of **magic charms** and particular articles of clothing (**veils**) in their ceremonies.

i. "Ezekiel's language suggests that these were more like witches or sorceresses who practised strange magic arts (cf. 1 Samuel 28:7)." (Taylor)

ii. "We can only guess at what, precisely, were the magic wristbands and head veils created by the sorceresses." (Vawter and Hoppe)

iii. "In Babylonia Jewish women were selling charms and spells. They were ready to do anything for even a small reward, putting a curse on the innocent, and promising a long and safe life for wrongdoers." (Wright)

d. **For the heads of people of every height to hunt souls**: God did not regard the work of these female false prophets as harmless or innocent.

God saw them as those who **hunt souls**, asking these women, **Will you hunt the souls of My people, and keep yourselves alive?**

> i. The practice of false prophetesses (and prophets) *hunting souls* has not ended. Those who seduce others with false words, with magic charms, special clothing, and other things are still among us.

> ii. "*Calmet* observes that there was scarcely a heresy in the primitive Church that was not supported and fomented by seducing women." (Clarke)

> iii. "It is not possible that the word for soul (Heb. *nepes*) could have the meaning of a disembodied spirit: this is a totally unhebraic concept. It means the total person, the self, not just a part of him." (Taylor)

e. **Will you profane Me among My people for handfuls of barley and for pieces of bread**: This explains the phrase, **keep yourselves alive**. They made a living for themselves through their false words, ceremonies, and actions.

> i. **Profane Me**: "With their sorcerous invocation of the divine name, the women have degraded Yahweh in the public's eyes to the level of the Babylonian deities and demons, who let themselves be manipulated by divination and witchcraft." (Block)

> ii. "Bread and morsels of bread. Mercenary sorceresses! that thus make sale of their predictions to feed their hungry bellies." (Poole)

> iii. Alexander had a different understanding of this **barley** and **pieces of bread**: "Barley and bread were also instruments of sorcery (v.19). Some have understood the bread and barley to represent the cheap payment these prophetesses would accept in return for their occult practices; but Hittite practices and later Syrian rituals demonstrate that divination was carried out with barley bread either as part of the pagan sacrificial ritual or as a means of determining whether the victim would live or die."

f. **By your lying to My people who listen to lies**: The false prophetesses were guilty of **lying** to God's own **people**, yet the people were guilty because they did **listen to lies**. If none of God's people listened to false prophets, there would be much fewer of them.

> i. "They had used deceptive and counterfeit means to dishearten the righteous, pulling them into their cultic snare and influence. At the same time they encouraged the wicked to disobey God's ways." (Alexander)

2. (20-21) Against the magic charms of the female false prophets.

'Therefore thus says the Lord God: "Behold, I *am* against your *magic* **charms by which you hunt souls there like birds. I will tear them from your arms, and let the souls go, the souls you hunt like birds. I will also tear off your veils and deliver My people out of your hand, and they shall no longer be as prey in your hand. Then you shall know that I** *am* **the Lord.**

a. **I am against your magic charms by which you hunt souls**: The false prophetesses used their **magic charms** and ceremonies to hunt and trap vulnerable souls.

i. "The women who made use of them were not, for this prophet, carnival gypsies whom one frequents for amusement; they were practitioners of the dark arts." (Vawter and Hoppe)

b. **I will tear them from your arms, and let the souls go**: God promised to defeat these false prophetesses and to rescue those trapped by their snares.

i. "God would strip them of their charms and amulets and then take His people back to their land, leaving these evil women behind to die." (Wiersbe)

c. **Then you shall know that I am the Lord**: God promised that through the defeat of the female prophets, and His rescue of those who were **prey** in their hands, He would reveal Himself.

3. (22-23) The terrible effect of the lies of the false prophets.

"**Because with lies you have made the heart of the righteous sad, whom I have not made sad; and you have strengthened the hands of the wicked, so that he does not turn from his wicked way to save his life. Therefore you shall no longer envision futility nor practice divination; for I will deliver My people out of your hand, and you shall know that I** *am* **the Lord.""'**

a. **Because with lies you have made the heart of the righteous sad, whom I have not made sad**: The work of the false prophets (both men and women) had at least two terrible effects. Their work brought sadness to the **heart of the righteous**, and it **strengthened the hands of the wicked**. Not only were the godly discouraged, but also the wicked would not **turn from his wicked way to save his life**. The false prophets convinced them there was no need to **turn**.

b. **Therefore you shall no longer envision futility nor practice divination; for I will deliver My people out of your hand**: God promised to put an end to the false prophets. Their visions were **futility** and their ceremonies were not worship, but **divination**. God promised to **deliver** His people from their deceptions.

i. "What is unmistakable is that they degraded the name of the Lord by linking it with superstitions and magical practices." (Feinberg)

Ezekiel 14 – Noah, Daniel, and Job

A. Rebuking elders and prophets.

1. (1-3) The inquiry and the idols of the elders of Israel.

Now some of the elders of Israel came to me and sat before me. And the word of the LORD came to me, saying, "Son of man, these men have set up their idols in their hearts, and put before them that which causes them to stumble into iniquity. Should I let Myself be inquired of at all by them?

a. **Some of the elders of Israel came to me**: These **elders** had visited Ezekiel before (Ezekiel 8:1). These were the leaders of the Israelite community in exile.

i. "Rulers and chieftains of the captives in Babylon, pretending to be far better than those elders at Jerusalem, complained about in Ezekiel 8:11-12, but indeed no better; nay, so much the worse, because they had lost the fruit of all their afflictions, and were as arrant hypocrites." (Trapp)

ii. "They had come presumably in the hope of hearing some oracle about the length of their exile or giving news of affairs at home in Jerusalem. The oracle was given, but it was not what they expected." (Taylor)

iii. "They pretend they want to listen to the prophet. It is like coming to church with a big Bible under your arm, pretending you want to serve the Lord." (McGee)

b. **These men have set up idols in their hearts**: God gave Ezekiel supernatural insight into the **hearts** of these leaders. Like the leaders mentioned in Ezekiel 8:10-12 and 8:16, these were idol worshippers. Their **idols** were not evident outwardly but **in their hearts**. This secret idolatry made **them to stumble into iniquity**.

i. "The word of the Lord revealed to him that whatever their outward attitude might be, they were at heart idolaters, and he was charged to declare to them that while idolatry remained in their heart they were necessarily estranged from Jehovah." (Morgan)

ii. "The charge against them is that they have been infected by their Babylonian environment and the attractions of its idolatrous religion. Nothing had changed outwardly in their allegiance to the Lord, but they had taken *idols into their hearts.*" (Taylor)

iii. "They were like the people in Isaiah's day who drew near to God with words but not with their hearts (Isaiah 29:13). Jesus said that the Pharisees in His day were guilty of the same sin (Matthew 15:8–9)." (Wiersbe)

iv. Ananias and Sapphira (Acts 5) and the rich young ruler (Matthew 19:16-26) are New Testament examples of those who looked spiritual on the outside but had idols in their hearts. No wonder John closed his first letter, *little children, keep yourselves from idols* (1 John 5:21).

c. **Should I let Myself be inquired of at all by them?** Knowing the hidden sin in their lives, God asked Ezekiel an obvious and important question. This question, with the assumed answer of "no," showed that God had no *obligation* to answer the inquiry of these men who harbored such secret sin.

i. "This verse is important for those who come to Scripture seeking guidance. No true direction can be given to those who have erected idols in their hearts." (Alexander)

ii. "Can these men seriously consult me? Is it fit I should give counsel to obstinate, resolved sinners, who come to inquire, but will not hearken? Should I help them in their distress, who depend on idols which I hate?" (Poole)

2. (4-5) God's promise to the idol-loving inquirers.

"Therefore speak to them, and say to them, 'Thus says the Lord GOD: "Everyone of the house of Israel who sets up his idols in his heart, and puts before him what causes him to stumble into iniquity, and then comes to the prophet, I the LORD will answer him who comes, according to the multitude of his idols, that I may seize the house of Israel by their heart, because they are all estranged from Me by their idols.'"

a. **I the LORD will answer him who comes, according to the multitude of his idols:** God promised that the ones with such hidden idolatry and sin in their lives would receive an answer from Him, but it would be an answer of *judgment.* It would be an answer **according to the multitude of his idols.**

i. "No oracle will be given, but *I the Lord will answer him myself,* in actions and not in words. The words have a sinister ring about them." (Taylor)

b. **That I may seize the house of Israel by their heart**: This is a powerful and eloquent statement of one of the great reasons for God's judgment upon Israel in the Babylonian conquest and captivity. He did it to **seize** them **by their heart**. Their hearts were far from God, and He intended to grab hold of their hearts again.

i. "God told Ezekiel that the Jewish people had deserted Him to follow after idols and that He would discipline them in order to 'recapture' their hearts." (Wiersbe)

ii. "As the verb [**seize**] conveys the forceful seizing of prisoners (1 Sam 15:8; 1 Kings 13:4) or an animal (Ezek 19:4, 8) and the conquest of a city (Deut 20:19; Josh 8:8) or parents seizing a rebellious son (Deut 21:19), so the Lord's heart for Israel to return to him is seen in his laying hold of those who have gone astray in idolatry." Alexander)

c. **Because they are all estranged from Me by their idols**: This was *why* their hearts were distant from God. As an unfaithful spouse might give their heart to another, so Israel unfaithfully gave their heart to the **idols** of the Canaanites and other surrounding nations.

3. (6-8) A call to repentance and a promise of judgment.

"Therefore say to the house of Israel, 'Thus says the Lord GOD: "Repent, turn away from your idols, and turn your faces away from all your abominations. For anyone of the house of Israel, or of the strangers who dwell in Israel, who separates himself from Me and sets up his idols in his heart and puts before him what causes him to stumble into iniquity, then comes to a prophet to inquire of him concerning Me, I the LORD will answer him by Myself. I will set My face against that man and make him a sign and a proverb, and I will cut him off from the midst of My people. Then you shall know that I *am* the LORD.

a. **Repent, turn away from your idols, and turn your faces away from all your abominations**: This was God's word to those among Israel who sought Him. If they inquired of Him, God had a simple response: **repent**. Then God defined repentance as *turning away* from **idols** and **abominations**.

i. This included both those **of the house of Israel** and foreigners in Israel (**the strangers who dwell in Israel**). "What the text says simply is that all Israelites, native and [strangers], have through their idolatry cut themselves off from Yahweh's prophetic communication. God will now deal with them directly." (Vawter and Hoppe)

b. **Then comes to a prophet to inquire of him concerning Me**: The people of Israel – such as the elders described in Ezekiel 14:1-3 – were secretly immersed in idolatry, yet they still went **to a prophet to inquire** about God's will.

c. **I will set My face against that man and make him a sign and a proverb**: God promised to oppose such double-hearted men. God knew the truth about those who pretended to serve God on the outside but were filled with idolatry on the inside, and He would oppose them and judge them according to that truth.

i. **Set My face against that man**: "I will look him to death." (Trapp)

ii. **A proverb**: "Just as the name 'Nimrod' has become proverbial for hunting prowess (Genesis 10:9), and 'Babel' for incomprehensible speech (Genesis 11:9), so the name 'Israel' would become proverbial for divinely imposed disaster." (Block)

iii. "The punishment outlined echoes the wording of Deuteronomy 28:37 and the earlier warning in Leviticus 20:3, 5-6. God would set Himself against that man until he was destroyed from the midst of Israel." (Feinberg)

4. (9-11) God's promised punishment of the prophets.

"And if the prophet is induced to speak anything, I the LORD have induced that prophet, and I will stretch out My hand against him and destroy him from among My people Israel. And they shall bear their iniquity; the punishment of the prophet shall be the same as the punishment of the one who inquired, that the house of Israel may no longer stray from Me, nor be profaned anymore with all their transgressions, but that they may be My people and I may be their God," says the Lord GOD.'"

a. **If the prophet is induced to speak anything**: From the context, we understand that Ezekiel spoke here of *false prophets*. When the idol-hearted people went to a false prophet to inquire of the LORD, God could very well give them an answer (**I the LORD have induced that prophet**).

i. "**The prophet,** viz. the prophet who makes this his trade and gain, the false prophet, who speaks all serene and quiet, in hope of reward for his kind answer to those that desired to hear what might please them more than what God commanded, promised, or threatened." (Poole)

ii. **I the LORD have induced that prophet**: "I had not only a permissive, but an active hand in that imposture; not as a sin, but as a punishment of other sins. See 1 Kings 22:20, Job 12:16, Jeremiah 4:10, 2 Thessalonians 2:11." (Trapp)

iii. "Yahweh answers insincerity with insincerity. Unrepentant kings and unrepentant people, who seek confirmation of their perverse ways, and who clamor for reassurances of well-being, do not deserve a straight answer." (Block)

iv. "When the false prophet, sensing the desires of his idolatrous inquirers, gave them a prediction, a prophetic word in keeping with their wishes, thus aiding their apostasy and delusion, the prophet himself had been deceived by his wicked heart; and ultimately it was the Lord who had enticed him. There is an elimination of secondary causes as in Isaiah 45:7 and Amos 3:6." (Feinberg)

b. **I will stretch out My hand against him and destroy him from among My people Israel**: God's ultimate response to that false prophet would be to destroy him. Even if God used the false prophet to give the idolater the deception they longed for, God would still send judgment upon the false and wicked prophet.

i. "By giving the people lying prophets, who proclaim to the people exactly what they want to hear, Yahweh ensures the people's judgment." (Block)

ii. Wright saw in this a warning to those who have a gift and are unfaithful with it. "If we have some great gift and are being used in the service of God, and then try to use it in our own interests, or divorce it from the requirements of Christian living, God may turn the gift against us. A theologian, who abandons revealed truth for clever ideas of his own, first deceives himself, and then, by divine rule, becomes blind to the truth."

c. **The punishment of the prophet shall be the same as the punishment of the one who inquired**: God would bring judgment upon the false prophet just as much as He brought it upon the secret idolater who sought the false prophet.

i. "There is so great parity in the folly and impiety of both seducing prophets and the seduced people, that it is hard to say whose sin is greatest. Their punishment shall be by the Lord made as like as they made their sin, and both shall be cut off and destroyed." (Poole)

ii. "Neither shall excuse other; but as they have sinned together, so shall they suffer together." (Trapp)

d. **That the house of Israel may no longer stray from Me, nor be profaned anymore**: Once more, God explained the ultimate reason for His great judgment upon Israel. It was so that they would be corrected of their sins and **no longer stray** as before. Israel would have a restored relationship with God (**that they may be My people and I may be their God**).

> i. "Yahweh's desire is for a people who will never *stray* from him again. The word [**stray**] derives from the realm of animal husbandry but is also applied to persons who are lost." (Block)

> ii. This declared purpose of God was fulfilled in history. When Israel came back into the land in the days of Ezra and Nehemiah, they did not have the same problem with idolatry as before. In some sense, the Babylonian conquest and captivity "cured" Israel of idolatry.

> iii. "Again Ezekiel stressed that this judgment had a positive purpose. The judgment would cause the house of Israel no longer to stray from the Lord or defile themselves by their transgressions." (Smith)

B. Noah, Daniel, and Job.

1. (12-14) No hope for Judah during famine.

The word of the LORD came again to me, saying: "Son of man, when a land sins against Me by persistent unfaithfulness, I will stretch out My hand against it; I will cut off its supply of bread, send famine on it, and cut off man and beast from it. Even *if* these three men, Noah, Daniel, and Job, were in it, they would deliver *only* themselves by their righteousness," says the Lord GOD.

a. **When a land sins against Me by persistent unfaithfulness, I will stretch out My hand against it**: God said that there was a sense in which **a land** could sin against Him. Of course, people sin and real estate does not. Yet since God gives responsibility over certain real estate to certain people, there is a sense in which **a land** can indeed sin – and become a target of God's judgment.

> i. **Persistent unfaithfulness**: "It is used of the sin of Achan in relation to the devoted thing (the *herem*, Joshua 7:1) and of a wife's adulterous act (Numbers 5:12), both of which incurred the death penalty. The meaning here is similarly of a land which by its unfaithfulness deserves the ultimate in punishment." (Taylor)

b. **I will cut off its supply of bread, send famine on it**: This was God's promised judgment upon a land – agricultural failure and the **famine** that results from it. The lack of food would **cut off man and beast from it.**

c. **Even if these three men, Noah, Daniel, and Job, were in it, they would deliver only themselves**: The sin of Israel was so deep and serious that even if three of the most righteous men of Israel's history were present in the land, it would not stop God's judgment against the land. They would

deliver only themselves by their righteousness, and not the nation as a whole.

> i. "Here he makes the point that a nation cannot shelter under the goodness of a few individuals." (Wright)

> ii. "This is an assertion of personal and individual responsibility that runs athwart the old idea of communal virtue and vice in which all participated as a people." (Vawter and Hoppe)

> iii. "The intercession even of the holiest of men shall not avert my judgments. *Noah*, though a righteous man, could not by his intercession preserve the old world from being drowned. *Job*, though a righteous man, could not preserve his children from being killed by the fall of their house. Daniel, though a righteous man, could not prevent the captivity of his country." (Clarke)

> iv. "Jerusalem was more culpable than Sodom. A few righteous men would have delivered Sodom. Here none could turn away the wrath." (Alexander)

> v. This text teaches us "the prayers of the greatest intercessors cannot avail if men persist in their unbelief." (Spurgeon)

d. **Noah, Daniel, and Job**: The choice of these three men is fascinating. All three were men who were tested and proven faithful, men of faith who were rescued by their trust in God.

- **Noah** was a righteous and obedient man (though later shown to be flawed), yet his righteousness did not save his world, only himself and his immediate family.

- **Daniel** was alive and in Babylon in Ezekiel's day. His leadership and godliness were so evident to everyone that God could cite *him* as an example of great **righteousness** even in his own lifetime.

- **Job** was not, properly, even an Israelite (the same could be said of **Noah**). The reality of his relationship with God was demonstrated through the most difficult of testing and misery.

> i. "Questions have been raised about the inclusion of the name of Daniel, but he was a well-known contemporary of Ezekiel at the court of Babylon.... Daniel's fame for wisdom and piety was already widespread in Ezekiel's day." (Feinberg)

> ii. "Daniel was now alive and in his prime; Ezekiel, his contemporary and fellow prophet, envieth him not, but celebrateth him; as also Peter doth Paul. [2 Peter 3:15-16]" (Trapp)

iii. "From this account we may infer that *Job* was as *real* a *person* as *Noah* or *Daniel*; and of their identity no man has pretended to doubt." (Clarke)

2. (15-16) No hope for Judah during desolation.

"If I cause wild beasts to pass through the land, and they empty it, and make it so desolate that no man may pass through because of the beasts, *even though* these three men *were* in it, *as* I live," says the Lord GOD, "they would deliver neither sons nor daughters; only they would be delivered, and the land would be desolate.

a. **If I cause wild beasts to pass through the land, and they empty it**: In the previous verses God described the judgment of famine. Here God spoke of the judgment of **wild beasts** that would drive out the people of the land.

i. When the Babylonians depopulated the land of Israel, it gave much more territory to the **wild** animals of the forest and wilderness. This happens even in the present day when villages and towns depopulate; animals such as wolves come in and make life dangerous for any who may remain.

ii. "God gave the Jews victory over the residents 'little by little' so that the land wouldn't revert to its natural state and the wild animals take over (Deuteronomy 7:22)." (Wiersbe)

iii. "As lions, wolves, bears, serpents, &c. Great hurt hath been done not only by such, as Numbers 21:6, 2 Kings 2:24; 2 Kings 17:25-26, Joshua 24:12; but also by tamer creatures when set on by God." (Trapp)

b. **Even though these three men were in it**: God promised that even the presence of the **three men** (Noah, Daniel, and Job) would not spare the land of Israel from the judgment of the wild beasts soon to come.

i. "In all the procedures of divine judgment the principle of individual responsibility can never be relaxed. Hence the need of personal piety – the absolute necessity that men and women should pray for themselves- that each one should repent for himself, that each one should believe for himself; and that each one should in his own proper person be born again by the effectual operation of the Spirit of God. No proxy in these matters is possible." (Spurgeon)

3. (17-18) No hope for Judah during war.

"Or *if* I bring a sword on that land, and say, 'Sword, go through the land,' and I cut off man and beast from it, even *though* these three men

were in it, *as* I live," says the Lord G<small>OD</small>, "they would deliver neither sons nor daughters, but only they themselves would be delivered.

a. **If I bring a sword on that land**: Famine (Ezekiel 14:12-14) and wild beasts (Ezekiel 14:15-16) were not the only judgments God could send against Israel. He could also bring the **sword** of invading armies against them.

b. **Even though these three men were in it**: God promised that even the presence of the **three men** (Noah, Daniel, and Job) would not spare the land of Israel from the judgment of the sword soon to come.

4. (19-20) No hope for Judah during a plague.

"Or *if* I send a pestilence into that land and pour out My fury on it in blood, and cut off from it man and beast, even *though* Noah, Daniel, and Job *were* in it, *as* I live," says the Lord G<small>OD</small>, "they would deliver neither son nor daughter; they would deliver *only* themselves by their righteousness."

a. **If I send a pestilence into that land**: We can think of these four judgments as Ezekiel's version of the four horsemen: famine, wild beasts, war, and now **pestilence**.

b. **Even though Noah, Daniel, and Job were in it**: God promised that even the presence of the **three men** (Noah, Daniel, and Job) would not spare the land of Israel from the judgment of pestilence soon to come.

i. "It is very remarkable how evil men believe in goodness, and in hours of danger hope that its influence will protect them. I was once told by a multi-millionaire, who was completely materialised, and had become boastfully cynical concerning Christianity, that perhaps the piety of his wife would secure him entry into heaven." (Morgan)

5. (21-23) The lesson from a remnant.

For thus says the Lord G<small>OD</small>: "How much more it shall be when I send My four severe judgments on Jerusalem—the sword and famine and wild beasts and pestilence—to cut off man and beast from it? Yet behold, there shall be left in it a remnant who will be brought out, *both* sons and daughters; surely they will come out to you, and you will see their ways and their doings. Then you will be comforted concerning the disaster that I have brought upon Jerusalem, all that I have brought upon it. And they will comfort you, when you see their ways and their doings; and you shall know that I have done nothing without cause that I have done in it," says the Lord G<small>OD</small>.

a. **How much more it shall be when I send My four severe judgments on Jerusalem**: God promised to send these **four severe judgments** upon Jerusalem and Judah. When they came, they would be *God's* **severe judgments**, and they would bring death to both **man and beast**.

b. **Yet behold, there shall be left in it a remnant**: This is an unusual reference to a **remnant**, because it does not seem to refer to a righteous remnant, but a wicked one. We understand this from the phrase **their ways and their doings**, which almost always had a negative meaning.

> i. **Their ways and their doings**: "Most recent commentators recognize that the context demands that these words refer to 'unrighteous doings' for which due punishment has been meted out, and Cooke points out that in Ezekiel *doings* always has a bad sense. So the remnant of the fugitives would be wicked men." (Taylor)

> ii. "This 'unspiritual remnant' will provide evidence of Yahweh's justice in annihilating the nation. Instead of responding to their narrow escape with a change in behavior, their pattern of impious conduct will be on display for the entire exilic community to observe." (Block)

c. **You will see their ways and doings**: At the time Ezekiel spoke this, there were still many more exiles to come from Jerusalem and Judah to Babylon. When this **remnant** survived and arrived in Babylon, the Jews already in Babylon would see their wicked lives and *know* that the judgment Ezekiel spoke of was well deserved.

> i. "This, of course, does not exclude righteous survivors (9.4-6), but tells the exiles that when they find these fresh exiles flooding into Babylonia, they will see that Ezekiel has not been exaggerating the black picture he has drawn of them." (Wright)

d. **Then you will be comforted**: The comfort would come in the understanding of God's ways and judgments. God would send these **sons and daughters** to be a living example of God's righteousness in the **disaster** of the deserved judgment of God.

> i. "It would all take place in order to convince the exiles of God's justice, that he had not brought about the destruction of Jerusalem *without cause*." (Taylor)

e. **You shall know that I have done nothing without cause**: In the end, Israel would know something of God's comfort, but also His righteousness. They would understand that God was righteous in all He did, even in His **severe judgments**.

i. "We do not know the cause of so much that crushes us to the ground. But if we did know it as well as we shall know it some day, we should have no difficulty in reconciling God's dealings with His perfect love." (Meyer)

Ezekiel 15 – The Parable of the Wood of the Grapevine

A. The example of the wood of the grapevine.

1. (1-3) The uselessness of the wood of the grapevine.

Then the word of the LORD came to me, saying: "Son of man, how is the wood of the vine *better* than any other wood, the vine branch which is among the trees of the forest? Is wood taken from it to make any object? Or can *men* make a peg from it to hang any vessel on?

a. **The wood of the vine**: Many times in the Scriptures, God used **the vine** as an illustration of Israel and later, the community of the Messiah.

- The vine represented the future blessings of the Messiah (Genesis 49:11).
- Vines fat with grapes were an early sign of the fertility and abundance of Canaan (Numbers 13:23).
- A bad vine could illustrate the wickedness of man (Deuteronomy 32:32).
- Jotham used a vine as a figure in a story (Judges 9:12-13).
- Israel was compared to a vine (Psalm 80:8-19).
- Israel was like a vineyard (Isaiah 5:1-7).
- Israel was like a vine full of fruit (Hosea 10:1).
- Israel started out as a noble vine (Jeremiah 2:21).
- Ezekiel used the image of the vine and vineyard later (Ezekiel 17:5-10 and 19:10-14).
- Later Jesus used the vine to illustrate the rebellious Israel of His day (Luke 20:9-19) and also to picture the relationship He had with His people (John 15).

i. We sense that in using this illustration, Ezekiel answered a question or a protest: *God won't judge us; we are His chosen people, we are His special vine. We have been burned by past crises, but God will deliver us.* Ezekiel wanted to destroy this false sense of confidence in Israel's status as God's special vine.

ii. "This oracle disputes Israel's false claims to security based on their being the royal vine, the privileged people of God." (Block)

iii. "This parable implies that the exiles had asked about God's consistency. They understood that they were his chosen people, his choice vine. How could he destroy them? They had been through the fire of two invasions and deportations by the Babylonians, but each time they had endured and sprouted up again." (Alexander)

iv. In fact, Israel's past status as God's special vine made them more responsible and accountable, not less. "Grace places high demands on its recipients, and unless one matches one's claims with adherence to his will, one may well wake up one day to the reality that far from being his or her protector and patron, God has actually become the adversary." (Block)

b. **How is the wood of the vine better than any other wood**: God asked Ezekiel to compare the wood of the grapevine to the wood of **the trees of the forest**. If a grapevine has grapes on it, then there is an obvious use for the vine. Yet if there is no fruit, then the value of the **wood** itself should be considered.

i. It's interesting to consider that nowhere in Ezekiel 15 is there mention of *fruit*, either in the presence or absence of it. This was a dramatic way Ezekiel communicated that at this point in Israel's history, there was absolutely no fruit to speak of. It was a non-issue.

ii. "He makes no allusion to that which is always the chief idea in the use of that figure, its fruit. He only thinks of it as wood." (Morgan)

iii. "A vine would never be cultivated for the sake of its *wood*; it is really *worthless* but as it bears *fruit*. What is *Israel*? Good for nothing, but as God influenced them to bring forth fruit to his glory. But now that they have ceased to be *fruitful*, they are *good* for nothing, but, like a withered branch of the vine, to be burnt." (Clarke)

c. **Is wood taken from it to make any object?** The wood of the grapevine is useless to make a table, a tool, or even a **peg**. The wood from **the trees of the forest** can be used for many things, but not the wood that comes from the grape **vine**.

i. "Because the vine is crooked, it cannot be used for building. Because it burns so rapidly, it is of little value for fuel. Because it is soft, it cannot be employed where anything needs to hang on it." (Feinberg)

ii. "It is good for nothing; no, not so much as to make a pin or a peg of to hang a hat or bridle on, because it is a sappy and brittle wood. Think the same of that empty vine, the profligate professor, being abominable, disobedient, and unto every good work reprobate." (Trapp)

iii. "Savourless salt is good for nothing: fruitless vines are utterly useless: professors who bear no fruit are worse than useless, they cumber the ground. Let us abide in Christ, that He may bear fruit through us." (Meyer)

iv. **Peg**: "It developed the meaning of someone who could be relied upon, as in Isaiah 22:23ff.; Zechariah 10:4; cf. also Ezra 9:8. Israel was neither useful nor dependable." (Taylor)

2. (4-5) The burning of the wood of the grapevine.

Instead, it is thrown into the fire for fuel; the fire devours both ends of it, and its middle is burned. Is it useful for *any* work? Indeed, when it was whole, no object could be made from it. How much less will it be useful for *any* work when the fire has devoured it, and it is burned?

a. **It is thrown into the fire for fuel**: This is the only real use for the wood that comes from a grapevine. This is especially true if it is already partially burned (**the fire devours both ends of it**). It is then no longer **useful for any work**.

i. "Ezekiel's contribution to the 'vineyard story' is to point out the worthlessness of the vine if it doesn't bear fruit. If a tree becomes useless, you can at least cut it down and make something useful out of the wood; but what can you make out of the wood of a vine?" (Wiersbe)

ii. "Unlike metal, firing wood does not enhance its intrinsic value." (Block)

iii. "God, the Divine Carpenter, has not been able to make anything out of the vine nation. Now that it has been partly charred by the fires of judgement, it is even more useless, and it must be burnt up." (Wright)

b. **When it was whole, no object could be made from it**: If the wood had no value before it was partially burned, surely it has less value when partially burned.

i. "This is notoriously useless, not being firm enough even for making a peg to hang a pot from, and it is of even less value when it has been charred in a fire." (Taylor)

ii. "Ezekiel takes a traditional figure connoting the 'messianic' character of Israel as the repository of God's favor and turns it against itself in almost cynical fashion as a symbol of discarded worthlessness." (Vawter and Hoppe)

B. Jerusalem is like the wood of the grapevine.

1. (6-7) The people of Jerusalem are like the useless wood of the grapevine.

"Therefore thus says the Lord GOD: 'Like the wood of the vine among the trees of the forest, which I have given to the fire for fuel, so I will give up the inhabitants of Jerusalem; and I will set My face against them. They will go out from *one* fire, but *another* fire shall devour them. Then you shall know that I *am* the LORD, when I set My face against them.

a. **So I will give up the inhabitants of Jerusalem**: God said that the people of Jerusalem were like **the wood of the vine among the trees of the forest**. They had no fruit and the remaining wood was of no use. Like **the wood of the vine** they were fit only for burning.

i. **Which I have given to the fire for fuel**: "Yahweh is the one who throws the wood into the fire, and the wood represents their own compatriots, *the residents of Jerusalem.*" (Block)

b. **I will set My face against them**: In the strongest terms, God promised to oppose the people of Jerusalem with His very presence.

c. **They will go out from one fire, but another fire shall devour them**: Like the partially burned piece of grapevine wood, the people of Jerusalem would emerge from one calamity only to be devoured by another.

i. "The application is then made to Jerusalem: insignificant and not worthy to be compared with the nations and cities round about; then charred in the fires of enemy invasion in the days of Jehoiachin; spared from total destruction in 597 BC, but fit for nothing more than to be thrown back into the fire to be utterly consumed." (Taylor)

ii. "There can be no failure in Him Who is the True Vine; but if a branch in Him beareth not fruit it is taken away, cast forth, and burned in the fire. Such is the teaching of our Lord." (Morgan)

d. **Then you shall know that I am the LORD**: By telling them the severity of the judgment before it happened, this work through the prophet would help reveal God to the people of Israel when the great judgment came upon them.

2. (8) The reason for the coming desolation upon Jerusalem.

Thus I will make the land desolate, because they have persisted in unfaithfulness,' says the Lord GOD."

a. **Thus I will make the land desolate**: God promised to depopulate the land of Israel, make the land virtually empty of His covenant people.

i. "The disintegration of the spiritual relationship between Yahweh and Israel will result in the desolation of the land. As if further guarantees were necessary, the concluding signatory formula seals the Jerusalemites' fate." (Block)

b. **Because they have persisted in unfaithfulness**: It wasn't only the sin of Israel that brought God's judgment, but their *persistent* sin. They wouldn't stop their idolatry and wickedness.

i. "The reason for this fiery judgment was once more made clear: Judah had been unfaithful to the Lord and his covenant. They had failed to be a blessing to the world." (Alexander)

ii. **Persisted in unfaithfulness**: "Not one single trespass, but they have been so perpetually trespassing that it seemed a continued act, and all done with greatest aggravation." (Poole)

Ezekiel 16 – The Harlot Wife of Yahweh

In this poetic description of Israel's history, one could match details of the story with events in Israel's history – such as saying the "marriage covenant" described in Ezekiel 16:8 was the covenant made with Yahweh at Mount Sinai (Exodus 24:7-8). Still, we don't have to find a specific event or season of Israel's history for each detail; this is prophetic poetry, and truly describes the relationship in its impressions.

"Here, in the longest chapter in Ezekiel, the story is told in detail in all its sordid, loathsome character, so that God's infinite abhorrence of Israel's sin may be clearly seen. According to Rabbi Eliezer ben Hyrcanus in the Mishna, the chapter was not to be read nor translated in public." (Charles Feinberg)

"A very extraordinary chapter this sixteenth of Ezekiel! A minister could scarcely read it in public: he certainly would not like to explain its metaphors to a general audience." (Charles Spurgeon)

"Although there are many metaphors here, yet all is not metaphorical. Where there was so much idolatry, there must have been adulteries, fornications, prostitutions, and lewdness of every description." (Adam Clarke)

A. Israel rescued and adorned.

1. (1-5) Jerusalem's humble beginning.

Again the word of the LORD came to me, saying, "Son of man, cause Jerusalem to know her abominations, and say, 'Thus says the Lord GOD to Jerusalem: "Your birth and your nativity *are* from the land of Canaan; your father *was* an Amorite and your mother a Hittite. As for your nativity, on the day you were born your navel cord was not cut, nor were you washed in water to cleanse *you;* you were not rubbed with salt nor wrapped in swaddling cloths. No eye pitied you, to do any of these things for you, to have compassion on you; but you were thrown out into the open field, when you yourself were loathed on the day you were born.

a. **Cause Jerusalem to know her abominations**: This word of the Lord through Ezekiel concerns Jerusalem and the depths of her wickedness. Throughout this chapter, **Jerusalem** is used as an accurate representative of the people of Israel as a whole.

> i. "Ezekiel was charged by God to declare his message to Jerusalem as representative of all Judah, and even the entire nation." (Feinberg)

b. **Your birth and your nativity are from the land of Canaan**: This was true in the prior sense of God's promise to Abraham (Genesis 12:1-3) and when Israel as a nation came back to the land in the days of Joshua. The land of Israel was occupied by Canaanite tribes such as the **Amorite** and the **Hittite** tribes.

> i. "Amorite and Hittite were general names for the people of Canaan who occupied the land before Abraham.... Being the most powerful of the nations in Canaan, they represented them all." (Feinberg)

> ii. **Are from the land of Canaan**: "The statement is heavy with sarcasm, however, for the term 'Canaanite' was a byword for moral decadence." (Taylor)

> iii. **Your mother a Hittite**: "Sometimes the ill nature of a father is corrected in the child by the sweetness of the mother, but you Jews were not so happy, your mother was as bad every whit as your father." (Poole)

c. **On the day you were born**: God used a vivid description to show how humble and poor Israel's beginnings were. There was none to care for her at birth; all other nations were against her from the beginning (**no eye pitied you**). Israel was hated from birth (**you yourself were loathed on the day you were born**). If not for the care of their covenant God, they would have perished.

> i. **You were not rubbed with salt**: "In salting the child the skin is rubbed with salt to make it firm and clean." (Feinberg)

> ii. "Cutting the cord, washing, rubbing down with salt, and clothing the newborn were also customary legal acts of legitimation. In the neglect and abandonment of the infant in the open field, the parent legally relinquished all rights to and responsibilities for the child." (Block)

> iii. **Thrown out into the open field**: "This is an allusion to the custom of some heathen and barbarous nations, who exposed those children in the open fields to be devoured by wild beasts who had any kind of deformity, or whom they could not support." (Clarke)

iv. **Thrown out into the open field** shows how lost and vulnerable they were without God. "Cast out into the open field, left in a wilderness where it is not likely that any should pass by, thrown where the cold can smite by night and the heat can blast by day, left where the wild beast goeth about, seeking whom he may devour-such is the estate of human nature: unclothed, unarmed, helpless, exposed to all manner of ravenous destroyers." (Spurgeon)

2. (6-7) God's favor transforms Jerusalem.

"And when I passed by you and saw you struggling in your own blood, I said to you in your blood, 'Live!' Yes, I said to you in your blood, 'Live!' I made you thrive like a plant in the field; and you grew, matured, and became very beautiful. *Your* breasts were formed, your hair grew, but you *were* naked and bare.

a. **When I passed by you and saw you struggling**: Continuing the illustration from the previous verses, God took note of Israel in their humble, hated state. They would have perished (**struggling in your own blood**) if not for God's grace-filled intervention.

i. In Deuteronomy 7:7-8, God explained the reason He set His attention on Israel to rescue them: *The LORD did not set His love on you nor choose you because you were more in number than any other people, for you were the least of all peoples; but because the LORD loves you, and because He would keep the oath which He swore to your fathers.*

ii. It wasn't because Israel was so amazing or so holy. They were weak, poor, struggling, and near death. But God **passed by** and took notice.

b. **I said to you in your blood, "Live!"**: When all their circumstances and all the other nations said *die* to Israel, God said **live**. He brought life to them and **made** them **thrive like a plant in the field**.

i. "He pronounces the sentence of life upon the child, otherwise sentenced to certain death. His passion is reflected in the emphatic twofold declaration, *In your blood, live!*" (Block)

c. **You grew, matured, and became very beautiful**: Under God's care Israel became larger, stronger, and more mature. They became **very beautiful** and came into young adulthood (**your breasts were formed, your hair grew**).

i. According to Block, **your hair grew** refers to the metaphorical young woman's pubic hair. "With the passing of the age of innocence and the arrival of sexual maturity, nakedness assumes moral overtones. Whereas the earlier nakedness had made the foundling vulnerable to the elements and marauding animals, now she stands exposed to dangers of a different sort." (Block)

d. **But you were naked and bare**: Israel grew and matured, but had not become so self-sufficient that they no longer needed God.

i. "The foundling became a beautiful young woman, yet it is stated that she was naked and bare. The implication may be that she was without wealth and without the benefits of culture and civilization, as the world sees them." (Feinberg)

3. (8) God's loving covenant with Jerusalem.

"When I passed by you again and looked upon you, indeed your time *was* **the time of love; so I spread My wing over you and covered your nakedness. Yes, I swore an oath to you and entered into a covenant with you, and you became Mine," says the Lord GOD.**

a. **I spread My wing over you and covered your nakedness**: In the figure used by the Lord to describe Israel and His relationship to them, they were grown yet still greatly neglected and needy. They needed God's protection (**spread My wing**) and His provision (**covered your nakedness**), and God gave them both.

i. **Spread My wing over you**: "The phrase in v. 8 describes the symbolic act whereby the husband took his wife under his protection (Ruth 3.9)." (Wright)

b. **I swore an oath to you and entered into a covenant with you**: Above protecting and providing for Israel, God entered into a **covenant** relationship with them. It was a covenant marriage, and God could say, "**you became Mine**."

i. "In earthly inter-relationships, the marriage relationship is the highest in sanctity, because it is the highest in the experience of Love. By this figure, then, God sets forth for us what His heart feels for us, and what He desires from us in return. His love is of the strongest and tenderest, and He looks for a return of that love in uttermost loyalty." (Morgan)

4. (9-14) God's care and generosity adorn Jerusalem.

"Then I washed you in water; yes, I thoroughly washed off your blood, and I anointed you with oil. I clothed you in embroidered cloth and gave you sandals of badger skin; I clothed you with fine linen and covered you with silk. I adorned you with ornaments, put bracelets on your wrists, and a chain on your neck. And I put a jewel in your nose, earrings in your ears, and a beautiful crown on your head. Thus you were adorned with gold and silver, and your clothing *was of* **fine linen, silk, and embroidered cloth. You ate** *pastry of* **fine flour, honey, and oil. You were exceedingly beautiful, and succeeded to royalty. Your fame**

went out among the nations because of your beauty, for it *was* perfect through My splendor which I had bestowed on you," says the Lord GOD.

a. **I washed you in water**: God described His care and adornment of Israel. He cleaned them and **anointed** them with fragrant **oil**. He **clothed** them in fine clothes and **sandals of badger skin**. God **adorned** them with all kinds of jewelry, and even put **a beautiful crown** on Israel's head.

i. **Covered you with silk**: "The word for 'silk' in verse 10 is a Hebrew word which does not occur elsewhere. The clothing was costly." (Feinberg)

ii. **Embroidered cloth…badger skin…fine linen**: "These expressions occur elsewhere most frequently in the descriptions of the tabernacle, its curtains, and the priestly vestments. References to the luxury leather of which her sandals are made (*tahas*) occur only in contexts involving the tabernacle." (Block)

iii. "The *badgers' skin* (AV) is the same as the material used in the covering of the tabernacle (Numbers 4:6ff.). The various translations give *sealskin* (RV), *porpoise skin* (RV mg.), *leather* (RSV). 'Badger' is certainly not right, because the skin had to be both suitable for shoes and also large enough for one of them to cover the ark. The likeliest candidate is the dugong, a seal-like animal of the order Siremia, which is found in the Red Sea; its skin is used by the bedouin for making sandals." (Taylor)

b. **You ate pastry of fine flour, honey, and oil**: God provided richly for Israel's every need.

i. "Furthermore, her special food…'fine flour' and 'oil,' figured prominently in the sacred offerings. In short, Jerusalem, the bride of Yahweh, is clothed with the garments that 'clothe' the sanctuary and is fed with the 'food' of its offerings." (Block)

c. **You were exceedingly beautiful, and succeeded to royalty**: Because of God's generous love and care, Israel excelled in beauty and was raised to royal status. They became famous among the nations, and it was all because of God's **splendor** that He had **bestowed** upon them. It was not of themselves.

i. "During the reign of King David and during Solomon's early years, Jerusalem was indeed a queenly city and Israel a prosperous kingdom. As long as Israel, Jehovah's wife, obeyed His Word and kept His covenant, He blessed her abundantly just as He promised. He gave her healthy children, fruitful flocks and herds, abundant harvests, and protection from disease, disaster, and invasion." (Wiersbe)

ii. "Incredibly, the charge that Ezekiel would later level at the king of Tyre applied to this poor foundling: 'Your heart was lifted up on account of your beauty; you corrupted your wisdom on account of your splendor.'" (Block)

iii. From a new covenant perspective, it is staggering to think and to believe that we have even more in Jesus Christ than Israel had when they were blessed under the old covenant. Every aspect of God's blessing to Israel under the old covenant (washing, anointing, clothing, providing, adorning, crowning, etc.) is given in greater measure and glory in the new covenant.

iv. F.B. Meyer described how we should react to God's amazing gifts towards us: "Let us dare to believe that it is so. Accept and value your position. In Christ, we are more than tolerated; we are loved. We are more than forgiven; we are arrayed in fair garments. The King greatly delights in us. In His eyes, and because His beauty is upon us, we are all fair."

B. Israel the proud harlot.

1. (15-19) Jerusalem acts like a harlot.

"But you trusted in your own beauty, played the harlot because of your fame, and poured out your harlotry on everyone passing by who *would have* it. You took some of your garments and adorned multicolored high places for yourself, and played the harlot on them. *Such* things should not happen, nor be. You have also taken your beautiful jewelry from My gold and My silver, which I had given you, and made for yourself male images and played the harlot with them. You took your embroidered garments and covered them, and you set My oil and My incense before them. Also My food which I gave you—the pastry of fine flour, oil, and honey *which* I fed you—you set it before them as sweet incense; and *so it was*," says the Lord God.

a. **You trusted in your own beauty**: This pride was the root of Israel's decline. They forgot that they were nothing when God found them and that He had bestowed their beauty upon them. Brought to beauty by God's blessing, they **trusted** in the blessing God gave instead of in God Himself.

i. Ezekiel 16:15-35 is one of the strongest denunciations of Israel's sin found in the entire Bible. "Rebukes of Israel's sin by the prophets of

Israel are many and well known, but none is so vivid, vehement, sordid and piercing as these words." (Feinberg)

ii. "God had warned Israel not to forget him when she came into all the benefits that he would give her in the Promised Land (Deuteronomy 6:10–12). This exhortation was soon forgotten by the nation's leaders." (Alexander)

iii. To deserve such a strong rebuke, Israel began by forgetting an important principle: everything good they were, and all the good they had, were the gift of God's grace to them. Many centuries later the Apostle Paul wrote of this same principle for Christians: *For who makes you differ from another? And what do you have that you did not receive? Now if you did indeed receive it, why do you boast as if you had not received it?* (1 Corinthians 4:7).

iv. If it was possible for blessed Israel to trust in her own beauty, so it is possible for the disciple of Jesus. F.B. Meyer spoke of the Christian's proper attitude: "Let us not presume. We have nought of our own. When the temptation tries us to pride ourselves on our goodness; to arrogate to ourselves a special position because of our superiority to others; to assume that we can be independent of our immortal Lover— then let us remember what we were."

b. **Played the harlot because of your fame**: God gave Israel a place of status and royalty among the nations, but they used that **fame** to seek after the idols of the pagan nations. They ran after pagan idols like a harlot runs after customers (**poured out your harlotry on everyone passing by**).

i. "It is an ill sign in any of us when God's blessings are themselves made into idols. If thou beginnest to worship thy wealth, thy health, thy children, thy learning, or anything that God has given thee, this is exceedingly provoking to the Most High; it is a breach of the marriage covenant between thy soul and God." (Spurgeon)

ii. **Played the harlot**: "The verb [**harlot**, root *znh*] and other derivatives occur twenty-one times in this description of Jerusalem's unrestrained nymphomaniacal adventures with her lovers." (Block)

iii. "The Christian reader may, not surprisingly, feel nauseated at the indelicate realism of Ezekiel's language, but Ezekiel meant it that way. He was telling of ugly sins and he made the parable fit the facts." (Taylor)

iv. "Although the root *naap* [adultery] is more fitting to describe Israel's covenantal infidelity, *znh* [harlotry] offers a more forceful rhetorical tool. The innocent young woman, graciously elevated to the status of queen, has become a whore." (Block)

c. **You took some of your garments and adorned multicolored high places**: Israel took the very blessings God adorned her with and she used those blessings to adorn the places of pagan idolatry. The **gold** and **silver** God gave them were used in sexually charged idol worship (**male images and played the harlot with them**).

> i. **Multicolored high places**: "The *gaily decked shrines* (RSV) indicate the colourful hangings of the tents that were set up at the high places (see note on 6:3), which were seen by Ezekiel to be places for feasting, fornication, idolatry and child-sacrifice." (Taylor)

> ii. **Male images**: "*Priapi* are here meant, which were carried about in the ceremonies of Osiris, Bacchus, and Adonis; and were something like the *lingam* among the Hindoos.... This was done at the worship of Bacchus in Egypt: and they who wish to see more may consult *Herodotus* lib. ii, c. 48, 49. In this *phallic* worship the women were principally concerned." (Clarke)

2. (20-22) Jerusalem sacrifices their sons and daughters to idols.

"Moreover you took your sons and your daughters, whom you bore to Me, and these you sacrificed to them to be devoured. *Were* your *acts* of harlotry a small matter, that you have slain My children and offered them up to them by causing them to pass through *the fire?* And in all your abominations and acts of harlotry you did not remember the days of your youth, when you were naked and bare, struggling in your blood.

a. **These you sacrificed to them to be devoured**: Israel became so degenerate in her devotion to idols that she offered her own **sons** and **daughters** and **sacrificed** them to the pagan idols such as the detestable Molech.

> i. **To be devoured**: "Instead of presenting her children to Yahweh, her husband, this woman presented them *as food* to the pagan images that she had made! The expression *le ekol* (lit. 'for eating') portrays the children as idols' diet." (Block)

b. **By causing them to pass through the fire**: Their idolatry went so far that they actually participated in the Canaanite cult of child sacrifice. Even King Ahaz (2 Kings 16:3) and King Manasseh (2 Kings 21:6) took part in this horrific practice. The pagan god (or, *demon*, more accurately) Molech was worshipped by heating a metal statue representing the god until it was red hot, then placing a living infant on the outstretched hands of the statue, while beating drums drowned out the screams of the child until it burned to death.

i. Sadly, even a man as great as Solomon at least sanctioned the worship of Molech and built a temple to this idol (1 Kings 11:7). One of the great crimes of the northern tribes of Israel was their worship of Molech, leading to the Assyrian captivity (2 Kings 17:17). King Manasseh of Judah gave his son to Molech (2 Kings 21:6). Up to the days of King Josiah of Judah, Molech worship continued, because he destroyed a place of worship to that idol (2 Kings 23:10).

ii. There is little or no archaeological evidence for child sacrifice among the Israelites of this period. This means that either the practice was very rare or diligently covered up. This may be God's way of saying that even if the practice was rare, it was an abomination to Him.

c. **You did not remember the days of your youth**: Israel's haughty pride was rooted in their failure to **remember**. They no longer remembered their poor and humble beginning, and how all the protection, provision, and adornment they enjoyed was the blessing and gift of God.

3. (23-26) Jerusalem's great wickedness.

"Then it was so, after all your wickedness—'Woe, woe to you!' says the Lord GOD — *that* you also built for yourself a shrine, and made a high place for yourself in every street. You built your high places at the head of every road, and made your beauty to be abhorred. You offered yourself to everyone who passed by, and multiplied your acts of harlotry. You also committed harlotry with the Egyptians, your very fleshly neighbors, and increased your acts of harlotry to provoke Me to anger.

a. **Woe, woe to you**: This was God's sorrowful lament over wicked Israel. God's protest came from great depth of feeling.

i. "The repeated woe is partly threat and partly lament." (Feinberg)

b. **You also built for yourself a shrine, and made a high place for yourself in every street**: As they grew worse in wickedness, Israel began to multiply their idolatry. It became widespread and common over the entire land.

i. **Made a high place**: "*Gab*, a *stew* or *brothel*…. So my old MS. Bible, *a bordel house*. 'Thou hast builded thy stewes and bordell houses in every place.'–*Coverdale's* Bible, 1535. *Bordel* is an *Italian* word: how it got so early into our language I know not. Our modern word *brothel* is a corruption of it." (Clarke)

c. **You offered yourself to everyone who passed by**: Israel's unfaithfulness to God was not only in every place, but seemingly also to every pagan god, even the gods of **the Egyptians**. They did it all to **provoke** God **to anger**.

i. **You offered yourself**: Literally, this is *you opened your feet*. It was an indelicate way of saying "you spread your legs for everyone." Ezekiel used this shocking language to jolt his jaded listeners.

ii. **Your very fleshly neighbors**: This is more shocking language. "The prophet describes this lover in obscenely physical terms: *your neighbors with the huge organs.*" (Block) There are several places in the Old Testament where the penis is euphemistically referred to as *flesh*: Ezekiel 23:20, 44:7, 9; Genesis 17:11, 14, 23, 24, 25; Exodus 28:42; and Leviticus 15:2-19.

C. The depths of the sin of Israel the harlot.

1. (27-29) Foreign lovers turn upon Jerusalem the harlot.

"Behold, therefore, I stretched out My hand against you, diminished your allotment, and gave you up to the will of those who hate you, the daughters of the Philistines, who were ashamed of your lewd behavior. You also played the harlot with the Assyrians, because you were insatiable; indeed you played the harlot with them and still were not satisfied. Moreover you multiplied your acts of harlotry as far as the land of the trader, Chaldea; and even then you were not satisfied.

a. **Therefore, I stretched out My hand against you**: After a long time and great provocation, God began to act against Israel. He **diminished** their provision and gave them to their enemies the Philistines (**gave you up to the will of those who hate you**). Israel's idolatry was so great it made the **Philistines** blush.

i. **Diminished your allotment**: "God's reaction was that he was provoked to anger (26), for which his appointed punishment was to diminish her *allotted portion* (27), which refers to loss of territory by enemy annexation. We know from the Taylor Prism that Sennacherib did just that in 701 BC." (Taylor)

b. **You also played the harlot with the Assyrians**: Their idolatry became worse, multiplying so far they not only went after the gods of the **Assyrians** and the Babylonians (**as far as the land of the trader, Chaldea**), they also formed political alliances with those nations. The temptation was not only to idolatry but also to reliance upon, and alliances with, foreign nations.

i. "In time and when it suited her pleasure, she turned to the Assyrians. The historical books recount the pro-Assyrian policy of both Ahaz

and Manasseh (see II Kings 16:7 ff.; Hosea 5:13; 8:9; Amos 5:26)."
(Feinberg)

2. (30) Degenerate Jerusalem.

"How degenerate is your heart!" says the Lord GOD**, "seeing you do all these *things*, the deeds of a brazen harlot.**

a. **How degenerate is your heart**: God saw that the problem with Israel went far deeper than their actions. Their **heart** had become proud and dissatisfied with their covenant God. This decline was truly **degenerate**.

b. **The deeds of a brazen harlot**: Israel's decline began in the **heart**, but it did not end there. In their wickedness and idolatry they **did the deeds** of unashamed prostitutes.

3. (31-34) Jerusalem *worse* than a harlot.

"You erected your shrine at the head of every road, and built your high place in every street. Yet you were not like a harlot, because you scorned payment. *You are* an adulterous wife, *who* takes strangers instead of her husband. Men make payment to all harlots, but you made your payments to all your lovers, and hired them to come to you from all around for your harlotry. You are the opposite of *other* women in your harlotry, because no one solicited you to be a harlot. In that you gave payment but no payment was given you, therefore you are the opposite."

a. **Yet you were not like a harlot, because you scorned payment**: Israel practiced their idolatry every place (**at the head of every road** and a **high place in every street**), yet in one way they were significantly worse than a literal **harlot** – they received *no benefit of any kind* from their idolatry, still they persisted in it.

i. "In Ezekiel 16:30–34 in a piece of fine sarcasm Ezekiel portrays Israel literally as a nymphomaniac whose promiscuous lust has caused her to reverse the usual order involved in prostitution. She has hired rather than been hired by her clients." (Vawter and Hoppe)

b. **You are an adulterous wife, who takes strangers**: The sense is that the harlot does it for pay, but the **adulterous wife** for free, merely for the thrill of transgression and a combination of weakness and hardness of heart.

i. Israel as the **adulterous wife** is the theme of Ezekiel's predecessor, the prophet Hosea – as well as many other prophets.

c. **Men make payments to all harlots, but you made your payments to all your lovers**: Israel was like the adulterous wife who not only gives herself away for free but also buys lavish gifts for her illicit **lovers**.

d. **No one solicited you to be a harlot**: In her metaphorical harlotry, Israel had no pimp. She was not forced or persuaded to do what she did; it came from her degenerate heart (Ezekiel 16:30). Even though it cost her (**you gave payment**), she still continued to be unfaithful to her God.

> i. "But is the church today any less guilty? Members of local churches commit the same sins we read about in the newspapers, but the news doesn't always get to the headlines. Congregations are being torn apart because of professed Christians who are involved in lawsuits, divorces, immorality, family feuds, crooked business deals, financial scandals, and a host of other activities that belong to the world." (Wiersbe)

D. God's message to Israel the harlot.

1. (35-39) Judgment announced against Jerusalem the harlot.

'Now then, O harlot, hear the word of the LORD! Thus says the Lord GOD: "Because your filthiness was poured out and your nakedness uncovered in your harlotry with your lovers, and with all your abominable idols, and because of the blood of your children which you gave to them, surely, therefore, I will gather all your lovers with whom you took pleasure, all those you loved, *and* all those you hated; I will gather them from all around against you and will uncover your nakedness to them, that they may see all your nakedness. And I will judge you as women who break wedlock or shed blood are judged; I will bring blood upon you in fury and jealousy. I will also give you into their hand, and they shall throw down your shrines and break down your high places. They shall also strip you of your clothes, take your beautiful jewelry, and leave you naked and bare.

a. **O harlot, hear the word of the LORD**: God didn't address Israel by a noble name. Their degenerate heart deserved a shocking address.

> i. **O harlot**: "A name good enough for such an odious housewife, the shame of her sex. He is not worthy of an honest name whose deeds are not honest." (Trapp)

> ii. **Because your filthiness was poured out**: Block believes this refers to "the female genital fluid produced at sexual arousal." But most commentators believe this is a reference to the issue of a venereal disease: "Thy filthiness issuing from thee by reason of thine overly frequent and excessive adulteries. He meaneth the infamous fluxes of whores, saith Diodat." (Trapp) It is properly translated in our version *filthiness, poisonous filth*. Does it not refer to that *venereal virus* which is engendered by promiscuous connexions?" (Clarke)

b. **I will gather all your lovers with whom you took pleasure, all those you loved, and all those you hated**: The LORD spoke as the one who knows human nature. He knew that when people run after illicit lovers – either literally or spiritually – some they may love, but others they will hate.

> i. "Appropriately, it is Israel's 'lovers' who will execute God's vengeance upon her. By that they add to the depth of her shame. They show how cheaply they had valued what she had to offer them and the real contempt in which they held her." (Vawter and Hoppe)

> ii. "For these reasons God would gather all her lovers—those she had loved, i.e., the Egyptians, and those she had hated, i.e., the Chaldeans. These would come against Jerusalem from every direction." (Smith)

c. **I will gather them from all around against you and will uncover your nakedness to them**: God promised to humble – even to humiliate – Israel before her pagan neighbors. The beauty and adornment she had traded upon before the nations would be stripped away, and they would see what Israel was without God.

> i. This wasn't shame for the sake of shame; this was for the sake of repentance and restoration.

> ii. "Jerusalem had bared her body to all passersby. Now God provides her with all the exposure she wants, and more. If she wants to be a public spectacle, he offers his aid. Naked he had found her; naked he would leave her. The hell that awaited her was not the creation of some demonic force or external power, but of her own making." (Block)

d. **I will judge you as women who break wedlock or shed blood are judged**: God would bring the punishment of death upon Israel. He would not kill the nation completely, but reign death upon them in judgment. God promised to bring this judgment with passion: **I will bring blood upon you in fury and jealousy.**

> i. "The first step in her retributive judgment at the hands of the Lord would be public exposure before both her lovers and her enemies. Public exposure of profligate women and stoning of them were well-known customs in ancient Israel." (Feinberg)

e. **I will also give you into their hand**: God promised that the judgment to come upon Israel would come through the very lovers she gave herself to. The neighboring nations, and their gods by proxy, would conquer and humiliate stubborn Israel.

i. **They shall also strip you**: "It is opprobrium to a man to be stripped, more to a woman; this Jewish adulteress shall be stripped, that her nakedness appear." (Poole)

2. (40-43) Describing the coming judgment against Jerusalem the harlot.

"They shall also bring up an assembly against you, and they shall stone you with stones and thrust you through with their swords. They shall burn your houses with fire, and execute judgments on you in the sight of many women; and I will make you cease playing the harlot, and you shall no longer hire lovers. So I will lay to rest My fury toward you, and My jealousy shall depart from you. I will be quiet, and be angry no more. Because you did not remember the days of your youth, but agitated Me with all these *things*, surely I will also recompense your deeds on *your own* head," says the Lord GOD. "And you shall not commit lewdness in addition to all your abominations.

a. **They shall also bring up an assembly against you**: The armies of the nations surrounding Israel would come against her in a divinely appointed judgment. The judgment would be complete, with the **stones** of attack, the **swords** of war, and the **fire** of destruction.

b. **I will make you cease playing the harlot, and you shall no longer hire lovers**: The judgment God would bring upon them would be something of a cure for Israel's gross idolatry. After this judgment and exile, they would never have the same problem with the idols of the nations.

c. **So I will lay to rest My fury toward you**: God's judgment against and anger towards Israel was not to last forever. When their hearts were turned away from their gross idolatry, God would change His disposition toward them.

d. **Because you did not remember the days of your youth**: God repeats the idea from Ezekiel 16:22. Their self-destructive pride was based on their failure to remember that all the good they had was a blessing and gift from God.

i. "In order that she might remember him once again, God would bring this discipline on her. Though mankind may forget God, his love prevents him from forgetting his own. God takes his commitments in personal relationships seriously." (Alexander)

E. The past, present, and future of Jerusalem the harlot and her "family."

1. (44-45) The mother of Jerusalem the harlot.

"Indeed everyone who quotes proverbs will use *this* proverb against you: 'Like mother, like daughter!' You *are* your mother's daughter,

loathing husband and children; and you *are* the sister of your sisters, who loathed their husbands and children; your mother *was* a Hittite and your father an Amorite.

a. **Like mother, like daughter**: This **proverb** would be accurately said of Israel in Ezekiel's day. The idea from Ezekiel 16:3 is repeated: *your father was an Amorite and your mother a Hittite* – and Israel acted just like those pagan nations.

b. **You are your mother's daughter…you are the sister of your sisters**: God had called Israel to be *different* from the pagan nations, and instead she became just like them.

c. **Who loathed their husbands**: It is strange and shocking that Israel would be like those who hated their husbands. Spiritually speaking, Yahweh was the covenant husband of Israel, *who was a perfect husband*. This bad marriage was entirely the responsibility of one party, not both.

i. Israel "was weary of the best Husband, that while she doted on abominable adulterers, did most contemptuously disregard her Husband, and forsake him." (Poole)

2. (46-47) The sisters of Jerusalem the harlot.

"Your elder sister *is* Samaria, who dwells with her daughters to the north of you; and your younger sister, who dwells to the south of you, *is* Sodom and her daughters. You did not walk in their ways nor act according to their abominations; but, as *if that were* too little, you became more corrupt than they in all your ways.

a. **Your elder sister is Samaria**: Here God focused on Jerusalem and the southern kingdom it was the capital of. The city of **Samaria** was the capital city of the long-conquered northern kingdom of Israel (1 Kings 16:24-29). Once-faithful Jerusalem had become just as corrupt as her **elder sister**, **Samaria**.

b. **Your younger sister…is Sodom**: It was bad enough to be identified with **Samaria**, but Jerusalem's state was far worse than that. She was like **Sodom**, with all her infamous corruptions (Genesis 13:13, 19:1-24).

i. "Ezekiel calls Samaria the "elder sister" and Sodom the "younger sister" not out of any chronological interest (the Hebrew terms are, literally, "big" and "small," respectively). Ezekiel has in view their historical importance to those whom the prophet addressed." (Vawter and Hoppe)

ii. Some think the associations with **Samaria** and **Sodom** were only poetic. "Ezekiel probably has two groups in mind. Samaria represents those who in the past were a breakaway from Judah. Sodom represents the dregs of Canaanite society, and would be those who had not had any allegiance to Jehovah (cf. Matthew 10.15; 11.23,24)." (Wright)

c. **But, as if that were too little, you became more corrupt than they in all your ways**: Even worse, Jerusalem became **more corrupt** than Sodom. This was a staggering accusation for God to make, yet it was true.

> i. "Jerusalem's sin had been the more heinous in that she had professed to set the standard for her sisters, whereas she had been more abominable than they." (Morgan)

3. (48-50) Comparing Jerusalem to her sister Sodom.

"*As* I live," says the Lord God, "neither your sister Sodom nor her daughters have done as you and your daughters have done. Look, this was the iniquity of your sister Sodom: She and her daughter had pride, fullness of food, and abundance of idleness; neither did she strengthen the hand of the poor and needy. And they were haughty and committed abomination before Me; therefore I took them away as I saw *fit*.

a. **Neither your sister Sodom nor her daughters have done as you**: Introducing this word with a solemn vow (**as I live**), God repeated the accusation from the previous verse.

b. **This was the iniquity of your sister Sodom**: Point by point, God listed some of the sins of Sodom. The sins listed here are alluded to in Genesis, but not specifically detailed. Some wrongly take this to mean that God did not consider the sexual depravity described in Genesis 19:1-24 to be sin, but this is a clear and willful misunderstanding of the text. These were sins at the root of the depravity described in Genesis 19, and in addition to that depravity.

- **She and her daughter had pride**: Genesis 13:10 says that the land of Sodom was *like the garden of the* LORD. It was the kind of city that citizens take great pride in.

- **Fullness of food and abundance of idleness**: Being well watered everywhere, like the garden of the Lord (Genesis 13:10), there was agricultural abundance in Sodom. This made them self-reliant, sinfully independent, and overly invested in entertainments and comforts.

- **Neither did she strengthen the hand of the poor and needy**: With her great abundance, the people of Sodom should have been more generous and giving to the **poor and needy**. Yet in their selfishness and **abundance of idleness** they were not generous or helpful.

- **They were haughty and committed abomination**: Ancient Sodom was filled with pride and terrible idolatry (**abomination**). The sexual depravity described in Genesis 19 was no doubt connected with the environment of unrestrained idolatry.

    i. "The sins of Sodom here include what we know of from Genesis18.20-19.11, but go wider into the luxuries and sins of civilized prosperity (Genesis13.10)." (Wright)

    ii. "This material ease fostered sexual perversion (Genesis 13:13; 18:20; 19:4–5). This passage stands as both an exhortation and a warning against such wickedness and life styles today." (Alexander)

    iii. **Committed abomination**: "That unnatural filthiness which taketh its name from them. This in the Levant is not held a vice, and in Mexico it is one of the Spanish virtues." (Trapp)

    c. **Therefore I took them away as I saw fit**: God brought His judgment to Sodom, and He would bring it to Jerusalem and Judah, who in many ways were *worse* than Sodom.

4. (51-52) Comparing Israel to her sister Samaria.

"Samaria did not commit half of your sins; but you have multiplied your abominations more than they, and have justified your sisters by all the abominations which you have done. You who judged your sisters, bear your own shame also, because the sins which you committed were more abominable than theirs; they are more righteous than you. Yes, be disgraced also, and bear your own shame, because you justified your sisters.

    a. **Samaria did not commit half of your sins**: Since Samaria fell some 130 years before Jerusalem, Judah had much more time to indulge in sin. As well, they had far more light with the presence of the temple, the institution of the priesthood, and better kings.

    i. "Judah was more guilty because she had more privileges from the Lord." (Feinberg)

    b. **And have justified your sisters by all the abominations which you have done**: Jerusalem's heart and deeds were so bad that it made Samaria and Sodom look **justified** in comparison.

    i. Jesus made a similar comparison more than once (Matthew 10:15, 11:23-24).

    ii. "Any woman who puts these women in a good light should be ashamed of herself." (Block)

c. **You who judged your sisters, bear your own shame also**: Jerusalem and Judah proudly thought themselves better than Samaria and Sodom, but this proud judgment only made them guiltier. Jerusalem would **be disgraced also** and **bear** their **own shame**.

> i. "Ezekiel lives among people who feel shame because Yahweh, in whom they had placed their trust, had reneged on his covenant commitment and failed to stand up for them. The purpose of this entire oracle has been to turn the tables on the Israelites' complaint. The charge of betrayal is to be leveled not against Yahweh but against themselves." (Block)

5. (53-59) A promise of restoration for Jerusalem and her sisters.

"When I bring back their captives, the captives of Sodom and her daughters, and the captives of Samaria and her daughters, then *I will also bring back* the captives of your captivity among them, that you may bear your own shame and be disgraced by all that you did when you comforted them. When your sisters, Sodom and her daughters, return to their former state, and Samaria and her daughters return to their former state, then you and your daughters will return to your former state. For your sister Sodom was not a byword in your mouth in the days of your pride, before your wickedness was uncovered. It was like the time of the reproach of the daughters of Syria and all *those* around her, and of the daughters of the Philistines, who despise you everywhere. You have paid for your lewdness and your abominations," says the LORD. **For thus says the Lord GOD: "I will deal with you as you have done, who despised the oath by breaking the covenant.**

a. **When I bring back their captives**: God promised some kind of restoration for **Sodom** and **Samaria**, and that Jerusalem would also be restored, and their captives brought back. The promise to bring back the captives of Samaria is easily understood, and we may see its fulfillment. The fulfillment of this promise to Sodom is more difficult to understand.

> i. "But the restoration of Sodom will pose no difficulty for the omnipotence of God; her restoration was mentioned first to do away with all boasting." (Feinberg)

b. **That you may bear your own shame**: Part of the reason God promised to restore the captivity of Samaria and Sodom was to humble Jerusalem and Judah. They would know that they were not the *unique* objects of God's favor and restoration. His love was wider than that.

i. "There will, however, be a day of restoration for Sodom, Samaria and Jerusalem, but this will bring nothing but a heightened sense of shame and further humiliation for the harlot city." (Taylor)

ii. **Your sister Sodom was not a byword**: "In former times self-righteous Jerusalem would not even mention the name of Sodom. Jerusalem, however, was humbled when her own wickedness was made public through divine judgment." (Smith)

c. **You have paid for your lewdness and your abominations**: The day would come when God's season of discipline and judgment over Jerusalem and Judah would pass. In some sense cured of their previous idolatry, they could move forward in humility instead of pride.

6. (60-63) Remembering the old covenant, promising an everlasting covenant.

"Nevertheless I will remember My covenant with you in the days of your youth, and I will establish an everlasting covenant with you. Then you will remember your ways and be ashamed, when you receive your older and your younger sisters; for I will give them to you for daughters, but not because of My covenant with you. And I will establish My covenant with you. Then you shall know that I *am* the Lord, that you may remember and be ashamed, and never open your mouth anymore because of your shame, when I provide you an atonement for all you have done," says the Lord God.'"

a. **Nevertheless I will remember My covenant with you in the days of your youth**: Despite the certainty of the coming judgment, God would not forget His **covenant** with Israel. They would continue to have a special place in His plan of the ages, and therefore in His heart.

b. **Then you will remember your ways and be ashamed**: The restoration would bring humility to Israel, not only toward God but also towards those they had previously despised and judged (**when you receive your older and younger sisters**).

c. **And I will establish My covenant with you**: The idea is repeated again for emphasis. The coming judgment would be so great that Israel would be tempted to believe there was no more hope for them with God. Yet again and again Yahweh promised to **establish** His **covenant** with them again.

i. "God says that not only will He make good on the past covenants but He is also going to make a new covenant with them. Unfortunately, these passages of Scripture are not studied very much at all. When they are, they make it very clear that God still has a future purpose with the nation Israel." (McGee)

d. **When I provide you an atonement for all you have done**: Through Ezekiel, the LORD hinted at the nature of the future covenant. The idea of a God-provided **atonement** is an important aspect of the new covenant, already mentioned in Ezekiel 11:17-21. This would be the true and ultimate restoration of Israel.

Ezekiel 17 – The Parable of the Two Eagles and the Vine

"From the beauty of its images, the elegance of its composition, the perspicuity of its language, the rich variety of its matter, and the easy transition from one part of the subject to another, this chapter forms one of the most beautiful and perfect pieces of its kind that can possibly be conceived in so small a compass." (Adam Clarke)

A. The parable of the two eagles and the vine.

1. (1-2) A riddle and a parable.

And the word of the LORD came to me, saying, "Son of man, pose a riddle, and speak a parable to the house of Israel,

a. **Son of man, pose a riddle, and speak a parable**: Ezekiel the prophet was told to speak a saying that would be something of a **riddle** and something of a **parable**. It was a **riddle** in that the meaning was a bit of a puzzle to understanding; it was a **parable** in that it told a story illustrating spiritual and material truth.

i. "It is a riddle in that its meaning needs to be explained; there is a deeper meaning which underlies the figurative form, for something in its presentation is obscure. It is a parable in that it is an allegory." (Feinberg)

ii. "Riddles exercise the wit, and parables help the memory, and excite both attention and affection." (Trapp)

iii. "The manner in which plants and animals relate in the story, carrying on as if they were humans, would have amused any audience, and undoubtedly contributed to the prophet's reputation as a 'spinner of riddles' (Ezekiel 20:49)." (Block)

b. **To the house of Israel**: Once again God referred to what was primarily the kingdom and tribe of Judah as the **house of Israel** as a whole. The parable describes the events between the time of King Jehoiachin's exile

(597 BC, when also Nebuchadnezzar placed Zedekiah on the throne of Judah) and the year Zedekiah revolted against Babylon because he trusted in the promise of Egypt's help (588 BC).

> i. "In the allegory of a foundling in the previous chapter Ezekiel was dealing with the spiritual and moral malady of Israel. In this message he was concerned with her political folly and wickedness." (Morgan)

2. (3-6) The first eagle of the parable.

And say, 'Thus says the Lord GOD:
"A great eagle with large wings and long pinions,
Full of feathers of various colors,
Came to Lebanon
And took from the cedar the highest branch.
He cropped off its topmost young twig
And carried it to a land of trade;
He set it in a city of merchants.
Then he took some of the seed of the land
And planted it in a fertile field;
He placed *it* by abundant waters
***And* set it like a willow tree.**
And it grew and became a spreading vine of low stature;
Its branches turned toward him,
But its roots were under it.
So it became a vine,
Brought forth branches,
And put forth shoots.

> a. **A great eagle**: The parable concerns a large and majestic **eagle** that **came to Lebanon** and took the **highest branch** from a **cedar** tree. The eagle then **carried it to a land of trade**.

> > i. "It is interesting to note that often the eagle was used symbolically in the OT to represent God's punitive power (Deuteronomy 28:49) and the speed with which a conqueror advanced (Isaiah 46:11; Jeremiah 48:40; 49:22)." (Alexander)

> b. **He took some of the seed of the land**: Then the eagle used some of the **seed** from the land of the cedar tree, and he **planted it in a fertile field**, where it **became a spreading vine**, spreading **forth branches**.

3. (7-8) The second eagle of the parable.

"But there was another great eagle with large wings and many feathers;
And behold, this vine bent its roots toward him,

And stretched its branches toward him,
From the garden terrace where it had been planted,
That he might water it.
It was planted in good soil by many waters,
To bring forth branches, bear fruit,
And become a majestic vine.'"

a. **There was another great eagle**: The second **eagle** appears suddenly, and the vine previously mentioned **bent its roots** and **stretched its branches** toward the second eagle.

i. "What strikes the listener/reader is this bird's passivity. In contrast to the first eagle, this bird takes no actions; he is simply there." (Block)

b. **That he might water it**: The vine did this in the hope that the second eagle would care for the vine, protect it, and give it the right conditions for growth and prosperity – which *it already had under the first eagle*. The hoped-for result was that it would **become a majestic vine**.

i. "In the absence of any explanation for the vine's action, the audience is left to reflect on the vine's ingratitude and stupidity." (Block)

4. (9-10) God's observations upon this vine.

"Say, 'Thus says the Lord GOD:
"Will it thrive?
Will he not pull up its roots,
Cut off its fruit,
And leave it to wither?
All of its spring leaves will wither,
And no great power or many people
Will be needed to pluck it up by its roots.
Behold, *it is* **planted,**
Will it thrive?
Will it not utterly wither when the east wind touches it?
It will wither in the garden terrace where it grew.'"'"

a. **Will it thrive?** God asked the question, revealing the fate of the vine. The rhetorical questions show that it would not **thrive**; that the first eagle would **pull up its roots, cut off its fruit, and leave it to wither**.

i. "The critical issue is, Will the vine survive after it has turned away from the first eagle and oriented itself toward the second?" (Block)

b. **Will it not utterly wither when the east wind touches it?** Though the vine stretched out roots and branches to the second eagle, the second eagle would not be able to shelter it against the coming storm. The vine would perish.

i. "The redirection of the vine's branches toward the second eagle (instead of having them spread out low on the ground) and its roots upward (instead of going deeper into the fertile and well-watered soil) had rendered the plant extremely vulnerable to the wind's withering force." (Block)

ii. "The vine was still Jehovah's, and the eagles were also within His power.... Therefore the transplanting of the vine was of no avail." (Morgan)

B. The meaning and application of the parable.

1. (11-15) The meaning of the parable of the two eagles.

Moreover the word of the LORD came to me, saying, "Say now to the rebellious house: 'Do you not know what these *things mean?*' Tell *them,* 'Indeed the king of Babylon went to Jerusalem and took its king and princes, and led them with him to Babylon. And he took the king's offspring, made a covenant with him, and put him under oath. He also took away the mighty of the land, that the kingdom might be brought low and not lift itself up, *but* that by keeping his covenant it might stand. But he rebelled against him by sending his ambassadors to Egypt, that they might give him horses and many people. Will he prosper? Will he who does such *things* escape? Can he break a covenant and still be delivered?

a. **Do you not know what these things mean?** Ezekiel explained the meaning of his riddle/parable, so his listeners could not claim the excuse that they did not understand.

- The first, *great eagle* represented **the king of Babylon.**
- Lebanon represented **Jerusalem.**
- The highest branch of the cedar represented Judah's **king** (Jehoiachin) **and princes.**
- The seeds and the vine represented **the king's offspring** (Zedekiah).
- The first eagle **made a covenant** with Zedekiah and **put him under oath.**
- The first eagle **took away the mighty of the land**, not only King Jehoiachin, but also other notable men such as Daniel and his companions. He did this to keep Zedekiah **low**, and so that Zedekiah would keep **his covenant.**
- The king of Babylon took **them with him to Babylon**, which was called the *city of merchants.*

- Just as the vine stretched out its roots and branches toward the second eagle, so Zedekiah **rebelled against** him **by sending his ambassadors to Egypt**, which represented the second eagle. Zedekiah hoped for **horses and many people** from Egypt.

    i. **Do you not know**: "Are ye so blockish that you do not know what is meant? or are you so secure that you will not consider it, but run on your own ruin?" (Poole)

    ii. The Bible uses an eagle as a symbol of Babylon in some other places (Jeremiah 48:40, 49:22, and Daniel 7:4).

    iii. Adam Clarke on the use of *a city of merchants* in Ezekiel 17:4: "Babylon; for which this city was the most celebrated of all the cities of the east. Its situation procured it innumerable advantages; its two rivers, the *Tigris* and *Euphrates*, and the *Persian Gulf*, gave it communication with the richest and the most distant nations."

    iv. Regarding the second eagle of Ezekiel 17:7: "This was Egypt, specifically Pharaoh Hophra who came to the throne of Egypt in 588 B.C. To him Zedekiah foolishly looked for help to throw off the Babylonian yoke after he had been befriended by Nebuchadnezzar." (Feinberg)

b. **Will he prosper? Will he who does such things escape?** When the vine in the parable turned to the second eagle, it had great hope of life and vitality (Ezekiel 17:8). These rhetorical questions reminded everyone that the vine would find no help from the second eagle, and Zedekiah would find no help from Egypt.

c. **Can he break a covenant and still be delivered?** Fundamentally, Zedekiah was a covenant breaker, who ignored the promises of loyalty and submission he made to Nebuchadnezzar, the king of Babylon (2 Kings 24:20). God expected Zedekiah to be loyal to the **covenant** he made to Nebuchadnezzar and would punish him for breaking the covenant.

    i. "Both Jeremiah and Ezekiel accused him of disloyalty, and urged submission to Babylon again (Jeremiah 37.6-10; 38.17-23)." (Wright)

    ii. "Zedekiah was surrounded by favorable conditions for his reign, represented in the parable by the fruitful soil, the many waters and the planting as a willow tree (Isaiah 44:4). The benevolent attitude of Nebuchadnezzar helped Zedekiah to prosper in his rule. If he had remained faithful to his oath of fealty to Nebuchadnezzar, the kingdom of Judah could have continued to prosper as a tributary kingdom." (Feinberg)

2. (16-18) God's estimation of Zedekiah.

'*As* I live,' says the Lord GOD, 'surely in the place *where* the king *dwells* who made him king, whose oath he despised and whose covenant he broke—with him in the midst of Babylon he shall die. Nor will Pharaoh with *his* mighty army and great company do anything in the war, when they heap up a siege mound and build a wall to cut off many persons. Since he despised the oath by breaking the covenant, and in fact gave his hand and still did all these *things*, he shall not escape.'"

a. **In the midst of Babylon he shall die**: Zedekiah did indeed die in Babylon, and in the most terrible of circumstances. 2 Kings 25:7 describes the terrible judgment on Zedekiah: *they killed the sons of Zedekiah before his eyes, put out the eyes of Zedekiah, bound him with bronze fetters, and took him to Babylon.* Jeremiah 52:11 says that Zedekiah remained in Babylon until his death.

b. **Nor will Pharaoh with his mighty army and great company do anything in the war**: Despite whatever promises or assurances Pharaoh gave to Zedekiah, he and the Egyptians were of no help at all against the Babylonians. It was a foolish alliance.

c. **Since he despised the oath by breaking the covenant**: God promised severe judgment on Zedekiah because he did not keep his word and honor the **covenant** he made with Nebuchadnezzar. His fate was sealed; **he shall not escape**.

i. **Since he despised the oath**: "This God particularly resents. He had bound himself by oath, in the presence of Jehovah, to be faithful to the covenant that he made with Nebuchadnezzar, and he took the first opportunity to break it; therefore he shall not escape." (Clarke)

ii. "The sanctity of an oath was ingrained in Israel. Even an oath made by fraud was to be honored; for example, that with the Gibeonites (cf. Joshua 9 with II Samuel 21:1-2). Jeremiah had warned Zedekiah against treachery and duplicity." (Feinberg)

iii. "Violation of a sacred oath was an offense against Yahweh. God would bring down on Zedekiah's head all the stipulations of self-malediction which he pronounced upon himself in his oath to Nebuchadnezzar." (Alexander)

3. (19-21) God's promise to capture Zedekiah.

Therefore thus says the Lord GOD: "*As* I live, surely My oath which he despised, and My covenant which he broke, I will recompense on his own head. I will spread My net over him, and he shall be taken in My snare. I will bring him to Babylon and try him there for the treason

which he committed against Me. All his fugitives with all his troops shall fall by the sword, and those who remain shall be scattered to every wind; and you shall know that I, the LORD, have spoken."

a. **I will spread My net over him**: Jeremiah 52:6-9 tells the story of how Zedekiah and some other high-ranking men of the government tried to escape when the Babylonians came against Jerusalem. They did not succeed, because God had **spread** His **net over him**.

b. **I will bring him to Babylon and try him there for the treason which he committed against Me**: When Zedekiah broke his covenant with the king of Babylon, he also committed **treason** against Yahweh Himself. As Jeremiah repeatedly counseled, Zedekiah and the other Judeans should have surrendered themselves to the Babylonians and the judgment God ordained to bring through them.

i. God prophetically said of Zedekiah, **My oath which he despised**. God regarded it not only as an oath to Nebuchadnezzar, but to Him also. "The implications of this attitude are far-reaching. It indicates that agreements entered into and obligations incurred by worshippers of God are as binding as if they had been made with God in person." (Taylor)

ii. "Why were they being judged for all the past sins of their nation? It was not fair! Ezekiel would respond, declaring that they would be judged for the contemporary lack of trust in the Lord, which they had shown by their tendency to rely on Egypt for security and by the corruption of their regent, Zedekiah." (Alexander)

c. **All his troops shall fall by the sword, and those who remain shall be scattered**: There would be no recovery from the fall of Zedekiah's reign. Judea would be conquered completely.

i. "As plainly as he could declare it, Ezekiel showed that Judah's political disaster was traceable to moral weakness and deceit. When once the hand was given in token of agreement, that word should have been all the bond needed." (Feinberg)

4. (22-24) The hope and promise of restoration.

Thus says the Lord GOD: "I will take also *one* of the highest branches of the high cedar and set *it* out. I will crop off from the topmost of its young twigs a tender one, and will plant *it* on a high and prominent mountain. On the mountain height of Israel I will plant it; and it will bring forth boughs, and bear fruit, and be a majestic cedar. Under it will dwell birds of every sort; in the shadow of its branches they will dwell. And all the trees of the field shall know that I, the LORD, have

brought down the high tree and exalted the low tree, dried up the green tree and made the dry tree flourish; I, the LORD, have spoken and have done *it.*"

a. **I will also take one of the highest branches of the high cedar and set it out**: Returning to the images of the parable, God promised that He was *not* finished with Israel and her kings. He would take the **highest** of the branches, would **crop off from the topmost of its young twigs a tender one**, and replant it on **a high and prominent mountain**.

i. **A tender one**: "The 'tender one' is the Messiah, the Son of David (see Isaiah 11:1; 53:2; Jeremiah 23:5-6; 33:15; Zechariah 6:12; Revelation 22:16)." (Feinberg)

ii. "The word 'sprig' links on to the Messianic title of 'branch' in Isaiah 11.1; Jeremiah 23.5; 33.15; Zechariah 3.8; 6.12. Three Hebrew words are used. Ezekiel's word is the feathery top of a tree; the other words describe the shoot coming from the stump of the line of David." (Wright)

iii. "I will raise up *another monarchy*, which shall come in the *line of David*, namely, the *Messiah*; who shall appear as a *tender plant*, as to his incarnation; but he shall be *high* and *eminent*; his Church, the royal city, the highest and purest ever seen on the face of the earth." (Clarke)

iv. "Ezekiel believed—but only in his fashion—in a restoration of the Davidic dynasty. The prophet hoped that the dynasty would rule over a new and renewed Israel in the times to come." (Vawter and Hoppe)

v. "The 'high mountain' Ezekiel wrote about is probably Mount Zion, where Messiah will reign over His people." (Wiersbe)

b. **On the mountain height of Israel I will plant it; and it will bring forth boughs, and bear fruit, and be a majestic cedar**: This is Ezekiel's version of the great prophecy of Isaiah 11:1: *There shall come forth a Rod from the stem of Jesse, and a Branch shall grow out of his roots.* Out of what was thought to be dead, God promised to bring wonderful and productive growth.

i. **I will plant it**: "After the failure of the two great eagles to make a success of establishing the state of Israel under their extensive and powerful patronage, God says, *I myself* (emphatic) *will plant it* upon a high mountain where it will grow and be conspicuous and attract the birds of the air to shelter under its protection." (Taylor)

ii. **Under it will dwell birds of every sort**: "All nations, the Gentiles as well as the Jews, shall build, breed, and multiply under the kingdom of Christ; it shall be no more confined to the Jews, but extend to the

Gentiles also. There they shall find peace and safety; and this repeated confirms the certainty of the promise." (Poole)

c. **All the trees of the field shall know that I, the LORD, have brought down the high tree and exalted the low tree**: Through God's dealing with kings such as Zedekiah, and His future work through the Messiah, God would exalt Himself among all the nations.

i. "God is governing, and there is no escape from Him. Eagles, and vines, are under His control. Happy are they who frame their policies by consulting Him, and order their ways in fear." (Morgan)

ii. **Brought the high tree down**: "Look over history, and you will see that everything gigantic in stature and colossal in dimensions, whatsoever has been great to human apprehension, grasping at earthly fame, has become an object for God's penetrating arrows, and a subject for his withering blight." (Spurgeon)

iii. **Exalted the low tree**: "You remember Joseph in the dungeon, Israel in Egypt, Hannah in the family of Elkanah, David when Samuel would have passed him by, Hezekiah when Sennacherib rebuked him. Are not all these instances of God exalting the low tree?" (Spurgeon)

iv. "Yahweh remains sovereign over history. When his people experience calamity, his hand is in it. When foreign nations sweep down on them, they come as his agents. No nation has ever become so powerful that he cannot bring it down in a moment; and no people is so low that he cannot exalt it." (Block)

v. "The chapter began with judgment and punishment; it ends with mercy and grace. The dethroned and blind Zedekiah is overshadowed by God's King who is full of power and glory. Kingdoms are but the lengthened shadows of kings." (Feinberg)

Ezekiel 18 – The Responsibility of the Individual Soul

A. The answer to a false proverb.

1. (1-3) A proverb to use no longer.

The word of the LORD came to me again, saying, "What do you mean when you use this proverb concerning the land of Israel, saying:

**'The fathers have eaten sour grapes,
And the children's teeth are set on edge'?**

"As I live," says the Lord GOD, "you shall no longer use this proverb in Israel.

a. **What do you mean when you use this proverb**: God spoke to Israel regarding a **proverb** that was commonly used among the Jewish people of Ezekiel's day.

i. This was such a popular proverb in that day that it is also quoted in Jeremiah 31:29 30, and in a similar form in Lamentations 5.7.

ii. "The people of Israel responded to the preaching of men like Jeremiah and Ezekiel with clichés and proverbs, not with reasoned argument." (Smith)

b. **The fathers have eaten sour grapes, and the children's teeth are set on edge**: The proverb was a protest, a complaint. The idea was that the present generation was being unjustly punished for what their **fathers** did. One would think that if **the fathers have eaten sour grapes**, then the *fathers* would have the sour taste in their teeth. According to the proverb, the fathers didn't have the sour taste and the children did.

i. The proverb "reflects a materialistic fatalism, a resignation to immutable cosmic rules of cause and effect, an embittered paralysis of the soul, that has left the exiles without hope and without God." (Block)

ii. "Both Jeremiah and Ezekiel saw this as a pernicious doctrine, because it inevitably led to a spirit of fatalism and irresponsibility. If the fault could really be laid at the door of a previous generation, those on whom the judgment was falling could reasonably shrug off any sense of sin and accuse God of injustice." (Taylor)

iii. "Men are still using this proverb, and so using it as to show that they think the saying is true. As a matter of fact, no saying more false was ever coined. It is based upon a one-sided philosophy of heredity. The proverb is at once an attempt to escape from responsibility for sin; and a protest against punishment." (Morgan)

c. **The fathers have eaten sour grapes, and the children's teeth are set on edge**: This popular proverb both expressed and promoted a popular idea. The idea was that God was unfair; unfair in *not* punishing the fathers as they deserved, and unfair in punishing the present generation.

i. It seems those who quoted this wicked proverb and hoped to accuse God by it found refuge in twisting Exodus 20:4-6. "They had failed, as many do today, to see the force of the words 'hate me' and 'love me.' Thus, if they individually loved God, they could not be suffering the penalty of their fathers' sins." (Feinberg)

ii. "The second commandment (Exod. 20.5,6) had spoken of the cumulative disaster that mounts up when generation after generation refuses to repent. This is also the teaching of Jesus Christ (Matthew 23.35,36). Ezekiel asserts that each generation is responsible for breaking the evil tradition or for maintaining the good one." (Wright)

d. **You shall no longer use this proverb in Israel**: God did not accept the proverb just because it was a popular message. Proverbs were a popular form of media or messaging in the ancient world, and through His prophet God commanded that this false message be exposed, answered, and spoken against.

i. Just because the proverb was popular did not mean that it was true.

2. (4) The answer to the false proverb.

"Behold, all souls are Mine;
The soul of the father
As well as the soul of the son is Mine;
The soul who sins shall die.

a. **Behold, all souls are Mine**: God began His answer to the false proverb by declaring an important principle. **All souls** belong to God, the souls of the fathers as well as the children. If Israel complained that previous generations escaped the consequences of their sin, God assured that He had authority over all.

    i. "The idea of Yahweh's lordship over all human life is ancient. After all, he is the source and creator of all, and he sustains life with his own breath." (Block)

    ii. "Let us ever get down to the beginnings of things, when we state God's claims on men. Instead of only pleading with them, let us boldly assert God's claims upon them. All souls are His: of the African as of the European; of the heathen as well as of the Christian born; of the toiling, sorrowing, sinning, as of those that stand in the sunlit circle." (Meyer)

b. **The soul who sins shall die**: Because God has authority over all **souls** (including **the father** and **the son**), God promised to pronounce judgment over every guilty soul. None who should be punished for their **sins** would escape that judgment.

    i. "The word *souls* must not be understood in terms of disembodied spirits. The Hebrew soul (*nepes*) represented the totality of the person or the life-force within him." (Taylor)

    ii. Some believe that Ezekiel only dealt with physical life or death in these passages. The problem with this is that surely, there were relatively good and innocent people who physically died in the judgment that came upon Jerusalem and Judea. The book of Job and all our personal experience teach us that sometimes the wicked prosper in this life and the righteous suffer. Ezekiel must have the eternal life and death of people primarily in mind.

    iii. "Sheer fact, of which Ezekiel was as fully aware as we are, makes it impossible to limit it to physical death, but physical death in Scripture is linked with eternal death." (Wright)

3. (5-9) The promise of life to the righteous man.

But if a man is just
And does what is lawful and right;
If he has not eaten on the mountains,
Nor lifted up his eyes to the idols of the house of Israel,
Nor defiled his neighbor's wife,
Nor approached a woman during her impurity;
If he has not oppressed anyone,
***But* has restored to the debtor his pledge;**
Has robbed no one by violence,
***But* has given his bread to the hungry**

And covered the naked with clothing;
If he has not exacted usury
Nor taken any increase,
But has withdrawn his hand from iniquity
And executed true judgment between man and man;
If he has walked in My statutes
And kept My judgments faithfully—
He *is* just;
He shall surely live!"
Says the Lord GOD.

a. **But if a man is just and does what is lawful and right**: In the previous line God promised that *the soul who sins shall die.* Yet, **if a man is just**, God will not condemn his soul to death. Ezekiel then began to describe the nature of the **just** man.

- **If he has not eaten on the mountains**: He does not eat the ritual meals that accompanied the idol sacrifices made on the high places.

- **Nor lifted up his eyes to the idols**: He does not look to or give honor to the **idols** cherished by others in **the house of Israel**.

- **Nor defiled his neighbor's wife**: He does not commit adultery and reserves sex for the bond of marriage.

- **Nor approached a woman during her impurity**: He observes the laws of ritual purity described in Leviticus 15:19-31.

- **If he has not oppressed anyone, but has restored to the debtor his pledge**: He has the heart of justice commanded by the law of Moses (as in Deuteronomy 24:12-13 and other passages).

- **Has robbed no one by violence, but has given his bread to the hungry**: He is not a taker, but a giver to others.

- **If he has not exacted usury**: He obeys God's commands regarding financial dealings with others, honoring God with his money.

- **And executed true judgment between man and man**: He is a man of justice and righteousness in his dealings with others and between others.

    i. **Has not exacted usury**: "Such interest was allowed by the law of Moses in dealing with foreigners (Deuteronomy 23:20), but was strictly forbidden in loans to Israelites (Exodus 22:25; Deuteronomy 23:19)." (Feinberg)

    ii. Clarke on the Hebrew word for **usury**: "*Nasach* signifies to *bite; usury* is properly so termed, because it *bites* into and *devours* the *principal*.

Usury signifies, with us, exacting *unlawful interest* for money; and taking the *advantage* of a man's necessities to advance him cash on *exorbitant profit.* This *bites* the *receiver* in his *property,* and the *lender* in his *salvation.*"

b. **If he has walked in My statutes and kept My judgments faithfully**: All of the preceding is a general description of the man (or woman) who is faithful to the covenant Israel made with God in the days of Moses. Today we relate with God by a new and better covenant, but we still understand the heart of God's ancient law for today.

c. **He is just; he shall surely live**: God promised that this righteous one would ultimately **live** before Him. He would not ultimately suffer in the age to come for the sins of previous generations.

i. In Ezekiel 18, the prophet will use three examples: a righteous man (18:5-9), his wicked son (18:10-13), and his righteous grandson (18:14-18). "Three kings of Judah fit these descriptions-Hezekiah, Manasseh and Josiah." (Feinberg)

4. (10-13) The wicked son of the righteous father.

"**If he begets a son *who is* a robber**
Or a shedder of blood,
Who* does any of these *things
And does none of those *duties,*
But has eaten on the mountains
Or defiled his neighbor's wife;
If he has oppressed the poor and needy,
Robbed by violence,
Not restored the pledge,
Lifted his eyes to the idols,
***Or* committed abomination;**
If he has exacted usury
Or taken increase—
Shall he then live?
He shall not live!
If he has done any of these abominations,
He shall surely die;
His blood shall be upon him.

a. **If he begets a son who is a robber or a shedder of blood**: If the righteous man mentioned in Ezekiel 18:5-9 has a son who is wicked, who **does none of those duties**, then that son will bear his own guilt.

b. **But has eaten on the mountains**: In each detail, Ezekiel described the wicked man as essentially the reverse image of the man described in Ezekiel 18:5-9.

> i. "Whereas the former does everything to preserve life, even that of the poor, to the latter others' lives are expendable if they interfere with that person's own selfish pursuits." (Block)

c. **Shall he then live? He shall not live**: Though this wicked man had a righteous father, he would have to answer for his own sin. **His blood shall be upon him**. To answer the proverb mentioned in Ezekiel 18:2, this wicked man ate the sour grapes and it will be his teeth that are set on edge.

> i. **His blood shall be upon him**: "Heb. it is plural, *bloods*: both the blood of the innocent which he murdered, and his own blood, which thereby he forfeited, the blood of his own soul and life, that is, the whole blame of his misery in time and eternity, shall lie upon himself, who brought all those sorrows on himself by his own wickednesses." (Poole)

5. (14-18) The righteous son of the wicked father.

"*If,* however, he begets a son
Who sees all the sins which his father has done,
And considers but does not do likewise;
Who has not eaten on the mountains,
Nor lifted his eyes to the idols of the house of Israel,
Nor defiled his neighbor's wife;
Has not oppressed anyone,
Nor withheld a pledge,
Nor robbed by violence,
But has given his bread to the hungry
And covered the naked with clothing;
Who has withdrawn his hand from the poor
And not received usury or increase,
But has executed My judgments
And walked in My statutes—
He shall not die for the iniquity of his father;
He shall surely live!
"*As for* his father,
Because he cruelly oppressed,
Robbed his brother by violence,
And did what *is* not good among his people,
Behold, he shall die for his iniquity.

a. **If, however, he begets a son who sees all the sins which his father has done**: Ezekiel used the example of the wicked man portrayed in Exodus 18:10-13 and his **son**. If the son **considers but does not do likewise**, he may live a righteous life.

> i. "He shall no more be affected by his father's *crimes*, than his father was *benefited* by his *grandfather's righteousness*." (Clarke)

b. **Who has not eaten on the mountains**: Ezekiel described the righteous man in the same terms of faithfulness to the covenant as earlier in the chapter (Ezekiel 18:5-9).

> i. "This man's conduct is presented as the antithesis of his father's and a virtual carbon copy of his grandfather's." (Block)

c. **He shall not die for the iniquity of the father**: If the son is righteous, he will not suffer for the sins of the wicked father. To answer the proverb of Ezekiel 18:2, if the father ate the sour grapes, the son's teeth *would not* be set on edge.

d. **As for his father**: The righteousness of the son would not justify the wicked father. Because of his many sins, **he shall die for his iniquity**. Again, in the terms of the proverb of Ezekiel 18:2, the wicked father ate the sour grapes, and they would set *his* teeth on edge.

B. The principle of the responsibility of the individual soul.

1. (19-20) Explaining the principle of each soul bearing its own guilt.

"Yet you say, 'Why should the son not bear the guilt of the father?' Because the son has done what is lawful and right, and has kept all My statutes and observed them, he shall surely live. The soul who sins shall die. The son shall not bear the guilt of the father, nor the father bear the guilt of the son. The righteousness of the righteous shall be upon himself, and the wickedness of the wicked shall be upon himself.

a. **Why should the son not bear the guilt of the father?** God invited questioning Israel to look at the question from a different angle. Father and son are linked; why shouldn't the son be guilty because of what the father did?

> i. God's question sounds a bit crazy to our modern individualistic ears. It is often hard for us to relate to cultures where there is a much stronger sense of family and community solidarity, where what one does affects the entire clan or community.

> ii. "We have to reflect that, however reasonable it may appear to us, habituated as we are to the sense of personal responsibility, it was a revolutionary idea to present to Ezekiel's contemporaries. They were

more at home with the idea of collective righteousness and blame."
(Vawter and Hoppe)

iii. "Communal solidarity and corporate responsibility were facts, to
which experience bore witness. Ezekiel's aim is to show that they are
not the only facts. God's redeemed community is a nation of righteous
or repentant individuals." (Taylor)

b. **Because the son has done what is lawful and right**: God repeated
the principle that He looks at people as *individuals* before Him. There are
certainly *some* ways that God may bless or judge people in community, but
in regard to eternity God looks at each individual life.

c. **The soul who sins shall die**: As God judges each man and woman
individually, the righteous will be justified and the wicked will be
judged. They will not be justified or condemned on the basis of family or
community; **the son shall not bear the guilt of the father, nor the father
bear the guilt of the son**.

d. **The righteousness of the righteous shall be upon himself, and the
wickedness of the wicked shall be upon himself**: This principle is stated
so clearly and repeatedly in Ezekiel 18 that there is no mistaking either
its truth or importance. Yet it must be said that there are two significant
exceptions to this principle.

i. The New Testament clearly teaches us that the guilt of Adam was
passed on to the entire human race, and the righteousness of Jesus
Christ is passed on to all who believe upon Him (Romans 5:12-19).
These two men – absolutely unique in all humanity as representative
heads of humanity – see their respective wickedness and righteousness
upon others.

2. (21-23) God's desire for the wicked to turn.

**"But if a wicked man turns from all his sins which he has committed,
keeps all My statutes, and does what is lawful and right, he shall surely
live; he shall not die. None of the transgressions which he has committed
shall be remembered against him; because of the righteousness which
he has done, he shall live. Do I have any pleasure at all that the wicked
should die?" says the Lord God, "*and* not that he should turn from his
ways and live?**

a. **He shall surely live**: For emphasis, God repeated this principle again
and again. The door of repentance and restoration is open to any **wicked
man**. The thief on the cross, who because he turned, entered into paradise
after a wicked life, later showed this (Luke 23:39-43).

i. "One can sense Ezekiel's excitement as he announces the verdict for those who meet these conditions: *He shall surely live! He shall not die!* The past rebellious acts will be discounted, and his present righteousness will be all that matters." (Block)

b. **None of the transgressions which he has committed shall be remembered against him**: God promised not a probationary restoration to the wicked man who turns, but full restoration.

i. "Leave your own, and you shall never suffer for others' sins." (Poole)

ii. "The lesson from these two examples is obvious and answered their questions: *people determine their own character and destiny by the decisions that they make.* Neither the exiles in Babylon nor the citizens in Jerusalem were the prisoners and victims of some cosmic determinism that forced them to act as they did." (Wiersbe)

c. **Do I have any pleasure at all that the wicked should die?** In this God explained a basic principle about His nature and dealings with humanity. God takes no special **pleasure** in the death of **the wicked**. God's heart is for the wicked man to repent, to **turn from his ways and live**. God is *not* sadistic and cruel, making repentance impossible because He loves to see humanity suffer.

i. "This is what Ezekiel's audience needs to deliver them from their bondage of depression and despair—a new vision of God, a God who is on the side of blessing and life, not on the side of the curse and death." (Block)

ii. "Sinful mankind normally sees judgment as God's delight. Nothing could be further from God's desire, else he would not have sent his only Son to be judged on the cross for the sin of the whole world (1 John 2:1–2)." (Alexander)

iii. "It is the Lord's longing and will and purpose that men should be saved. Such a longing should be shared by every preacher who ventures to speak about the judgment of God." (Taylor)

iv. The fact that God does not take **pleasure** in the death of **the wicked** does not mean that it will not happen. God's general desire for all humanity is that they would repent, turn to Him and be saved; yet He will not spare the requirements of justice and holiness for those who refuse to **turn** to Him.

v. "And if God can have *no pleasure* in the *death of the wicked*, he cannot have made a *decree* to abandon him to the evil of his nature, and then damn him for what he could not avoid: for as God can *do* nothing with which he is *not pleased*, so he can *decree* nothing with which he is *not pleased*. But he is 'not pleased with the death of a sinner,' therefore he cannot have *made a decree* to bring him to this *death*." (Clarke)

3. (24) God's promise of judgment to the righteous who turns away.

"But when a righteous man turns away from his righteousness and commits iniquity, and does according to all the abominations that the wicked *man* does, shall he live? All the righteousness which he has done shall not be remembered; because of the unfaithfulness of which he is guilty and the sin which he has committed, because of them he shall die.

a. **But when a righteous man turns away from his righteousness**: God promised no refuge for the apparently **righteous man** who **turns** to the **abominations** and idolatry of the wicked.

b. **All the righteousness which he has done shall not be remembered**: This is tragic but true. A man or woman known for a righteous life can have it "forgotten" before God *and* man by a turn to wickedness. When that is the case, God promised that **because of** his sins **he shall die.**

i. "Although v. 24 raises difficulties in the N.T. context of the final perseverance of the saints, such warnings must stand in Scripture. No person – believer or unbeliever – ever has the right to say, 'Because I was righteous once, it does not matter whether I am plunging into sin now.'" (Wright)

4. (25-29) God's final declaration of the fairness of His ways.

"Yet you say, 'The way of the LORD is not fair.' Hear now, O house of Israel, is it not My way which is fair, and your ways which are not fair? When a righteous *man* turns away from his righteousness, commits iniquity, and dies in it, it is because of the iniquity which he has done that he dies. Again, when a wicked *man* turns away from the wickedness which he committed, and does what is lawful and right, he preserves himself alive. Because he considers and turns away from all the transgressions which he committed, he shall surely live; he shall not die. Yet the house of Israel says, 'The way of the Lord is not fair.' O house of Israel, is it not My ways which are fair, and your ways which are not fair?

a. **Is it not My way which is fair, and your ways which are not fair?** For emphasis, God once more repeats the principles of His judgment and the reason for them. Israel was **not fair** for hoping to find either guilt or innocence in other generations. Each soul would stand on its own before God.

i. "While they claim to be victims of an immutable universal law that locks their fate to the conduct of their parents, they really perceive themselves to be at the mercy of a capricious God, whose actions are unpredictable and arbitrary." (Block)

b. **Yet the house of Israel says**: Because the error was so deeply ingrained, so God's counter to their error had to be strong and repetitive.

5. (30-32) The summary statement and call to action.

"Therefore I will judge you, O house of Israel, every one according to his ways," says the Lord GOD. "Repent, and turn from all your transgressions, so that iniquity will not be your ruin. Cast away from you all the transgressions which you have committed, and get yourselves a new heart and a new spirit. For why should you die, O house of Israel? For I have no pleasure in the death of one who dies," says the Lord GOD. "Therefore turn and live!"

a. **Therefore I will judge you, O house of Israel, every one according to his ways**: The error in believing in communal or family salvation or damnation is so serious and dangerous that God unmistakably emphasized the individual's responsibility before God.

i. "It may be true that in my physical being I have inherited tendencies to some forms of evil from my father; but in the fact of my essential relation to God there are forces available to me more and mightier than all these tendencies. Neither righteousness nor evil is hereditary." (Morgan)

b. **Repent, and turn from all your transgressions, so that iniquity will not be your ruin**: Because of the principle of individual responsibility before God, it is absolutely essential for each soul to **repent** and prevent their **iniquity** from becoming their **ruin**.

i. "People may not bank on a treasury of past good deeds to ensure their future well-being, nor need they despair of a treasury of evil that prevents them from enjoying life." (Block)

c. **And get yourselves a new heart and a new spirit**: In this, Ezekiel pointed all his listeners and readers to look forward to the new covenant (Deuteronomy 30:1-6, Jeremiah 23:1-8, Jeremiah 31:31-34, Jeremiah 32:37-41, Ezekiel 11:16-20, Ezekiel 36:16-28, Ezekiel 37:11-14, 37:21-28). This would make the life transformation so desired by those who **repent** actually possible.

i. "Later Ezekiel would develop how a new heart and spirit would ultimately be appropriated by Israel (36:26). Repentance was available to the people of Israel in Ezekiel's day." (Alexander)

d. **For I have no pleasure in the death of the one who dies**: Once again in this section, God emphasized this principle (first stated in Ezekiel 18:23). God considered it important that all understand that God is *not willing that any should perish but that all should come to repentance* (2 Peter 3:9).

> i. "Remember that the Lord Jesus *wept* at the tomb of Lazarus, even though He was going to bring him back into this life. By man came death, not through the working of God, but because of man's sin." (McGee)

> ii. **Why should you die**: "Why should you go to *hell* while the kingdom of God is open to receive you? Why should you be the *devil's slaves*, when ye may be *Christ's freemen*! WHY WILL YE DIE?" (Clarke)

e. **Therefore turn and live**: God ended this prophecy with a strong, dramatic exhortation and application. God's people should **turn** and **live**. They should not have fatalistic confidence or despair in their forefathers or descendants. God has offered a way for mankind to come to Him, and they must come as individuals.

> i. "To those who presume on the grace of God, it sends a stern warning; to those who despair of life, it offers hope. In both respects it provides a healthy corrective to a systemic approach to human evil and suffering that would absolve the individual of responsibility for his or her own life and destiny." (Block)

Ezekiel 19 – Two Laments

A. The lamentation of the lions.

1. (1) A lamentation for the leaders of Israel.

"Moreover take up a lamentation for the princes of Israel,

a. **Take up a lamentation**: Ezekiel 19 is the collection of two laments, two sorrowful songs over the condition of Israel in Ezekiel's day. It is a **lamentation** both by its poetic arrangement and by its subject matter.

i. **Lamentation**: "*Qina* is a technical term for a special kind of musical composition, the dirge, which was composed and sung at the death of an individual, though it is also used of laments at the destruction of a nation or people." (Block)

ii. "This pattern apparently attempted to imitate the drumbeat (or its equivalent) of a funeral dirge: BOOM BOOM BOOM-pause-BOOM BOOM." (Vawter and Hoppe)

iii. "Ezekiel expressed the Lord's sadness over the Judean leadership's failure by chanting this elegy over her final rulers prior to their deaths." (Alexander)

b. **For the princes of Israel**: This **lamentation** mainly concerns the later kings of **Israel**. Significantly, God here called them **princes** rather than kings, even though it refers to three of the later kings of Judah. It is also significant that God referred to them as **princes of Israel**, even though the northern kingdom was long before conquered and scattered.

i. This **lamentation** for the **princes of Israel** was fitting considering how badly the last several kings ruled and the judgment that answered their wickedness. "His zeal for the Davidic covenant, however, did not allow him to see three of its inheritors disappear into exile without profound sorrow and emotion. This was no taunt-song. The judgment of the Lord could be very grievous, and Ezekiel felt it keenly." (Taylor)

ii. "So long as a descendant of David occupied the throne in Jerusalem, the Judeans could hope in divine protection. After all, Yahweh had made an eternal covenant with David (2 Samuel 7); he would surely not abandon his designated ruler or the people he represented. Ezekiel's aim in this 'dirge' is to demolish another false theological pillar on which the nation's sense of security was based. Yahweh's covenant with David is hereby suspended." (Block)

2. (2-4) The lioness, and the mighty lion taken to Egypt.

And say:
'What *is* your mother? A lioness:
She lay down among the lions;
Among the young lions she nourished her cubs.
She brought up one of her cubs,
And he became a young lion;
He learned to catch prey,
And he devoured men.
The nations also heard of him;
He was trapped in their pit,
And they brought him with chains to the land of Egypt.

a. **A lioness**: The **lioness** was **mother** to the princes mentioned in the previous verse. The **lioness** is best understood as Israel or Jerusalem itself, who **lay down among the lions** by taking her place in the community of nations.

i. "The lioness must have been a personification of Judah, just as in verse 10 (cf. Genesis 49:9; Numbers 23:24; 24:9; Revelation 5:5; and Isaiah 29:1-used of Jerusalem)." (Feinberg)

ii. "'The lion of Judah' was probably as proverbial a term in Ezekiel's days as 'the Russian bear' or 'the American eagle' is in our own times." (Vawter and Hoppe)

iii. "Lions, incidentally, were common in Palestine until shortly after the Crusades, and Hebrew had five different words to describe them (all of which occur in Job 4:10f., and three of which are found here in verse 2)." (Taylor)

b. **She brought up one of her cubs**: This refers to Jehoahaz, the son of King Josiah (also called Shallum in Jeremiah 22:10-12). Jehoahaz reigned only for a few months in 609 B.C. His reign was short but evil and brutal (**he devoured men**).

i. Jehoahaz "soon showed his fierce, haughty, cruel, and bloody disposition, as appears 2 Kings 23:30-32, though he continued but three months, and some odd days, wherein to play his pranks." (Poole)

c. **They brought him with chains to the land of Egypt**: King Jehoahaz of Judah was taken prisoner to Egypt in 609 B.C. (2 Kings 23:31-33), after a three-month reign.

i. **He was trapped in their pit**: "Just as it was customary for a community to gather together to catch a lion or wild beast, so Jehoahaz was taken by force by Pharaoh Necho to the land of Egypt." (Feinberg)

3. (5-7) The second lion's power.

'**When she saw that she waited,** *that* **her hope was lost,**
She took another of her cubs *and* **made him a young lion.**
He roved among the lions,
And became a young lion;
He learned to catch prey;
He devoured men.
He knew their desolate places,
And laid waste their cities;
The land with its fullness was desolated
By the noise of his roaring.

a. **She took another of her cubs and made him a young lion**: This was King Jehoiachin of Judah, who reigned from 609 to 597 B.C. He also learned the ways of lions and **devoured men**.

i. **Another of her cubs**: "A brat of the same breed, and of no better condition. Judea changed her lords oft, but not her miseries." (Trapp)

b. **He knew their desolate places, and laid waste their cities**: For a time Jehoiachin seemed to rule with power and authority. Others heard and were affected **by the noise of his roaring**.

4. (8-9) The young lion's capture.

Then the nations set against him from the provinces on every side,
And spread their net over him;
He was trapped in their pit.
They put him in a cage with chains,
And brought him to the king of Babylon;
They brought him in nets,
That his voice should no longer be heard on the mountains of Israel.

a. **The nations set against him from the provinces on every side**: When Jehoiachin rebelled against his Babylonian overlords Nebuchadnezzar brought an army against him from the many **nations** and **provinces** under his empire.

> i. "Again the nations about Israel were aroused into action against the perpetrator of these deeds, not because of their superior righteousness, but because of the judgment of God on the king." (Feinberg)

b. **They put him in a cage with chains, and brought him to the king of Babylon**: Jehoiachin was taken as a prisoner to Babylon in 597 B.C. He never returned, **that his voice should no longer be heard on the mountains of Israel**.

> i. "Perhaps the most remarkable detail in the story so far is the nations' motive for capturing this lion: to silence the sound of his roar, that is, to stop his terrifying predatory behavior *on the mountains of Israel*. The surrounding peoples pose as liberators of Israel from this lion!" (Block)

> ii. "The cage was that used for a dog or a lion. Ashurbanipal of Assyria said of a king of Arabia, 'I put him into a kennel. With jackals and dogs I tied him up and made him guard the gate, in Nineveh.'" (Feinberg)

> iii. "The term (*sugar*, 'cage') is probably a loanword from the Akkadian *sigaru*, which can mean an animal cage or a neckband for prisoners. It is very likely that Ezekiel played on the word, using it literally for a neckband for Jehoiachin and at the same time using the sense of 'animal cage' in the imagery of the passage." (Alexander)

> iv. "He was carried that long journey in chains, enough to change his roaring lion-like into the roarings of a desperate, miserable captive." (Poole)

> v. "In this brief parable, the Lord made it clear that these two kings of Judah thought themselves to be great leaders, but they ignored the Word of God and He cut them down after their brief reigns." (Wiersbe)

B. The lamentation of the vine.

1. (10-11) The fruitful vine.

'Your mother *was* like a vine in your bloodline,
Planted by the waters,
Fruitful and full of branches
Because of many waters.
She had strong branches for scepters of rulers.
She towered in stature above the thick branches,
And was seen in her height amid the dense foliage.

a. **Your mother was like a vine**: Ezekiel returned to the familiar image of the **vine** as a representation of Israel. The picture is of a fruitful and strong kingdom (**fruitful and full of branches**).

i. "The vine traditionally symbolized Israel itself (cf., e.g., Isaiah 5:1-7; Zechariah 8:12-13), especially as it was destined for resurgence. For Ezekiel at this point, there is no resurgence in sight." (Vawter and Hoppe)

b. **She had strong branches for scepters of rulers**: Ezekiel probably had in mind the most glorious years of Israel's monarchy, the reigns of David and Solomon. In those years God lifted Israel up among the nations and **she towered in stature**.

i. **Strong branches**: "This kingdom equaled, if not excelled, the greatest neighbour kingdoms, and her kings, as David, Solomon, &c. exceeded all their neighbour kings in riches and power." (Poole)

2. (12-14) Plucked up and planted in the wilderness.

But she was plucked up in fury,
She was cast down to the ground,
And the east wind dried her fruit.
Her strong branches were broken and withered;
The fire consumed them.
And now she *is* **planted in the wilderness,**
In a dry and thirsty land.
Fire has come out from a rod of her branches
And **devoured her fruit,**
So that she has no strong branch—a scepter for ruling.'"
This *is* **a lamentation, and has become a lamentation.**

a. **But she was plucked up in fury**: There came a day when God no longer blessed Israel and her kings. When they persistently rebelled against Him, **she was cast down to the ground**. As a result of God's judgment, **her strong branches were broken and withered**, with the **strong branches** representing her later kings.

b. **Now she is planted in the wilderness**: God transplanted the vine and took it to an unpleasant place, Babylon. Babylon wasn't a *literal* wilderness, but it was certainly one for God's exiled kings and people.

i. **Planted in the wilderness**: "Nebuchadnezzar planted them in policy and for his advantage, they planted themselves out of necessity, and God planted them there in just correcting mercy, and will give them root, and make them thrive, and transplant them after seventy years, and set them on the mountains of Israel again." (Poole)

ii. **In the wilderness**: "Babylon was no wilderness, but fruitful beyond credulity, But the poor captive Jews had little joy from it, for some time at least." (Trapp)

c. **Fire has come out from a rod of her branches and devoured her fruit**: The worst damage to the vine came from one of **her** own **branches**. The corruption and destruction came from within. This particular **rod of her branches** represents Zedekiah, who was king at the destruction of Jerusalem in 587 B.C.

i. "Note that the destructive fire comes from the stem of the vine itself. Thus Jerusalem and the royal house are the cause of their own destruction." (Wright)

ii. "Plucked up in fury, her strong rulers ceased, and out of her rods went forth a fire that destroyed. That is to say, Judah's final destruction had come through those having rule over her, and the reference undoubtedly was to Zedekiah." (Morgan)

d. **So that she has no strong branch, a scepter for ruling**: Zedekiah was the last of the kings of the line of David, until the Messiah establishes His reign as promised to David in 2 Samuel 7:11-16. From Zedekiah until Jesus the royal line of David went underground.

i. "None to speak of till Shiloh come. Rulers indeed they had after this and governors, [Haggai 2:21] but no kings of their own nation." (Trapp)

ii. "The foolish rebellion of Zedekiah against Babylon was the cause of the ruin which befell Judah. No strong branch remained on the vine to serve as a scepter to rule. The deportation of Zedekiah brought a temporary halt to the rule of the house of David." (Smith)

e. **This is a lamentation, and has become a lamentation**: These two parables described and prophesied the tragedy of the last few kings of Judah. When kings and leaders over the people of God are ungodly and become rightful targets of God's judgment, there is truly a reason for **lamentation**.

i. "His message was a lamentation for the destruction already carried out; it would be a lamentation for the desolation yet to be accomplished." (Feinberg)

ii. "Had the nation of Israel obeyed the Lord, it would have become and remained a mighty lion and a fruitful vine that would have brought glory to the name of the Lord." (Wiersbe)

Ezekiel 20 – Israel's History of Sin, God's History of Mercy

A. God's mercy to Israel in Egypt and the wilderness.

1. (1-4) Elders of Israel visit Ezekiel to inquire of the LORD.

It came to pass in the seventh year, in the fifth *month,* on the tenth *day* of the month, *that* certain of the elders of Israel came to inquire of the LORD, and sat before me. Then the word of the LORD came to me, saying, "Son of man, speak to the elders of Israel, and say to them, 'Thus says the Lord GOD: "Have you come to inquire of Me? *As* I live," says the Lord GOD, "I will not be inquired of by you."' Will you judge them, son of man, will you judge *them?* Then make known to them the abominations of their fathers.

a. **It came to pass in the seventh year**: This took place some two years after the prophecies of Ezekiel 1-3 (Ezekiel 1:2) and one year after the prophecies of Ezekiel 8 (Ezekiel 8:1).

b. **Certain of the elders of Israel came to inquire of the LORD, and sat before me**: As happened previously in Ezekiel 14:1, the **elders** of Israel in exile came to Ezekiel as a recognized prophet, to **inquire of the LORD** through him.

c. **I will not be inquired of by you**: This was God's initial response to the elders of Israel, much the same as He said to them the last time they **inquired** of God (Ezekiel 14:3). He said it strongly with an oath (**As I live**).

i. "For some unexplained reason the enquiry is an impertinent one and needs only a rehearsal of Israel's past sins to show that history has answered the question for them." (Taylor)

ii. "Nay, but you act a deep hypocrisy, being already resolved on your own course, and yet now pretend you would know my counsel. It is

181

a sharp reproof of their wickedness, and God utterly refuseth to be inquired of by such." (Poole)

d. **Then make known to them the abominations of their fathers**: Following in Ezekiel 20 is a strong description and denunciation of Israel's **abominations** through their history, together with remarkable promises of restoration and mercy.

2. (5-7) God's oath to Israel.

"Say to them, 'Thus says the Lord GOD: "On the day when I chose Israel and raised My hand in an oath to the descendants of the house of Jacob, and made Myself known to them in the land of Egypt, I raised My hand in an oath to them, saying, 'I *am* the LORD your God.' On that day I raised My hand in an oath to them, to bring them out of the land of Egypt into a land that I had searched out for them, 'flowing with milk and honey,' the glory of all lands. Then I said to them, 'Each of you, throw away the abominations which are before his eyes, and do not defile yourselves with the idols of Egypt. I *am* the LORD your God.'

a. **On the day when I chose Israel and raised My hand in an oath to the descendants of the house of Jacob**: God referred to an **oath** He made to Israel **in the land of Egypt**. We have no record of this specific oath, but it is simply a restatement of aspects of the covenant God made with Abraham, Isaac, and Jacob (Genesis 12:1-3).

i. Something of that **oath** is shown in Exodus 6:8: *And I will bring you into the land which I swore to give to Abraham, Isaac, and Jacob; and I will give it to you as a heritage: I am the LORD.*

b. **I raised My hand in an oath to them, to bring them out of the land of Egypt into a land...the glory of all lands**: God repeated the promise originally given to Abraham and his covenant descendants, renewing it for the generation yet in Egypt. God promised to take them out of Egypt, and into Canaan, which He called **the glory of all lands**.

i. **Raised My hand in an oath**: "I bound myself in a covenant to them to continue to be their God, if they should be faithful, and continue to be my people. Among the Jews the *juror* lifted up his right hand to heaven; which explains Psalm 144:8: 'Their right hand is a right hand of falsehood.' This is a form used in England, Scotland, and Ireland." (Clarke)

ii. **A land that I had searched out for them**: "After the manner of man God speaks, as if he had been the spy to go from place to place to search out the best, and to appoint it for them; it was his wise and good providence which assigned this land to them." (Poole)

iii. **The glory of all lands**: "It was so then, it is not so now, since the Jews were disprivileged and dejected; but as in the earthly paradise, after man fallen, the rose fell off, the brier whereon it grew remained; so here." (Trapp)

c. **Each of you, throw away the abominations which are before his eyes**: God not only gave Israel an oath; while the people of God were still in Egypt, God gave them a command. The command was to **throw away** the **idols of Egypt**. They were to have nothing to do with the gods of Egypt.

i. "The fact that they turned so easily to fresh idols like the golden calf, indicates that many, as Ezekiel says, must have been attracted also by Egyptian religious practices." (Wright)

3. (8-9) God's mercy to Israel's early disobedience to Him while still Egypt.

But they rebelled against Me and would not obey Me. They did not all cast away the abominations which were before their eyes, nor did they forsake the idols of Egypt. Then I said, 'I will pour out My fury on them and fulfill My anger against them in the midst of the land of Egypt.' But I acted for My name's sake, that it should not be profaned before the Gentiles among whom they *were,* in whose sight I had made Myself known to them, to bring them out of the land of Egypt.

a. **But they rebelled against Me and would not obey Me**: Even while in Egypt, Israel did not listen to God and truly **forsake the idols of Egypt**. In response, God said He would judge (**I will pour out My fury on them**).

i. "They continued attached to the *idolatry* of Egypt; so that, had I consulted my *justice* only, I should have consumed them *even in Egypt* itself." (Clarke)

ii. "They did not forsake the idols of Egypt; it is probable there were some among them that carried with them (as Rachel did her father's) the idols of Egypt." (Poole)

iii. There were several evidences of Israel's idolatry in Egypt:

- The worship of the golden calf at Mount Sinai (Exodus 32:1-6).
- The idolatry practiced in Egypt: *Put away the gods which your fathers served on the other side of the River and in Egypt. Serve the LORD!* (Joshua 24:14)
- The choice of golden calves as objects of worship by Jeroboam (1 Kings 12:26-33).

b. **But I acted for My name's sake, that it should not be profaned before the Gentiles**: Despite Israel's sin, God extended His grace and mercy to Israel while still in Egypt. He did this to preserve His reputation among the Gentiles, and fulfilled His promise **to bring them out of the land of Egypt**.

> i. "When God could find no basis in them for extending to them His mercy and grace, He did it solely for His name's sake, that is, for His own glory." (Feinberg)

> ii. "The divine reputation depends on the fate and welfare of his people. All of God's dealings with Israel were public—before the eyes of the nations. Israel was to be the agent through whom the nations would come to know that he is Yahweh." (Block)

4. (10-17) God's mercy to a disobedient Israel in the wilderness.

"Therefore I made them go out of the land of Egypt and brought them into the wilderness. And I gave them My statutes and showed them My judgments, 'which, *if* a man does, he shall live by them.' Moreover I also gave them My Sabbaths, to be a sign between them and Me, that they might know that I *am* the LORD who sanctifies them. Yet the house of Israel rebelled against Me in the wilderness; they did not walk in My statutes; they despised My judgments, 'which, *if* a man does, he shall live by them'; and they greatly defiled My Sabbaths. Then I said I would pour out My fury on them in the wilderness, to consume them. But I acted for My name's sake, that it should not be profaned before the Gentiles, in whose sight I had brought them out. So I also raised My hand in an oath to them in the wilderness, that I would not bring them into the land which I had given *them,* 'flowing with milk and honey,' the glory of all lands, because they despised My judgments and did not walk in My statutes, but profaned My Sabbaths; for their heart went after their idols. Nevertheless My eye spared them from destruction. I did not make an end of them in the wilderness.

> a. **Therefore I made them go out of the land of Egypt and brought them into the wilderness**: Despite the sins described in Ezekiel 20:8, God did as He described in Ezekiel 20:9. God set them free from slavery and Egypt and set them on the road to Canaan, the Promised Land.

> > i. **I made them go out**: "Though greatly oppressed and degraded, they were not *willing* to leave their *house of bondage.* I was obliged to *force them away.*" (Clarke)

> b. **I gave them My statutes and showed them My judgments**: God did much more than bring Israel out of Egypt. He brought them to Mount Sinai where He gave them His law. He gave them *His* **Sabbaths** as a **sign between them and** Himself. God did it all to separate Israel to Himself.

i. "Had they attended to these things, they should have *lived by them*. They would have been holy, healthy, and happy." (Clarke)

ii. "The Sabbath was the central sign of the old covenant (cf. Isaiah 56:2, 4). Repeatedly it is shown that the law of the Sabbath was not legislation by which they could gain life but rather the sign of the covenant between God and Israel." (Feinberg)

iii. "The phrase 'the man who obeys them will live by them' (v.13) reflects Leviticus 18:5. It is not a reference to eternal salvation by works." (Alexander)

c. **Yet the house of Israel rebelled against Me in the wilderness**: There were many times when Israel did this. One of the most notable was their sin with the golden calf (Exodus 32:1-8). Even in the wilderness, they **greatly defiled** God's **Sabbaths**.

i. **Their heart went after their idols**: "Heb., Their dungy deities; those dirty delights carried them sheer away from God and goodness. Any beloved sin will do so." (Trapp)

d. **I said I would pour out My fury on them in the wilderness**: As He did in Egypt (Ezekiel 20:8), God said He would judge Israel in the wilderness. Yet as He did before, God held back His judgment acting **for** His **name's sake**, to preserve His reputation **before the Gentiles**.

e. **I did not make an end to them in the wilderness**: Israel certainly *deserved* God's judgment in the wilderness, but God mercifully brought them into the Promised Land.

5. (18-20) God's appeal to Israel's next generation in the wilderness.

"But I said to their children in the wilderness, 'Do not walk in the statutes of your fathers, nor observe their judgments, nor defile yourselves with their idols. I *am* the LORD your God: Walk in My statutes, keep My judgments, and do them; hallow My Sabbaths, and they will be a sign between Me and you, that you may know that I *am* the LORD your God.'

a. **But I said to their children in the wilderness**: The generation that came from Egypt would not trust or obey God as they should. God mercifully spoke to the next generation and told them to not repeat the same mistakes as their fathers.

b. **I am the LORD your God: Walk in My statutes, keep My judgments, and do them**: God gave that generation, born and raised in the wilderness, the path and the opportunity to **walk** in His ways.

6. (21-24) God's further mercy to Israel in the wilderness.

"Notwithstanding, the children rebelled against Me; they did not walk in My statutes, and were not careful to observe My judgments, 'which, *if* a man does, he shall live by them'; but they profaned My Sabbaths. Then I said I would pour out My fury on them and fulfill My anger against them in the wilderness. Nevertheless I withdrew My hand and acted for My name's sake, that it should not be profaned in the sight of the Gentiles, in whose sight I had brought them out. Also I raised My hand in an oath to those in the wilderness, that I would scatter them among the Gentiles and disperse them throughout the countries, because they had not executed My judgments, but had despised My statutes, profaned My Sabbaths, and their eyes were fixed on their fathers' idols.

a. **Notwithstanding, the children rebelled against Me**: Sadly, the generation born and raised in the wilderness did not obey God. God said, **they did not walk in My statutes, and were not careful to observe My judgments**.

b. **I said I would pour out My fury on them and fulfill My anger against them in the wilderness**: As He did regarding Israel in Egypt (Ezekiel 20:8) and the generation that came out of Egypt (Ezekiel 20:13), God said that He would judge the generation of Israel born and raised in the wilderness.

c. **Nevertheless I withdrew My hand and acted for My name's sake**: Once again, God spared Israel and did so with an eye towards His reputation among the Gentiles.

d. **I raised My hand in an oath to those in the wilderness, that I would scatter them among the Gentiles and disperse them throughout the countries**: In the late wilderness period, God promised Israel that if they persisted in disobedience and rebellion, He would **scatter** them to the nations (Deuteronomy 4:27 and 28:64). Ezekiel and the elders he spoke to experienced the fulfillment of that **oath**.

i. "But even as early as the wilderness era God had predicted Israel's worldwide scattering among the nations (Deuteronomy 28:64-68). The Babylonian captivity was only a partial realization of this prophecy by Moses." (Feinberg)

7. (25-26) In His judgment, God allows Israel to suffer the consequences of their sin.

"Therefore I also gave them up to statutes *that were* not good, and judgments by which they could not live; and I pronounced them unclean because of their ritual gifts, in that they caused all their firstborn to pass through *the fire,* **that I might make them desolate and that they might know that I am the** L**ORD.**'"

a. **I also gave them up to statutes that were not good**: Since Israel rejected God's law (Ezekiel 20:8, 20:13, 20:16), God allowed them to live under the law of other nations – laws that **were not good** and **judgments by which they could not live**.

i. "Ezekiel was declaring that in retribution the Lord allowed them to go after their own ways in order to punish them according to their deeds. The passage is speaking in the sense of a judicial sentence…. Disobedience leads to greater sin. Sin becomes its own punishment." (Feinberg)

ii. "God gave them to the customs and consequences of the religion they had chosen." (Wright)

iii. "When they had rebelled against the Lord, despised his statutes, and polluted his Sabbaths-in effect cast him off, and given themselves wholly to their idols, then he *abandoned* them, and they abandoned themselves to the customs and ordinances of the heathen." (Clarke)

b. **I pronounced them unclean because of their ritual gifts**: Israel served and gave honor to the pagan idols in the most **unclean** and terrible ways, ultimately including child sacrifice (**they caused all their firstborn to pass through the fire**).

c. **That I might make them desolate and that they might know that I am the** L**ORD**: These great sins while in the land eventually brought the long-withheld judgment of God.

B. God's mercy to disobedient Israel in the Promised Land.

1. (27-28) Israel's idolatry in the Promised Land.

"Therefore, son of man, speak to the house of Israel, and say to them, 'Thus says the Lord G**OD: "In this too your fathers have blasphemed Me, by being unfaithful to Me. When I brought them into the land** *concerning* **which I had raised My hand in an oath to give them, and they saw all the high hills and all the thick trees, there they offered their sacrifices and provoked Me with their offerings. There they also sent up their sweet aroma and poured out their drink offerings.**

a. **In this too your fathers have blasphemed Me**: Ezekiel here retraces some of Israel's history, beginning at the nation as they received Canaan as God's gift. Even then they were **unfaithful** to God when He **brought them into the land**.

b. **They saw all the high hills and all the thick trees, there they offered their sacrifices**: In terrible ingratitude, Israel used the very **hills** and **trees** God gave to them to offer their sacrifices to pagan idols. The sacrifices were of all kinds, including incense (**sweet aroma**) and wine (**drink offerings**).

i. "The crowning rebellion of Israel's history was that when finally, in the mercy of God, they entered into the land of promise, they promptly took over the heathen Canaanite hill-top shrines as their own places of sacrifice." (Taylor)

2. (29-32) God refuses to speak to an Israel that will not listen to Him.

Then I said to them, 'What *is* this high place to which you go?' So its name is called Bamah to this day."' Therefore say to the house of Israel, 'Thus says the Lord God: "Are you defiling yourselves in the manner of your fathers, and committing harlotry according to their abominations? For when you offer your gifts and make your sons pass through the fire, you defile yourselves with all your idols, even to this day. So shall I be inquired of by you, O house of Israel? *As* I live," says the Lord God, "I will not be inquired of by you. What you have in your mind shall never be, when you say, 'We will be like the Gentiles, like the families in other countries, serving wood and stone.'

a. **What is this high place to which you go?** Israel used the tops of hills and mountains for idol altars and sacrifice so often that the term **high place** was used for any place of idolatry, no matter what the elevation (as in Ezekiel 16:24-25). The name **Bamah** means *high place*.

i. **Bamah**: "A high place; a name good enough in itself, but, as used by them, as odious to all good hearts as a brothel house is to a chaste matron. She is the worse to pass by it, and spitteth at it. So should we in like case." (Trapp)

b. **Are you defiling yourselves in the manner of your fathers**: This was the critical question Ezekiel asked of the elders who came to him as a prophet to inquire of the Lord (Ezekiel 20:1). After spelling out a long history of Israel's sin and idolatry, the elders were those and represented those who did **defile yourselves with all your idols, even to this day**. *Nothing had changed.*

i. "Why this rehearsal of the nation's sins of the past to the prophet's countrymen in exile? The reason is clear: their father's sins were mirrored in their own lives, as is demonstrated in the course of the message." (Feinberg)

ii. Yet God used the period of exile to refine and change Israel. When they emerged from their Babylonian exile, they no longer had the same problem with idolatry as they had before. They certainly had other sins and failings, but seemed to be "cured" of their outward idolatry of pagan gods.

c. **So shall I be inquired of by you, O house of Israel?** The elders originally came to seek a word from God through the prophet Ezekiel (Ezekiel 20:1). God made it clear that He owed no special revelation to such a disobedient people. If we want to hear God's voice and receive His guidance, it is always best to obey what He has already said and walk in the path already revealed.

i. "It is as though he expressed surprise that those who had continued in sin and emulated the disobedience of their forefathers should still expect to receive fresh revelations from God." (Feinberg)

ii. "Are you fit to come and ask counsel of me, whom you have so shamelessly, so obstinately forsaken and reproached? Can you expect I should answer you?" (Poole)

d. **We shall be like the Gentiles, like the families in other countries**: God forcefully rebuked the elders, and many others among Israel's exiles, for their unspoken and hidden sins. They almost *looked forward* to the opportunity to live **like the families in other countries** and to forsake the Lord, **serving wood and stone**. God had to correct this evil attitude or Israel would completely assimilate into the countries where they were exiled.

i. "Ye wish to be naturalized among *idolaters*, and make a part of such nations. But this *shall not be at all*; you shall be preserved as a *distinct people*. Ye shall not be permitted to mingle yourselves with the people of those countries: even *they*, idolaters as they are, will *despise* and *reject* you." (Clarke)

ii. **We shall be like the Gentiles**: "The more pleasure we may have in forbidden paths, the more sharp the anguish through which we shall have to retrace our steps. We cannot be as the nations. We cannot serve wood and stone. We cannot go our own way." (Meyer)

3. (33-36) God's strong promise of restoration.

"*As* I live," says the Lord God, "surely with a mighty hand, with an outstretched arm, and with fury poured out, I will rule over you. I will bring you out from the peoples and gather you out of the countries where you are scattered, with a mighty hand, with an outstretched arm, and with fury poured out. And I will bring you into the wilderness of the peoples, and there I will plead My case with you face to face. Just

as I pleaded My case with your fathers in the wilderness of the land of Egypt, so I will plead My case with you," says the Lord God.

a. **Surely with a mighty hand, with an outstretched arm, and with fury poured out, I will rule over you**: God said this with a vow (**As I live**), emphasizing the fact that though Israel had in many ways forsaken Him, *He* had not forsaken them. God would **rule over** them on His own terms.

i. "The insidious attitude of assimilation to the idolatrous ways of the heathen will not be allowed to happen." (Taylor)

ii. "If one reads these verses dispassionately, that they proffer not salvation to the existing Israel but the opposite. The only 'mercy' that Yahweh promises, the only surcease of exile where Israel finds itself, is that it may be confronted by its Master. The result of this confrontation is that Israel will come to realize the enormity of its guilt. The people will loathe the evil that they have done." (Vawter and Hoppe)

b. **I will bring you out from the peoples and gather you**: God had fulfilled His promise to scatter disobedient Israel. Soon He would fulfill His promise to restore them, and with the same energy and intent as His previous judgment.

c. **I will bring you into the wilderness of the peoples, and there I will plead My case with you face to face**: God promised to deal with Israel in their return from exile much as He dealt with them when they came out of Egypt. He would prove to them His love and faithfulness, and so **plead** His **case with** Israel.

i. **Into the wilderness**: "So the final period of Israel's history, the dispersion in exile, is seen as a reversion to the wilderness life which had preceded the settlement in Canaan." (Taylor)

ii. **Face to face**: "The emphasis is not on the intimacy of the relationship between deity and human but on the directness of the encounter. This time there will be no cloud or mediator to shield Israel from the awesome divine majesty." (Block)

4. (37-38) God promises correction and covenant.

"I will make you pass under the rod, and I will bring you into the bond of the covenant; I will purge the rebels from among you, and those who transgress against Me; I will bring them out of the country where they dwell, but they shall not enter the land of Israel. Then you will know that I *am* the Lord.

a. **I will make you pass under the rod, and I will bring you into the bond of the covenant**: God promised that the time of exile would be a necessary corrective and that the **covenant** He had with Israel would be again restored. The correction would begin by selecting those who were restored to the land, as a shepherd identified his flock **under the rod**.

> i. **Under the rod**: "The idiom derives from the custom of a shepherd standing at the entrance of the fold and using his rod to count, examine, and sort his sheep." (Block)
>
> ii. "As a shepherd's staff is employed to count the sheep (Jeremiah 33:13), so the Lord will bring the entire flock under the rod, this time with the purpose of separating the godly from the wicked." (Feinberg)

b. **I will purge the rebels from among you**: God promised that not all those in exile would return. **Rebels** and **those who transgress** would **not enter the land of Israel**. This purging work would be another way God would reveal Himself to Israel (**then you will know that I am the LORD**).

> i. We see from these promises a *partial* fulfillment in the return from the Babylonian captivity under Ezra and Zerubbabel, and a greater and more perfect fulfillment in the millennial age.
>
> ii. Smith spoke to the sooner, partial fulfillment: "Centuries before in the wilderness of Egypt the Lord had discriminated between those who were destined to enter the land of promise, and those who were not. So now the Babylonian exile would serve to discriminate between those who were to be permitted to return, and those who would be denied."
>
> iii. Wiersbe spoke to the later, ultimate fulfillment: "Israel will be restored to her covenant relationship to the Lord and will experience the blessings of the New Covenant (18:31; 36:26–27). 'I will purge out the rebels' (20:38) and they will not be allowed to enter the land of Israel and enjoy the blessings of the messianic kingdom."

C. God reveals Himself in restoration and mercy.

1. (39) A challenge to choose Yahweh or the idols.

"As for you, O house of Israel," thus says the Lord GOD: "Go, serve every one of you his idols—and hereafter—if you will not obey Me; but profane My holy name no more with your gifts and your idols.

a. **As for you, O house of Israel**: Having walked through Israel's history of sin and God's history of mercy to Israel, having brought the matter to the present day, and having spoken of the future, now Yahweh gave them a challenge.

b. **Go, serve every one of you his idols**: God called His people to a decision point. If they wanted to serve their **idols**, then they might as well make up their minds and do it. Let them become Babylonians in every regard now that they were in Babylon.

c. **But profane My holy name no more with your gifts and your idols**: What God did *not* want from Israel was a divided heart. When they brought Yahweh worship from hearts also given to idols, it profaned God and His name. In New Testament phrasing, God called Israel to be hot or cold, but no longer lukewarm (Revelation 3:15-16).

2. (40-41) Gathered again to properly worship God.

For on My holy mountain, on the mountain height of Israel," says the Lord GOD, "there all the house of Israel, all of them in the land, shall serve Me; there I will accept them, and there I will require your offerings and the firstfruits of your sacrifices, together with all your holy things. I will accept you as a sweet aroma when I bring you out from the peoples and gather you out of the countries where you have been scattered; and I will be hallowed in you before the Gentiles.

a. **On My holy mountain...all the house of Israel...shall serve Me**: God promised that when Israel was restored to the land, the people would once again **serve** Him in a way that He would **accept**. This was fulfilled when the temple was rebuilt under Ezra and Zerubbabel.

i. **Shall serve Me**: "They will render priestly service to God, for the word 'serve' is the technical term for priestly ministry (cf. for this commission Exodus 19:6)." (Feinberg)

b. **I will accept you as a sweet aroma when I bring you out from the peoples**: God clearly longed for Israel's restoration to the land. When God brought them back from where He had **scattered** them, it would be like a pleasing sacrifice. It would also glorify God **before the Gentiles**.

3. (42-44) God revealed in His restoration and mercy.

Then you shall know that I *am* the LORD, when I bring you into the land of Israel, into the country *for* which I raised My hand in an oath to give to your fathers. And there you shall remember your ways and all your doings with which you were defiled; and you shall loathe yourselves in your own sight because of all the evils that you have committed. Then you shall know that I *am* the LORD, when I have dealt with you for My name's sake, not according to your wicked ways nor according to your corrupt doings, O house of Israel," says the Lord GOD.'"

a. **Then you shall know that I am the LORD, when I bring you into the land of Israel**: God's restoration of Israel to the land would be a powerful revelation of Himself, both to Israel and to the world. This was true of the return from the Babylonian exile; it was also true of Israel's 1948 return to the land.

b. **For which I raised My hand in an oath to give to your fathers**: God promised the land to Abraham (Genesis 12:1-3) and his covenant descendants. It was their land, and it remained their land even after God scattered them from the land because of their disobedience.

c. **There you shall remember your ways and all your doings with which you were defiled**: Restored Israel would no longer be given over to the same sins as they were before the exile. They would **loathe** themselves **because of all the evils that** they **have committed.**

> i. **You shall remember your ways**: "Recognition is the first thing in reformation." (Trapp) "As elsewhere *zakar* [**remember**] does not mean simply 'to recall to mind,' but 'to acknowledge, take account of, accept responsibility for,' their conduct." (Block)

> ii. "These promises may, in a certain limited sense, be applied to the restoration from the Babylonish captivity; but they must have their proper fulfilment when the Jews shall accept Jesus as their Saviour, and in consequence be brought back from all their dispersions to their own land." (Clarke)

d. **I have dealt with you for My name's sake, not according to your wicked ways**: The overwhelming mercy of God toward Israel would be a powerful revelation of Yahweh's existence and character (**then you shall know that I am the** Lord).

> i. "Israel would have new understanding of Jehovah, and come to know that the perpetual reason for His operation was the glory of His name, and not merely punishing them for their evil ways, that is to say, the punishment of Jehovah was never merely vindictive, but always a process moving toward the realisation of His original intention of good to the nations of the earth." (Morgan)

D. Judgment like a forest fire.

"In the Hebrew text of Ezekiel, verse 45 of this chapter is the beginning of chapter 21, where the connection is clear and the figure is explained in direct prophetic discourse." (Feinberg)

1. (45-48) Judgment on the forest of the south.

Furthermore the word of the Lord **came to me, saying, "Son of man, set your face toward the south; preach against the south and prophesy against the forest land, the South, and say to the forest of the South, 'Hear the word of the** Lord**! Thus says the Lord** God**: "Behold, I will**

kindle a fire in you, and it shall devour every green tree and every dry tree in you; the blazing flame shall not be quenched, and all faces from the south to the north shall be scorched by it. All flesh shall see that I, the LORD, have kindled it; it shall not be quenched.""

a. **Son of man, set your face toward the south**: God told Ezekiel to **preach against the south**, that is, the land of Judah, which lies south of where Ezekiel was (Babylon). Here Judah and Jerusalem are represented as a forest ready to be burned. Jerusalem was as full of people as the forest is full of trees.

    i. "The Hebrew uses three different words [for **south**] (*temana*, *darom*, and *negeb*). Of these the first two are general poetic words to describe the southerly direction, whereas the third refers to a named geographical area, called in modern Israel the Negev, which lay to the south of the Judean hills." (Taylor)

    ii. "'Preach against the south' (RSV) is a pallid equivalent of the Hebrew, which is more actually 'spit toward the south'—the word occurs in Ezekiel only in this passage." (Vawter and Hoppe)

    iii. "The southern forest referred to the southern kingdom of Judah, a forested area in biblical times, even into the upper Negev." (Alexander)

b. **Behold, I will kindle a fire in you**: The Babylonian army would come with devastating judgment against Judea and Jerusalem. The judgment would be so complete that it would burn both the **green tree** and the **dry tree** – those obviously ready to burn in the coming judgment, and those who were relatively righteous and innocent.

    i. "Ezekiel characterizes Yahweh as an enemy who ignites the forest, setting off a conflagration that does not cease until every twig has burned up." (Block)

    ii. "That fire would consume every green tree as well as every dry one. The thought is that both the righteous and the wicked would suffer from the devastation caused by the Chaldean invaders." (Smith)

c. **All flesh shall see that I, the LORD, have kindled it**: God's judgment against Israel would be so powerful and complete that the whole world would take notice.

2. (49) The prophet's complaint.

Then I said, "Ah, Lord GOD! They say of me, 'Does he not speak parables?'"

a. **Ah, Lord GOD**: This was another of Ezekiel's passionate pleas to God.

b. **Does he not speak in parables?** The elders of Israel (Ezekiel 20:1) and others rejected or even despised Ezekiel's message because they claimed it was hard to understand. Their failure to understand was willful and would be judged.

i. "Men find difficulty in understanding a message which is distasteful to them.... It is well known that to the unwilling heart any message from God appears to be difficult of comprehension." (Feinberg)

Ezekiel 21 – The Sword of Yahweh's Judgment

"No chapter in the Bible speaks more prominently and fully of the sword of the Lord than does this chapter which has been called the sword song or the prophecy of the sword." (Charles Feinberg)

A. The sword of the LORD comes against Jerusalem.

1. (1-5) The work of Yahweh's sword.

And the word of the LORD came to me, saying, "Son of man, set your face toward Jerusalem, preach against the holy places, and prophesy against the land of Israel; and say to the land of Israel, 'Thus says the LORD: "Behold, I *am* against you, and I will draw My sword out of its sheath and cut off both righteous and wicked from you. Because I will cut off both righteous and wicked from you, therefore My sword shall go out of its sheath against all flesh from south *to* north, that all flesh may know that I, the LORD, have drawn My sword out of its sheath; it shall not return anymore."'

a. **Set your face toward Jerusalem, preach against the holy places, and prophesy against the land of Israel**: It's a terrible thing to have God speak **against** a land, especially one so favored as He gave to Israel. Yet God was not only against the land; more pointedly He was against the *people* (**Behold, I am against you**).

b. **I will draw My sword out of its sheath and cut off both righteous and wicked**: When God's judgment came against the nation, it would not be against specific individuals. It would come against the people in general and **both righteous and wicked** would find themselves under His sword.

i. **Both righteous and wicked**: "The teaching here regarding the cutting off of both righteous and wicked does not contradict the teaching of chapter 18 that only the soul that sins shall die (cf. Ezekiel 18:20). The former passage spoke of final judgment, while this passage speaks of temporal judgment. As regards final judgment, the righteous will not be destroyed along with the wicked. In temporal judgments, however, both often suffer equally." (Smith)

ii. "Accordingly, the statement describes the indiscriminate nature of war, which recognizes only two parties, victors and the victims; there is no concern to subdivide the latter, particularly according to that nation's definitions of righteous and wicked." (Block)

iii. "The vision of that glittering, furbished, active sword is indeed a terrible one. But it is the Sword of Jehovah. Observe how that fact is kept in mind." (Morgan)

c. **That all flesh may know that I, the LORD, have drawn My sword**: The magnitude and severity of God's judgment would be a revelation to the watching world. They would know that only God Himself could be behind such a great judgment.

i. The forest fire of Ezekiel 20:46-48 becomes a sword which will slay the righteous and the wicked, just as the fire would burn both the green and the dry tree.

2. (6-7) The sighs of the prophet.

Sigh therefore, son of man, with a breaking heart, and sigh with bitterness before their eyes. And it shall be when they say to you, 'Why are you sighing?' that you shall answer, 'Because of the news; when it comes, every heart will melt, all hands will be feeble, every spirit will faint, and all knees will be weak *as* water. Behold, it is coming and shall be brought to pass,' says the Lord GOD."

a. **Sigh therefore, son of man, with a breaking heart**: God did not want Ezekiel to be an unemotional messenger of judgment. God wanted the heart of the prophet to display the same **breaking heart** that God Himself had.

i. **With a breaking heart**: This is literally *breaking loins*. "A phrase expressing deep emotional distress. The loins were regarded as the seat of strength, and so this represents complete nervous and physical collapse (cf. Ezekiel 29:7; Psalm 69:23; Nahum 2:10)." (Taylor)

ii. "Literally means 'breaking of loins.' 'Loins' in the OT are viewed as the center of physical strength and the seat of emotions. When they are 'broken,' the strength is gone and one is helpless. The emotions are shattered." (Alexander)

b. **Because of the news; when it comes, every heart will melt**: The people of Jerusalem and Judah heard from Ezekiel, Jeremiah, and other prophets that judgment was coming, and they didn't take the message seriously. Yet when the armies of Babylon actually came and they heard **the news** of it, they would be completely broken. **Every spirit will faint, and all knees will be weak as water**.

> i. The phrase **all the knees will be weak as water** is especially vivid, and used also in Ezekiel 7:17. "There is a vivid account of the panic that will follow. The RSV's 'all knees [are] weak as water' means 'all knees will run water': a euphemism for the loss of bladder control in moments of terror." (Vawter and Hoppe)

> ii. "Hebrew, Shall go into water – that is, they shall bepiss themselves for fear, saith Jerome; they shall be all on a cold sweat, say others; or their knees shall shake, *instar aquae tremulae,* like trembling water, and knock together, as Belshazzar's did. [Daniel 5:6]" (Trapp)

c. **Behold it is coming and shall be brought to pass**: This judgment was certain, and it broke the heart of prophets like Ezekiel and Jeremiah to consider what great devastation would come upon the land.

3. (8-17) The prophecy of Yahweh's sword.

Again the word of the LORD came to me, saying, "Son of man, prophesy and say, 'Thus says the LORD!' Say:

'A sword, a sword is sharpened
And also polished!
Sharpened to make a dreadful slaughter,
Polished to flash like lightning!
Should we then make mirth?
It despises the scepter of My son,
As it does **all wood.**
And He has given it to be polished,
That it may be handled;
This sword is sharpened, and it is polished
To be given into the hand of the slayer.'
"Cry and wail, son of man;
For it will be against My people,
Against all the princes of Israel.
Terrors including the sword will be against My people;
Therefore strike *your* **thigh.**
"Because *it is* **a testing,**
And what if *the sword* **despises even the scepter?**
The scepter **shall be no** *more*,"
says the Lord GOD.
"You therefore, son of man, prophesy,
And strike *your* **hands together.**

The third time let the sword do double *damage.*
It *is* the sword *that* slays,
The sword that slays the great *men,*
That enters their private chambers.
I have set the point of the sword against all their gates,
That the heart may melt and many may stumble.
Ah! *It is* made bright;
It is grasped for slaughter:
"Swords at the ready!
Thrust right!
Set your blade!
Thrust left—
Wherever your edge is ordered!
"I also will beat My fists together,
And I will cause My fury to rest;
I, the LORD, have spoken."

a. **A sword, a sword is sharpened and also polished**: In this poetically powerful prophecy regarding the instrument of God's judgment against Judah and Jerusalem, the first emphasis is on the *readiness* of God's **sword** against His people. It is **sharpened to make a dreadful slaughter**.

i. **A dreadful slaughter**: "In secular usage, *tabah* normally refers to the slaughtering of domestic animals for consumption, but with humans as objects the term may be applied to bloody massacres, which is what is envisioned here." (Block)

ii. **Should we then make mirth?** "In view of the fearful prospect, Ezekiel asked whether this was the hour for mirth, an hour of enjoyment and complacency. The implication was that any imagined basis for confidence was false." (Feinberg)

b. **It despises the scepter of My son**: The **son** referred to here is probably the ruler of Judah, Zedekiah – or, the nation itself. God's sword of judgment had no regard for his right to reign, for Zedekiah's **scepter**. It would destroy it as a metal sword does **wood**. This idea is repeated again in this prophecy (Ezekiel 21:13).

i. "Despising the king of Judah (v. 13), the sword of Babylon would turn Judah's scepter into nothing but a stick!" (Wiersbe)

c. **To be given into the hands of the slayer**: The army of Babylon would come against Judah and Jerusalem, but *only* because God put the sword of judgment **into the hands of the slayer.**

i. **Strike your hands together**: "Therefore, the injunction to 'clap your hands,' a gesture in which God even joins, with the stamping of the feet (cf. 6:11; 25:6) is a sign of defiance. It encourages the murderous work of the sword and exults over the inglorious end of this callous people." (Vawter and Hoppe)

d. **The third time let the sword do double damage**: Nebuchadnezzar had already invaded and subjected Jerusalem twice. The next time – **the third time** – he would do far more **damage**.

i. "The sword has been *doubled*, and it shall come the *third time*. Nebuchadnezzar came against Judea THRICE. 1. Against *Jehoiakim*. 2. Against *Jeconiah*. 3. Against *Zedekiah*. The sword had already been *doubled*; it is to come now the *third time*, i.e., against Zedekiah." (Clarke)

e. **Swords at the ready! Thrust right**: To emphasize the idea that all this is done at Yahweh's direction, God presents Himself as something of a general over the army of judgment. He directs even the **thrust** of the blade and will not cease until He says, "**I will cause My fury to rest.**"

i. "Since he and other prophets often reinforced their messages with dramatic signs, he has perhaps drawn a sword and is whirling it round, making it flash in the sun, and shouting his words in disjointed sentences." (Wright)

B. The path of the sword

1. (18-21) Two paths for the sword of judgment.

The word of the LORD came to me again, saying: "And son of man, appoint for yourself two ways for the sword of the king of Babylon to go; both of them shall go from the same land. Make a sign; put *it* at the head of the road to the city. Appoint a road for the sword to go to Rabbah of the Ammonites, and to Judah, into fortified Jerusalem. For the king of Babylon stands at the parting of the road, at the fork of the two roads, to use divination: he shakes the arrows, he consults the images, he looks at the liver.

a. **Appoint for yourself two ways for the sword of the king of Babylon to go**: In a vivid description, God explained to Ezekiel that the **sword of the king of Babylon** – his army used as the instrument of God's judgment – stood at a crossroads, deciding to next go to either **Rabbah of the Ammonites** or **to Judah, into fortified Jerusalem**.

i. **Make a sign**: "The use of *yad* (lit. "hand") for signpost suggests a roadsign on which is carved the form of a hand with fingers pointing in the direction specified." (Block)

ii. **Rabbah of the Ammonites**: "In Greco-Roman times Rabbath was called Philadelphia; it is the modern Amman in Transjordan, the Old Testament Rabbath-Ammon." (Feinberg)

b. **He shakes the arrows, he consults the images, he looks at the liver**: Ezekiel pictured Nebuchadnezzar **at the parting of the road**, using all the methods pagans used to get guidance from their gods.

i. **He shakes the arrows**: "First, he *has shaken the arrows,* a practice known as belomancy or rhabdomancy. The action consisted of shaking two inscribed arrows and then drawing one as one draws a lot, on the assumption that the gods had determined which one was selected." (Block)

ii. **He consults the images**: "The next way of divining was by asking counsel of his idol, or image, which being made artificially by the skill of their juggling priests and conjurers, with little help they could give answers, and the image spake aloud what the sorcerer spake more softly, somewhat like the artificial whispering places which convey the voice, from unseen persons." (Poole)

iii. **He looks at the liver**: "Here we have a truly authentic Babylonian divinatory process, which had come into Canaan. A 'science' had grown up around this divinatory technique. It also spawned a professional priesthood that confidently predicted a proper course of action by examining the color and the internal segmentation of the livers of newly slaughtered animals." (Vawter and Hoppe)

iv. "Even Nebuchadnezzar's superstition was overruled by God in order to carry out His purpose on Judah (for Babylon's divinations see Isaiah 47:8-15). The king thought he was deciding by the help of his gods, but God was determining the course of his action." (Feinberg)

2. (22-23) The decision to go to Jerusalem.

In his right hand is the divination for Jerusalem: to set up battering rams, to call for a slaughter, to lift the voice with shouting, to set battering rams against the gates, to heap up a *siege* mound, and to build a wall. And it will be to them like a false divination in the eyes of those who have sworn oaths with them; but he will bring their iniquity to remembrance, that they may be taken.

a. **In his right hand is the divination for Jerusalem**: At the parting of the roads, Nebuchadnezzar decided to go to **Jerusalem**. He would come against the city with his **battering rams** and bring a great **slaughter**.

> i. **Battering rams**: "Engines made to beat down walls; and they had this name from the iron or brass head, which usually was at the end of it, like unto the head of a ram." (Poole)

> ii. **To heap up a siege mound**: "Open pitched battles were fought only if an army thought it could match the enemy sword for sword. Otherwise the troops would retreat within their defensive walls, a strategy that could succeed especially if the invading forces were far from home and lacked efficient supply lines. This would be Jerusalem's only hope in the face of the Babylonians." (Block)

b. **It will be to them like a false divination**: It would be false in the sense that though Nebuchadnezzar sought the pagan gods with their superstitions of divination, *Yahweh was actually guiding him*. As much as the people of Judah and Jerusalem may have prayed the king of Babylon would *not* come against them, God would guide him to them to **bring their iniquity to remembrance**.

> i. **Those who have sworn oaths**: "Zedekiah, his princes, and nobles, who swore allegiance to the king of Babylon first, and afterward conspired with Egypt, and by new and contrary oaths perjured themselves, provoked as well as dishonoured God, and enraged Nebuchadnezzar to revenge their perfidiousness." (Poole)

3. (24-27) The humbling of the prince of Judah.

"Therefore thus says the Lord GOD: 'Because you have made your iniquity to be remembered, in that your transgressions are uncovered, so that in all your doings your sins appear—because you have come to remembrance, you shall be taken in hand. 'Now to you, O profane, wicked prince of Israel, whose day has come, whose iniquity *shall* end, thus says the Lord GOD:

"Remove the turban, and take off the crown;
Nothing *shall remain* the same.
Exalt the humble, and humble the exalted.
Overthrown, overthrown,
I will make it overthrown!
It shall be no *longer*,
Until He comes whose right it is,
And I will give it *to Him*.'"

a. **Because you have made your iniquity to be remembered**: Because Judah sinned so memorably before God, it was to be expected that He would in fact remember them in judgment. They prayed and hoped that God and Nebuchadnezzar would forget about them, but they would not.

b. **Now to you, O profane, wicked prince of Israel**: After generations of hardened and persistent sin, it could be said that the **day has come** for judgment and of the prince of Israel (probably Zedekiah), his **iniquity shall end**.

c. **Remove the turban, and take off the crown**: All the emblems of royalty and leadership would be removed from Zedekiah; **nothing shall remain the same**. He would be humbled, and the humble of the land would be its only inhabitants.

> i. "The miter [**turban**] was the headdress of the high priest (Exodus 28:37); the crown, of course, belonged to the king. Priesthood and royalty were related in Israel. Now they were both to be interrupted, set aside for a time." (Feinberg)

> ii. "The removal of the priesthood and the kingship from Judah were pictured, respectively, in the removal of the high priest's turban (Exodus 28:4, 37, 39; 29:6; 39:28, 31; Leviticus 8:9; 16:4) and the king's crown (v.26)." (Alexander)

> iii. **Exalt the humble**: "Jeconiah; it is probable the prophet foretells the advance of this captive king, which came to pass in the 37th year of Jeconiah's captivity, in the first year of Merodach, 2 Kings 25:27-29 Jeremiah 52:31, who exalted his seat above all the captive kings in Babylon." (Poole)

d. **Overthrown, overthrown, I will make it overthrown**: The idea is repeated three times both for great emphasis and because Nebuchadnezzar subjugated Jerusalem three times, with the third bringing complete destruction and conquest.

> i. "Our King is always engaged in destruction, that He may the better occupy Himself with construction. He overthrows our cities of brick that He may build them of marble. He removes the things that can be shaken, as things that are made, that the things which cannot be shaken may remain." (Meyer)

e. **Until He comes whose right it is, and I will give it to Him**: Zedekiah was the last of a long line descended from David to reign in some sense over Jerusalem and Israel. He and his reign would be **overthrown**, and no descendant of David would sit on the throne **until He comes whose right it is** – that is, until God's Messiah, the true Son of David comes. This was wonderfully and obviously fulfilled in Jesus Christ and still waits for its ultimate fulfillment.

i. "Verse 27 is one of the great Messianic promises of the O.T., although it is often overlooked. It is similar to the promise of Genesis 49.10, (RSV). After the exile there were no more kings of David's line. Zerubbabel, who was leader soon after the return, was of David's line, but was never king." (Wright)

ii. "This was Judah's only hope in the midst of their current judgment. When Judah would ultimately be purified, then the 'scepter' (Messiah) would rule over his people." (Alexander)

iii. "From Zedekiah down to the Lord Jesus there has been no one in the line of David who ever sat on that throne. Ezekiel is saying that no one would ever be able to do so. The Lord Jesus is the only One who will. Right now He is sitting at God's right hand, waiting until His enemies are made His footstool when He comes to this earth to rule." (McGee)

iv. "The coming of the Lord for His church in the rapture is recalled in every celebration of the Lord's Supper: 'till He come.' Israel also has an 'until He come.' The Messiah will restore access to God in high-priestly ministry and righteous rule in royal ministry." (Feinberg)

v. "Whatever the king of Judah thought to establish by his wit and power, God would overthrow. Nothing should stand, however carefully constructed, till the Messiah came to take up the kingdom and rule with meekness and righteousness." (Meyer)

4. (28-32) The coming reproach of the Ammonites.

"And you, son of man, prophesy and say, 'Thus says the Lord God concerning the Ammonites and concerning their reproach,' and say:

'A sword, a sword *is* drawn,
Polished for slaughter,
For consuming, for flashing—
While they see false visions for you,
While they divine a lie to you,
To bring you on the necks of the wicked, the slain
Whose day has come,
Whose iniquity *shall* end.
'Return *it* to its sheath.
I will judge you
In the place where you were created,
In the land of your nativity.

I will pour out My indignation on you;
I will blow against you with the fire of My wrath,
And deliver you into the hands of brutal men *who are* skillful to
destroy.
You shall be fuel for the fire;
Your blood shall be in the midst of the land.
You shall not be remembered,
For I the LORD have spoken.'"

a. **Thus says the Lord GOD concerning the Ammonites**: When God
said that Nebuchadnezzar would stand at the parting of the roads and be
guided by God to go to Jerusalem, it did not mean that God would *not*
bring judgment against the Ammonites. The land of Ammon was on the
eastern side of the Jordan River, in the modern-day kingdom of Jordan.

i. "Since Ammon would mock and mistreat Judah in her collapse
before Babylonia, Ezekiel sang the same 'sword song' to Ammon."
(Alexander)

ii. "This prophecy against them was fulfilled about *five* years after the
taking of Jerusalem. See Joseph. Ant. lib. x. c. 11; and Jeremiah 27; 48;
49; Ezekiel 25." (Clarke)

b. **A sword, a sword is drawn**: The sword of God's judgment would
also come against the Ammonites. God promised, **I will judge you in
the place where you were created, in the land of your nativity**. The fire
of God's wrath would **blow against** the Ammonites. Unlike Israel, they
would eventually disappear as a people (**you shall not be remembered**).

i. **I will blow against you**: "As those who melt down metals blow upon
the metal in the fire, that the fire might burn the fiercer, and consume
the dross." (Poole)

ii. **You shall not be remembered**: "Their ultimate fate will be worse
than Israel's and worse even than Egypt's, for they will be *no more
remembered*. To the Semitic mind nothing could be more terrible: no
prospect of restoration, no continuance in succeeding generations, no
memorial, not even a memory. Oblivion." (Taylor)

Ezekiel 22 – The Bloody City and the Judgment to Come Upon It

A. The corruption of Jerusalem and her leaders.

1. (1-5) The guilt and the judgment of Jerusalem, the bloody city.

Moreover the word of the LORD came to me, saying, "Now, son of man, will you judge, will you judge the bloody city? Yes, show her all her abominations! Then say, 'Thus says the Lord GOD: "The city sheds blood in her own midst, that her time may come; and she makes idols within herself to defile herself. You have become guilty by the blood which you have shed, and have defiled yourself with the idols which you have made. You have caused your days to draw near, and have come to *the end of* your years; therefore I have made you a reproach to the nations, and a mockery to all countries. *Those* near and *those* far from you will mock you as infamous *and* full of tumult.

a. **Will you judge the bloody city?** With a double call, God told Ezekiel to pronounce judgment upon Jerusalem, **the bloody city**. Jerusalem was guilty of many sins, and large among them was injustice leading to death and violence. Perhaps Jerusalem was not as **bloody** as many pagan cities, but they had the word, prophets, and priests of God. They were rightly held to a much higher standard.

i. At this point in her history, Jerusalem was no longer the *holy city*, the *beautiful city*, or God's special city. She was **the bloody city**, for her many crimes that showed disregard for human life. Many centuries later Stephen spoke of the bloodguilt of Jerusalem: *Which of the prophets did your fathers not persecute?* (Acts 7:52)

ii. **The bloody city**: "Jerusalem is so named because of the many deeds of violence and oppression committed in her. The plural of the original for 'blood' points to numerous acts of bloodshed." (Feinberg)

iii. "Ezekiel seems to have borrowed this phrase from Nahum, who had in the previous century arraigned Nineveh as 'the bloody city' par excellence." (Block) *Jerusalem seemed as bad as Nineveh!*

b. **Show her all her abominations**: This refers to another of Jerusalem's many sins, that of gross idolatry. Ezekiel noted, **she makes idols within herself to defile herself**. They were defiled by their unfaithfulness to God and by the actual immoral practices connected to the worship of these pagan idols.

i. **In her own midst**: "This aggravates their murders, and makes them more bloody, in that it was done where so many were, that should have been safety to the innocent; it was not done in a wilderness." (Poole)

c. **You have caused your days to draw near**: The coming judgment upon Jerusalem was their own fault. God was gracious and patient with them over many generations, but eventually they had **come to the end of your years**.

d. **Those near and those far from you will mock you as infamous and full of tumult**: Jerusalem could expect no sympathy from the surrounding nations, both **near** and **far**. They would be **a reproach to the nations and a mockery to all countries**.

2. (6-12) The many sins of Israel and her princes.

"Look, the princes of Israel: each one has used his power to shed blood in you. In you they have made light of father and mother; in your midst they have oppressed the stranger; in you they have mistreated the fatherless and the widow. You have despised My holy things and profaned My Sabbaths. In you are men who slander to cause bloodshed; in you are those who eat on the mountains; in your midst they commit lewdness. In you men uncover their fathers' nakedness; in you they violate women who are set apart during their impurity. One commits abomination with his neighbor's wife; another lewdly defiles his daughter-in-law; and another in you violates his sister, his father's daughter. In you they take bribes to shed blood; you take usury and increase; you have made profit from your neighbors by extortion, and have forgotten Me," says the Lord GOD.

a. **Look, the princes of Israel**: In the first five verses of Ezekiel 22, God rebuked the sinful city. Then He focused His rebuke on the actual sinners in the city, beginning with **the princes of Israel**.

i. Though the twelve tribes of Israel did not exist as their own nation or nations for more than 100 years (since the fall of the northern kingdom of Israel), yet God still referred to the leaders of His people as **the princes of Israel**.

b. **Each one has used his power to shed blood in you**: Instead of using their **power** in ways that would honor God and serve His people, the **princes of Israel** used their power in violent, self-serving ways.

> i. "The social disintegration within Jerusalem was reflected first and foremost in the manner in which power was exercised." (Block)

> ii. "Judicial murders were evidently intended (see II Kings 21: 16; 24:4)." (Feinberg)

c. **In your midst they have oppressed the stranger; in you they have mistreated the fatherless and the widow**: These were those whom the princes of Israel should have cared for. Instead of caring for families (**father and mother**) and the vulnerable of society, they used and despised them.

> i. "The Jews were commanded to honor their fathers and mothers (Exodus 20:12), and so are believers today (Ephesians 6:1–3). God even attached a special promise to this commandment—'that your days may be long upon the land'—and now the Jews were about to be exiled from their land." (Wiersbe)

d. **You have despised My holy things and profaned My Sabbaths**: The sins of the princes of Israel were not only against their community; they were also against God Himself. They sinned against God's glory when they sacrificed and feasted to idols **on the mountains**.

> i. **Profaned My Sabbaths**: "The plural form indicates that the charge extends beyond the violation of the weekly Sabbaths to sacred days (and years) as well." (Block)

e. **One commits abomination with his neighbor's wife**: A further area of sin among the princes of Israel was their sexual immorality and perversion. They not only committed adultery (**with his neighbor's wife**), but they also committed incest with a **daughter-in-law** or **sister**.

> i. "No type of impurity could stay their evil desires (Lev. 18:19; 20:18). In their excesses they acted more like beasts than creatures of reason. God has placed restraints in every realm of human life with infinite wisdom, and it is worse than folly to disregard these warnings." (Feinberg)

> ii. **They violate women**: "A double sin was committed when men 'humbled,' i.e., raped, a woman during her menstruous period." (Smith)

f. **They take bribes to shed blood; you take usury and increase**: The final area of sin exposed among the princes of Israel was their financial exploitation against their own community. They lent money in unjust ways and **made profit from your neighbors by extortion**.

> i. "The precise transgressions that are listed are less important than their cumulative effect that is the burden of Ezekiel's charge." (Vawter and Hoppe)

> ii. This terrible list describes the sins of the *leaders* of Jerusalem and Judah. If this was the conduct of the leaders, it is to be expected that the conduct of the commoners was as bad or worse. In addition, the social cost of these sins was much worse among the commoners, who had fewer resources to help lessen the effects of their sins.

> iii. **And have forgotten Me**: "But at the heart of all these outward displays of wickedness was the main cause: 'You have forgotten me, declares the Sovereign Lord.' When one forgets God and leaves his ways, the path into every kind of abomination opens before him." (Alexander)

3. (13-16) God beats His fists against Jerusalem's corrupt leaders.

"Behold, therefore, I beat My fists at the dishonest profit which you have made, and at the bloodshed which has been in your midst. Can your heart endure, or can your hands remain strong, in the days when I shall deal with you? I, the LORD, have spoken, and will do *it*. I will scatter you among the nations, disperse you throughout the countries, and remove your filthiness completely from you. You shall defile yourself in the sight of the nations; then you shall know that I *am* the LORD.""

a. **Therefore, I beat My fists at the dishonest profit which you have made**: In the strongest terms possible, God said He would oppose these corrupt leaders of Jerusalem. He hated their **dishonest profit** and the **bloodshed** that came from their dishonest courts.

b. **Can your heart endure, or can your hands remain strong, in the days when I shall deal with you?** After shocking them with His beating **fists**, God then spoke to the princes of Israel with clear logic. They should soberly consider if they could stand against the great judgment God promised to bring (**I, the LORD, have spoken, and will do it**).

> i. **In the days when I shall deal with you**: "The Babylonians are but men, but I the Lord your God, whom you have provoked, am with them; they are my weapons of war and I strike by them, and thou shalt never be able to subsist under it. Flatter not thyself, the Lord will do it as he hath spoken it." (Poole)

c. **I will scatter you among the nations**: As in previous passages, God promised to not only conquer Judah and Jerusalem but to **scatter** them in exile. When they sat defiled **in the sight of the nations**, then they would understand Yahweh and how He revealed Himself in judgment.

i. **Then you shall know that I am the LORD**: "Thou shalt know me by my punishments, whom thou wouldst not know by my benefits." (Trapp)

B. The furnace of judgment.

1. (17-19) Gathering into God's furnace of judgment.

The word of the LORD came to me, saying, "Son of man, the house of Israel has become dross to Me; they *are* all bronze, tin, iron, and lead, in the midst of a furnace; they have become dross from silver. Therefore thus says the Lord GOD: 'Because you have all become dross, therefore behold, I will gather you into the midst of Jerusalem.

a. **The house of Israel has become dross to Me**: Once Israel was regarded as God's precious possession. Through their sin and rebellion, God now regarded them as **dross** – the worthless impurities that come from the refining of metal.

i. "The prophet's point is that far from being regarded as Yahweh's special treasure, the house of Israel is nothing more than slag, the waste produced in the extraction of silver from ore." (Block)

b. **I will gather you into the midst of Jerusalem**: When Nebuchadnezzar's army came into Judah, many in the surrounding cities and towns fled into Jerusalem, thinking it would be the safest place. They were really being gathered there for judgment.

2. (20-22) The judgment of melting in God's furnace.

As *men* gather silver, bronze, iron, lead, and tin into the midst of a furnace, to blow fire on it, to melt *it;* so I will gather *you* in My anger and in My fury, and I will leave *you there* and melt you. Yes, I will gather you and blow on you with the fire of My wrath, and you shall be melted in its midst. As silver is melted in the midst of a furnace, so shall you be melted in its midst; then you shall know that I, the LORD, have poured out My fury on you.'"

a. **So I will gather you in My anger and in My fury, and I will leave you there and melt you**: God promised to make Jerusalem like a great furnace. Not only would the armies of Babylon burn the city, but it would be a melting of Israel itself. God would **blow on** the refining fire to make it hotter.

i. "Ye must be put in the furnace, and subjected to the most intense fire, till your impurities are consumed away. No *ordinary* means will avail any thing; the most *violent* must be resorted to." (Clarke)

ii. "In such an hour the methods of patience and mercy are useless; it is only by the fiery furnace that the dross can be destroyed, and the corrupted silver be recovered." (Morgan)

b. **As silver is melted in the midst of a furnace, so shall you be melted in its midst**: This severe announcement of judgment had within it a glimmer of hope. When the refiner melts the **silver** (or other precious metal) it isn't to destroy it, but to purify it. As terrible as the burning of Jerusalem and exile would be, it would purify Israel even through the judgment.

i. That metal is refined *at all* shows that there is the abiding presence of the refiner supervising the process, and that there is something precious that may be yet reclaimed and drawn out.

ii. "The OT references to fire or furnace (e.g., Deuteronomy 4:20) are symbols for excruciating pain and suffering. These also evoke the notion of fire as a purifying agent and of 'smelting' as a way to spiritual regeneration (cf. Isaiah 1:25)." (Vawter and Hoppe)

C. The sins of prophets, priests, princes, and people.

1. (23-25) The sin of Israel's prophets.

And the word of the LORD came to me, saying, "Son of man, say to her: 'You *are* a land that is not cleansed or rained on in the day of indignation.' The conspiracy of her prophets in her midst is like a roaring lion tearing the prey; they have devoured people; they have taken treasure and precious things; they have made many widows in her midst.

a. **You are a land that is not cleansed**: Israel's corruption was so widespread and deep that it was as if the entire **land** was dirty and defiled. One of God's great purposes in the coming judgment and exile was to spiritually and morally cleanse the land.

i. **Or rained on**: "According to Old Testament promise rain was one of the blessings in the material realm which attended a walk of obedience. It was withheld to turn their hearts back to the Lord." (Feinberg)

b. **The conspiracy of her prophets in her midst is like a roaring lion tearing the prey**: The false prophets of Israel worked together in something like a **conspiracy**, taking from and devouring the people instead of serving them. The sin of prophets who fundamentally take instead of give is still a great problem among those who promote themselves as prophets.

i. "The indictment of the royal house in Israel is based on their practice of exacting wealth from their people, almost certainly to the accompaniment of violence and murder." (Taylor)

ii. **The conspiracy**: "A contrivance, or framing among themselves a design, to speak all alike flattering, smooth words, and give out promises of peace and safety, when there was no peace." (Poole)

iii. **They have made many widows in her midst**: "The prophets were directly responsible for the multiplication of widows in the land because their husbands went out to battle against the will of the Lord after being deceived by the prophets of lies and flatteries." (Feinberg)

2. (26) The sin of Israel's priests.

Her priests have violated My law and profaned My holy things; they have not distinguished between the holy and unholy, nor have they made known *the difference* between the unclean and the clean; and they have hidden their eyes from My Sabbaths, so that I am profaned among them.

a. **Her priests have violated My law and profaned My holy things**: The **priests** of Israel did not take their appointed role to serve and teach the people. Their own lives were corrupt (**violated My law**) and they performed their priestly service in disgraceful ways (**profaned My holy things**).

i. "Even they whose lips should preserve knowledge, have not instructed the people: they *have violated my law*, not only in their private conduct, but in their careless and corrupt manner of serving in my temple." (Clarke)

b. **They have not distinguished between the holy and the unholy**: This was one of the important jobs of the priests of Israel. They were to help the people understand how the law of God applied to their daily lives by declaring things and conduct as **holy** or **unholy**, as **unclean** or **clean**. But they did not know the difference themselves and so could not instruct the people they were intended to serve.

i. "The charge to Aaron in Leviticus 10:11 to teach the Israelites all the statutes spoken by Yahweh through Moses is the most explicit. But Moses places this burden on the tribe of Levi in his final blessing: 'They shall teach your ordinances to Jacob, and your law to Israel' (Deuteronomy 33:10)." (Block)

c. **They have hidden their eyes from My Sabbaths**: The priests failed in their basic responsibilities to honor God's law themselves, and to teach the people to do so. Therefore God was **profaned among them**, when He should have been glorified among His own priests.

3. (27-29) The sins of Israel's princes, prophets, and people.

Her princes in her midst *are* like wolves tearing the prey, to shed blood, to destroy people, and to get dishonest gain. Her prophets plastered them with untempered *mortar*, seeing false visions, and divining lies for them, saying, 'Thus says the Lord GOD,' when the LORD had not spoken. The people of the land have used oppressions, committed robbery, and mistreated the poor and needy; and they wrongfully oppress the stranger.

a. **Her princes in her midst are like wolves tearing the prey**: When the leaders should have been like faithful shepherds, they were instead like vicious wolves. Their interest was not in the glory of God and the welfare of His people; it was **to shed blood, to destroy people, and to get dishonest gain**.

b. **Her prophets plastered them with untempered mortar**: The **false visions** and divined **lies** of the false prophets were spoken in the name of the LORD. Yet those supposed revelations were like a wall made with mortar that had no cement. It looked nice from the outside, but had no strength and could never stand on the critical day.

i. "The prophets had whitewashed their own impure motives and led the people astray by falsely claiming to have God's authority." (Alexander)

ii. "They were meticulous about claiming the same divine authority as the true prophets, even using the same sacred formula 'Thus saith the Lord,' but the Lord had no relation to their claims or messages." (Feinberg)

c. **The people of the land have used oppressions**: The princes of Israel corruptly mistreated and abused others (Ezekiel 22:6-12). It was no surprise that the **people of the land** imitated the behavior of their leaders, preying upon each other and those who were weaker with violence and oppression.

i. "The people of the land were the prominent land-owning citizens (Ezekiel 12:19), often officers in the army, and they fell right in line with the princes and priests." (Wiersbe)

4. (30-31) The vain search for a man to stand in the gap.

So I sought for a man among them who would make a wall, and stand in the gap before Me on behalf of the land, that I should not destroy it; but I found no one. Therefore I have poured out My indignation on them; I have consumed them with the fire of My wrath; and I have recompensed their deeds on their own heads," says the Lord GOD.

a. **So I sought for a man among them who would make a wall**: The image of the **wall** connects back with the false and weak wall of the false prophets just a few verses before this (Ezekiel 22:28). The false prophets built with *untempered mortar*; God looked for a man to bring strength, stability, and security to Israel.

> i. *God looks for such men.* The problem isn't that God doesn't want such people or has not called them. If there is a problem, it is because God seeks and finds none. He **found no one** with the character or wisdom or real relationship with God to build such strength, stability, and security among His people.

> ii. "Presumably Jeremiah was an exception to Ezekiel's general condemnation, but he had no kingly status and few listened to his words. Any nation which lacks godly leadership, as Israel did at that time, must surely be on the way out." (Taylor)

> iii. "Jeremiah himself had scoured the city, looking for a godly man (Jeremiah 5:1–6), but his quest was a failure." (Wiersbe)

b. **And stand in the gap before Me on behalf of the land**: The man God sought was not only a builder, but just as importantly was a man of prayer. Like Abraham (Genesis 20:7) and Moses (Exodus 32:9-14) and David (2 Samuel 24:15-18), God looked for one who would, through prayer, **stand in the gap** between a holy God and His disobedient, rebellious, profane people. This man **in the gap** would fight for and hopefully rescue God's people in prayer.

c. **But I found no one**: Here is the tragedy. God hoped for one who would lead and pray to avert the judgment, but there was none. There were godly people to be sure (such as Jeremiah), but none to fill this role at that time.

> i. "He then concluded by describing the utter hopelessness of the case. There was no man to stand in the gap, therefore the fire of wrath must proceed on its way." (Morgan)

> ii. Fortunately, *God did find a Man to stand in the gap.* This is a powerful description of Jesus and His work for His people. He is the wall of strength, stability, and security for God's people. He is the one who ever lives to pray for His people (Hebrews 7:25). God **found no one** in Ezekiel's day, but in Jesus Christ has provided this ultimate wall-builder and Man in the gap.

d. **Therefore I have poured out My indignation on them**: Because of the great sin and corruption of the princes, prophets, priests, and people; because there was no one to lead or pray **in the gap**, the judgment God promised was sure to come. It could not be turned back.

i. "Thus, the reprobation of Israel was vindicated, not only on account of its pollution, but in order to its ultimate restoration, for there was no force in her which could lead her back to the God from Whom she had departed." (Morgan)

ii. **I have...I have...I have**: "With the entire nation so given over to every displeasing act, and no one to intervene for them, judgment alone remained for them. So sure was this visitation that Ezekiel thrice expressed it as having already occurred." (Feinberg)

Ezekiel 23 – Oholah and Oholibah

A. The sins and judgment of Oholah (Samaria and the kingdom of Israel).

1. (1-4) Two symbolic sisters, Oholah and Oholibah.

The word of the LORD came again to me, saying:
"Son of man, there were two women,
The daughters of one mother.
They committed harlotry in Egypt,
They committed harlotry in their youth;
Their breasts were there embraced,
Their virgin bosom was there pressed.
Their names: Oholah the elder and Oholibah her sister;
They were Mine,
And they bore sons and daughters.
As for their names,
Samaria is Oholah, and Jerusalem is Oholibah.

    a. **There were two women, the daughters of one mother**: Ezekiel 23 presents two symbolic sisters, representing the kingdoms of Israel and Judah. This story of the two sisters is not a perfect illustration of the relationship between Yahweh and Israel; the Lord did not have two wives. But the story of the two sisters is a powerful description of how Judah followed in the sinful steps of Israel.

        i. There are many parallels between Ezekiel 16 and 23; both chapters confront Israel as an unfaithful wife to Yahweh. Yet there are also important differences. "The mood set by the opening lines contrasts sharply with Ezekiel 16:2–5, which had intentionally evoked great sympathy for the foundling in the minds of the hearers. The women introduced here are not to be pitied." (Block)

    b. **They committed harlotry in Egypt**: Ezekiel states a theme that will be repeated several times in this chapter. This is that *Israel was unfaithful to*

Yahweh from the very start, worshipping idols in Egypt. Symbolically, their worship of Egyptian idols was like giving their bodies to those gods (**their breasts were there embraced, their virgin bosom was there pressed**).

> i. While they were still in Egypt, God told Israel to forsake the Egyptian idols – and they did not (Ezekiel 20:5-8).

> ii. As previously noted in Ezekiel 20, there were several evidences of Israel's idolatry in Egypt:

> • The worship of the golden calf at Mount Sinai (Exodus 32:1-6).

> • The idolatry practiced in Egypt: *Put away the gods which your fathers served on the other side of the River and in Egypt. Serve the LORD!* (Joshua 24:14)

> • The choice of golden calves as objects of worship by Jeroboam (1 Kings 12:26-33).

c. **Their names: Oholah the elder and Oholibah her sister**: God gave these two symbolic sisters names. The elder was **Oholah**, which means *Her Own Tabernacle*, with the sense that she rejected God's temple and the service that attended it. The younger was **Oholibah**, which means *My Tabernacle is In Her*, with the sense that she was home to God's temple and its service.

> i. "Both incorporate the word *ohel*, 'tent,' Oholah suggesting 'her own tent,' and Oholibah 'my tent in her.'" (Block)

d. **They were Mine, and they bore sons and daughters**: These sisters belonged to Yahweh by the principles of election, redemption, and marriage covenant. They were "mothers" to many **sons and daughters**.

e. **Samaria is Oholah, and Jerusalem is Oholibah**: To avoid any misunderstanding, God stated it clearly. **Oholah** represented **Samaria**, the capital of the northern kingdom of Israel, and **Oholibah** represented **Jerusalem**, the capital of the southern kingdom of Judah.

> i. "The city of Samaria is called the elder because she preceded Judah in both defection and in captivity." (Feinberg)

2. (5-8) The story of Oholah, the elder sister.

"Oholah played the harlot even though she was Mine;
And she lusted for her lovers, the neighboring Assyrians,
Who were **clothed in purple,**
Captains and rulers,
All of them desirable young men,
Horsemen riding on horses.
Thus she committed her harlotry with them,

All of them choice men of Assyria;
And with all for whom she lusted,
With all their idols, she defiled herself.
She has never given up her harlotry *brought* **from Egypt,**
For in her youth they had lain with her,
Pressed her virgin bosom,
And poured out their immorality upon her.

a. **Oholah played the harlot**: Once again God used the idea of harlotry to symbolically express the idolatry of Israel. In particular, the northern kingdom of Israel gave herself to idolatry from the start (1 Kings 12:26-33).

b. **She lusted for her lovers, the neighboring Assyrians**: Before the Assyrians conquered Israel she followed her attraction to their gods, their power, their protection, and their ways. This repeats an irony expressed before in Ezekiel; when God's people reject Him and embrace the idols of the nations, He allows those nations to conquer His people.

i. We imagine the small kingdom of Israel looking with awe and envy upon the mighty empire of the Assyrians. Though they feared them, they also noticed their power and wealth, their influence and fame. Israel thought that by worshipping Assyria's gods, adopting their morals, and embracing their customs they also could gain some of that power and fame. They foolishly rejected their covenant God and embraced idolatry.

ii. "Samaria had no true faith in the living God, so she looked to the Assyrians to help her. The picture here is that of a prostitute seeking a lover to care for her and the language is quite graphic. Samaria not only welcomed Assyria's soldiers but also Assyria's idols, and the religion of the Northern Kingdom became a strange mixture of Mosaic Law and Assyrian idolatry (2 Kings 17:6–15)." (Wiersbe)

iii. "The Black Obelisk of Shalmaneser III illustrates Jehu prostrating himself before the Assyrian king (the date would be about 840 BC, at the beginning of Jehu's reign) and offering gifts, possibly with a view to buying support against Hazael of Damascus." (Taylor)

iv. "2 Kings also describes the paying of tribute by Israel to Assyria in the reigns of Menahem (c. 745–738 BC) and Hoshea (c. 732–724 BC); see 2 Kings 15:19ff.; 17:3." (Taylor)

c. **Who were clothed in purple, captains and rulers, all of them desirable young men**: There was nothing holy or even spiritual in Israel's attraction to the Assyrians and their gods. It was purely on a fleshly, materialistic basis.

i. "Horses and horsemen were mentioned because the Assyrians, as the Egyptians, used cavalry prominently." (Feinberg)

ii. "The Hebrew had never found it easy to resist the temptations and allurements of more sophisticated civilizations than his own, whether they were the fleshpots of Egypt or the dashing gallants of the Assyrian cavalry regiments." (Taylor)

iii. "Her total lack of restraint is emphasized by the threefold repetition of *kol*, 'all,' in Ezekiel 23:7." (Block)

d. **She has never given up her harlotry brought from Egypt**: The idea from Ezekiel 23:3 is repeated specifically for Oholah, the kingdom of Israel. She started out by giving herself to Egyptian idols and continued giving herself to the idols of the nations.

3. (9-10) Judgment upon Oholah.

"Therefore I have delivered her
Into the hand of her lovers,
Into the hand of the Assyrians,
For whom she lusted.
They uncovered her nakedness,
Took away her sons and daughters,
And slew her with the sword;
She became a byword among women,
For they had executed judgment on her.

a. **Therefore I have delivered her into the hand of her lovers**: Because Israel gave herself to foreign gods and morals, God allowed them to be conquered by those foreign nations. It was God's way of saying, "You reject Me and lust after these; now you must be conquered by them and live under them."

i. "Throughout the Scriptures it may be discerned that divine retribution operates in such a way that the source of sinful pleasure becomes the source of punishment. Samaria's lovers became her destroyers." (Feinberg)

b. **They uncovered her nakedness, took away her sons and daughters, and slew her with the sword**: When the Assyrians conquered Israel in 722 b.c. they did this. Assyria humiliated Samaria and Israel, took her **sons and daughters** captive, and killed many **with the sword**. This was well known to Ezekiel's listeners and readers, having happened more than 100 years before. Samaria and Israel had become **a byword** for well-deserved judgment.

B. The sins and judgment of Oholibah (Jerusalem and the kingdom of Judah).

1. (11-13) Oholibah (Jerusalem) imitates the sins of Oholah (Samaria).

"Now although her sister Oholibah saw *this,* **she became more corrupt in her lust than she, and in her harlotry more corrupt than her sister's harlotry.**

"She lusted for the neighboring Assyrians,
Captains and rulers,
Clothed most gorgeously,
Horsemen riding on horses,
All of them desirable young men.
Then I saw that she was defiled;
Both *took* **the same way.**

a. **Although her sister Oholibah saw this**: There was at least one significant way that the sins of Jerusalem were much worse than the sins of Samaria. Jerusalem had the example of Samaria to take warning from and to learn by. They did not. They **saw** Samaria's sin *and the judgment that came upon her*, yet followed in the same ways.

i. The focus is upon Jerusalem's idolatry with the gods of Assyria and Babylon and Egypt, but that idolatry was often connected with real or hoped-for political alliances. They lusted after the gods of these great empires *and* their protection.

b. **She became more corrupt in her lust than she**: In the end, Jerusalem was more depraved than Samaria. Ezekiel will develop that theme starting at verse 16.

c. **She lusted for the neighboring Assyrians**: Even as the northern kingdom of Israel lusted after Assyrian power, wealth, fame, and influence, so did the southern kingdom of Judah. Jerusalem **lusted for** the material and fleshy emblems of that mighty empire the same way as Samaria (Ezekiel 23:5-6). They were both **defiled**; **both took the same way**.

i. King Ahaz of Judah gave gifts and made an alliance with the Assyrians (2 Kings 16:7-10). The prophet Isaiah spoke against this lust for the neighboring Assyrians (Isaiah 7:3-17).

ii. "He went up to Damascus to meet Tiglath–pileser, king of Assyria, and he saw there an altar he thought was the prettiest altar he'd ever seen. So he sent Urijah the priest to get the pattern of it in order to make one just like it (2 Kings 16:10–18)." (McGee)

2. (14-16) Oholibah (Jerusalem) *surpasses* the sins of Oholah (Samaria).

But she increased her harlotry;
She looked at men portrayed on the wall,
Images of Chaldeans portrayed in vermilion,
Girded with belts around their waists,
Flowing turbans on their heads,
All of them looking like captains,
In the manner of the Babylonians of Chaldea,
The land of their nativity.
As soon as her eyes saw them,
She lusted for them
And sent messengers to them in Chaldea.

a. **She increased her harlotry**: It was bad enough that Jerusalem imitated the sins of Samaria; it was far worse that she **increased** her rejection and rebellion.

b. **She looked at men portrayed on the wall**: The media of that day gave the people of Jerusalem the enticements to go after the morals, customs, and idols of the Babylonians. The **images of Chaldeans** seduced them to follow their sins, even as they had previously done with the Assyrians (Ezekiel 23:12-13).

i. "Bas-reliefs were common decorations in Mesopotamian palaces and temples. Perhaps this statement was an allusion to some Judean envoys who were sent to Babylonia and saw the witness of her great power demonstrated on such walls." (Alexander)

ii. "Rich clothes are oft but fine covers of the foulest shame. If every silken suit did cover a sanctified soul, it would be brave." (Trapp)

c. **The land of their nativity**: This probably refers to the fact that according to Genesis 11:27-32, Abraham, the father of all the Jewish peoples, originally came from Chaldea (the region of Babylon). God called Abraham *out of* Babylonian idolatry; now his descendants returned to it.

d. **Sent messengers to them in Chaldea**: Long before the Babylonians conquered Judah, they *sent* receptive messengers to her. They *pursued* the Babylonians, and eventually the same Babylonians conquered the people of Judah.

i. "There is no direct reference elsewhere to overtures to Babylon, but foreign alliances produced foreign standards of life and religion (e.g. 2 Kings 16.10 f.; Isaiah 2.6; Jeremiah 7.18)." (Wright)

ii. **As soon as her eyes saw them**: "Here began the mischief.... many have died of the wound in the eye." (Trapp)

3. (17-21) The disgusting idolatry and immorality of Jerusalem.

"Then the Babylonians came to her, into the bed of love,
And they defiled her with their immorality;
So she was defiled by them, and alienated herself from them.
She revealed her harlotry and uncovered her nakedness.
Then I alienated Myself from her,
As I had alienated Myself from her sister.
"Yet she multiplied her harlotry
In calling to remembrance the days of her youth,
When she had played the harlot in the land of Egypt.
For she lusted for her paramours,
Whose flesh *is like* the flesh of donkeys,
And whose issue *is like* the issue of horses.
Thus you called to remembrance the lewdness of your youth,
When the Egyptians pressed your bosom
Because of your youthful breasts.

a. **The Babylonians came to her, into the bed of love**: Ezekiel continues with the familiar theme using gross sexual promiscuity to illustrate Jerusalem's idolatry. This was accurate as a spiritual illustration but was also connected to literal reality because many of the rites connected with the Babylonian idols were sexual in nature, especially sex with prostitutes representing the idol. Truly, **they defiled her with their immorality**.

i. "If a Christian choose worldly prosperity, or his own reputation, or any earthly object apart from God, it is through this that he will suffer. The things that he has loved will be raised up against him, just as Israel, that had dallied with Babylon, was carried into captivity to Babylon." (Meyer)

b. **I alienated Myself from her**: A faithful husband would distance himself from a promiscuous wife; even so, God **alienated** Himself from Jerusalem as He had previously done in regard to Samaria (**her sister**).

c. **She multiplied her harlotry**: God disciplined Jerusalem by distancing Himself from her. Her response was to return to her roots, to the idolatry of her **youth, when she had played the harlot in the land of Egypt.**

d. **She lusted for her paramours**: Jerusalem ran after her idol-lovers in the most gross and disgusting ways. Ezekiel said she lusted after their potency, represented by large sexual organs (**whose flesh is like the flesh of donkeys**) and large emissions of semen (**whose issue is like the issue of horses**). The idea was that potent, mighty people could protect Judah. Ezekiel used this shocking language to jolt his complacent and jaded listeners and readers.

i. "She lusted after the Egyptians who had a reputation for sexual potency, i.e., military power. She relived the 'lewdness' of her youth in Egypt, i.e., she revived Egyptian cults and customs long forgotten." (Smith)

ii. Ezekiel's language here is admittedly coarse, and apparently more so in the original Hebrew. Yet the modern preacher should note that he did not use the coarse terms to entertain his listeners and readers, nor to make himself seem contemporary and cool. The coarse language was used to shock, and to reflect God's own disgust with Jerusalem's sins. Furthermore, this coarse language stands out for its rarity, and its use should never be used to justify any kind of regular use in the pulpit or even everyday conversation.

iii. "In Egyptian hieroglyphics the horse represents a lustful person. Asses and horses are proverbially lustful (Jeremiah 2:24; 5:8; 13:27). Thus was described the return to her first degradation." (Feinberg)

iv. "The original is still more rough than the translation; and surely there is no need of a *comment* to explain imagery that is but too generally understood." (Clarke)

4. (22-27) Judgment on Oholibah.

"Therefore, Oholibah, thus says the Lord God:
'Behold, I will stir up your lovers against you,
From whom you have alienated yourself,
And I will bring them against you from every side:
The Babylonians,
All the Chaldeans,
Pekod, Shoa, Koa,
All the Assyrians with them,
All of them desirable young men,
Governors and rulers,
Captains and men of renown,
All of them riding on horses.
And they shall come against you
With chariots, wagons, and war-horses,
With a horde of people.
They shall array against you
Buckler, shield, and helmet all around.
'I will delegate judgment to them,
And they shall judge you according to their judgments.

I will set My jealousy against you,
And they shall deal furiously with you;
They shall remove your nose and your ears,
And your remnant shall fall by the sword;
They shall take your sons and your daughters,
And your remnant shall be devoured by fire.
They shall also strip you of your clothes
And take away your beautiful jewelry.
'Thus I will make you cease your lewdness and your harlotry
Brought from the land of Egypt,
So that you will not lift your eyes to them,
Nor remember Egypt anymore.'

a. **Therefore, Oholibah, thus says the Lord GOD**: God's judgment against Jerusalem was all the more deserved because they were **Oholibah** – meaning, *My Tabernacle is In Her*. The great blessing of the temple and priesthood in their midst made their accountability much greater.

b. **I will stir up your lovers against you**: Jerusalem and Judah would find that those they gave themselves to would not treat them well. They would come **against** Oholibah **from every side**, with officers and leaders from many nations. They would come with powerful weapons (**buckler, shield, and helmet**) and instruments of war (**chariots, wagons, war-horses**).

i. "Those who had previously come to her to make love, now come from all sides to make war." (Block)

ii. "Pekod is a tribe east of the Tigris (Jeremiah 50.21), and Shoa and Koa have been identified with other tribes in the same area." (Wright)

iii. "The intention seems merely to accumulate familiar inimical names to designate the 'host' (Ezekiel 23:46) that will be summoned up to execute the Lord's vengeance." (Vawter and Hoppe)

c. **They shall deal furiously with you**: The armies assembled against Jerusalem would not treat her gently or like lovers. They would kill and maim her, strip her of her beautiful **clothes** and **jewelry**.

i. **They shall deal furiously**: Block quoted an excerpt from the annals of Assyrian king Ashurnasirpal II (883–859): "I felled with the sword 800 of their combat troops, I burnt 3,000 captives from them. I did not leave one of them alive as a hostage. I captured alive Hulaya their city ruler. I made a pile of their corpses. I burnt their adolescent boys (and) girls. I flayed Hulaya their city ruler (and) draped his skin over the wall of the city Damdammusa. I razed, destroyed, (and) burnt the city.... Moving on from the city Kinabu I approached the city

Tela. The city was well fortified.... I felled 3,000 of their fighting men with the sword. I carried off prisoners, possessions, oxen (and) cattle from them. I burnt many captives from them. I captured many troops alive: I cut off of some their arms (and) hands; I cut off of others their noses, ears (and) extremities. I gouged out the eyes of many troops. I made one pile of the living (and) one of heads. I hung their heads on trees around the city. I burnt their adolescent boys (and) girls. I razed, destroyed, burnt (and) consumed the city."

d. **Thus I will make you cease your lewdness and your harlotry**: The severe judgment of the conquest of Jerusalem and the exile would be like strong medicine to the Jewish people. They would no longer run after their idol lovers as they did before. The last remnants of the sins **brought from the land of Egypt** would be purged and forgotten.

5. (28-31) Jerusalem delivered over to those who hate her.

"For thus says the Lord GOD: 'Surely I will deliver you into the hand of those you hate, into the hand *of those* from whom you alienated yourself. They will deal hatefully with you, take away all you have worked for, and leave you naked and bare. The nakedness of your harlotry shall be uncovered, both your lewdness and your harlotry. I will do these *things* to you because you have gone as a harlot after the Gentiles, because you have become defiled by their idols. You have walked in the way of your sister; therefore I will put her cup in your hand.'

a. **Surely I will deliver you into the hand of those you hate.... they will deal hatefully with you**: Though Jerusalem went after the nations and their gods as if they were her lovers, there was never *real* love between them – they were never lovers that truly desired the best for each other. Jerusalem wanted what she could *get* from the nations and their idols, and they wanted the same from her. Jerusalem would suffer the terrible fate of being given over to the ones she hated.

i. "There is a profound psychological truth in verses 28 and 29 (cf. 17). Sex without love only too often ends in frustration and hatred (2 Samuel 13.15)." (Wright)

b. **The nakedness of your harlotry shall be uncovered**: Instead of love and glory, Jerusalem and Judah would find shame. They had not been benefited or blessed by their idolatry; they had **become defiled by their idols**.

i. "Using the image of punishing a prostitute, he described how the invaders would strip the nation, expose her lewdness, and mutilate her body. It isn't a very beautiful picture." (Wiersbe)

c. **You have walked in the way of your sister; therefore I will put her cup in your hand**: More than 100 years before, Samaria and Israel fell against the invading Assyrians. Now Jerusalem and Judah would suffer the same fate, drinking from the same **cup** of judgment.

i. Being *Oholibah* (having the temple) instead of *Oholah* (rejecting the temple) made no difference if it did not result in faithfulness to Yahweh and His covenant. If the people of Jerusalem thought having the temple would save them from judgment, that God would never allow the Babylonians to destroy the temple, they needed to learn from the story of Oholah and Oholibah.

C. Drinking the cup of judgment, receiving the penalty of adultery.

1. (32-35) Drinking Samaria's cup.

"Thus says the Lord GOD:

'You shall drink of your sister's cup,
The deep and wide one;
You shall be laughed to scorn
And held in derision;
It contains much.
You will be filled with drunkenness and sorrow,
The cup of horror and desolation,
The cup of your sister Samaria.
You shall drink and drain it,
You shall break its shards,
And tear at your own breasts;
For I have spoken,'
Says the Lord GOD.
"Therefore thus says the Lord GOD:
'Because you have forgotten Me and cast Me behind your back,
Therefore you shall bear the *penalty*
***Of* your lewdness and your harlotry.'"**

a. **You shall drink of your sister's cup**: Jerusalem will not only hold Samaria's cup of judgment (Ezekiel 23:31), they will surely **drink** it. The cup of judgment is **the deep and wide one** and **it contains much**. The on-looking nations will offer no sympathy; they will offer only **scorn** and **derision**.

b. **You will be filled with drunkenness and sorrow, the cup of horror and desolation**: The cup Samaria drank was terrible, as the record of the city's last days showed (2 Kings 17:1-23). Now Jerusalem would drink the same cup of judgment; they must **drink and drain it**. In their misery, they would harm themselves (**tear at your own breasts**).

> i. "Drinking that cup would result in national 'drunkenness,' i.e., confusion, which in turn would lead to scorn and derision by other nations. That cup would produce sorrow, astonishment and desolation." (Smith)

> ii. "Judah would not only drink to the full the cup of God's wrath, but she would even gnaw the shards of the cup. Ezekiel vividly portrayed the utter despair of the outcast who would drink herself to madness, tearing at her breasts." (Feinberg)

> iii. "She who had shamelessly craved the fondling of her breast by her lovers will tear them off in her inexpressible grief." (Block)

c. **Because you have forgotten Me and cast Me behind your back**: This great penalty would come upon Jerusalem and Judah because they *forgot* God and wanted Him to *disappear*. Ignoring God and wanting to have nothing to do with Him is a great sin, and worthy of judgment.

2. (36-39) Some of the specific sins of Oholah (Samaria) and Oholibah (Jerusalem).

The Lord also said to me: "Son of man, will you judge Oholah and Oholibah? Then declare to them their abominations. For they have committed adultery, and blood is on their hands. They have committed adultery with their idols, and even sacrificed their sons whom they bore to Me, passing them through *the fire*, to devour *them*. Moreover they have done this to Me: They have defiled My sanctuary on the same day and profaned My Sabbaths. For after they had slain their children for their idols, on the same day they came into My sanctuary to profane it; and indeed thus they have done in the midst of My house.

a. **Declare to them their abominations**: God has thus far mostly spoken in a symbolic way about the sins of Samaria and Jerusalem, using the figure of sexual immorality to illustrate their idolatry. Now God will speak directly and literally about their sins.

b. **They have committed adultery, and blood is on their hands**: They were unfaithful to their marriage covenants and unfaithful to their communities, committing adultery and practicing violence under the cover of law.

c. **And even sacrificed their sons whom they bore to Me**: They **sacrificed** their children in tribute to the terrible idol Molech, burning their infants to death.

d. **They have defiled My sanctuary on the same day and profaned My Sabbaths**: They would offer their children to Molech on one of the **Sabbaths** and **on the same day** go to the temple **to profane it**.

i. "They dared to worship in the temple of God on the same day that they made their sacrifice of their children to Molech worship." (Feinberg)

ii. "Note that *both* sisters are charged with the defilement of the Jerusalem sanctuary: a reminder that the separation of Israel from Jerusalem was still remembered with bitterness." (Taylor)

3. (40-45) The comfortable harlotry of the lewd sisters.

"Furthermore you sent for men to come from afar, to whom a messenger *was* sent; and there they came. And you washed yourself for them, painted your eyes, and adorned yourself with ornaments. You sat on a stately couch, with a table prepared before it, on which you had set My incense and My oil. The sound of a carefree multitude *was* with her, and Sabeans *were* brought from the wilderness with men of the common sort, who put bracelets on their wrists and beautiful crowns on their heads. Then I said concerning *her who had grown* old in adulteries, 'Will they commit harlotry with her now, and she *with them?*' Yet they went in to her, as men go in to a woman who plays the harlot; thus they went in to Oholah and Oholibah, the lewd women. But righteous men will judge them after the manner of adulteresses, and after the manner of women who shed blood, because they *are* adulteresses, and blood *is* on their hands.

a. **Furthermore you sent for men to come from afar**: After plainly stating the sins of Samaria and Jerusalem in the previous section, Ezekiel returned to the symbol of the harlot to represent their unfaithfulness to God.

b. **You washed yourself for them, painted your eyes, and adorned yourself**: They happily and carefully prepared themselves for their unfaithfulness to Yahweh. They worshipped idols in comfortable and ornate surroundings.

i. **Painted your eyes**: "Like a decayed harlot, madest up thy defects with paint." (Poole)

c. **On which you had set My incense and My oil**: God had appointed sacred incense and oil for the service of the temple. Jerusalem was so corrupt that they took these sacred things and used them in idolatry.

i. "The irony was that she used the gifts which God had bestowed upon her to advance the cause of idolatry. She created a festive atmosphere, the sound of a multitude at ease. The harlot was not particular about who shared her table and her bed. Men of the common sort and even drunkards from the desert were all welcome." (Smith)

d. **The sound of a carefree multitude was with her**: They *loved* their idolatry. Their rebellion against God made them feel **carefree** and popular with the **multitude**. Foreigners came and rewarded them for their idolatry.

> i. "This seems to be an account of an idolatrous festival, where a riotous multitude was assembled, and fellows of the baser sort, with *bracelets* on their arms and *chaplets* on their heads, performed the religious rites." (Clarke)

e. **Then I said concerning her who had grown old in adulteries**: All the while, they became like old, tired, worn-out prostitutes. Their young years of attractiveness and allure were a distant memory and they were merely **lewd women**. Their unfaithfulness to God made them age poorly.

> i. "In Joshua 9:4–5 the verb *bala* is used of worn-out sacks, wineskins, sandals, and garments. Sarah uses the term in Genesis 18:12 to describe her own old age, specifically her having passed the age of childbearing. The prophet's usage implies that Oholibah's adulterous behavior has left her worn out." (Block)

f. **But righteous men will judge them after the manner of adulteresses**: Their illusion of glamorous prostitution could never last. Any **righteous** man would perceive they were simply unfaithful **adulteresses**, and that **blood is on their hands**.

4. (46-49) The sisters are judged as adulteresses.

"For thus says the Lord God: 'Bring up an assembly against them, give them up to trouble and plunder. The assembly shall stone them with stones and execute them with their swords; they shall slay their sons and their daughters, and burn their houses with fire. Thus I will cause lewdness to cease from the land, that all women may be taught not to practice your lewdness. They shall repay you for your lewdness, and you shall pay for your idolatrous sins. Then you shall know that I *am* the Lord God.'"

a. **Bring up an assembly against them, give them up to trouble and plunder**: In a remarkably understated way, this refers to the literal invading armies that came against Samaria and Jerusalem.

b. **The assembly shall stone them with stones and execute them**: The punishment for adultery according to the Law of Moses was execution. This penalty had already been carried out against Samaria; it would soon be carried out regarding Jerusalem.

i. **Shall stone them...and burn their houses with fire:** "The punishment will be the common penalty for all adulteresses and shedders of blood: death by stoning, to which is added destruction of their property with fire (cf. Leviticus 20:10; Deuteronomy 21:21)." (Taylor)

ii. "The similarity of this penalty with the state of siege of a city bombarded with sling-stones and incendiary missiles can scarcely have been coincidence. The shame of the guilty person's end under Mosaic law will be exactly matched by the fate of Samaria and Jerusalem." (Taylor)

c. **Thus I will cause lewdness to cease from the land:** As before stated in Ezekiel 23:27, the punishments of conquest and exile would have a cleansing effect upon Jerusalem and Judah. The particular sin of gross idolatry would never again be the same problem as it was before the exile.

d. **Then you shall know that I am the Lord GOD:** The severity of conquest and exile had a purpose greater than punishment. The ultimate purpose was to reveal God in both His holy judgments and gracious restorations.

Ezekiel 24 – The Death of the Prophet's Wife

A. The parable of the boiling cauldron.

1. (1-2) The start of the siege of Jerusalem.

Again, in the ninth year, in the tenth month, on the tenth *day* of the month, the word of the LORD came to me, saying, "Son of man, write down the name of the day, this very day—the king of Babylon started his siege against Jerusalem this very day.

> a. **In the ninth year, in the tenth month, on the tenth day of the month**: As God commanded, Ezekiel carefully recorded the day of this prophecy. This was a nation-changing and life-changing date, long remembered. To relate this to 21st century United States events, it was an iconic date like 9-11 which remembers attacks against the United States on September 11, 2001.

> > i. This exact date is also recorded in 2 Kings 25:1, Jeremiah 39:1, and Jeremiah 52:4.

> > ii. "It is also known from Zechariah 8:19 that this date became a fast for the exiles, as commemorating one of the critical days in the fall of the holy city." (Taylor)

> b. **The king of Babylon started his siege against Jerusalem**: The day was important because it was the start of what God had long promised – the final siege, conquest, and destruction of Jerusalem.

2. (3-5) Jerusalem like a cooking pot, a boiling cauldron.

And utter a parable to the rebellious house, and say to them, 'Thus says the Lord GOD:

"Put on a pot, set *it* on,
And also pour water into it.
Gather pieces *of meat* in it,
Every good piece,

The thigh and the shoulder.
Fill *it* with choice cuts;
Take the choice of the flock.
Also pile *fuel* bones under it,
Make it boil well,
And let the cuts simmer in it."

a. **Put on a pot, set it on**: We don't know if Ezekiel literally acted out this parable, or simply told the story. Either way, the meaning is the same. The picture is of a cooking **pot** or cauldron, filled with water and **pieces of meat**.

i. "The word for *cauldron* [**pot**] normally refers to any large wide-mouthed pottery utensil used for washing or cookery, though in this instance we find in verse 11 that it is made of copper." (Taylor)

ii. "Like most preachers Ezekiel uses an illustration more than once, varying the application according to the point of his message. He has used the picture of the cauldron in Ezekiel 11:3-12. Now he takes it up again. Jerusalem is the cooking pot, and its people are the meat that is to be cooked." (Wright)

iii. From the description, Jerusalem would be a remarkable feast for Nebuchadnezzar and his armies. "The cook does not appear to be fixing an ordinary dinner; rather, an extraordinarily sumptuous meal is implied by the emphasis on the quality and quantity of meat being prepared." (Block)

b. **Pile fuel bones under it**: With a fire feeding on **bones**, the command was to make the pot **boil well** so that its contents would **simmer** and cook.

i. Most commentators consider the picture to be of animal bones, but Block makes the case for it to be the chilling picture of a fire fueled by *human* bones: "Since the feminine plural form is used elsewhere in Ezekiel only of human bones, an interpretive element has already been introduced: the contents of the pot about to be destroyed are not animal bones—they are human."

3. (6-8) Woe to the bloody city of Jerusalem.

'Therefore thus says the Lord GOD:
"Woe to the bloody city,
To the pot whose scum *is* in it,
And whose scum is not gone from it!
Bring it out piece by piece,
On which no lot has fallen.
For her blood is in her midst;

She set it on top of a rock;
She did not pour it on the ground,
To cover it with dust.
That it may raise up fury and take vengeance,
I have set her blood on top of a rock,
That it may not be covered."

a. **Woe to the bloody city**: Since it was the very day that Jerusalem was surrounded by Nebuchadnezzar's siege army, there is no doubt that the **bloody city** was Jerusalem. It was a **bloody city** in at least two ways. First, it was the city where much innocent blood had been shed, often under the cover of authority (Ezekiel 21:13 and many other passages). Second, it was the city where much blood would be shed under Nebuchadnezzar's attack.

b. **To the pot whose scum is in it**: As Jerusalem boiled and cooked, its worst qualities would become evident to everyone. Most commentators believe that **scum** here is better understood as *rust*, especially in light of its reddish color.

> i. "Some translate the word as 'scum,' but 'rust' is correct. It was a symbol of the corrosion and corruption of the city and may have represented the blood of victims slain through intrigue and oppression." (Feinberg)

> ii. **Whose scum is in it**: "Filthiness, her abominations, all her lewdness, are still within her; they have not been punished, restrained, or cast out by the execution of just and good laws; but the citizens have with obstinacy, impenitence, and with impudence continued in them." (Poole)

> iii. **Bring it out piece by piece**: "Pull out the flesh indiscriminately; let no piece be *chosen* for *king* or *priest*; thus showing that all should be involved in one indiscriminate ruin." (Clarke)

> iv. "The people of Jerusalem may have thought they were choice cuts, but as far as Ezekiel is concerned they were unfit for consumption; no lot would fall on Jerusalem." (Block)

c. **Her blood is in her midst**: The death and bloodshed coming to Jerusalem would prevent proper burial. The bloody dead would not be covered with dirt and **dust**; their dead bodies would lie horrifically exposed. This was another example of God's **fury** and **vengeance** against Jerusalem and Judah.

> i. "The blood in Ezekiel 24:7 is that of murder, wrongful conviction, and human sacrifice. Blood unjustly shed cries for vengeance (Genesis 4.10; Job 16.18)." (Wright)

> ii. "According to Genesis 4:10, blood which was uncovered called for God's vindication of it (cf. Isaiah 26:21). When blood was not covered

with dust, there was a violation of the Mosaic law (Leviticus 17:13)." (Feinberg)

iii. This principle was even true of animal blood. "The Mosaic law required that whenever a game animal or bird was slain, the blood was to be poured out and covered with earth (Deuteronomy 12:16, 24; 15:23). To leave it exposed was to provoke the wrath of God, the source and guarantor of all life." (Block)

4. (9-13) Further woe to the bloody city.

'Therefore thus says the Lord GOD:
"Woe to the bloody city!
I too will make the pyre great.
Heap on the wood,
Kindle the fire;
Cook the meat well,
Mix in the spices,
And let the cuts be burned up.
"Then set the pot empty on the coals,
That it may become hot and its bronze may burn,
That its filthiness may be melted in it,
That its scum may be consumed.
She has grown weary with lies,
And her great scum has not gone from her.
Let her scum *be* in the fire!
In your filthiness *is* lewdness.
Because I have cleansed you, and you were not cleansed,
You will not be cleansed of your filthiness anymore,
Till I have caused My fury to rest upon you.

a. **Woe to the bloody city**: Jerusalem's woe did not end with the tragedies described in the previous section. There was much more to describe.

b. **I too will make the pyre great**: The fire under the cooking pot is now described as a **pyre** – a burning for the dead. The fire will be huge, and the contents of the pot will first **be burned up** – then, the pot itself will **become hot and its bronze may burn**. All of Jerusalem's impurities, her **scum**, will **be consumed** in the judgment coming upon her.

i. "Let the siege be *severe*, the carnage great, and the ruin and catastrophe complete." (Clarke)

ii. "The great opportunity had passed by. And therefore, says the Lord, the fire will be an agent of destruction with no purificatory features whatever. The fire—now the final destruction of Jerusalem by the Babylonians—will be heaped up, and the pot will be reduced to molten metal. There will be no regeneration, only total destruction." (Vawter and Hoppe)

c. **Because I have cleansed you, and you were not cleansed**: Through many generations God sent His prophets to His people. They had the institutions of the temple, the sacrifices, the feasts, and the priesthood. All of these should have been cleansing, purifying agents upon His people – yet they were not. Therefore God would not cleanse them anymore; in His fury He would judge them.

i. **Because I have cleansed you**: "One can only surmise to which historical events Ezekiel alludes. Josiah's recent attempts at reformation (2 Kings 22–23) must be in view, but Hezekiah's earlier efforts would also be included (2 Kings 18:4, 22; 2 Chronicles 31)." (Block)

ii. "Ezekiel's entire prophecy implies that God's wrath will cease and Israel will be cleansed completely when God begins to restore Israel to the land of Canaan in the end time." (Alexander)

iii. **Lewdness**: "A word that denominates the *worst kinds of impurity; adultery, incest*, &c., and the *purpose, wish, design*, and *ardent desire* to do these things. Hers were not *accidental* sins, they were *abominations by design*." (Clarke)

5. (14) The certainty of God's pronouncement.

I, the LORD, have spoken *it;*
It shall come to pass, and I will do *it;*
I will not hold back,
Nor will I spare,
Nor will I relent;
According to your ways
And according to your deeds
They will judge you,"
Says the Lord GOD.'"

a. **I, the LORD, have spoken it; it shall come to pass**: God wanted to leave no doubt that this would happen just as He had said. The terrible calamity announced for Jerusalem and Judah would surely happen.

b. **According to your ways and according to your deeds**: Under the covenant Israel made with God at Mount Sinai, they would be blessed in their obedience and cursed in their disobedience. Their wicked **ways** and **deeds** would **judge** them.

B. The death of Ezekiel's wife.

1. (15-17) God tells Ezekiel his wife will die and how he must react.

Also the word of the LORD came to me, saying, "Son of man, behold, I take away from you the desire of your eyes with one stroke; yet you shall neither mourn nor weep, nor shall your tears run down. Sigh in silence, make no mourning for the dead; bind your turban on your head, and put your sandals on your feet; do not cover *your* lips, and do not eat man's bread *of sorrow*."

a. **I take away from you the desire of your eyes with one stroke**: God brought Ezekiel a shocking message regarding his wife (touchingly referred to as **the desire of your eyes**). The message was that she would suddenly and unexpectedly die (**I take away…with one stroke**).

i. **The desire of your eyes**: "Whether it refer to the beauty of her person or no, it certainly refers to the amiableness of her disposition, and the agreeableness of her to the prophet." (Poole)

ii. "In these verses we catch a glimpse of the inner Ezekiel which rarely appears through his apparently harsh and unyielding exterior. His austerity and rigid self-discipline, his passion for truth and for the honour of God's holy name, very nearly conceal the tender heart that lies within." (Taylor)

iii. **With one stroke**: "With pestilence, palsy, or some similar sudden death. This was no small trial of the prophet's patience and obedience. Let us learn to hang loose to all outward comforts." (Trapp)

iv. Wiersbe observed that in some way or another, the wife of a Biblical prophet was connected with their mission or message.

- Abraham was a prophet (Genesis 20:7) who twice lied about his wife and got into trouble.

- Moses was a prophet and was criticized for the wife he chose (Numbers 12:1).

- Isaiah's wife was a prophetess (Isaiah 8:3). She bore him at least two sons whose names were signs to the people of Judah.

- The Prophet Jeremiah wasn't allowed to have a wife (Jeremiah 16:1–4), and this was a sign to the Jews that judgment was coming, and it was not time for marrying.

- Hosea's wife became a prostitute and he had to buy her out of the slave market (Hosea 1–3).

b. **Yet you shall neither mourn nor weep**: Ezekiel was strangely forbidden to grieve or even **weep** over the loss of **the desire of** his **eyes**. The command was strong: **nor shall your tears run down**, and no visible signs of mourning were permitted.

> i. According to Leviticus 21:1-4, God restricted the mourning of the priests. This can be seen as an extension of that principle.

> ii. "He was not forbidden to sorrow, for even our Lord wept at the grave of Lazarus. He was only prohibited from a loud manifestation of it, which was in contrast to the usual loud wailing on such occasions." (Feinberg)

> iii. "The general truth may be found in Jeremiah 16:5, where it is shown that all personal sorrow will be eclipsed in the hour of universal calamity." (Feinberg)

> iv. **Sigh in silence**: "In that we see the understanding heart of God. He knew the sorrow of His servant's soul, both personal and public, and did not rebuke it. In days when public testimony demands that we rise superior to private sorrows, it is good to know that He understands the difficulty, and does not forbid the sigh." (Morgan)

> v. "The word 'sigh' is normally used of the noisy groaning of wounded men and is a reminder of the ritual lamentations that were regularly laid on for funeral occasions." (Taylor)

2. (18-19) The death of Ezekiel's wife.

So I spoke to the people in the morning, and at evening my wife died; and the next morning I did as I was commanded. And the people said to me, "Will you not tell us what these *things signify* to us, that you behave so?"

a. **So I spoke to the people in the morning**: Presumably, Ezekiel spoke as he had many times before, reporting what God had told him to proclaim. This time the message was both strange and sad. As a prophet, he told them that his wife would die. We can only wonder what Ezekiel had told his wife the night before.

b. **At evening my wife died**: This was a great loss to Ezekiel, one that many have suffered. The title, *the desire of your eyes* (Ezekiel 24:16), points to a dear and loving relationship. Throughout the book, Ezekiel is presented to us as a man of deep feeling and emotion who often mourned and wept over the fate of Jerusalem and Judah. He certainly was deeply affected by this sudden loss of a dear companion and spouse.

c. **The next morning I did as I was commanded**: Remarkably, Ezekiel obeyed God. However overwhelming the feeling may have been to mourn and weep, Ezekiel was determined to honor God by obeying Him despite his feelings and the quite understandable circumstances.

i. "Obedience must be yielded to God even in the most difficult duties, and conjugal love must give place to our love to him." (Trapp)

ii. This strange incident teaches us many things about mourning and grief over the loss of a loved one.

- Such sudden and dear losses may happen to anyone, including great prophets and servants of God.

- This was *unusual*. We never read again in the Scriptures of such a loss of a dear one and such a commanded non-reaction. In its specifics, we should never regard this strange incident as a pattern of God's work.

- Mourning and weeping over the loss of a loved one is so natural and to be expected that Ezekiel needed an express command from God *not* to do it.

- In obedience to God and under the power of the Holy Spirit, God's people are not absolute slaves to their emotions.

d. **Will you not tell us what these things signify to us, that you behave so?** The strange event had the intended effect. The people were shocked and mystified at Ezekiel's sudden loss and strange behavior.

i. "By this time the captives were familiar enough with Ezekiel's methodology to realize that the absence of emotion at the death of his beloved wife must have some prophetic meaning. They therefore asked the prophet to explain his conduct." (Smith)

3. (20-24) God explains the sign to the people: death without the ability to mourn.

Then I answered them, "The word of the LORD came to me, saying, 'Speak to the house of Israel, "Thus says the Lord GOD: 'Behold, I will profane My sanctuary, your arrogant boast, the desire of your eyes, the delight of your soul; and your sons and daughters whom you left behind shall fall by the sword. And you shall do as I have done; you shall not cover *your* lips nor eat man's bread *of sorrow*. Your turbans shall be on your heads and your sandals on your feet; you shall neither mourn nor weep, but you shall pine away in your iniquities and mourn with one another. Thus Ezekiel is a sign to you; according to all that he has done

you shall do; and when this comes, you shall know that I *am* the Lord God.'"

a. **Then I answered them**: The tragic event and the strange reaction had a divine purpose. Under the inspiration of the Holy Spirit, Ezekiel had an answer for their legitimate question, and the answer was not fate, chance, or ignorance.

b. **Behold, I will profane My sanctuary, your arrogant boast, the desire of your eyes, the delight of your soul**: As a husband finds a proper source of joy, confidence, and security in his relationship with his wife, so Israel had an improper source of confidence and security in the temple (**your arrogant boast**). As Ezekiel's wife suddenly died, so the **sanctuary** would suddenly and soon perish.

i. Both in exile and in the land, in Ezekiel's day the people of Israel had an irrational and dangerous confidence in the mere *existence* of the temple. They thought, "This is God's house. It is dear to Him and to us. He will never allow it to be conquered." God shattered this mistaken confidence.

ii. We note how God referred to the temple that had become an idol and false source of hope for Judah:

- **Your arrogant boast**, thought to guarantee their security.
- **The desire of your eyes**, that most precious to them.
- **The delight of your soul**, that which delighted them most.

c. **Your sons and daughters whom you left behind shall fall by the sword**: The captives in Babylon had many **sons and daughters** still in Jerusalem and Judah, and many of those dear ones would die in the judgment that had now come upon the land.

d. **You shall do as I have done**: When all this tragedy comes upon their dear ones and their dear temple, the people would have to respond as Ezekiel did. Their shock would make them unable to mourn "normally," and perhaps the Babylonian culture would also hinder their expressions of grief.

i. "Ezekiel had not wept, and Israel would not weep either: because in both cases the tragedy was too deep and stunning for any expression of grief to prove adequate." (Taylor)

ii. "Yet no mourning is to take place, for this is a judgment that calls not for mutual consolation but for mutual shame and recrimination." (Vawter and Hoppe)

iii. "They would experience a grief which is beyond tears, a despondency which could not be expressed with outward acts.... The only outward expression which would be heard among them would be a quiet moan." (Smith)

e. **When this comes, you shall know that I am the Lord GOD**: The consistent purpose of God throughout the book of Ezekiel is the revelation of Himself even through tragedy and crisis. In all their unexpressed sorrow, there would be a revelation of the **Lord GOD**.

i. They should *not* have mourned the conquest of Jerusalem and the destruction of the temple because it was deserved, and it was clearly announced long ahead of time. In contrast, the death of Ezekiel's wife was neither deserved nor announced long ahead – yet he was commanded to not mourn. It was much truer that Israel should not mourn the conquest of Judah, Jerusalem, and the temple.

4. (25-27) God explains the sign to Ezekiel.

'And you, son of man—*will it* not *be* in the day when I take from them their stronghold, their joy and their glory, the desire of their eyes, and that on which they set their minds, their sons and their daughters: on that day one who escapes will come to you to let *you* hear *it* with *your* ears; on that day your mouth will be opened to him who has escaped; you shall speak and no longer be mute. Thus you will be a sign to them, and they shall know that I *am* the LORD.'"

a. **In the day when I take from them their stronghold, their joy and their glory, the desire of their eyes**: The beginning of Ezekiel 24 marked the start of Nebuchadnezzar's siege of Jerusalem. The day would soon and inevitably come when the temple (**stronghold**) and all else they held dear would be conquered and destroyed.

b. **On that day your mouth will be opened to him who has escaped; you shall speak and no longer be mute**: There was, in some sense, a restriction on the distribution of Ezekiel's message that waited for Jerusalem to finally fall. The day would soon come when that restriction would end.

i. "When some one who shall have escaped from Jerusalem, having arrived among the captives, shall inform them of the destruction of the city, the temple, the royal family, and the people at large; till then he might suppress his tears and lamentations. And we find from Ezekiel 33:21, that one did actually escape from the city, and informed the prophet and his brethren in captivity that the *city was smitten*." (Clarke)

c. **You shall speak and no longer be mute**: Ezekiel's loosened tongue will mean that he will begin to prophesy in a much more hopeful tone. The judgment had been measured out in all its strength; now God could begin to rebuild and do so with true hope. The ultimate restoration would be glorious.

> i. "His prophecies of doom will no longer need to be uttered. He will be able to act as a shepherd and a watchman to his people. He will be free to work constructively towards the building up of a new community, a new Israel." (Taylor)

> ii. "His ministry would change. He would be able to comfort and encourage them with words of hope rather than oracles of doom and stony silence. This prophet who previously had been so negative would become at that time the great encourager." (Smith)

d. **Thus you will be a sign to them, and they shall know that I am the** **LORD**: In the end, both the prophet and his God, the covenant God of Israel, would be vindicated and revealed.

> i. "That day will be marked by two significant events: Yahweh will pull the rug out from under the people by removing the ground of all their hopes, and he will vindicate his prophet by confirming his sign value for the nation." (Block)

Ezekiel 25 – Judgment on the Nations Near Judah

A. Judgment upon Ammon.

1. (1-5) Against the Ammonites.

The word of the LORD came to me, saying, "Son of man, set your face against the Ammonites, and prophesy against them. Say to the Ammonites, 'Hear the word of the Lord GOD! Thus says the Lord GOD: "Because you said, 'Aha!' against My sanctuary when it was profaned, and against the land of Israel when it was desolate, and against the house of Judah when they went into captivity, indeed, therefore, I will deliver you as a possession to the men of the East, and they shall set their encampments among you and make their dwellings among you; they shall eat your fruit, and they shall drink your milk. And I will make Rabbah a stable for camels and Ammon a resting place for flocks. Then you shall know that I *am* the LORD."

a. **Son of man, set your face against the Ammonites**: This begins a new section of the book of Ezekiel, from chapters 25 through 32. This section is concerned with the judgment of the nations surrounding Judah. God's general message is that though He had a first and proper focus on the sins of His people, He had not forgotten, and would not neglect, the judgment of the pagan nations surrounding Judah and Jerusalem.

i. In Ezekiel 24:26-27 the prophet announced a coming day when one who escaped the conquered Jerusalem would come to Babylon to tell the sad news that the siege that began (Ezekiel 24:1-2) was completed and the city was destroyed. The fulfillment of that promise is recorded in Ezekiel 33:21-22. In between, Ezekiel prophesied concerning the nations surrounding Israel.

ii. "What the nations didn't realize was that the destruction of Jerusalem wasn't just a punishment of the Jews; it was also a warning to the Gentiles." (Wiersbe)

iii. "The principle of I Peter 4:17-18 is pertinent throughout this section. If God judged His own people, in justice He must judge the nations for their sins as well." (Feinberg)

iv. "Although the Old Testament prophets addressed their messages primarily to their own people, or to a part at least of God's covenant community, it was characteristic of them to survey the other nations of the world in order to demonstrate the Lord's sovereignty over the heathen as well as over Israel. This is the pattern in Isaiah (chapters 13–23), in Jeremiah (chapters 46–51) and also in Amos (chapters 1, 2)." (Taylor)

v. "The principle which is operative in Matthew 25:31-46 is seen as applicable here also: the nations are judged on the basis of their treatment of 'my brethren.'" (Feinberg)

vi. Of the section between Ezekiel 25 and 32, "There seems to be a fascination with the number seven. There are seven nations that the prophet addresses. The seventh nation is Egypt, which has seven prophecies devoted to it. In the seventh of these, the text surveys seven nations." (Vawter and Hoppe)

vii. "It is remarkable that Ezekiel in his predictions did not mention judgment on Babylon, which was God's instrument of wrath on Israel. In this particular, contrast the extended prophecies in Isaiah, Jeremiah and elsewhere." (Feinberg)

viii. "Ezekiel, like Jeremiah, believed that Babylon was God's instrument of judgment against an unfaithful Israel. To resist Babylon was to resist the divine will. That is why Jeremiah counseled submission to Babylon and why Ezekiel did not include Babylon among the nations he condemned." (Vawter and Hoppe)

b. **Against the Ammonites**: The **Ammonites** lived in the area on the east side of the Jordan River, north of the Moabites. Their lands are included in what is today Jordan, and the capital of Jordan is named *Amman* because of this connection.

i. "In spite of its limited territory between the mountainous area of southern Gilead and the eastern desert, Ammon's importance and wealth were significant. It enjoyed unrivalled domination of the King's Highway. This important commercial artery ran the length of the Transjordanian highlands from the Gulf of Aqabah to Damascus." (Vawter and Hoppe)

c. **Because you said, "Aha!" against My sanctuary when it was profaned**: The Ammonites felt no pity or sorrow for the fall of Jerusalem and the destruction of the temple. This may be understandable in terms of political or national rivalry, but they should have mourned the desecration of the **sanctuary** of the true God, the creator of heaven and earth. They did not, and it made them liable for judgment.

d. **And against the land of Israel when it was desolate, and against the house of Judah when they went into captivity**: The sins of the Ammonites against the people of Israel went back a long time. They did not sorrow, and instead rejoiced, when Israel was conquered more than 100 years before and did the same when Judah later **went into captivity**.

i. "Ammon evidently took advantage of Babylon's victory and·grabbed whatever land and property that they could. This is implied in Ezekiel 25:3 and is confirmed by Jeremiah 49.1. Here is the temporarily strong nation taking advantage of the weaker neighbour." (Wright)

ii. "According to Ezekiel 21:18-20 Nebuchadnezzar had set out against Judah and Ammon. But there is no record of an attack on Ammon; apparently it had capitulated and turned against Judah (Ezekiel 21:28; Zephaniah 2:8-11)." (Feinberg)

e. **Therefore, I will deliver you as a possession to the men of the East**: It made them happy that Israel and Judah were conquered; soon they also would be conquered. The **men of the East** would come to **eat** their **fruit** and **drink** their **milk**, and they would occupy the cities of **Rabbah** and **Ammon**.

i. **Men of the East**: "Opinions vary as to the identity of the children of the east: some take them to be the Bedouin, the nomadic tribes beyond the Jordan (Judges 6:3); others feel they are the Ishmaelites; and yet others think they are doubtless the Babylonians." (Feinberg)

ii. "The fulfilment of this prediction is not noted in Scripture: but *Josephus* tells us, that about *five* years after the taking of Jerusalem, Nebuchadnezzar turned his arms against the *Ammonites* and *Moabites*, and afterwards against *Egypt*; and having subdued those nations, he returned to Babylon. *Josephus* Antiquities, l. x., c. ii." (Clarke)

2. (6-7) The guilt of the Ammonites.

'For thus says the Lord God: "Because you clapped *your* hands, stamped your feet, and rejoiced in heart with all your disdain for the land of Israel, indeed, therefore, I will stretch out My hand against you, and give you as plunder to the nations; I will cut you off from the peoples, and I will cause you to perish from the countries; I will destroy you, and you shall know that I *am* the Lord."

a. **Because you clapped your hands, stamped your feet, and rejoiced in heart**: The sin first mentioned in Ezekiel 25:3 is now enlarged upon. They showed great **disdain for the land of Israel** and therefore for the God of Israel.

> i. "The Ammonites were clapping their hands and stamping their feet with glee over Jerusalem's fall." (Block)

> ii. **Give you as plunder to the nations**: "For a prey, or for meat, so the word will bear. The greedy, covetous soldier shall make thy wealth his prey; the hungry enemy shall eat thee up." (Poole)

b. **I will cause you to perish from the countries**: As a nation, the Ammonites would pass into history, even though individual Ammonites would have a future through their descendants. Jeremiah 49:3 promised some kind of eventual restoration for the Ammonites.

> i. "The pronouncement of the Lord was that Ammon and Moab were not to be remembered among the nations. Both were absorbed by the Arabs." (Feinberg)

B. Judgment upon Moab, Edom, and the Philistines.

1. (8-11) Moab and Seir numbered among the Ammonites.

'Thus says the Lord GOD: "Because Moab and Seir say, 'Look! The house of Judah *is* like all the nations,' therefore, behold, I will clear the territory of Moab of cities, of the cities on its frontier, the glory of the country, Beth Jeshimoth, Baal Meon, and Kirjathaim. To the men of the East I will give it as a possession, together with the Ammonites, that the Ammonites may not be remembered among the nations. And I will execute judgments upon Moab, and they shall know that I *am* the LORD."

a. **Moab and Seir**: By ancestry, the people of Moab and Seir were cousins to Israel. The ancestor of **Moab** came from the incestuous pairing of Lot and his daughter (Genesis 19:37). **Seir** was a notable city of the Edomites, who were also cousins to Israel, being the descendants of Jacob's twin brother Esau.

> i. Moab was something of a cousin to Israel. They feared Israel as they came from Egypt towards Canaan (Numbers 22:3-4) and Balak king of Moab hired Balaam to curse Israel (Numbers 22:5-8). When Israel came into Canaan sometimes Moab attacked and ruled over them (Judges 3:12-14).

> ii. Later Ruth the Moabite was the great-grandmother of King David, and David sent his parents to Moab for their protection when Saul

hunted him (1 Samuel 22:3-4). When he was king, David fought against and defeated Moab (2 Samuel 8:2) and they became a vassal kingdom to Israel, sometimes rebelling (2 Kings 1:1, 2 Kings 3:4-5).

iii. The Edomites also lived in the lands east of the Jordan River and the Dead Sea, toward the southern mountains and deserts.

b. **Look! The house of Judah is like all the nations**: This was the mocking claim of the people of Moab and Seir. Sadly, the people of **Judah** gave them a reason to say this by acting **like all the nations**. Still, their *joy* in the decline and fall of God's people made them guilty.

i. **Judah is like all the nations**: "To the Moabites, the fall of Jerusalem proved that the Jews were just like any other people. 'If you are such a special nation,' they argued, 'why have you experienced such a humiliating defeat?'" (Wiersbe)

ii. "The Mesha Stone recounts the king of Moab's boast that his god Chemosh had vanquished Israel (ANET, pp. 320–21)." (Alexander)

iii. "The Moabite taunt is not only against her neighbor, but also a direct assault on Yahweh himself, who had granted this status to his people." (Block)

c. **To the men of the East I will give it as a possession**: The fate of Moab and Seir would be the same as that of the Ammonites. They would be conquered and occupied by **the men of the East**.

i. "Ammon was joined with Moab in the passage, and the Jewish historian Josephus records that Nebuchadnezzar came to fight against Ammon and Moab in the fifth year after the destruction of Jerusalem." (Feinberg)

ii. "It is worth noting that not long after this both Ammon and Moab were overrun by Nabatean tribesmen and ceased to have any independent existence as nations." (Taylor)

2. (12-14) More on Edom's guilt and judgment.

'Thus says the Lord God: "Because of what Edom did against the house of Judah by taking vengeance, and has greatly offended by avenging itself on them," therefore thus says the Lord God: "I will also stretch out My hand against Edom, cut off man and beast from it, and make it desolate from Teman; Dedan shall fall by the sword. I will lay My vengeance on Edom by the hand of My people Israel, that they may do in Edom according to My anger and according to My fury; and they shall know My vengeance," says the Lord God.

a. **Because of what Edom did against the house of Judah by taking vengeance**: When Nebuchadnezzar came against Judah, it seems that the Edomites not only approved, they helped, and did so with **vengeance**. Mentions of this are found in the short book of Obadiah, in Psalm 137:7, and Lamentations 4:21.

> i. "The phrase 'taking vengeance' is literally 'revenging with revenge'; it was to be an unrelieved, unabated revenge." (Feinberg)

> ii. "The Edomites were the most inveterate enemies of the Jews from the very earliest times, and ever did all that they could to annoy them." (Clarke)

> iii. "What the Edomites actually did we cannot say for sure, but they certainly sided with Nebuchadrezzar against Jerusalem and after the exile there is evidence of Edomite occupation of southern Judah." (Taylor)

> iv. "He may use others as His rod, just as at certain epochs of their national history He used Moab or Edom. But when the work of refining is done, He will lay the instruments aside, and even punish, if there has been an excess of malice." (Meyer)

b. **I will also stretch out My hand against Edom**: God brought judgment to Judah first, but would **also** bring it to Edom and their cities (**Teman** and **Dedan**). The judgment would be great, affecting both **man and beast**. In some way, God would also use His **people Israel** in the process of judgment.

> i. **And beast**: "Either their cattle should be driven away by the plundering soldier, or devoured by the mighty numerous army of Nebuchadnezzar, or wasted with murrain [plague, disease], or all should concur to unstock their pastures." (Poole)

> ii. "While differing slightly in form, the expression 'from Teman and Dedan' is reminiscent of the common phrase 'from Dan to Beer-sheba,' which delimited the extremities of Israel." (Block)

> iii. "The basis of Edom's economy was its control of that portion of the King's Highway that passed through its territory. Once the Babylonians ended this control in the 6th century, the Edomites were in serious economic trouble. By the 4th century the Nabateans replaced the Edomites, and the latter moved into southern Judah." (Vawter and Hoppe)

> iv. "Edom also was overrun, and, eventually, in 109 B.C. it was finally subjugated by the Jewish leader, John Hyrcanus." (Wright)

v. "This was fulfilled by the Maccabees, who not only defeated them and brought them under complete subjection, but obliged them to receive circumcision, *Joseph.* Antiquities l. xiii., c. 17; 1 Maccabees 5:65; 2 Maccabees 10:16." (Clarke)

3. (15-17) Judgment against the Philistines.

'Thus says the Lord GOD: "Because the Philistines dealt vengefully and took vengeance with a spiteful heart, to destroy because of the old hatred," therefore thus says the Lord GOD: "I will stretch out My hand against the Philistines, and I will cut off the Cherethites and destroy the remnant of the seacoast. I will execute great vengeance on them with furious rebukes; and they shall know that I *am* the LORD, when I lay My vengeance upon them."'"

a. **Because the Philistines dealt vengefully and took vengeance with a spiteful heart**: The Philistines were ancient enemies of Israel, populating many of the seacoast cities in the land of Canaan. There was **old hatred** between the Philistines and Israel, and when the Babylonians invaded they put as much misery on Judah as they could.

i. "These inhabitants of the southern part of the coastal strip of Palestine were also inveterate foes of Israel during her early history, but they had no ties of kinship and were originally Mediterranean 'sea peoples' from the Aegean." (Taylor)

ii. Feinberg on the long history of conflict between the Philistines and Israel: "They constantly harassed and oppressed Israel until subjugated by David, who broke their power after their repeated attacks in the reign of Saul (1 Samuel 13:17; 14). They were conquered by Jehoshaphat (2 Chronicles 17:11); subjugated by Uzziah (2 Chronicles 26:6); strong under Jehoram (2 Chronicles 21:16); powerful under Ahaz (2 Chronicles 28:18); subdued by Hezekiah (2 Kings 18:8; Isaiah 14:31); and confederate against Jerusalem (Psalm 83:7)."

b. **I will stretch out My hand against the Philistines**: God promised to bring His judgment against them, against the related **Cherethites**, those who lived along **the seacoast**.

i. "Nebuchadnezzar punished them because they had assisted the Tyrians during the time he was besieging their city." (Clarke)

ii. "When Ezekiel announced that the Lord would cut off the Cherethites, he was playing on words, as 'cut off the cutters off.'" (Feinberg)

iii. "David had a group of Cherethite mercenaries as well as others from Gath (2 Samuel 15.18)." (Wright)

c. **And they shall know that I am the** LORD: As with the Ammonites (Ezekiel 25:7), the Moabites and Edomites (Ezekiel 25:12), God would reveal Himself to these pagan, disobedient nations through His judgment. God's purpose was always greater than just judgment or vengeance; there was, and always is, the strong purpose of His self-revelation.

i. **With furious rebukes:** "In fierceness of anger, and without pity. They, as other stupid nations, will not see till they feel, and then they shall confess it is the hand of an angry, but just, and mighty God." (Poole)

ii. "Philistia has to face the most severe form of judgment since the prophet does not mention any human agent of punishment. God will pass judgment on the Philistines directly." (Vawter and Hoppe)

iii. "It is solemn to consider that all four nations of this chapter showed vindictive jealousy and hatred toward Israel. The nations of earth refused to learn that God meant every word in the Abrahamic covenant of Genesis 12:1-3, 7. No nation under heaven could touch Israel for ill without bringing down upon them the wrath of almighty God." (Feinberg)

iv. "Here is the one purpose of Jehovah in His dealings with all nations. Those who fail to find Him in the light of His revelation of Himself by law or in the natural order, he brings to know Him through judgment." (Morgan)

Ezekiel 26 – Greedy Tyre is No More

A. Certain judgment against Tyre.

1. (1-2) Announcing the fall of Tyre.

And it came to pass in the eleventh year, on the first *day* of the month, *that* the word of the LORD came to me, saying, "Son of man, because Tyre has said against Jerusalem, 'Aha! She is broken who *was* the gateway of the peoples; now she is turned over to me; I shall be filled; she is laid waste.'

a. **It came to pass in the eleventh year, on the first day of the month**: The last time marker given was at Ezekiel 24:1, telling of how the siege of Jerusalem began *in the ninth year, in the tenth month, on the tenth day of the month*. Though Ezekiel does not give us the name of *which* month this **word of the LORD came** to him, most think that Ezekiel received the prophecy regarding **Tyre** a little more than 14 months later.

i. Most commentators believe these prophecies regarding Tyre were given shortly after the fall of Jerusalem because they focus on Tyre's joy at the fall of Zion. Some believe that instead they were written in the "prophetic perfect," speaking of future events with such certainty that the idea is that they have already happened.

b. **Tyre**: This was the great and ancient city of the Phoenicians on the Mediterranean coast north of Israel (in modern-day Lebanon). **Tyre** and her sister city Sidon (about 20 miles or 32 kilometers north of Tyre) were important seaports for the whole region.

i. "Tyre was an ancient city of the Phoenicians, appearing for the first time in the Bible in Joshua 19:29.... The city was actually composed of two parts, one on the mainland and the other on a rocky island about a half mile from the coast." (Feinberg)

ii. "As a commercial centre, Tyre was famous for her glassware and for her dyed materials, using the purple dye made from the local *murex* shell-fish." (Taylor)

iii. "Tyre, to the world of her age, was what Venice was in the Middle Ages, and London to-day. She was strong in the sea; the carrying trade of the world was in her hands. Carthage, which was able to conflict with Rome, was her daughter; and the coasts of Cornwall were visited by her merchant vessels. In the days of Ezekiel she was a proud and populous city." (Meyer)

c. **Because Tyre has said against Jerusalem**: God promised judgment against the city-kingdom of Tyre because she said she would benefit from Jerusalem's fall. Now that Jerusalem was **broken**, Tyre said: "**she is turned over to me; I shall be filled; she is laid waste**."

i. This strong opposition was not always the policy of Tyre towards Jerusalem. Hiram, the King of Tyre, was a true friend of King David (2 Samuel 5:11) and helped David and later Solomon in supplies and expertise in building the temple (1 Kings 5:1-12; 1 Chronicles 14:1; 2 Chronicles 2:3 and 2:11).

ii. Though Tyre and Israel were friendly in the reigns of David and Solomon, they drifted apart later. Tyrians sold Jews as slaves *to* the Greeks and Edomites (cf. Joel 3:4-8; Amos 1:9-10)." (Feinberg)

iii. "Earlier Tyre had treacherously broken a pact (Amos 1:9), and she is selected as an example of proud self-sufficiency by Isaiah (Isaiah 23) as well as by Ezekiel." (Wright)

d. **She is turned over to me; I shall be filled; she is laid waste**: Tyre was happy at the fall of Jerusalem because it was good for her trading business. In some way the kingdom of Judah was a competitor or hindrance to the economy of Tyre. Blind with greed, Tyre had no spiritual sense or values, only material and economic values. If destroying God's city, temple, and people were good for business, then it made Tyre happy.

i. "Jerusalem's fall enhanced Tyre's control over commerce in the eastern Mediterranean. That is precisely how Tyre reacted to the Babylonian devastation of Jerusalem. This callous venality prompted Ezekiel's words of judgment." (Vawter and Hoppe)

ii. Proverbs 17:5 says, *He who is glad at calamity will not go unpunished.* This was true of Tyre.

iii. "God is against any nation whose life has become so materialized by commercial prosperity that she can rejoice over the calamities of other nations, because such calamities increase her opportunities of barter and amassing of wealth….Any nation to-day which gauges her attitude towards other nations by what their rise or fall may contribute to her wealth has God against her." (Morgan)

2. (3-6) The destruction to come to Tyre.

"Therefore thus says the Lord GOD: 'Behold, I *am* against you, O Tyre, and will cause many nations to come up against you, as the sea causes its waves to come up. And they shall destroy the walls of Tyre and break down her towers; I will also scrape her dust from her, and make her like the top of a rock. It shall be *a place for* spreading nets in the midst of the sea, for I have spoken,' says the Lord GOD; 'it shall become plunder for the nations. Also her daughter *villages* which *are* in the fields shall be slain by the sword. Then they shall know that I am the LORD.'

a. **Behold, I am against you, O Tyre**: God said He was **against** Tyre because of her wicked and opportunistic attitude toward Jerusalem and Judah. She hoped to benefit from the misfortune and judgment of God's people. There were, no doubt, many other sins that made Tyre guilty, yet in faithfulness to His covenant to Abraham (Genesis 12:1-3), God would judge Tyre based on how they treated His covenant people, the Jews.

i. When God is **against you**, none can help. "Neither can thine Apollo help or deliver thee out of my hands; no, though thou chain that idol and nail him to a post, that thou mayest be sure of him; for so these Tyrians did when Alexander besieged their city and took it." (Trapp)

b. **Will cause many nations to come against you, as the sea causes its waves to come up**: Tyre was famous for its remarkably secure defenses, especially because when under attack they could retreat to a seemingly unconquerable portion of the city that was an island. Nevertheless, God promised that one day **many nations** would come against them as unstoppable as the **waves** of the sea.

i. God was faithful to bring **many nations** against Tyre in successive waves of conquest and destruction:

• Nebuchadnezzar laid siege to Tyre for 13 years and eventually conquered them (about 586-573 BC).

• The Persians conquered and brought Tyre to submission around 525 BC.

• Alexander the Great destroyed the city in just the manner described in 332 BC.

• Antiochus III conquered and subjugated Tyre.

• Rome conquered and subjugated Tyre.

- The Saracens in the 14th century AD finally obliterated the city of Tyre.

c. **They shall destroy the walls of Tyre and break down her towers**: Despite her strongly defended position, God promised that Tyre would indeed be destroyed. Throughout history, **many nations** would come and continually crash against her like the **waves** of the sea. The destruction would be so complete that the city would be bare **like the top of a rock**, and **a place for spreading nets in the midst of the sea**.

    i. **The top of a rock**: The name **Tyre** means, "rock." When God said He would make her a bare outcropping of rock, it was a play upon her name.

    ii. "The magnificent structures of the commercial capital of the Mediterranean will be replaced by fishermen's nets, spread out on the bare rock to dry, in the midst of the sea." (Block)

d. **Also her daughter villages which are in the fields**: The many villages and small cities allied with Tyre would also be destroyed. Her colony cities scattered around the broader world would be crippled. Judgment would be complete.

    i. "The colonies of Phoenicia were in Cyprus, Rhodes, Malta, Spain, Sicily, Sardinia, the Balearic Islands and Africa, with all looking to Tyre as their headquarters, and sending annual gifts to the Tyrian Heracles." (Feinberg)

3. (7-11) The destruction to come from Nebuchadnezzar's army.

"For thus says the Lord GOD: 'Behold, I will bring against Tyre from the north Nebuchadnezzar king of Babylon, king of kings, with horses, with chariots, and with horsemen, and an army with many people. He will slay with the sword your daughter *villages* in the fields; he will heap up a siege mound against you, build a wall against you, and raise a defense against you. He will direct his battering rams against your walls, and with his axes he will break down your towers. Because of the abundance of his horses, their dust will cover you; your walls will shake at the noise of the horsemen, the wagons, and the chariots, when he enters your gates, as men enter a city that has been breached. With the hooves of his horses he will trample all your streets; he will slay your people by the sword, and your strong pillars will fall to the ground.

a. **I bring against Tyre from the north Nebuchadnezzar king of Babylon**: God promised that the same king who destroyed Jerusalem would also attack and subdue Tyre. Nebuchadnezzar would bring much death and destruction, complete with **battering rams** and **axes** to break down towers.

i. Throughout the book of Ezekiel many references have been made to the king of Babylon, but Ezekiel 26:7 is the first mention of **Nebuchadnezzar** by name. Here, Ezekiel actually used a slightly different form of his name (*Nebuchadrezzar*), often used in Babylonian writings.

ii. "This spelling of his name was thought to be more correct than Nebuchadnezzar, being closer to the Babylonian *Nabukudurri-usur*, but both forms are found in the Hebrew Bible and Nebuchadnezzar may have been the common western Aramaic form." (Taylor)

iii. "The strategy described here reflects thorough knowledge of military tactics, containing all the elements normally associated with siege warfare." (Block)

b. **Because of the abundance of his horses, their dust will cover you**: The army of Nebuchadnezzar would be so massive that their horses would kick up a cloud of **dust** big enough to cover the city. The whole city would **shake at the noise of the horsemen, the wagons, and the chariots** of Babylon.

c. **He will slay your people by the sword**: Nebuchadnezzar laid siege against the mainland portion of Tyre for 13 years and conquered that part of the city, subjugating all of Tyre under his rule.

i. "Nebuchadnezzar now turned his attention to Tyre, which held out on its island for thirteen years. It is now known from inscriptions that Nebuchadnezzar eventually forced its submission and put a puppet king on the throne. Ezekiel. 29.18 records that he did not obtain enough spoil from the city to pay for all the efforts he had made." (Wright)

ii. **Your strong pillars will fall to the ground**: "The pillars spoken of were actually obelisks, and were probably those mentioned by the historian Herodotus as erected in the temple of Heracles at Tyre. One was of gold and the other of emerald, which shone brilliantly at night, and were dedicated to Melkarth, god of Tyre (cf. 1 Kings 7:15). These impressive pillars would be demolished by the invader." (Feinberg)

4. (12-14) The destruction to come from succeeding waves of invaders.

They will plunder your riches and pillage your merchandise; they will break down your walls and destroy your pleasant houses; they will lay your stones, your timber, and your soil in the midst of the water. I will put an end to the sound of your songs, and the sound of your harps shall be heard no more. I will make you like the top of a rock; you shall be *a*

place for spreading nets, and you shall never be rebuilt, for I the LORD
have spoken,' says the Lord GOD.

a. **They will plunder your riches**: There is a subtle but significant change
from Ezekiel 26:7-11 to 26:12-14. In verses 7-11 the destruction is
described as the effect of a *he* – that is, Nebuchadnezzar. Starting at verse
12, the destruction comes at the hands of **they** – that is, the succeeding
waves of many nations of invaders and conquerors mentioned in Ezekiel
26:3-6.

> i. "Commentators have long noticed the change of pronoun from the
> 'he' of the previous verses to the 'they' of verse 12. It is rightly understood
> that Ezekiel was carrying the picture beyond Nebuchadnezzar to other
> invaders as well who would complete what he began." (Feinberg)

b. **They will break down your walls and destroy your pleasant houses**:
In the centuries after Nebuchadnezzar's conquest of Tyre, many other
nations came against her like the waves of the sea prophesied in Ezekiel
26:3-6. One of the most notable was Alexander the Great in 332 BC, who
brought great destruction.

c. **They will lay your stones, your timber, and your soil in the midst of
the water**: When Alexander the Great came against Tyre, most of the people
retreated to the island portion of the city which even Nebuchadnezzar could
not conquer. In a remarkable feat of engineering and vision, Alexander's
armies took the rubble of the mainland city and built a causeway, a solid
road built up through the water out to the island part of the city and
conquered it – *just as Ezekiel prophesied.*

> i. "Certainly Alexander the Great literally threw Tyre's 'stones, timber
> and rubble into the sea' when he built a one-half mile causeway out to
> the island fortress to conquer the city." (Alexander)

> ii. "The American archaeologist Edward Robinson saw forty or fifty
> marble columns beneath the water along the shores of Tyre." (Feinberg)

d. **I will make you like the top of a rock; you shall be a place for spreading
nets**: Once again the doom and destruction of Tyre is announced, even as
in Ezekiel 26:4-5. Eventually, the final wave of destruction came against
Tyre from the Saracens in the fourteenth century AD. They destroyed the
city so thoroughly that its remains have only been found with great time
and difficulty. It truly became **a place for spreading nets**.

> i. It is worth noting that in mercy, God delayed this final destruction of
> Tyre for many centuries, even until the 14th century. In New Testament
> times, "The Lord Jesus did bring his preaching and healing ministry
> to this heathen city (Matt 15:21; Mark 7:24–31; Luke 6:17). Her

responsibility and judgment would be less than that of the Galileans who rejected Christ's constant ministry to them (Matt 11:21–22; Luke 10:13–14)." (Alexander)

ii. The Apostle Paul also visited Tyre and met with believers there (Acts 21:3-4). Adam Clarke quoted Calmet, who wrote that many faithful martyrs came from Tyre in its Christian period.

iii. There is a modern city of Tyre, but it isn't really built on the same spot as the ancient city – and has never come close to reaching the grandeur and importance of ancient Tyre.

B. Down to the Pit.

1. (15-18) The nations lament over Tyre.

"Thus says the Lord GOD **to Tyre: 'Will the coastlands not shake at the sound of your fall, when the wounded cry, when slaughter is made in the midst of you? Then all the princes of the sea will come down from their thrones, lay aside their robes, and take off their embroidered garments; they will clothe themselves with trembling; they will sit on the ground, tremble** *every* **moment, and be astonished at you. And they will take up a lamentation for you, and say to you:**

"How you have perished,
O one inhabited by seafaring men,
O renowned city,
Who was strong at sea,
She and her inhabitants,
Who caused their terror *to be* **on all her inhabitants!**
Now the coastlands tremble on the day of your fall;
Yes, the coastlands by the sea are troubled at your departure.'"

a. **Will the coastlands not shake at the sound of your fall**: The fall of the great city of Tyre would be a horror and a warning to the other cities on the Mediterranean coast.

b. **They will sit on the ground, tremble every moment, and be astonished at you**: The **princes** of those other cities on the Mediterranean coast would humble themselves in great fear that the same destruction would come upon them.

i. **Come down from their thrones**: "The Hebrew word can refer to any chair of an official (1 Samuel 4:13), not exclusively to the royal throne, although it is used mainly in that connection." (Feinberg)

c. **How you have perished**: The lamentation of the princes of the seacoast cities will mourn the loss of such a great, **renowned**, **strong** city. Tyre's fall would make them **troubled**, knowing that similar judgment could come upon them.

> i. "In Ezekiel 26:17-18 we have a brief lamentation over the fall of the city. Keep in mind that in ancient days, the prophets sometimes used funeral lamentations in a satirical manner to poke fun at the enemies of God." (Wiersbe)

> ii. **Who was strong at sea**: "The strength of Tyre was so great, that Alexander despaired of being able to reduce it unless he could *fill up that arm of the sea that ran between it and the main land.* And this work cost his army *seven months* of labour." (Clarke)

2. (19-21) Tyre brought down to the pit.

"For thus says the Lord GOD: 'When I make you a desolate city, like cities that are not inhabited, when I bring the deep upon you, and great waters cover you, then I will bring you down with those who descend into the Pit, to the people of old, and I will make you dwell in the lowest part of the earth, in places desolate from antiquity, with those who go down to the Pit, so that you may never be inhabited; and I shall establish glory in the land of the living. I will make you a terror, and you *shall be no more;* though you are sought for, you will never be found again,' says the Lord GOD."

> a. **I will bring you down with those who descend into the Pit**: God promised to not only bring **the deep upon you, and great waters** to **cover you**, but to take them deeper still, down to **the Pit** of God's eternal judgment.

> > i. **Pit**: "Refers primarily to a cistern in which rainwater is trapped and stored, but it was also applied to empty cisterns used as dungeons (Exodus 12:29; Jeremiah 37:16; 38:6–13), or convenient places in which to dump corpses (Jeremiah 41:7–9)." (Block)

> > ii. **Pit**: "The Hebrew word *bor* means 'a well, a pit, a cistern,' but it also refers to the pit of death (Psalms 28:1 and 88:4-6) and sometimes is an equivalent of *sheol,* the realm of departed spirits." (Wiersbe)

> b. **I will make you dwell in the lowest part of the earth**: This wasn't speaking of geography, such as the Dead Sea region (1400 feet or 430 meters below sea level). This speaks of the realm of the dead, where the lost are judged. These are **places desolate from antiquity**.

> > i. **The lowest part of the earth**: "Another description of the grave, from the situation, and from the solitudes or desolation of it. In brief, when Tyre, as a dead man, shall be buried, forgotten and perish utterly, and my hand hath done it, then it shall be known my hand hath avenged

and punished all her insolence, inhumanity, and covetousness that she discovered when she rejoiced at Jerusalem's fall." (Poole)

ii. "Other ancient Near Easterners recognized the realm of the dead to be ruled by the god of the netherworld, the 'King of Terrors,' as far as Ezekiel and all orthodox Yahwists are concerned, Yahweh exercises full control over life and death. His sovereignty knows no bounds (Ps. 139:8). He opens and closes the doors of Sheol and he consigns his enemies to it." (Block)

c. **I shall establish glory in the land of the living**: The judgment and fall of cities such as Tyre do not defeat God's plan; it advances it. His agenda remains the same, to **establish glory in the land of the living**.

i. **Land of the living**: "Represents the sphere in which humans live, in contrast to the netherworld, the realm of the dead, and the heavens, the domain of God." (Block)

ii. "The point is that Tyre would disappear from the land of the living—from the stage of history—and never be found again." (Smith)

d. **I will make you a terror, and you shall be no more**: The judgment God would bring upon Tyre would bring fear and **terror** into the heart and mind of all who heard it. When Tyre had served this final purpose in God's plan, then they would **be no more**. Their destruction would be so complete that archaeologists would do their work with difficulty: **though you are sought for, you will never be found again**.

i. "Tyre would never again exist and play an important role in history as she had in the past. Though some might look for her, she would not be found." (Alexander)

ii. **Though you are sought for, you will never be found again**: What a contrast to this are the words of Jeremiah 50:20: "'In those days the iniquity of Israel shall be sought for, and there shall be none; and the sins of Judah, and they shall not be found.' Refuse the love of God, and you are doomed; you will leave no enduring record. Trust in Him, and your sins will be blotted out as if they had never been." (Meyer)

iii. **Never be found again**: "Unlike the surrounding nature religions, in which one of the deities (Baal in Canaan, Tammuz in Babylon) was thought to die each autumn and be banished to the netherworld, where he remained until his annual resurrection in the spring, when Yahweh banishes someone to Sheol and closes the door to the Pit, it is sealed. No one consigned to Sheol ever returns." (Block)

Ezekiel 27 – The Shipwreck of Tyre

"Ezekiel's description is considered a classic on the nature, scope and variety of the commerce of the ancient world, together with an invaluable geographic list of the chief cities concerned." (Charles Feinberg)

A. The glorious ship of Tyre.

1. (1-3a) A lamentation for Tyre.

The word of the LORD came again to me, saying, "Now, son of man, take up a lamentation for Tyre, and say to Tyre, 'You who are situated at the entrance of the sea, merchant of the peoples on many coastlands, thus says the Lord GOD:

a. **Take up a lamentation for Tyre**: This continues a series of songs and prophesies of judgment against ancient Tyre, making up Ezekiel 26, 27, and 28.

> i. "The words 'merchant' and 'merchandise' are used twenty-one times in this chapter, because Tyre was a mercantile city." (Wiersbe)

b. **You who are situated at the entrance of the sea**: As noted in Ezekiel 26:1-2, Tyre was a famous commercial center of the Phoenicians, north of Israel.

> i. **You who are situated**: "Tyre is portrayed as the ruler of the seas, occupying the entrances of the seas. In this context the verb *yasab*, which normally means 'to sit, dwell,' speaks of occupying with authority, that is, ruling." (Block)

2. (3b-11) The kingdom of Tyre represented as a beautiful ship.

**"O Tyre, you have said,
'I *am* perfect in beauty.'
Your borders *are* in the midst of the seas.
Your builders have perfected your beauty.
They made all *your* planks of fir trees from Senir;**

They took a cedar from Lebanon to make you a mast.
Of oaks from Bashan they made your oars;
The company of Ashurites have inlaid your planks
With ivory from the coasts of Cyprus.
Fine embroidered linen from Egypt was what you spread for your sail;
Blue and purple from the coasts of Elishah was what covered you.
"Inhabitants of Sidon and Arvad were your oarsmen;
Your wise men, O Tyre, were in you;
They became your pilots.
Elders of Gebal and its wise men
Were in you to caulk your seams;
All the ships of the sea
And their oarsmen were in you
To market your merchandise.
"Those from Persia, Lydia, and Libya
Were in your army as men of war;
They hung shield and helmet in you;
They gave splendor to you.
Men of Arvad with your army *were* on your walls *all* around,
And the men of Gammad were in your towers;
They hung their shields on your walls *all* around;
They made your beauty perfect.

a. **I am perfect in beauty**: Prosperous and glistening on the shores of the Mediterranean Sea, Tyre was a proud city. They saw themselves as a city without limits (**your borders are in the midst of the seas**) and full of beauty (**your builders have perfected your beauty**).

i. "Three dimensions of her magnificence are highlighted: her superior construction (vv. 4b–6), her impressive decoration (v. 7), and her first-class personnel (vv. 8–11). Each facet of the description reflects a remarkable geographical and nautical awareness on the part of the prophet." (Block)

b. **Your planks...a mast.... your oars**: Tyre was pictured as a beautiful ship, made of the finest and most expensive woods from all around the world and with a sail made of **fine embroidered linen from Egypt**.

i. **They took a cedar from Lebanon to make you a mast**: "Attaining a height of 290 ft. or more, cedars provided appropriate raw material for the mast." (Block)

ii. **From the coasts of Elishah**: "Elishah is thought by some to be Enkomi on the east coast of Cyprus (also Genesis 10.4)." (Wright)

iii. **Spread for your sail**: Her **sail** was like a flag. "Fundamentally, *nes* denotes a standard or flag raised on a hill around which marshaled troops would rally. Accordingly, this sail served as a symbol of Tyrian self-assurance and pride. Wherever the ship traveled observers would recognize her and marvel at her beauty." (Block)

c. **Inhabitants of Sidon and Arvad were your oarsmen**: Not only was the "ship" of Tyre strong and beautiful, but it had the best crew imaginable. The **wise men** and **elders** watched over the ship, and they had the best soldiers on board (**those from Persia, Lydia, and Libya were in your army**).

i. "Sidon, the island city of Arvad, Zemer, and Gebal (known by the Greeks as Biblos), are all Phoenician coastal cities." (Wright)

ii. **Oarsmen**: "Large numbers of oarsmen were required to operate the merchant ships of the Mediterranean. According to Sennacherib's reliefs, Phoenician boats were biremes, having one row of oarsmen visible on the lower deck, and a second invisible row who plied the water from holes in the ship's hull." (Block)

iii. "A large Phoenician ship would have as many as 50 oarsmen in a crew of 200." (Wiersbe)

iv. According to Block, Arvad is modern Ruad, Gebal (also known as Byblos) is modern Jubeil, and Put is modern Libya.

v. **To caulk your seams**: "Those who repaired their vessels; *paying*, as it is termed, pitched hemp into the seams, to prevent the water from oozing through." (Clarke)

vi. **The men of Gammad**: "The valorous men (literally, *gammadim*) were perhaps from northern Syria. Certain translations render the word as a common noun – 'watchmen' or 'warriors' or 'valorous men.'" (Feinberg)

d. **They made your beauty perfect**: The combination of it all was overwhelming. The city-kingdom of Tyre was like a mighty, beautiful, well-run ship.

i. The description of such a magnificent ship made the shipwreck described in Ezekiel 27:26 all the more of a disaster. "Fitly here compared to a goodly ship, and her desolation to a dismal shipwreck." (Trapp)

3. (12-24) Tyre's trade with many nations and cities.

"Tarshish *was* your merchant because of your many luxury goods. They gave you silver, iron, tin, and lead for your goods. Javan, Tubal, and Meshech *were* your traders. They bartered human lives and vessels

of bronze for your merchandise. Those from the house of Togarmah traded for your wares with horses, steeds, and mules. The men of Dedan *were* your traders; many isles *were* the market of your hand. They brought you ivory tusks and ebony as payment. Syria *was* your merchant because of the abundance of goods you made. They gave you for your wares emeralds, purple, embroidery, fine linen, corals, and rubies. Judah and the land of Israel *were* your traders. They traded for your merchandise wheat of Minnith, millet, honey, oil, and balm. Damascus *was* your merchant because of the abundance of goods you made, because of your many luxury items, with the wine of Helbon and with white wool. Dan and Javan paid for your wares, traversing back and forth. Wrought iron, cassia, and cane were among your merchandise. Dedan *was* your merchant in saddlecloths for riding. Arabia and all the princes of Kedar *were* your regular merchants. They traded with you in lambs, rams, and goats. The merchants of Sheba and Raamah *were* your merchants. They traded for your wares the choicest spices, all kinds of precious stones, and gold. Haran, Canneh, Eden, the merchants of Sheba, Assyria, *and* Chilmad *were* your merchants. These *were* your merchants in choice items—in purple clothes, in embroidered garments, in chests of multicolored apparel, in sturdy woven cords, which were in your marketplace.

a. **Tarshish was your merchant**: The distant city of **Tarshish** (likely in southern Spain and also Jonah's intended destination, Jonah 1:3) was a trading partner with Tyre. Tyre sold them **luxury goods** and bought **silver, iron, tin, and lead** from them.

i. The long list of goods traded and transported by sea on the ships of Tyre is a remarkable insight into the trade and commerce of the ancient world. A few of note are:

- **Judah and the land of Israel**: "The Jews traded with the Tyrians in *wheat, stacte, balsam, honey, oil,* and *resin.*" (Clarke)

- **The choicest spices**: "All aromatic wares. Pliny reports of cinnamon that in his time a pound of it was worth a thousand denarii, that is, 150 crowns of our money. Galen writeth that it was hard to be found, except in the storehouses of great princes." (Trapp)

- "That Damascus traded in *qidda*, a costly perfume native to east Asia, reflects how well established the trade routes between the Levant and the Far East were in ancient times." (Block)

- "Eden represents an abbreviated form of Beth-eden, Assyrian *Bit* Adini, an Aramean state situated west of the Balikh and incorporated into the Assyrian empire by Shalmaneser III in 856." (Block)

- Adam Clarke rightly noted, "The *places* and the *imports* are as regularly entered here as they could have been in a European custom-house."

b. **Javan, Tubal, and Meshech were your traders**: The list of trading partners for Tyre was long – at least 20 mentioned in these verses. Though small in territory it was mighty in commerce and in many ways the trade of the world came through Tyre.

i. The long list of trading partners gives a sense that everyone in the world that traded by sea dealt with Tyre. Through the centuries commentators have disagreed on the exact location of many of these places. A few of note are:

- "Javan is the name for the Greek Ionians, and Tubal and Meshech are probably peoples to the south of the Black Sea." (Wright)

- "*Tubal* and *Meshech* were tribes in Asia Minor which are known both from cuneiform inscriptions and from the Histories of Herodotus, where they appear together as Moschoi and Tibarenoi. They were engaged in a flourishing slave trade with Tyre." (Taylor)

- "The Togarmah that traded horses, war-horses and mules was probably Armenia, for the Armenians were a people in the Taurus country noted for horses and mules according to the historians Xenophon, Strabo and Herodotus (cf. Genesis 10:3; Ezekiel 38:6)." (Feinberg)

c. **They bartered human lives**: Among the long list of goods bought and sold was this tragic entry – human slaves. Though a kind of slavery existed in ancient Israel, it had nothing to do with the practices of man-stealing and human trading that marked the institution of slavery in many other places. This treatment of human beings like property and mere tools for economic profit was contrary to God's law and the dignity of all humanity created in His image.

i. It seems that Tyre was especially guilty and cold-blooded in this practice. Long before Ezekiel's time, Amos rebuked Tyre for their traffic in slaves as a violation of the *covenant of brotherhood* (Amos 1:9-10).

ii. "That is, they trafficked in *slaves*. The bodies and souls of men were bought and sold in those days, as in our degenerate age." (Clarke)

d. **Which were in your marketplace**: The impressive list of peoples, places, trading, and merchandise shows what an economic powerhouse Tyre was. The absence of any mention of God shows that they cared only for business, with no regard to God their creator and redeemer.

i. "When these various places are located on a map of the ancient Near East, it can be seen that Tyre traded with almost every region: from Tarshish (Spain) to northeast Anatolia (Tubal, Beth Togarmah) on an east-west axis (through the Aegean), and from Arabia through Syria and Palestine on a north-south axis. Each area brought the products of its land to trade with Tyre." (Alexander)

ii. "What an array of merchandise, what a variety of wares, what a range of places, and all of it for self and pride! God was in none of it." (Feinberg)

B. The shipwreck of glorious Tyre.

1. (25-28) The sinking of the ship of Tyre.

"The ships of Tarshish were carriers of your merchandise.
You were filled and very glorious in the midst of the seas.
Your oarsmen brought you into many waters,
But the east wind broke you in the midst of the seas.
"Your riches, wares, and merchandise,
Your mariners and pilots,
Your caulkers and merchandisers,
All your men of war who *are* **in you,**
And the entire company which *is* **in your midst,**
Will fall into the midst of the seas on the day of your ruin.
The common-land will shake at the sound of the cry of your pilots.

a. **You were filled and very glorious in the midst of the seas**: The scene of a full, **glorious** ship in the **midst of the seas** was an appropriate picture of the city-kingdom of Tyre. They were happy and successful, sailed by their **oarsmen** into **many waters** (the cities and kingdoms mentioned in Ezekiel 27:12-24).

b. **But the east wind broke you in the midst of the seas**: Even the best and strongest of ships is vulnerable to the power of the **wind** and the **seas**. Everything was fine for Tyre *until it wasn't*. All her material prosperity could not help when **the east wind broke** her.

i. According to Psalm 48:7, *God* is the one who breaks ships with an east wind. God here is not specifically mentioned, but He is the ultimate cause of this judgment on Tyre.

ii. "The Bible and history make one cause in their revelation of the peril of material prosperity. There is nothing more calculated to destroy a people. And yet how slow man is to learn the lesson." (Morgan)

c. **The entire company which is in your midst, will fall into the midst of the seas**: When Tyre eventually sank, everyone and everything would go down with the ship. The day of ruin for Tyre would ruin all those who proudly boasted of her glory, wealth, and strength and the **cry** of the **pilots** would be heard as the ship sank.

i. **The cry of your pilots**: "When the ship was dashed against the rocks by the violence of the winds and the waves, and all hope of life was taken away, then a universal cry was set up by all on board. I have heard this cry, and nothing more dismal can be imagined, when the ship by a violent tempest is driving among *rocks* on a lee shore. Then 'All lost! Cut away the boat!' is more dreadful than the cry of *fire* at midnight." (Clarke)

ii. Adam Clarke wrote as one who had experienced the horror of shipwreck: "But what must they have felt who were on board? Reader, wert thou ever *shipwrecked*? Wert thou ever in a *hurricane* on a *lee rocky shore*, where the helm had lost its power, and the sails were rendered useless? Dost thou remember that apparently last moment, when the ship drove up to the tremendous rocks, riding on the back of a mountainous surge? Then what was the universal cry? Hast thou ever heard any thing so terrific? so appalling? so death and judgment-like? No. It is impossible. These are the circumstances, this is the cry, that the prophet describes; disorder, confusion, dismay, and ruin. And this is a scene which the present writer has witnessed, himself a part of the wretched, when all hope of life was taken away, the yawning gulf opened, and nothing presented itself to support body or soul but that GOD who gave to both their being, and ultimately rescued him and his forlorn companions from one of the worst of deaths, by heaving the ship from the rocks by the agency of a tremendous receding wave. My soul hath these things still in remembrance, and therefore is humbled within me."

2. (29-36) The world mourns over the sinking of the ship, Tyre.

"All who handle the oar,
The mariners,
All the pilots of the sea

Will come down from their ships *and* stand on the shore.
They will make their voice heard because of you;
They will cry bitterly and cast dust on their heads;
They will roll about in ashes;
They will shave themselves completely bald because of you,
Gird themselves with sackcloth,
And weep for you
With bitterness of heart *and* bitter wailing.
In their wailing for you
They will take up a lamentation,
And lament for you:
'What *city is* like Tyre,
Destroyed in the midst of the sea?
'When your wares went out by sea,
You satisfied many people;
You enriched the kings of the earth
With your many luxury goods and your merchandise.
But you are broken by the seas in the depths of the waters;
Your merchandise and the entire company will fall in your midst.
All the inhabitants of the isles will be astonished at you;
Their kings will be greatly afraid,
And *their* countenance will be troubled.
The merchants among the peoples will hiss at you;
You will become a horror, and *be* no more forever.'"'"

a. **All the pilots of the sea will come down from their ships**: The sailing men of the world would **stand on the shore** and loudly mourn the destruction of Tyre. They would display all the traditional signs of mourning (**dust, ashes**, going **bald**, and **sackcloth**).

i. "The people on the mainland are aghast, and the sailors on board other ships are horrified at the sinking of this Tyrian Titanic. Lesser vessels might be expected to perish in a Mediterranean squall, but surely not this proud monarch of the seas!" (Block)

ii. "All over the world a lament arose over the loss of the ship. The countryside quaked in fear over the news. International shipping came to a halt. Tough sailors throughout the world were distraught. Tyre's clients were confused. Commerce was disrupted. The inhabitants of the coast lands were appalled. Kings were afraid and troubled, merchants astonished." (Smith)

iii. "There is no gloating over Tyre's fall here. The fall of Tyre was a forceful reminder to Judah of its own precarious position before God.

It is similar to the loss of any ship at sea as a reminder to all sailors of what can happen to them. In the face of this, there is no room for gloating but only for grieving." (Vawter and Hoppe)

iv. "Making oneself bald was a mourning custom which was connected with pagan superstitions and was forbidden in the Mosaic legislation (Deuteronomy 14:1)." (Feinberg)

v. "As every country hath its peculiar manners and customs in mourning, so had these customs that expressed most vehement sorrows in gestures which we are not accustomed to." (Poole)

b. **You are broken by the seas in the depths of the waters**: In the midst of her prosperity and commercial success, the ship of Tyre would be **broken** and sink, losing all **merchandise and the entire company**.

i. "What a powerful conception of the great ship sinking in silence with all on board! One cry; the waves meet over her; and only a floating spar tells where she sank. O mariner! See to it that Christ is on board; for He only can still the tempest and speak peace, and guide thee out of the great waters." (Meyer)

ii. "In her apparent invincibility, Tyre represented the glory of human achievement. Because her successes were driven by avarice and pursued in defiance of God, however, she could not stand. The Lord of history always has the last word." (Block)

iii. "Tyre has a message for our age, and it is that riches without God are unable to satisfy the heart of man and often keep many from dependence upon God. Has not this spirit invaded the church, and does it not pervade the lives of too many Christians?" (Feinberg)

c. **All the inhabitants of the isles will be astonished at you**: The world would be **astonished**, **afraid**, and horrified at the judgment God brought upon Tyre.

i. "This great lamentation is an advance demonstration of what the whole world will do when Satan's system, 'Babylon the great,' collapses before the Lord returns to establish His kingdom (Revelation 18:17–19)." (Wiersbe)

ii. **Will hiss at you**: "Shall *shriek* for thee. This powerfully expresses the sensation made on the feelings of the spectators on the shore when they saw the vessel swallowed up." (Clarke)

iii. "All the seaboard princedoms gasp in astonishment, but the terror on their faces is really selfish fear for the consequences that will come to them before long." (Taylor)

iv. "As I walked through the ruins of Tyre I heard no music nor laughter. I could not see the buildings or the gold and silver. All I saw were broken pieces of pottery and the wreck and ruin of what had once been a great city." (McGee)

Ezekiel 28 – Against Satan, King of Tyre

A. The lamentation for the prince of Tyre.

1. (1-5) The sins of the prince of Tyre.

The word of the LORD came to me again, saying, "Son of man, say to the prince of Tyre, 'Thus says the Lord GOD:

"Because your heart *is* lifted up,
And you say, 'I *am* a god,
I sit *in* the seat of gods,
In the midst of the seas,'
Yet you *are* a man, and not a god,
Though you set your heart as the heart of a god
(Behold, you *are* wiser than Daniel!
There is no secret that can be hidden from you!
With your wisdom and your understanding
You have gained riches for yourself,
And gathered gold and silver into your treasuries;
By your great wisdom in trade you have increased your riches,
And your heart is lifted up because of your riches),"

a. **The word of the LORD came to me again**: This continues a series of prophecies Ezekiel made against Tyre, the great commercial harbor city of the Phoenicians, north of Israel.

b. **Say to the prince of Tyre**: The prophecies of Ezekiel 26 and 27 focused on Tyre as a city. Now Ezekiel will speak against the leader of the city, both in the sense of one man (**the prince of Tyre**) and a representation of the leadership of the city.

i. Ezekiel may have had a specific **prince of Tyre** in mind. "According to Phoenician annals the king of this time was Ithobal II (called Ithobalus II by Josephus). The prophecy has been dated shortly before the siege of Tyre by Nebuchadnezzar (585-573 b.c.) during the reign of Ithobal II." (Feinberg)

c. **Because your heart is lifted up**: The fundamental sin of the prince of Tyre was pride. He said of himself, "**I am a god**" and gloried in his position of greatness **in the midst of the seas**. This was true of both the city and the ruler.

> i. "Tyre regarded herself as all-powerful, superhuman and virtually eternal; she was possessed of wealth and wisdom above all other cities, and this led on to the incredible arrogance for which Tyre was notorious." (Taylor)

d. **Yet you are a man, and not a god**: The prince of Tyre had a high opinion of himself, but God knew who he was. He was no **god**, merely a **man**. In his pride, he thought of himself as **wiser than Daniel** and wealthy beyond need (**gathered gold and silver into your treasuries**).

> i. **You are a man**: "The king may imagine himself enthroned among the gods, but God sees reality for what it is, not what egomaniacs perceive it to be." (Block)

> ii. **Wiser than Daniel**: Even in his own day, Daniel was famous for his wisdom (Daniel 1:20, 2:20, and 2:48) and God-given insight. This arrogant claim further exposed the pride of the prince of Tyre.

> iii. The example of Daniel is also meaningful because Daniel "was a classic example of a man whose head was not turned by his success." (Taylor)

e. **Your heart is lifted up because of your riches**: The great wealth of the prince of Tyre made him feel proud and invincible. He was smart in business (**by your great wisdom in trade you have increased your riches**), but his heart was lifted so high he thought of himself as a god.

> i. Significantly, God did not condemn the prince of Tyre for the possession of riches, but for how those riches corrupted him. "Significantly, the prophet castigates him neither for his shrewdness nor for his amassed wealth. Neither brilliance nor riches is reprehensible; the problem arises in his response. The wisdom that had brought him his wealth led to hubris. It was this inordinate pride that provoked Yahweh's ire." (Block)

> ii. The prince of Tyre was not the first or the last ruler corrupted by wealth and success. "Others whose heads were turned by prosperity were Sennacherib (II Kings 18:33-35), Nebuchadnezzar (Daniel 3:15; 4:30); Pharaoh (Ezekiel 29:3); Herod (Acts 12:21-23)." (Feinberg)

2. (6-10) Judgment upon the prince of Tyre.

'Therefore thus says the Lord GOD:
"Because you have set your heart as the heart of a god,
Behold, therefore, I will bring strangers against you,
The most terrible of the nations;
And they shall draw their swords against the beauty of your wisdom,
And defile your splendor.
They shall throw you down into the Pit,
And you shall die the death of the slain
In the midst of the seas.
"Will you still say before him who slays you,
'I *am* a god'?
But you *shall be* a man, and not a god,
In the hand of him who slays you.
You shall die the death of the uncircumcised
By the hand of aliens;
For I have spoken," says the Lord GOD.'"

a. **Behold, therefore, I will bring strangers against you**: Having lifted his **heart as the heart of a god**, the prince of Tyre could expect judgment soon. It would come from **the most terrible of nations**, and they would destroy the **beauty** and **splendor** of Tyre.

i. "If the prince has the audacity to claim prerogatives of deity, then let him prepare for a direct confrontation with the divine Lord of history." (Block)

ii. **I will bring strangers against you**: "A foreign people, called strangers for their multitude, and to intimate how little regard they would have to the Tyrian glory; these strangers were the Babylonian forces." (Poole)

b. **They shall throw you down into the Pit**: This possibly referred to the actual ruler of Tyre in Ezekiel's day, or it referred to a future ruler of Tyre, or it was a vivid picture of the certainty of the downfall of Tyre's leadership.

i. **Splendor**: "The expression refers to the radiance, the awe-inspiring glow, inherent in divine and royal items." (Block)

ii. "Claims of deity and superhuman powers would mean nothing to the invaders, for they would be intent on defiling (literally, profaning) the luster of Tyre, which had made such outlandish claims to deity." (Feinberg)

c. **You shall be a man, and not a god**: God promised that the judgment to come upon Tyre from foreign nations would humble the prince of Tyre, exposing his humanity to the world.

> i. "This is the sad catastrophe of such as dream of a deity. Of which number were Caligula, Herod, Heliogabalus, Dioclesian, and other monsters, uncircumcised vice gods, as we may, in the worst sense, best term them." (Trapp)

> ii. "When you read Scripture, you find occasions when God judged arrogant rulers, such as Pharaoh, whom the Egyptians treated as a god (Ex. 5:2), Nebuchadnezzar (Dan. 4), and Herod Agrippa (Acts 12). World leaders who ignore the Lord and act as if they are gods will all be exposed and judged." (Wiersbe)

> iii. **You shall die the death of the uncircumcised**: "A disgraceful death is conveyed by the phrase 'the death of the uncircumcised' (v.10). Phoenicians practiced circumcision; so to be slain as an uncircumcised male would be to die a barbarian's death." (Alexander)

> iv. "Because the king of Tyre uses language of himself that is appropriate to God alone, the king must become reacquainted with his humanity. There is no better teacher than death. Gods do not die; humans do." (Vawter and Hoppe)

B. The lamentation for the King of Tyre.

1. (11-15) The glory of the privilege of the king of Tyre.

Moreover the word of the LORD came to me, saying, "Son of man, take up a lamentation for the king of Tyre, and say to him, 'Thus says the Lord GOD:

"You *were* the seal of perfection,
Full of wisdom and perfect in beauty.
You were in Eden, the garden of God;
Every precious stone *was* your covering:
The sardius, topaz, and diamond,
Beryl, onyx, and jasper,
Sapphire, turquoise, and emerald with gold.
The workmanship of your timbrels and pipes
Was prepared for you on the day you were created.
"You *were* the anointed cherub who covers;
I established you;
You were on the holy mountain of God;
You walked back and forth in the midst of fiery stones.

You *were* perfect in your ways from the day you were created,
Till iniquity was found in you.

a. **Take up a lamentation for the king of Tyre**: Ezekiel 28:1-10 spoke to the *prince of Tyre*, and here Ezekiel spoke to **the king of Tyre**. His clear and curious description of the **king of Tyre** shows that this was indeed a ruler over the *prince of Tyre*, ruling over him in a spiritual sense. In the context of a lament for an arrogant human king, God spoke of the sin and the fall of the spiritual power behind that king.

i. The idea of a prophet speaking to the spiritual ruler or authority *behind* an earthly ruler is also present in Isaiah 14, where the description of the King of Babylon seems to go beyond any earthly king and describes Satan himself (Isaiah 14:12-14). We also see this idea in Daniel 10:10-20, where the angel Michael described his battle with a spiritual opponent he called the *prince of Persia*.

ii. "This chapter and Isaiah 14 throw light on the fall of Satan, and indicate that he was a created being who fell through pride." (Wright)

iii. "As he viewed the thoughts and ways of that monarch, he clearly discerned behind him the motivating force and personality who was impelling him in his opposition to God. In short, he saw the work and activity of Satan, whom the king of Tyre was emulating in so many ways." (Feinberg)

b. **You were the seal of perfection, full of wisdom and perfect in beauty**: We immediately recognize this as describing a being higher than any earthly, human king. God did not describe the proud way the king of Tyre thought of himself, but as he actually was – a being of great **perfection**, **wisdom**, and **beauty**.

i. "Here we have the most graphic and illuminating portrayal of Satan to be found in the whole Bible. His original power and greatness, wisdom and beauty, and exalted position are all set forth." (Morgan)

ii. **Seal of perfection**: "Seals functioned as insignias of authority and authenticity. Possession of the seal of a superior was a mark of great honor, signifying that one had been deputized to sign documents on his or her behalf." (Block)

c. **You were in Eden, the garden of God**: These words to the king of Tyre show that this was no human king. The reference to **Eden** draws us back to the work of Satan in the form of a serpent described in Genesis 3. The power behind the prince of Tyre – the true **king of Tyre** – was Satan himself, the great adversary of God and humanity.

i. This clear identification makes us understand something about Satan. From Ezekiel 28 we learn of his high status before his fall. Satan himself was this being of great **perfection, wisdom,** and **beauty**.

d. **Every precious stone was your covering**: Before his fall, Satan was *adorned* with great glory and splendor. God Himself gave him such a **covering**, honoring the pre-fall Satan greatly.

i. The collection of gemstones not only speaks of prestige and honor, but also suggests priesthood, because many of these stones were also found in the high priest's breastplate (Exodus 28:17-20).

ii. "The stones listed in this verse are similar to those on the high priest's breastplate in Exodus 28:17–20. The order is different here in Ezekiel, which includes only nine of the twelve stones of Exodus 28:17–20. The LXX inserts all twelve stones from Exodus 28 into Ezekiel 28:13." (Alexander)

iii. Matthew Poole described the gemstones in this manner: "**The sardius;** of a red, and by some said to be the ruby. **Topaz;** of a yellowish green. **The diamond;** of clear, waterish, sparkling colour. **The beryl;** of a sea-green colour, the best. **The onyx** resembles the whiteness of the nail of a man's hand. **The jasper;** of divers colours, but the best green. **The sapphire;** of sky colour, or blue. **The emerald;** green interspersed with golden spots. **The carbuncle;** of flame colour."

e. **The workmanship of your timbrels and pipes was prepared for you**: Before his fall, Satan had a significant role in the music of heaven, surrounding God's throne. Isaiah 14:11 also makes mention of the *stringed instruments* associated with Satan before his fall.

i. Some take this to say that Satan was the "worship leader" in heaven because there are songs of worship mentioned in the Bible (Job 38:7; Revelation 5:9, 14:3, and 15:3).

f. **You were the anointed cherub who covers**: This tells us that Satan, before his fall, was one of the privileged angelic beings surrounding the throne of God (cherubim were seen before in Ezekiel 1). The cherubim surrounding God's throne cover it with their wings (pictured in the mercy seat of Exodus 25:20 and 37:9, the representation of God's throne). Satan was one of those covering cherubim.

i. **The anointed cherub**: "Not simply one cherub among many; he was *the* cherub par excellence." (Block)

ii. "The anointed cherub was none other than Satan himself in his position of honor about the throne of God." (Feinberg)

iii. "Hence, Satan may have been once the chief guardian of the throne of God." (Wright)

iv. Some commentators believe this section of Ezekiel 28 speaks in the figures of pagan mythology, or that it represents *Adam* in Eden, and not Satan. That may fit with the idea of Eden, but not with the idea of Adam as the **anointed cherub who covers**.

g. **I established You**: This tells us that Satan, before his fall, had the great privilege of being **established** by God. Grasping or ambition did not gain his position. God gave him this unique position of great beauty, wisdom, adornment, and musical skill as **the anointed cherub who covers**.

h. **You were on the holy mountain of God**: We should regard this as the heavenly Zion, the heavenly reality of which earth is a representation. In this privileged place, Satan had great freedom of movement (**you walked back and forth in the midst of fiery stones**).

i. Hebrews 12:22 presents the idea of the mountain of God, Zion, as a representation of heaven.

ii. The **fiery stones** likely describe some adornment or perhaps describe the angelic beings known as *seraphim* (Isaiah 6:2). The name *seraphim* literally means "burning ones" or "fiery ones" and the context of Isaiah 6 suggests that this was another name for the cherubim surrounding God's throne.

i. **Till iniquity was found in you**: Satan enjoyed this place of great status and honor *until* something happened; until **iniquity was found** in him. The following verses will describe something of the nature of that **iniquity**, as does Isaiah 14:12-15. Ezekiel here tells us of the *source* of the **iniquity** – Satan, the king of Tyre, himself. It was not *placed* in him by God, but **found in** him as a corruption of the good that God put in **the anointed cherub who covers**.

2. (16-19) The pride and iniquity of the king of Tyre.

**"By the abundance of your trading
You became filled with violence within,
And you sinned;
Therefore I cast you as a profane thing
Out of the mountain of God;
And I destroyed you, O covering cherub,
From the midst of the fiery stones.
"Your heart was lifted up because of your beauty;
You corrupted your wisdom for the sake of your splendor;
I cast you to the ground,**

I laid you before kings,
That they might gaze at you.
"You defiled your sanctuaries
By the multitude of your iniquities,
By the iniquity of your trading;
Therefore I brought fire from your midst;
It devoured you,
And I turned you to ashes upon the earth
In the sight of all who saw you.
All who knew you among the peoples are astonished at you;
You have become a horror,
And *shall be* no more forever."'"

a. **By the abundance of your trading you became filled with violence within, and you sinned**: Because Satan is spoken of here as the *king of Tyre*, God spoke of Satan's sins in the same terms as Tyre's sins. Tyre was a highly commercialized city-state focused only on winning a profit. Satan's **abundance** of **trading** was found in his *competitive spirit*, his desire to be exalted above his associates (Isaiah 14:13-14).

i. **The abundance of your trading**: The dishonest business practices of the leaders of Tyre were a reflection of the dishonest, deceptive dealings of the spiritual power behind them. Satan is the father of lies (John 8:44) and comes only to steal, kill, and destroy (John 10:10).

ii. "The reference to trade in v. 16 shows that there is a blend of the king of Tyre and his master. The king traded for his own power. Satan sold his glory for violent rebellion, and was cast out from the mountain of God." (Wright)

iii. This connection between Tyre and Satan shows that the devil can be in business just as much as in armies and war. "Tyre's strength and influence were commercial rather than military, and it is interesting and suggestive that in this connection we find the most graphic and illuminating portrayal of Satan to be found in the whole Bible." (Morgan)

b. **You became filled with violence**: Satan's desire to exalt himself above his associates (Isaiah 14:13-14) led to some kind of violence. This has first reference to some kind of battle in heaven (as in Revelation 12:7), but also to violence against humanity made in the image of God (John 10:10).

i. This **violence** against humanity is perhaps explained by the idea that Satan rejected God's plan to create an order of beings made in His image (Genesis 1:26), who would be beneath the angels in dignity (Hebrews 2:6-7a; 2 Peter 2:11), yet would be served by angels in the present (Hebrews 1:14; 2:7-8; Psalm 91:11-12) and would one day be lifted in honor and status above the angels (1 Corinthians 6:3; 1 John 3:2). Satan wanted to be the highest among all creatures, equal to God in glory and honor, and the plan to create man would eventually put men above angels. He was apparently able to persuade one-third of the angelic beings to join him in his rebellion (Revelation 12:3-4, 7, and 9).

ii. If this is the case, it explains well Satan's present strategy against man: to obscure the image of God in man through encouraging sin and rebellion, to cause man to serve him, and to prevent the ultimate glorification of man.

c. **Therefore I cast you as a profane thing**: This speaks of the expulsion of Satan from heaven, something that seems to still be in the future of God's plan of the ages (Revelation 12:7-9). In fact, there are four falls of Satan and this refers to the second of the four; or perhaps the phrase **I destroyed you** means this refers to the fourth fall of Satan.

- Satan fell from glorified to profane (Ezekiel 28:14-16). This is what Jesus spoke of in Luke 10:18 when He says He *saw Satan fall like lightning from heaven*. This is the only fall of Satan that has already happened.

- Satan will fall from having access to heaven (Job 1:12, 1 Kings 22:21, Zechariah 3:1) to restriction on the earth (Revelation 12:9).

- Satan will fall from his place on the earth to bondage in the bottomless pit for 1,000 years (Revelation 20:1-3).

- Finally, Satan will fall from the bottomless pit to the lake of fire, which we commonly know as *hell* (Revelation 20:10).

d. **Your heart was lifted up because of your beauty**: Satan's sin was prompted by *pride*. With a swelled heart, drunk on his own sense of **beauty** and **splendor**, he made himself an opponent of God, because *God resists the proud, but gives grace to the humble* (Proverbs 3:34, James 4:6, 1 Peter 5:5).

e. **I cast you to the ground, I laid you before kings**: Satan's fall would be public and dramatic. As all the world would note Tyre's fall, so all the world would note the fall of the king of Tyre, Satan himself. God's judgment will come upon Satan **in the sight of all**.

f. **You defiled your sanctuaries by the multitude of your iniquities, by the iniquity of your trading**: The focus on winning profit corrupted and eventually ruined ancient Tyre. The focus on winning glory and honor corrupted and will ruin Satan.

i. "Tyre boasted numerous sanctuaries, and the temples of Tyre were the reason it was called the Holy Island by the ancients. These temples were profaned because the king's sin was the occasion for their destruction." (Feinberg)

g. **You have become a horror**: Much like the reaction of the nations in Isaiah 14:16-17, Ezekiel records that the nations will be horrified at the judgment that will come upon Satan. They will be horrified because it will mean to them that they also will be judged, and they will be horrified when they consider how greatly Satan has deceived them, leading to their own damnation.

i. This was true of literal Tyre, and already fulfilled. "Instead of being an object of *adoration* thou shalt be a subject of horror, and at last be destroyed with thy city, so that nothing but thy name shall remain. It was entirely burnt by Alexander the Great, as it had been before by Nebuchadnezzar." (Clarke) It will also one day be true of Satan, the power and influence behind Tyre.

C. The prophecy against Sidon.

1. (20-23) God glorified through His judgment on Sidon.

Then the word of the LORD came to me, saying, "Son of man, set your face toward Sidon, and prophesy against her, and say, 'Thus says the Lord GOD:

"Behold, I *am* against you, O Sidon;
I will be glorified in your midst;
And they shall know that I *am* the LORD,
When I execute judgments in her and am hallowed in her.
For I will send pestilence upon her,
And blood in her streets;
The wounded shall be judged in her midst
By the sword against her on every side;
Then they shall know that I *am* the LORD.

a. **Set your face toward Sidon**: The city of **Sidon** was another Phoenician harbor city near Tyre. God had a word of judgment to speak against them.

i. **Sidon** "was a great city in Joshua's time, Joshua 11:8, 19:28, and built by Sidon, Canaan's son, Genesis 10:15 1 Chronicles 1:13; a famous mart full of merchants, like Tyre, and as full of sin as riches." (Poole)

ii. "In Ezekiel's day, Sidon was not a very important state. In comparison with Tyre, its neighbor 40 km. (15 mi.) to the south,

Sidon was insignificant though once it had been a formidable power."
(Vawter and Hoppe)

iii. "Usually the two cities are mentioned together (Isaiah 23:1–4;
Jeremiah 47:4; Joel 3:4), but here Sidon is singled out for judgment by
the Lord." (Wiersbe)

b. **I am against you, O Sidon; I will be glorified in your midst**: The
declaration that God will glorify *Himself* in Sidon gives the sense that they
had sinned against His glory. Through His judgments, God would reveal
Himself and show that He was **hallowed in her.**

i. "The fulfillment of this prophetic word is confirmed by
Nebuchadrezzar's Court Register, which mentions the king of Sidon
along with other notables from conquered states." (Block)

2. (24) Blessing to Israel in the judgments upon neighboring nations.

**"And there shall no longer be a pricking brier or a painful thorn for the
house of Israel from among all *who are* around them, who despise them.
Then they shall know that I *am* the Lord God."**

a. **There shall no longer be a pricking brier or a painful thorn for the
house of Israel**: When God brings His judgment upon Israel's neighbors
(as described in Ezekiel chapters 25-32), it will be a relief to Israel. They
would no longer be under threat from those **who despise them.**

i. "Perhaps there is an allusion to *Jezebel*, daughter of *Ethbaal*, king of
Sidon, and wife to Ahab, king of Israel, who was the greatest curse to
Israel, and the universal restorer of idolatry in the land, see 1 Kings
16:31. Sidon being destroyed, there would come no encourager of
idolatry from that quarter." (Clarke)

b. **Then they shall know that I am the Lord God**: God's display of
judgment against the nations would display to Israel (and the world) His
holy and righteous nature. They would know Him as *Yahweh* (**God**) and
as *Adonai* (Master, **Lord**).

3. (25-26) The promise to restore Israel.

**'Thus says the Lord God: "When I have gathered the house of Israel
from the peoples among whom they are scattered, and am hallowed in
them in the sight of the Gentiles, then they will dwell in their own land
which I gave to My servant Jacob. And they will dwell safely there,
build houses, and plant vineyards; yes, they will dwell securely, when
I execute judgments on all those around them who despise them. Then
they shall know that I *am* the Lord their God."'"**

a. **When I have gathered the house of Israel from the peoples among whom they are scattered**: Ezekiel looked forward to an aspect of the new covenant, the gathering of Israel once again as a people and into the land (Deuteronomy 30:3; Jeremiah 23:3, 32:37; Ezekiel 11:17, 36:24).

i. In God's design the Babylonian exile would not last forever. After 70 years of exile and captivity, the Jewish people were allowed to go back to the promised land. Only about 50,000 of them did in the days of Ezra and Nehemiah, and when they did they did not return to a safe and secure land. This means that the promises of gathering back to the land were only partially fulfilled in the return from Babylonian exile. As part of the new covenant promises, there was a greater and perfect fulfillment to come, which can rightly be said to have reached a significant milestone in 1948.

b. **Then they will dwell in their own land which I gave to My servant Jacob**: This *future, post-exilic* promise shows that God's plan for Israel *in their land* did not end with the Babylonian conquest of Jerusalem; nor has it ended today.

i. "This brief message would be a source of encouragement to the exiles. Moreover, it was only a preview of the fuller development of the restoration message that would be given in chapters 33–39." (Alexander)

ii. The Puritan commentator John Trapp was one of those who rejected the idea that God still has some distinct place for Israel in His continuing plan of the ages. His explanation of the promise of Ezekiel 28:25 was: "Provided that they cleave close to me; otherwise I will out them again." Yet such a condition is nowhere mentioned in this and similar promises.

iii. "One reason that so many theologians are believed when they say that God is through with the nation Israel is because God's people are not acquainted with Isaiah, Jeremiah, Ezekiel, Daniel, and the minor prophets. The theme song of these prophets is that God is *not* through with Israel as a nation." (McGee)

c. **They will dwell securely, when I execute judgments on all those around them who despise them**: With his eye on the coming new covenant, Ezekiel looked for a secure restoration of Israel to their land – something only partially fulfilled in the present time.

i. "This point is emphasized rhetorically by the repetition of *they will live securely* and the presentation of concrete symbols of security: the construction of houses and planting of vineyards." (Block)

ii. "All sources of danger, opposition, and ridicule for Israel would be removed from Canaan. Then they—both the antagonists and the Israelites—would realize that Yahweh alone is deity." (Smith)

d. **Then they shall know that I am the LORD**: This beautiful restoration to the land in true peace and security, especially as an aspect of the new covenant, will be yet another way Yahweh reveals Himself to Israel and the world.

i. "The holy people are the channel through whom the Holy God reveals himself. There is no mention of judgments upon Israel: that is presumably thought of as a thing of the past." (Taylor)

Ezekiel 29 – God Against "King Crocodile"

A. Against Egypt.

1. (1-3) God opposes the pride of Egypt and her Pharaoh.

In the tenth year, in the tenth *month,* on the twelfth *day* of the month, the word of the LORD came to me, saying, "Son of man, set your face against Pharaoh king of Egypt, and prophesy against him, and against all Egypt. Speak, and say, 'Thus says the Lord GOD:

"Behold, I *am* against you,
O Pharaoh king of Egypt,
O great monster who lies in the midst of his rivers,
Who has said, 'My River *is* my own;
I have made *it* for myself.'

a. **In the tenth year**: This prophecy regarding Egypt came to Ezekiel *before* the fall of Jerusalem. At this time there were still some in Judah and Jerusalem who hoped that Egypt would rescue them from the powerful Babylonians.

i. Ezekiel 29 begins a four-chapter series of prophecies against Egypt. This was necessary because even though Egypt held Israel in slavery for 400 years, Israel also had an impulse to look to Egypt in times of crisis that predated their years of slavery, going all the way back to Abraham's earliest days in Canaan (Genesis 12:10-20). Isaiah warned God's people, *Woe to those who go down to Egypt for help* (Isaiah 31:1). Even in Jeremiah's and Ezekiel's days, they still looked to Egypt for help *instead of* trusting God and His plan.

ii. "As we have realised in reading this prophecy and that of Jeremiah, the political peril had been that created by the look of these people toward Egypt. This accounted for the length and definiteness of these messages." (Morgan)

iii. "The date given in verse 1 is explicit. It was a year and two days after Nebuchadnezzar had invested Jerusalem (24:1-2; II Kings 25:1), and seven months before its destruction (II Kings 25:3-8)." (Feinberg)

b. **Set your face against Pharaoh king of Egypt**: Egypt had long been an enemy of the people of Israel, both as the place of their long slavery and as a constant temptation both spiritually and politically. Ezekiel was to set his **face against Pharaoh king of Egypt** because God said, "**Behold, I am against you.**"

> i. It might seem strange that an exiled prophet of little Israel thought he had the place to speak to great kingdoms like Egypt. Yet Ezekiel represented the God of the whole earth. "The secular historian saw Israel dwarfed into insignificance by mighty neighbours; the religious commentator, the prophet, saw the great powers held firmly in the hand of little Israel's mighty God." (Taylor)

> ii. "Although the prophet does not mention him by name, the pharaoh at the time was Hophra who attacked Nebuchadnezzar in the spring of 588. This forced the Babylonians to lift their siege of Jerusalem." (Vawter and Hoppe)

> iii. This is the same Pharaoh mentioned in Jeremiah 44:30: *Thus says the LORD: 'Behold, I will give Pharaoh Hophra king of Egypt into the hand of his enemies and into the hand of those who seek his life, as I gave Zedekiah king of Judah into the hand of Nebuchadnezzar king of Babylon, his enemy who sought his life.*

c. **O great monster who lies in the midst of his rivers**: God likened Egypt to one of the **great** crocodiles that lived in the Nile and other associated **rivers**.

> i. **Great monster**: "The term refers concretely to a marine creature, in this instance a crocodile, the ruler of the Nile, sprawled out in the channels of the river." (Block)

> ii. "Crocodile, the figure of Pharaoh; whose princes also and people are fitly compared to lesser fishes, and Egypt to waters, wherewith it aboundeth." (Trapp)

> iii. "Egyptian prayers encouraged the pharaoh to be a crocodile to his enemies." (Vawter and Hoppe)

> iv. "Pharaoh was compared to a ferocious crocodile, guarding the waters of the land—the Nile and all the canals—and attacking anybody who dared to challenge his claims." (Wiersbe)

d. **My River is my own; I have made it for myself**: This was the proud boast of Egypt and her Pharaoh. They believed that the great Nile **River** both belonged to them and was created by them. They refused to recognize and honor the God of Israel as the creator and owner of all.

i. "The river Nile watereth Egypt, and maketh it fruitful beyond credulity. They do but cast in the seed, and have four rich harvests in less than four months, say travellers. Hence the Egyptians were generally proud, riotous, and superstitious above measure." (Trapp)

ii. "The Nile was the source of Egypt's greatness. It provided rich alluvial soil along its banks, beyond which was desert. It provided a continuous supply of water to irrigate the land and to slake the thirst of the Egyptians and their animals. It provided a means of transportation that made it possible for Egypt to bring its bountiful harvests to market. There would be no Egypt without the Nile." (Vawter and Hoppe)

iii. "The Nile was in every way the secret of the wealth and power of that land and people. Here Pharaoh is represented, not as worshipping the River, but claiming to possess it, and to have created it." (Morgan)

iv. "Actually, instead of his making the river, the river made him, for without it the land would have been a desert." (Feinberg)

v. "It is a graphic method of again drawing attention to the fact that all forgetfulness of God amounts at last to self-deification. That is the sin of every king and of every people who fail to recognise God and to deal with Him." (Morgan)

2. (4-5) God's promise to capture Egypt and Pharaoh like a great crocodile.

But I will put hooks in your jaws,
And cause the fish of your rivers to stick to your scales;
I will bring you up out of the midst of your rivers,
And all the fish in your rivers will stick to your scales.
I will leave you in the wilderness,
You and all the fish of your rivers;
You shall fall on the open field;
You shall not be picked up or gathered.
I have given you as food
To the beasts of the field
And to the birds of the heavens.

a. **But I will put hooks in your jaws**: Speaking like a great hunter of crocodiles, Yahweh announced that He would stop, capture, and displace Egypt. They would be terribly disrupted, as a crocodile pulled out of the Nile with a hook.

i. "The crocodile normally was caught with hooks in the jaws and then pulled on dry land where it would be slaughtered (cf. Herodotus 2.70). This is the figure used in these verses. The crocodile god, Sebek, was very important to the Egyptians in the Nile delta area. He was considered Egypt's protector and at times was identified with the solar deity, Re (cf. Diodorus 1.35)." (Alexander)

ii. "For all his arrogant pretensions, the glorious lord of the Nile is no match for Yahweh, who toys with him as a fisherman plays with his catch, then throws him away as carrion, unfit for human consumption." (Block)

b. **All the fish in your rivers will stick to your scales**: Their prosperity and sustenance would be greatly affected. It was a coming **wilderness** season for Egypt, as if a crocodile were taken from the river and cast into an **open field**.

i. **The fish**: "The fish spoken of were the followers of the king. The king would involve his people in his fall because of their loyalty to him." (Feinberg)

c. **I have given you as food to the beasts of the field**: Pharaoh and Egypt would be disgraced, treated as something that others prey and feed upon. The great concern for burial and memorial among the pharaohs is evident from their still existing tombs. God promised their disgrace would be so great it would be as if they were not buried at all.

i. "The Egyptian pharaohs were diligent to prepare their burial places, but Hophra would be buried like an unwanted dead animal. What a humiliating way to bury a man who claimed to be a god!" (Wiersbe)

3. (6-7) God will glorify Himself through His judgment of Egypt.

"Then all the inhabitants of Egypt
Shall know that I *am* the LORD,
Because they have been a staff of reed to the house of Israel.
When they took hold of you with the hand,
You broke and tore all their shoulders;
When they leaned on you,
You broke and made all their backs quiver."

a. **Then all the inhabitants of Egypt shall know that I am the LORD**: The coming judgment upon Egypt would show them that Yahweh, the God of Israel, did in fact rule.

b. **When they leaned on you, you broke**: Judah hoped to rely on Egypt's power to help them against the Babylonian Empire, but they were like **a**

staff of reed to the house of Israel. Egypt was a target of God's judgment and could never help Judah who was also appointed for God's judgment.

i. "This is a clear reference to the half-hearted response of Pharaoh Hophra to Zedekiah's appeal for help (cf. Jeremiah 37:7). Little is known of this action except that it produced only a temporary lull in the siege of Jerusalem, but we can presume that it was little more than a token foray on the Egyptians' part." (Taylor)

ii. "The Egyptians had a reputation for making promises and not keeping them (2 Kings 18:20–21; Isaiah. 36:6)." (Wiersbe)

iii. "It was the sin of the Jews to trust Egypt; it was Egypt's great sin to falsify promise with the Jews, and for this God now punisheth Egypt." (Poole)

4. (8-12) A sword upon Egypt.

'**Therefore thus says the Lord GOD: "Surely I will bring a sword upon you and cut off from you man and beast. And the land of Egypt shall become desolate and waste; then they will know that I *am* the LORD, because he said, 'The River *is* mine, and I have made *it*.' Indeed, therefore, I *am* against you and against your rivers, and I will make the land of Egypt utterly waste and desolate, from Migdol *to* Syene, as far as the border of Ethiopia. Neither foot of man shall pass through it nor foot of beast pass through it, and it shall be uninhabited forty years. I will make the land of Egypt desolate in the midst of the countries *that are* desolate; and among the cities *that are* laid waste, her cities shall be desolate forty years; and I will scatter the Egyptians among the nations and disperse them throughout the countries."**

a. **Surely I will bring a sword upon you and cut off from you man and beast**: God's judgment would come through the **sword** of warfare, and it would lay waste to both **man and beast**. This judgment would come because of Egypt's pride, especially as it focused on the Nile (**The River is mine**).

i. Trapp on the repetition of **the River is mine, and I have made it**: "With this proud speech he is twice twitted. The Egyptians so trusted in their river Nile, as if they needed no help from heaven."

ii. **From Migdol to Syene**: "Like Israelite 'from Dan to Beer-sheba,' the expression 'from Migdol to Syene as far as the border of Cush' defines the borders of the country." (Block)

b. **Neither foot of man shall pass through it nor foot of beast pass through it**: God promised that there would be great devastation to Egypt lasting **forty years**. It would be a **desolate** nation, with **cities that are laid waste**.

> i. **Desolate forty years**: "Because no such forty-year period is known in Egyptian history, some claim a literal fulfillment of the prophecy was never intended and that it is to be taken as hyperbole. But there is nothing in the context that would indicate a shift from the literal to the figurative." (Feinberg)

c. **I will scatter the Egyptians among the nations**: As the leaders and people of Judah would be conquered and scattered, so would the Egyptians. God promised to **disperse them throughout the countries**.

> i. "Berosus, the historian of Babylon, states that Nebuchadnezzar, after he had conquered Egypt, took great numbers of the captives to Babylon. Others, undoubtedly, fled to neighboring areas as in similar cases." (Feinberg)

5. (13-16) A promise to restore Egypt.

'Yet, thus says the Lord GOD: "At the end of forty years I will gather the Egyptians from the peoples among whom they were scattered. I will bring back the captives of Egypt and cause them to return to the land of Pathros, to the land of their origin, and there they shall be a lowly kingdom. It shall be the lowliest of kingdoms; it shall never again exalt itself above the nations, for I will diminish them so that they will not rule over the nations anymore. No longer shall it be the confidence of the house of Israel, but will remind them of *their* iniquity when they turned to follow them. Then they shall know that I *am* the Lord GOD."'"

> a. **I will gather the Egyptians from the peoples among whom they were scattered**: God promised mercy and restoration to Egypt. He would **bring back the captives of Egypt**, even though they would **be the lowliest of kingdoms**, not reaching their previous heights of empire and influence.

> > i. "This is the only instance in the book where the prophet speaks of the restoration of a nation other than Israel and Judah." (Vawter and Hoppe)

> > ii. Wright explained his understanding of this promised and limited restoration: "The restoration of Egypt came under Greek rule, and Alexandria especially became an important centre of Judaism and Christianity, thus probably fulfilling Isaiah 19.19-25."

> > iii. **The lowliest of kingdoms**: "Egypt did suffer from Nebuchadnezzar's invasion, and its rule over the nations was broken and never regained. They declined under the Persians, the Ptolemies and Rome. Egypt has

been a weak country in the centuries since except for a momentary revival of power during the Middle Ages." (Feinberg)

b. **No longer shall it be the confidence of the house of Israel**: One reason God would bring Egypt low and **diminish them** was so that Israel would no longer put their misplaced trust in Egypt. The lowly, diminished state of Egypt would **remind them of their iniquity when they turned to follow them**.

B. Nebuchadnezzar will plunder Egypt.

1. (17-18) Nebuchadnezzar's lack of reward from the plunder of Tyre.

And it came to pass in the twenty-seventh year, in the first *month,* on the first *day* of the month, *that* the word of the LORD came to me, saying, "Son of man, Nebuchadnezzar king of Babylon caused his army to labor strenuously against Tyre; every head *was* made bald, and every shoulder rubbed raw; yet neither he nor his army received wages from Tyre, for the labor which they expended on it.

a. **It came to pass in the twenty-seventh year**: Ezekiel received this prophecy long after the one previously recorded in this chapter.

i. The **twenty-seventh year**: "That is, of the *captivity of Jeconiah, fifteen* years after the taking of *Jerusalem....* The *preceding* prophecy was delivered one year before the taking of Jerusalem; *this,* sixteen years after; and it is supposed to be the last which this prophet wrote." (Clarke)

ii. "Thus this is the latest of his dated prophecies, two years after the vision of chapters 40–48 (cf. Ezekiel 40:1), almost seventeen years later than the previous oracle (Ezekiel 29:1–19), and almost sixteen years later than the next dated oracle in the book (Ezekiel 30:20)." (Block)

b. **Nebuchadnezzar king of Babylon caused his army to labor strenuously against Tyre**: Nebuchadnezzar conducted a long siege against Tyre, one that in the end was not worth all he had invested in the siege. It could be said, **neither he nor his army received wages from Tyre**.

i. "The 1st-cent. A.D. Jewish historian and apologist Flavius Josephus stated that the Babylonian siege of Tyre lasted for thirteen years (*Antiquities* x. 11.1). Tyre consumed its treasures in its own defense or otherwise made them unavailable to the Babylonians." (Vawter and Hoppe)

ii. "The Tyrians, finding it at last impossible to defend their city, put all their wealth aboard their vessels, sailed out of the port, and escaped for Carthage; and thus Nebuchadnezzar lost all the spoil of one of the richest cities in the world." (Clarke)

iii. According to secular histories, "We do not know whether Tyre was captured by the Babylonian force or not, though a few years later Babylonian officials were in residence in the city and Babylonian suzerainty was acknowledged. All that Ezekiel tells us is that the rewards of the siege were not commensurate with the effort involved." (Taylor)

iv. "Though some perceive that this passage demonstrates the incomplete fulfillment of Ezekiel's prophecies against Tyre, such a position rests on silence. On the contrary, these verses demonstrate that God faithfully executed his word against Tyre through Babylonia as he promised. The Scriptures do not demand that complete fulfillment lay in this one siege alone." (Alexander)

v. **Every head was made bald, and every shoulder rubbed raw**: "These expressions could refer to the chafing effects of helmets and armor, but since the Babylonian strategies involved a siege rather than a battle, it is preferable to think in terms of the backbreaking work involved in carrying out a siege. The baldness and raw shoulders were the effects of carrying the vast amounts of dirt required to construct siege mounds and ramps, and probably also an unsuccessful attempt to build a causeway to the island fortress." (Block)

2. (19-21) God will give Egypt as plunder to Nebuchadnezzar.

Therefore thus says the Lord GOD: 'Surely I will give the land of Egypt to Nebuchadnezzar king of Babylon; he shall take away her wealth, carry off her spoil, and remove her pillage; and that will be the wages for his army. I have given him the land of Egypt *for* his labor, because they worked for Me,' says the Lord GOD. 'In that day I will cause the horn of the house of Israel to spring forth, and I will open your mouth to speak in their midst. Then they shall know that I *am* the LORD.'"

a. **Surely I will give the land of Egypt to Nebuchadnezzar**: Because the Babylonian king had received so little from his conquest of Tyre, God promised to compensate him by giving Nebuchadnezzar the **wealth**, **spoil** and **pillage** of Egypt.

i. "A fragmentary cuneiform text refers to Nebuchadrezzar's thirty-seventh year (568 B.C.) when the king of Babylon marched against Egypt, that is, within three years of this prophecy." (Block)

ii. "One fragmentary Babylonian text from the chronicles of the Chaldean king (B.M. 33041) implies that Babylonia invaded Egypt about 568/567 B.C. This is corroborated by Josephus (Antiquities X, 180–82 [ix.7]).” (Alexander)

b. **Because they worked for Me**: There was a real sense in which Nebuchadnezzar and the armies of Babylon **worked for** God as His instruments of judgment. It was completely within God's rights to reward these workers according to His will and wisdom.

i. F.B. Meyer connected this reward God promised to a pagan king to the reward God promises to those who build His church: “If He gave Egypt to a heathen king for his service in respect to Tyre, we may also expect Him to bestow a reward on those who have built gold, silver, and precious stones, into His holy temple.”

c. **In that day I will cause the horn of the house of Israel to spring forth**: As God allowed Egypt to be pillaged, He would also restore strength to Israel. In all this work, God would reveal Himself to Israel and the world (**they shall know that I am the LORD**).

i. Psalm 132:17 also makes mention of **the horn of the house of Israel**: *There I will make the horn of David grow; I will prepare a lamp for My Anointed.* Yet the context here seems to be more the restoration of *Israel* than the emergence of the Messiah.

ii. “The prophet added a word of promise for the Jews (v. 21), assuring them that there would come for them a time of restoration when He would give them new strength (the budding horn) for their new challenges.” (Wiersbe)

iii. “No Messiah—or any other ruler—came in Israel around 586 B.C. The symbol must refer to the strength and encouragement that Israel was to receive when she observed God's faithfulness to execute his judgment on her enemy, Egypt, in accord with both these prophecies and the Abrahamic covenant (Genesis 12:3).” (Alexander)

iv. **I will open your mouth to speak in their midst**: “This seems to mean that the skepticism of the captives regarding Ezekiel would be removed and they would come to regard him as a true prophet.” (Smith)

Ezekiel 30 – A Fire in Egypt

A. The day of the LORD against Egypt.

1. (1-4) Woe is the day of the LORD for Egypt.

The word of the LORD came to me again, saying, "Son of man, prophesy and say, 'Thus says the Lord GOD:

"Wail, 'Woe to the day!'
For the day *is* near,
Even the day of the LORD is near;
It will be a day of clouds, the time of the Gentiles.
The sword shall come upon Egypt,
And great anguish shall be in Ethiopia,
When the slain fall in Egypt,
And they take away her wealth,
And her foundations are broken down.

a. **Woe to the day**: God told Ezekiel to prophesy a **woe** to the coming **day of the LORD** against Egypt. There would be a day of God's intervention and vindication against Egypt, **a day of clouds** against them.

i. In context, this was an audacious statement. "Imagine an exile from Judah, a third-rate Palestinian state whose future was very much in doubt, asserting that Judah's national deity is about to bring an end to Egypt! When Ezekiel spoke these words, Egypt had existed for two and a half millennia. The pyramids, the symbol of the achievements of that great civilization, had stood already for two thousand years. What Egypt did is without parallel in human history, ancient or modern. In the face of this, Ezekiel had the temerity to declare that Egypt, its cities, its rulers, and its people were vulnerable to the judgment of Judah's God. It was either outrageous delusion or great faith that led the prophet to utter this oracle of judgment against Egypt." (Vawter and Hoppe)

ii. **Day of the Lord**: "From time to time a nation reaches a climax of oppression and moral decay from which God humbles and often destroys it. The final Day is yet to come when God will put down all sin wherever it is found. Thus previous Days of the Lord become patterns of the final Day." (Wright)

iii. The **day** of Egypt's reckoning would come. "The human heart is ever prone to put off the judgment of God, easily finding solace in the unfounded thought that if God's visitation be postponed long enough, it may never occur at all." (Feinberg)

iv. **A day of clouds**: Ezekiel probably had in mind God's judgment coming as a great, powerful storm upon Egypt, complete with dark and ominous clouds. "The Jews were led out of Egypt by a bright cloud (Exodus 13:21), but the Egyptians who once enslaved them will be under a dark cloud." (Wiersbe)

b. **The sword shall come against Egypt**: Judgment would come against Egypt and Ethiopia in the form of the **sword** of war against them. There would be many dead (**the slain fall**) and plunder for the enemy (**they take away her wealth**).

i. "Some two years, and you shall be miserably routed in the deserts of Libya; immediately after the civil war for eleven years together shall waste you; and then Nebuchadrezzar's forces will be upon you; so that, whereas there may be about sixteen or eighteen years between the prophecy and its fulfilling, here is thirteen or fourteen of them taken up with sorrows and afflictions, forerunners of the last." (Poole)

2. (5-9) Judgment upon the regions and peoples of Egypt.

"Ethiopia, Libya, Lydia, all the mingled people, Chub, and the men of the lands who are allied, shall fall with them by the sword." 'Thus says the Lord:

"Those who uphold Egypt shall fall,
And the pride of her power shall come down.
From Migdol *to* **Syene**
Those within her shall fall by the sword,"
Says the Lord God.
"They shall be desolate in the midst of the desolate countries,
And her cities shall be in the midst of the cities *that are* **laid waste.**
Then they will know that I *am* **the Lord,**
When I have set a fire in Egypt
And all her helpers are destroyed.
On that day messengers shall go forth from Me in ships

To make the careless Ethiopians afraid,
And great anguish shall come upon them,
As on the day of Egypt;
For indeed it is coming!"

a. **Ethiopia, Libya, Lydia**: The judgment of God through war would not only come against Egypt but against her whole sphere of influence. All those **allied** with her **shall fall with them by the sword**.

i. **All the mingled people**: "Who are the mingled people? The reference is so general that a positive identification cannot be made. They have been understood to be the foreigners who served in the Egyptian army as mercenary soldiers (cf. 27:10; Jeremiah 25:20, 24; 46:9, 21). Extrabiblical sources confirm the fact that Egypt made great use of hired soldiers from various nationalities. This is a possible, perhaps even a probable, interpretation of Ezekiel's meaning." (Feinberg)

b. **The pride of her power shall come down**: Egypt and her rulers were well known for their **pride**. God promised to bring this proud one **down**. God promised to set **a fire in Egypt**, and her allies would become **desolate countries**.

i. **When I have set a fire in Egypt**: "War is fitly compared to fire; it feeds upon the people." (Trapp)

ii. "Fire is a common figure in the Scriptures for war and its ravages (cf. Ezekiel 30:14, 16; Ezekiel 15:5; 39:6). Just as fire is all-consuming and irresistible, so the visitation of God would do its work of extermination and extirpation." (Feinberg)

iii. **All her helpers are destroyed**: "The destruction of so many and powerful aids shall prove that it was God's hand did it." (Poole)

c. **Great anguish shall come upon them**: Fearful judgment would come upon Ethiopia as well as upon Egypt. When the messengers sent by God (**shall go forth from Me**) came in ships to Ethiopia, they would also fear.

i. "Ships can ascend the Nile up to Syene or Essuan, by the *cataracts*; and when Nebuchadnezzar's vessels went up, they struck terror into the Ethiopians. They are represented here as the 'messengers of God.'" (Clarke)

ii. "This anguish would be caused by the fact that all who had helped her would be made desolate, thus sharing in her judgment." (Morgan)

iii. "Throughout her history she had made much use of the force and arms of her allies, but in the crucial and all-determining hour they would be useless to her." (Feinberg)

3. (10-12) Nebuchadnezzar's destruction of Egypt.

'Thus says the Lord GOD:
"I will also make a multitude of Egypt to cease
By the hand of Nebuchadnezzar king of Babylon.
He and his people with him, the most terrible of the nations,
Shall be brought to destroy the land;
They shall draw their swords against Egypt,
And fill the land with the slain.
I will make the rivers dry,
And sell the land into the hand of the wicked;
I will make the land waste, and all that is in it,
By the hand of aliens.
I, the LORD, have spoken."

a. **I will also make a multitude of Egypt to cease**: Through either death or captivity (Ezekiel 29:12), God would use **Nebuchadnezzar king of Babylon** to take many people from Egypt.

i. **His people with him, the most terrible of the nations**: "Nebuchadrezzar will not come alone. He will be accompanied by his troops and a host of alien forces described as 'the most barbarous of nations,' an expression that struck terror in the heart of anyone." (Block)

b. **I will make the rivers dry, and sell the land into the hand of the wicked**: God promised to bring widespread destruction upon Egypt, so great that even the water from the life-giving Nile to the associated **rivers** would seem to fail them. God would **make the land waste** through the armies of **aliens** He brought upon them.

i. "By *rivers*, we may understand the *various canals* cut from the Nile to carry water into the different parts of the land. When the Nile did not rise to its usual height these canals were quite dry." (Clarke)

ii. **I, the LORD, have spoken**: "Behind the *hand of foreigners*, who appear to act as his agents, is the word of God (*I, the Lord, have spoken*), which is the all-powerful ultimate agent which can turn spoken prophecy into actual fact." (Taylor)

4. (13-19) Judgment on the regions and cities of Egypt.

'Thus says the Lord GOD:
"I will also destroy the idols,
And cause the images to cease from Noph;
There shall no longer be princes from the land of Egypt;
I will put fear in the land of Egypt.

I will make Pathros desolate,
Set fire to Zoan,
And execute judgments in No.
I will pour My fury on Sin, the strength of Egypt;
I will cut off the multitude of No,
And set a fire in Egypt;
Sin shall have great pain,
No shall be split open,
And Noph *shall be in* distress daily.
The young men of Aven and Pi Beseth shall fall by the sword,
And these *cities* shall go into captivity.
At Tehaphnehes the day shall also be darkened,
When I break the yokes of Egypt there.
And her arrogant strength shall cease in her;
As for her, a cloud shall cover her,
And her daughters shall go into captivity.
Thus I will execute judgments on Egypt,
Then they shall know that I *am* the LORD.""'"

a. **I will also destroy the idols**: When God long before sent the plagues against Egypt (Exodus 7-11), each plague was directed against one of their **idols**. Now, many hundreds of years later, God promised to once again **destroy the idols** of Egypt, by bringing judgment to the land and exalting Himself over them.

i. "Herodotus writeth that Cambyses wasted with the sword Egypt and Ethiopia, killed their god Apis, and defaced all their idols. This he did, doubtless, rather in scorn of all religion than hatred of idolatry." (Trapp)

ii. "The Greek historian Herodotus related how Cambyses of Persia, son of Cyrus the Great, took Pelusium by setting before his army cats and dogs, sacred to Egypt, which the Egyptians would not attack." (Feinberg)

iii. "I have walked over what is supposed to be the ruins of Memphis, and all that is left of the idols is one great big statue of Raamses. It lies on its back, and a building has been erected around it to house the statue. That is the only thing left in Memphis. God did exactly what He said He was going to do. He made the idols to cease." (McGee)

iv. **I will put fear in the land of Egypt**: "When Yahweh begins to work in Egypt, there will be fear in the land, not the reverence of devotees toward their deities or kings, but terror before Yahweh himself. Neither foolish idols nor self-proclaimed pharaonic divinities will hold his devastating fury at bay." (Block)

b. **I will make Pathros desolate, set fire to Zoan**: Beginning with **Noph**, God listed many Egyptian cities that would specifically experience His judgment. Of the land as a whole, **arrogant strength shall cease in her**, and instead of a cloud of God's glory, a **cloud** of judgment **shall cover her**. Many of Egypt's **daughters** would **go into captivity**.

> i. "So many cities were mentioned in this section to show how universal the judgment would be." (Feinberg)

> ii. **Her daughters:** "Either metaphorically, i.e. the towns and villages about her, or literally, her children; her daughters only mentioned, because her sons were destroyed and slain." (Poole)

c. **Then they shall know that I am the LORD**: God would reveal Himself through His judgments. Every observant eye could and would see that the God of Israel, Yahweh (**the LORD**), was Lord and God.

> i. "During Israel's sojourn in Egypt, Pharaoh wouldn't recognize the Lord; but now the nation would learn that the Lord God of the Hebrews was indeed the only true and living God." (Wiersbe)

B. Pharaoh's broken arms.

1. (20-21) Yahweh breaks the arm of Pharaoh.

And it came to pass in the eleventh year, in the first *month,* on the seventh *day* of the month, *that* the word of the LORD came to me, saying, "Son of man, I have broken the arm of Pharaoh king of Egypt; and see, it has not been bandaged for healing, nor a splint put on to bind it, to make it strong enough to hold a sword.

a. **The eleventh year, in the first month**: This was another of Ezekiel's prophecies with a specific date. This fourth prophecy against Egypt was given about four months before the fall of Jerusalem.

> i. At that time, "Many were still looking to Egypt in hope of help from her. Indeed, as we saw in reading Jeremiah (chapter 37), Pharaoh had made a movement with his hosts out of Egypt, and this had caused the Chaldeans temporarily to abandon the siege of Jerusalem" (Morgan). God wanted Jerusalem and Judah to know that Egypt had no power, no strength to help her.

b. **I have broken the arm of Pharaoh**: As an act of judgment and as a demonstration of His strength, God metaphorically broke the arm of Pharaoh and it had **been bandaged for healing**. It was therefore not **strong enough to hold a sword**, leaving Pharaoh and Egypt defenseless.

i. "The breaking of the arm of Pharaoh may refer to the unsuccessful attempt of Egypt to help Jerusalem in the invasion of Nebuchadnezzar (see Jeremiah 37:5 ff.)."

ii. "The flexed arm was a common Egyptian symbol for the Pharaoh's strength. Often statues or images of the Pharaoh have this arm flexed, wielding a sword in battle. A king with great biceps was especially a popular concept under the Saites Dynasty of Ezekiel's day. In addition Hophra took a second formal title that meant 'possessed of a muscular arm' or 'strong-armed.'" (Alexander)

2. (22-23) Yahweh breaks both arms of Pharaoh.

Therefore thus says the Lord God: 'Surely I *am* against Pharaoh king of Egypt, and will break his arms, both the strong one and the one that was broken; and I will make the sword fall out of his hand. I will scatter the Egyptians among the nations, and disperse them throughout the countries.

a. **Will break his arms, both the strong one and the one that was broken**: The picture of the broken arm of Pharaoh depicted in Ezekiel 30:20-21 was not strong enough to communicate how helpless Pharaoh and Egypt would be against God's coming judgment. Therefore, according to the image, God also broke the other arm, **the strong one**. Egypt was *completely* defenseless (**I will make the sword fall out of his hand**).

b. **I will scatter the Egyptians among the nations**: As previously spoken in Ezekiel 29:12 and 30:26, conquest and captivity were to come upon defenseless Egypt.

3. (24-26) Egypt and Babylon.

I will strengthen the arms of the king of Babylon and put My sword in his hand; but I will break Pharaoh's arms, and he will groan before him with the groanings of a mortally wounded *man*. Thus I will strengthen the arms of the king of Babylon, but the arms of Pharaoh shall fall down; they shall know that I *am* the Lord, when I put My sword into the hand of the king of Babylon and he stretches it out against the land of Egypt. I will scatter the Egyptians among the nations and disperse them throughout the countries. Then they shall know that I *am* the Lord.'"

a. **I will strengthen the arms of the king of Babylon and put My sword in his hand**: Even as God weakened Egypt and made Pharaoh defenseless, God would also **strengthen** Nebuchadnezzar and even give him the **sword** of God's judgment. Pharaoh could only **groan** under the judgment God would bring.

i. "The effects of Yahweh's action against the pharaoh go beyond neutralizing his power. The prediction that *he will groan* [lit. 'groan groanings'] *before him like one slain* implies that Pharaoh himself will be killed." (Block)

ii. "By the time Nebuchadrezzar invaded Egypt, after the siege of Tyre was ended, Hophra had been killed in civil war. He had conducted a disastrous campaign in Libya, which brought on a major revolt from a rival faction under Ahmose, who was eventually responsible for doing him to death." (Taylor)

iii. God would do to both Egypt and Babylon as served His love, His righteousness, and His justice. He would work on, in, and through them to advance His plan of the ages.

iv. "These apparently mighty monarchs of Egypt and Babylon were both in the hands of Jehovah. Their apparent successes and failures resulted from His action. They were completely in His power." (Morgan)

b. **I will scatter the Egyptians among the nations**: The prediction of scattering and exile is repeated once more. God would do this, and through it reveal Himself among the nations (**Then they shall know that I am the Lord**).

Ezekiel 31 – Egypt Will Fall as Assyria Did Before

A. The glory of the mighty tree.

1. (1-2a) Introduction to the prophecy regarding Egypt.

Now it came to pass in the eleventh year, in the third *month*, on the first *day* of the month, *that* the word of the LORD came to me, saying, "Son of man, say to Pharaoh king of Egypt and to his multitude:

> a. **In the eleventh year, in the third month, on the first day**: This fifth prophecy of Ezekiel against Egypt was also given on a specific date. As the prophecy starting in Ezekiel 30:20, this one came in the **eleventh year**, about two months after that one. This was only about one month before the final, catastrophic fall of Jerusalem.

> > i. "In just a matter of a few weeks, Jerusalem will fall to the Babylonians. In the allegory of the tree, Ezekiel helps Judah to see its fate from a more universal perspective. Judah is not the only nation that stands under divine judgment. No king and no nation can escape that judgment—not even Egypt." (Vawter and Hoppe)

> b. **Say to Pharaoh king of Egypt and to his multitude**: This word was given to **Egypt**, both her ruler and her people. As the prophecy develops, it will focus on Assyria, but as an example of, and warning to, Egypt.

2. (2b-6) The strength and the greatness of the tree of Assyria.

'Whom are you like in your greatness?
Indeed Assyria *was* a cedar in Lebanon,
With fine branches that shaded the forest,
And of high stature;
And its top was among the thick boughs.
The waters made it grow;
Underground waters gave it height,
With their rivers running around the place where it was planted,
And sent out rivulets to all the trees of the field.

'Therefore its height was exalted above all the trees of the field;
Its boughs were multiplied,
And its branches became long because of the abundance of water,
As it sent them out.
All the birds of the heavens made their nests in its boughs;
Under its branches all the beasts of the field brought forth their young;
And in its shadow all great nations made their home.

a. **Whom are you like in your greatness?** The history and stature of Egypt gave clear evidence of their **greatness**. In Ezekiel's day, Egypt had stood as a mighty kingdom for thousands of years. Yet God found an example to teach Egypt, described in the following lines.

b. **Indeed Assyria was a cedar in Lebanon**: Using the figure of a great tree (as also in Ezekiel 17), God here used the empire of Assyria to teach Egypt how He could establish a great power, and then bring it down in judgment. **Assyria** was, in the recent past, a great empire.

i. A few commentators (such as Poole, Trapp, Clarke, and Taylor) believe that Ezekiel actually had in mind Assyria of the distant past – in the days of Nimrod and the tower of Babel (Genesis 11). This is unlikely, yet the sins of that early kingdom were the same sins that God judged later Assyria for and would soon judge Egypt for.

ii. Some others (such as Morgan) believe that the word we translate **Assyria** in Ezekiel 31:3 is better translated as "a tree," and the entire reference is to Egypt and the recently passed empire of Assyria is not in view at all. This is a remote possibility.

iii. Therefore it is best to regard this as a description of **Assyria**, which also spoke directly to Egypt. God spoke about **Assyria** *and* to Egypt, and did so in ideas that were true of them both. Egypt should learn from Assyria.

iv. "The context requires a symbol of imperial greatness with which Egypt could be compared. No standard would have been more suitable than Assyria, whose memory would surely still have been alive in the minds of Ezekiel and his hearers. After all, this great cedar had been felled within their lifetime." (Block)

v. "The argument the prophet presented was simple. Egypt boasted in its greatness, yet Egypt wasn't as great as Assyria, and Assyria was conquered by Babylon. Conclusion: if Babylon can conquer Assyria, Babylon can conquer Egypt." (Wiersbe)

c. **The waters made it grow**: Ezekiel described a tree watered from many sources, so it never lacked for nourishment. **Its branches became long because of the abundance of water**. Assyria was watered by mighty rivers (such as the Tigris and Euphrates) and watered by many tributary nations. The description also fits Nile-sustained Egypt.

i. "The great cedar, Assyria (v.3), was well-watered, perhaps an indirect reference to her great water sources in the Tigris and Euphrates rivers (v.4). Egypt, of course, equally prided herself in her unending supply of Nile water." (Alexander)

d. **In its shadow all great nations made their home**: The greatness of Assyria made them a place of shelter for other **nations**; something true of Egypt also. Before the final fall of the city, many in Jerusalem hoped that they would find protection under Egypt's power.

i. What Adam Clarke wrote of the Egyptians was also true of the Assyrians: "By means of the different nations under the Egyptians, that government became very opulent. These nations are represented as *fowls* and *beasts*, taking shelter under the protection of this great political Egyptian tree."

3. (7-9) The incomparable greatness of the mighty tree of Assyria.

'Thus it was beautiful in greatness and in the length of its branches, Because its roots reached to abundant waters. The cedars in the garden of God could not hide it; The fir trees were not like its boughs, And the chestnut trees were not like its branches; No tree in the garden of God was like it in beauty. I made it beautiful with a multitude of branches, So that all the trees of Eden envied it, That *were* in the garden of God.'

a. **Thus it was beautiful in greatness and in the length of its branches**: Assyria was noted not only for its power but also for its beauty and the broad reach of its influence. What was true of the already fallen empire of Assyria was also true of the soon to be judged Egypt.

b. **No tree in the garden of God was like it in beauty**: God represented the other nations of the world as other trees, such as **cedars**, or the **fir**, or the **chestnut**. None of them compared to Assyria in its day. Yet even this was the work of God; Yahweh said, "**I made it beautiful**."

i. **I made it beautiful**: "Reminds the hearer that, like the trees in the garden, the great cedar's glory is not of its own making; Yahweh has endowed it with the kind of superlative beauty that would evoke jealousy among all the other trees in the garden." (Block)

B. The ruin of the mighty tree.

1. (10-12) Directed by God, foreigners cut down the mighty tree of Assyria.

"Therefore thus says the Lord GOD: 'Because you have increased in height, and it set its top among the thick boughs, and its heart was lifted up in its height, therefore I will deliver it into the hand of the mighty one of the nations, and he shall surely deal with it; I have driven it out for its wickedness. And aliens, the most terrible of the nations, have cut it down and left it; its branches have fallen on the mountains and in all the valleys; its boughs lie broken by all the rivers of the land; and all the peoples of the earth have gone from under its shadow and left it.

a. **Because you have increased in height….and its heart was lifted up in its height**: The mighty "tree" of Assyria became proud and arrogant. God would judge and humble them through **the hand of the mighty one of the nations** (Nebuchadnezzar). God would use that same **mighty one** to bring judgment to Egypt.

i. "But in v. 10 we detect once more the Satanic impulse to pride (28.17), and so Egypt in her turn has to be brought low." (Wright)

ii. "Now you shall hear the sin and the fall of this great kingdom of Assyria. His mind could not longer bear so great prosperity, he lifts up himself, and in his pride forgets God who lifted him up and will cast him down." (Poole)

b. **Aliens, the most terrible of the nations, have cut it down**: God brought a foreign army as His lumberjack against Assyria and they **cut down** its greatness. He would do the same to Egypt. Each would no longer be a **shadow** of refuge for **all the peoples of the earth**.

i. "They are portrayed as rough lumberjacks, who chop the tree down and leave it lying on the mountains, its broken branches strewn up and down the mountains, valleys, and ravines of the land." (Block)

ii. "It is worthy of notice, that Nebuchadnezzar, in the *first* year of his reign, rendered himself master of *Nineveh*, the capital of the *Assyrian* empire…. This happened about *twenty* years before Ezekiel delivered this prophecy; on this account." (Clarke)

iii. The association of Egypt with Assyria can also be seen in light of the timing of this prophecy, just before the final fall of Jerusalem, when some in Jerusalem still looked to Egypt for help. Assyria was a great power, but an enemy to Judah and no friend. Egypt would also be of no help at all to Judah, especially in the last days before the Babylonian conquest.

2. (13-14) The ruin of the unmatched glory of the fallen tree.

'On its ruin will remain all the birds of the heavens,
And all the beasts of the field will come to its branches—

'So that no trees by the waters may ever again exalt themselves for their
height, nor set their tops among the thick boughs, that no tree which
drinks water may ever be high enough to reach up to them.

'For they have all been delivered to death,
To the depths of the earth,
Among the children of men who go down to the Pit.'

a. **On its ruin will remain all the birds of the heavens**: Fallen Assyria was still noted for its glorious past, for its **ruin**. Many would still **come to its branches**, but not to find shelter there (as before).

i. "His dead body shall want decent burial, as afterward did great Alexander's, great Pompey's, our William the Conqueror's, Richard III's, &c." (Trapp)

b. **So that no trees by the waters may ever again exalt themselves**: God would use His dealings with the Assyrians to be a lesson to all the nations of the world – *if they would listen*. They would see what happens to a great power when it becomes proud and arrogant.

i. "Let this ruin, fallen upon Egypt, teach all the nations that shall hear of it to be *humble*, because, however *elevated*, God can soon bring them down; and *pride* and *arrogance*, either in *states* or *individuals*, have the peculiar abhorrence of God. Pride does not suit the sons of men; it made devils of *angels*, and makes fiends of *men*." (Clarke)

c. **They have all been delivered to death**: God would teach the nations that they were all under the power of **death**, that each of them was mortal and would have a day of reckoning before the God of all creation.

i. "Sennacherib had a statue set up in Egypt, saith Herodotus, with this inscription, Let him that looketh upon my misery learn to be modest and to fear God." (Trapp)

ii. "God had an educative purpose in the fall of Assyria: to teach the nations the folly of striving for earthly might. The ultimate objective of the judgment was to deter others from the same disastrous course." (Feinberg)

iii. **Down to the pit**: "That place is the great leveler. All are equal in Sheol. When it reaches the abode of the dead, Egypt must accept its solidarity with other, less important nations." (Vawter and Hoppe)

iv. "Death is the great equalizer and the surest antidote to an excess of ambition." (Taylor)

3. (15-17) Mourning and fear because of the fall of the mighty tree of Assyria.

"Thus says the Lord GOD: 'In the day when it went down to hell, I caused mourning. I covered the deep because of it. I restrained its rivers, and the great waters were held back. I caused Lebanon to mourn for it, and all the trees of the field wilted because of it. I made the nations shake at the sound of its fall, when I cast it down to hell together with those who descend into the Pit; and all the trees of Eden, the choice and best of Lebanon, all that drink water, were comforted in the depths of the earth. They also went down to hell with it, with those *slain* by the sword; and *those who were* its *strong* arm dwelt in its shadows among the nations.

a. **In the day when it went down to hell, I caused mourning**: When God brought judgment upon Assyria, the other nations noticed and mourned. They grieved because they knew that they also could and would be targets of God's judgment.

i. "The proud king is seen passing to Sheol, the underworld of the dead, and commotion is caused there by his coming, and the other fallen ones find satisfaction in that he too is brought low." (Morgan)

ii. "No matter how high and mighty a tree may have been during its earthly existence, in death all are equal. The glorious cedar may have evoked jealousy in its earthly life (v. 9), but in Sheol it has nothing to be envied; all are on the same level." (Block)

b. **I restrained its rivers**: Using the symbol of the tree and the reason for its great size and strength, God cut off the supply of water to the tree.

i. In reference to Egypt, **I restrained her rivers** probably has reference to the many canals and waterworks the Egyptians made to feed from the Nile. When the Nile was low with water, not rising and flooding as normal, these canals were **restrained**, the **great waters were held back**, and agriculture greatly suffered in Egypt. This was a demonstration of God's judgment on Egypt (as in Ezekiel 29:10 and 30:12).

c. **I caused Lebanon to mourn**: This follows the image of the mighty tree from Ezekiel 31:1-14. Since Lebanon was famous for its mighty cedar trees, it mourned over Assyria's fall, even as **all the trees of the field wilted because of it**.

i. **I caused Lebanon to mourn**: "There is a subtle play on words in making Lebanon, which is literally the white mountain, to mourn or to be made black, for such is the meaning of the Hebrew original for the verb 'mourn.'" (Feinberg)

4. (18) A curse against Pharaoh and the kingdom of Egypt.

'To which of the trees in Eden will you then be likened in glory and greatness? Yet you shall be brought down with the trees of Eden to the depths of the earth; you shall lie in the midst of the uncircumcised, with *those* **slain by the sword. This** *is* **Pharaoh and all his multitude,' says the Lord God."**

a. **You shall be brought down with the trees of Eden to the depths of the earth**: If mighty Assyria and Egypt were exalted as high as **the trees of Eden**, they still were not beyond God's judgment. They could still **be brought down**.

i. "The mightiest, richest, and longest-lived kingdom I have represented, saith God, overthrown and destroyed; a kingdom thou canst not pretend to equal; and if not like this, what king or kingdom art thou like, that thou shouldst be invincible? Whoever thou art like in height and power, thou shalt be like them in thy fall and ruin." (Poole)

b. **You shall lie in the midst of the uncircumcised, with those slain by the sword**: The main instrument of God's judgment upon Egypt would be war (**by the sword**), and it would come through another people.

i. "Since the Egyptians practiced circumcision, to spend eternity with those who were uncircumcised would be the ultimate humiliation." (Smith)

ii. "The reference to the uncircumcised is especially forceful because the Egyptians did practice circumcision and were amazingly meticulous, as the pyramids show, about proper burial, so this placing of them on the level of those mentioned was the deepest disgrace possible to them. To the Egyptians those in this condition were outside the range of the civilized world." (Feinberg)

c. **This is Pharaoh and all his multitude**: The final verse of the prophecy again makes it clear that this is really a word against Egypt. In speaking of Assyria, God spoke to Egypt.

i. "If he perceives himself as the heir of the Assyrians' imperial might, then let him also share in their fate and the fate of all other glorious trees, including those of Eden. As the Assyrians had experienced, so the netherworld will reduce him to the lowest common denominator." (Block)

Ezekiel 32 – Egypt, Monster of the Seas, Destined for Hell

A. Pharaoh and Egypt as a monster of the sea.

1. (1-2) Pharaoh like a lion or a monster of the sea.

And it came to pass in the twelfth year, in the twelfth *month,* on the first day of the month, *that* the word of the LORD came to me, saying, "Son of man, take up a lamentation for Pharaoh king of Egypt, and say to him:

'You are like a young lion among the nations,
And you *are* like a monster in the seas,
Bursting forth in your rivers,
Troubling the waters with your feet,
And fouling their rivers.'

a. **In the twelfth year, in the twelfth month, on the first day of the month**: This prophecy came more than a year after the fall of Jerusalem. This **lamentation for Pharaoh king of Egypt** was given after any hope Judah had in Egypt for help was passed.

i. This point of Jewish history, "They perhaps wondered whether God would be faithful to punish the heathen nations as he had declared. Conversely Egypt had seen the collapse of Jerusalem and Judah, and Egypt may have begun to gloat in pride over her own survival and power." (Alexander)

b. **You are like a monster in the seas**: Pharaoh and his kingdom were mighty forces in the world, second only to Babylon – and Babylon had only recently subdued Egypt at the battle of Carchemish in 605 BC. Egypt was still a great force with the ability to influence and trouble other nations.

i. **Like a young lion among the nations…like a monster in the seas**: "Here we have Pharaoh's regard for himself as a lion, whereas he is no more than a crocodile stirring up mud and filth. So God will haul him out and throw him on land to be eaten by birds and beasts." (Wright)

ii. **Troubling the waters with your feet**: "Pharaoh thrashed about in the water and made a big scene, but all he did was muddy the waters and create problems by disobeying the Lord." (Wiersbe)

2. (3-8) God will slay and disgrace the sea monster representing Pharaoh.

"Thus says the Lord GOD:
'I will therefore spread My net over you with a company of many
people,
And they will draw you up in My net.
Then I will leave you on the land;
I will cast you out on the open fields,
And cause to settle on you all the birds of the heavens.
And with you I will fill the beasts of the whole earth.
I will lay your flesh on the mountains,
And fill the valleys with your carcass.

'I will also water the land with the flow of your blood,
***Even* to the mountains;**
And the riverbeds will be full of you.
When *I* put out your light,
I will cover the heavens, and make its stars dark;
I will cover the sun with a cloud,
And the moon shall not give her light.
All the bright lights of the heavens I will make dark over you,
And bring darkness upon your land,'
Says the Lord GOD.

a. **I will therefore spread My net over you**: Regarding Pharaoh as a great sea monster (Ezekiel 32:2), God promised to capture him in a great **net** and drag him to land (**I will leave you on the land**). There he would become food for both **birds** and **beasts**.

i. **Spread My net over you**: "With which both lions and crocodiles might be taken, and in which this lion and crocodile should certainly be taken; for God, whose hand never erreth, will spread the net." (Poole)

ii. **I will cast you out on the open fields**: "It was literally fulfilled in the deserts of Libya, where the slain of Hophra's army were left to be devoured by fowls and beasts. Metaphorically it is gathering a mixture of people, soldiers, like ravenous birds and beasts. from all parts to spoil Egypt." (Poole)

b. **I will also water the land with the flow of your blood**: The idea is that the defeat and death of Pharaoh would be a *good* thing for the world. It would be like **water** for the **land**. This also reminds us of the first plague that came upon Egypt in Moses' day (Exodus 7:19).

i. "The prophet has painted a disgusting if vivid picture of the earth drinking the excrement, blood, and other body fluids that are discharged when an animal is slain. One can scarcely imagine a more ignominious death." (Block)

c. **And bring darkness upon your land**: This reminds us of the ninth of the plagues that came upon Egypt in Moses' day, darkness for three days over the whole land (Exodus 10:21-29). God had judged Egypt before and would do it again. God exalted Himself over the idols of Egypt and would do it again.

i. **When I put out your light**: "The term *kaba*, which is used concretely of snuffing out a wick or a lamp, is occasionally used figuratively of death." (Block)

ii. "It would be as if 'a great darkness covered the land' (vv.7–8), demonstrating that Egypt's great sun gods were impotent to help." (Alexander)

3. (9-10) Fear and astonishment among the nations at Pharaoh's fall.

'I will also trouble the hearts of many peoples, when I bring your destruction among the nations, into the countries which you have not known. Yes, I will make many peoples astonished at you, and their kings shall be horribly afraid of you when I brandish My sword before them; and they shall tremble *every* moment, every man for his own life, in the day of your fall.'

a. **I will also trouble the hearts of many peoples**: When God brought judgment to Pharaoh and Egypt many others would be troubled.

i. "The effect of this downfall would be widespread, bringing desolation to his own land, supplying booty to other lands, and making men everywhere tremble in the presence of the judgment of Jehovah." (Morgan)

b. **Their kings shall be horribly afraid of you**: Many peoples and on-looking **kings** would be both **astonished** and **afraid**. They saw that if God's judgment could come to mighty Egypt, it could also come to them.

4. (11-16) Judgment by the sword of Babylon.

"For thus says the Lord GOD: 'The sword of the king of Babylon shall come upon you. By the swords of the mighty warriors, all of them the most terrible of the nations, I will cause your multitude to fall.

'They shall plunder the pomp of Egypt,
And all its multitude shall be destroyed.
Also I will destroy all its animals
From beside its great waters;
The foot of man shall muddy them no more,
Nor shall the hooves of animals muddy them.
Then I will make their waters clear,
And make their rivers run like oil,'
Says the Lord GOD.

'When I make the land of Egypt desolate,
And the country is destitute of all that once filled it,
When I strike all who dwell in it,
Then they shall know that I *am* the LORD.

'This *is* the lamentation
With which they shall lament her;
The daughters of the nations shall lament her;
They shall lament for her, for Egypt,
And for all her multitude,'
Says the Lord GOD."

a. **The sword of the king of Babylon shall come upon you**: Since the image of the **sword** usually stands for war, this was one more statement making it clear that God would bring judgment upon Egypt through war brought upon them by **the king of Babylon**. The Babylonians would **plunder the pomp of Egypt** and destroy a **multitude**.

i. Being a wealthy and mighty empire for so many centuries, Egypt had a lot of **pomp** to **plunder**.

ii. **Plunder the pomp**: "Break her strength, rob her treasures, sack her cities, captivate her people, and make the kingdom tributary, and so stain all her glory." (Poole)

iii. Some skeptics argue that this was a false prophecy because there is little secular historical confirmation that **the king of Babylon** conquered Egypt. Feinberg answers these objections well: "As already stated, Egypt was conquered by Nebuchadnezzar. The silence of the Greek Herodotus is far from decisive in this matter, for he was unable to read the Egyptian sources and received his information through secondary sources. Furthermore, the Egyptians were adept at covering their disasters. For example, Herodotus did not even mention the important Battle of Carchemish. Some consider the prophecy as completely fulfilled."

b. **I will also destroy all its animals**: War would also ravage the livestock of Egypt. The land and riverbanks would become **desolate** from either the **foot of man** or the **hooves of animals**.

> i. "So great will be the slaughter and devastation that Egypt will be uninhabited by either man or beast." (Taylor)

> ii. **All its animals**: "Egypt, a most moist and fat country, was full of cattle." (Trapp)

> iii. **Make their rivers run like oil**: "With no people and animals available to work the land and draw the water, the streams and canals wouldn't be muddied and the water would 'run like oil' with nothing to impede its flow." (Wiersbe)

> iv. **Then they shall know that I am the LORD**: "Now we learn Yahweh's ultimate goal in humiliating Egypt: the universal acknowledgment of his person and his involvement in human affairs." (Block)

c. **They shall lament for her, for Egypt**: Both a surviving remnant and those observing from other nations would **lament** in sorrow for the severe judgment brought upon Egypt.

> i. **This is the lamentation**: "The funeral speech of this kingdom; for this, as a funeral oration, tells us what was their ancient glory, and what is now their miserable reproach and loss." (Poole)

B. The seventh prophecy against Egypt.

1. (17-21) Egypt dragged down to the pit of the grave.

It came to pass also in the twelfth year, on the fifteenth *day* of the month, *that* the word of the LORD came to me, saying:

**"Son of man, wail over the multitude of Egypt,
And cast them down to the depths of the earth,
Her and the daughters of the famous nations,
With those who go down to the Pit:
'Whom do you surpass in beauty?
Go down, be placed with the uncircumcised.'
"They shall fall in the midst of *those* slain by the sword;
She is delivered to the sword,
Drawing her and all her multitudes.
The strong among the mighty
Shall speak to him out of the midst of hell**

With those who help him:
'They have gone down,
They lie with the uncircumcised, slain by the sword.'

a. **In the twelfth year, on the fifteenth day of the month**: This last of the seven prophecies against Egypt also happened in the **twelfth year**, the year after the fall of Jerusalem. Most agree that since no month is specifically mentioned, this happened the same month as the previous oracle (Ezekiel 32:1). This would be about two weeks later.

i. F.B. Meyer made a contemporary spiritual application of the idea of Ezekiel dating his words received from God: "We do well to observe special days in our diary of the years. The day of our conversion or consecration; the day of deliverance from overwhelming trouble; the day when He summoned us to some new duty; the day when Paradise shone around us with its golden sheen."

b. **Cast them down to the depths of the earth**: As in Ezekiel 31:14-17, Egypt's destiny was to go to *sheol*, to the pit, the **depths of the earth**. Though Egypt surpassed many **in beauty**, their destiny would be agony and disgrace, **placed with the uncircumcised**.

i. **Wail over the multitude of Egypt**: "Slain they were with the sword; but that was but a beginning of their sorrows, a trap door to eternal torment. Virgil, by a like figure, brings in Aeneas going down to hell, and there seeing Agamemnon, Dido, the Titans, Cyclopes, and other tyrants." (Trapp)

ii. "Whatever excellence Egypt may have imagined herself to possess would be as nothing, for her body would be consigned to the grave as with all the rest." (Feinberg)

iii. **The depths of the earth**: "Into hell, as that rich glutton in Luke 16:23, where our Saviour seemeth to allude to this place." (Trapp)

iv. **Whom do you surpass in beauty?** "How little does it signify, whether a mummy be well embalmed, wrapped round with rich stuff, and beautifully painted on the outside, or not. Go down into the *tombs*, examine the *niches*, and see whether one dead carcass be preferable to another." (Clarke)

v. **With the uncircumcised**: "Among profane and loathed carcasses; such the uncircumcised were in the opinion of the circumcised, and Herodotus in Euterpe saith the Egyptians were circumcised. However, in Scripture, a burial with the uncircumcised is a note of dishonour and contempt; thus for the king and princes." (Poole)

c. **The strong among the mighty shall speak to him out of the midst of hell**: In **hell**, Pharaoh and Egypt will be among many **strong**, many **mighty**. They will note the agony and disgrace of Egypt, to **lie with the uncircumcised, slain by the sword**.

i. The actual words of greeting are taunting and harsh, challenging Egypt's self-esteem as the most delightful nation on earth." (Block)

ii. Though this description is poetic and clouded by the Old Testament's shadowy understanding of the life to come, we still learn here that the soul is conscious in Sheol (**shall speak to him**).

iii. "The inhabitants of Sheol are not asleep but fully conscious. They are aware of one another and their relative positions; they also know that their assignment was determined by their conduct during their tenure 'in the land of the living.'" (Block)

2. (22-30) Egypt will join other nations in the pit of the grave.

"**Assyria** *is* **there, and all her company,**
With their graves all around her,
All of them slain, fallen by the sword.
Her graves are set in the recesses of the Pit,
And her company is all around her grave,
All of them slain, fallen by the sword,
Who caused terror in the land of the living.

"**There** *is* **Elam and all her multitude,**
All around her grave,
All of them slain, fallen by the sword,
Who have gone down uncircumcised to the lower parts of the earth,
Who caused their terror in the land of the living;
Now they bear their shame with those who go down to the Pit.
They have set her bed in the midst of the slain,
With all her multitude,
With her graves all around it,
All of them uncircumcised, slain by the sword;
Though their terror was caused
In the land of the living,
Yet they bear their shame
With those who go down to the Pit;
It was put in the midst of the slain.

"**There** *are* **Meshech and Tubal and all their multitudes,**
With all their graves around it,
All of them uncircumcised, slain by the sword,

Though they caused their terror in the land of the living.
They do not lie with the mighty
Who are fallen of the uncircumcised,
Who have gone down to hell with their weapons of war;
They have laid their swords under their heads,
But their iniquities will be on their bones,
Because of the terror of the mighty in the land of the living.
Yes, you shall be broken in the midst of the uncircumcised,
And lie with *those* slain by the sword.

"There *is* Edom,
Her kings and all her princes,
Who despite their might
Are laid beside *those* slain by the sword;
They shall lie with the uncircumcised,
And with those who go down to the Pit.
There *are* the princes of the north,
All of them, and all the Sidonians,
Who have gone down with the slain
In shame at the terror which they caused by their might;
They lie uncircumcised with *those* slain by the sword,
And bear their shame with those who go down to the Pit.

a. **Assyria is there**: In his poetry, Ezekiel pictured *the strong among the mighty* in hell (Ezekiel 32:21), each noticing Egypt under God's judgment as she joined them in disgrace and damnation.

i. "Each empire, with its ruler, imagines that it has found the secret of immortality, but one follows another to death." (Wright)

ii. "Some of those named had not yet disappeared from the pages of history, but their doom foretold of God was nonetheless sure and was viewed as having occurred." (Feinberg)

iii. **Assyria**: "From early times the neo-Assyrian emperors gloated over their ruthless ferocity." (Block)

b. **Assyria is there... There is Elam... There are Meshech and Tubal... There is Edom... the princes of the north... all the Sidonians**: Each of these mighty peoples would see Egypt join them in hell, coming to share their place with the **slain**, all **in shame at the terror which they caused by their might**. Egypt's destiny was to share the disgrace and shame of other judged nations.

i. **Meshech and Tubal**: "Interpreters are not agreed on the identity of the people called Meshech and Tubal. Some regard them as remnants of the old Hittite people who were driven into the mountainous country in the eastern region of Asia Minor. Others identify them with the Scythians, seeing them as one people." (Feinberg)

ii. "Meshech and Tubal experienced an even more humiliating fate for they had been even more ruthless. They were 'the terror of the mighty in the land of the living.' Therefore Meshech and Tubal rested with those who had been stripped of their weapons." (Smith)

3. (31-32) The sword of judgment upon Egypt.

"Pharaoh will see them
And be comforted over all his multitude,
Pharaoh and all his army,
Slain by the sword,"
Says the Lord GOD.
"For I have caused My terror in the land of the living;
And he shall be placed in the midst of the uncircumcised
With *those* slain by the sword,
Pharaoh and all his multitude,"
Says the Lord GOD.

a. **Pharaoh will see them and be comforted**: Ezekiel ironically mentioned some small comfort that would come to Pharaoh on the day he entered hell. The **comfort** would come from knowing he was not the only one to suffer such shame and disgrace in judgment.

i. "This is the only consolation Pharaoh can find. He is in the company of every kind of fallen greatness." (Wright)

ii. "Pharaoh also, who said he was *a god*, shall be found among the vulgar dead." (Clarke)

iii. "The prophet's declaration that 'Pharaoh shall see them, and shall be comforted,' is appalling, as it reveals that the only comfort that can come to him is the profound sense of the operation of infinite justice in the punishment of all, himself included, who have been guilty of the abominations which have issued in the judgment of Jehovah." (Morgan)

b. **For I have caused My terror in the land of the living**: God closed His words of judgment to Egypt through Ezekiel with another solemn warning of the judgment, the **terror**, that He would surely bring.

i. "The oracle affirms that Yahweh is the Lord not only of individuals but also of history. The rise and fall of nations may appear attributable to charismatic and gifted leaders, but behind all international movements one must acknowledge the supreme hand of Yahweh, who alone fixes the times and seasons of their lives, sets the limits to their conduct, determines the nature of their downfall, appoints the agents of judgment, and in the process accomplishes his goal: the universal recognition of his power and his person." (Block)

Ezekiel 33 – The Prophet as Watchman

A. Ezekiel the watchman.

1. (1-6) The principle of the watchman.

Again the word of the LORD came to me, saying, "Son of man, speak to the children of your people, and say to them: 'When I bring the sword upon a land, and the people of the land take a man from their territory and make him their watchman, when he sees the sword coming upon the land, if he blows the trumpet and warns the people, then whoever hears the sound of the trumpet and does not take warning, if the sword comes and takes him away, his blood shall be on his *own* head. He heard the sound of the trumpet, but did not take warning; his blood shall be upon himself. But he who takes warning will save his life. But if the watchman sees the sword coming and does not blow the trumpet, and the people are not warned, and the sword comes and takes *any* person from among them, he is taken away in his iniquity; but his blood I will require at the watchman's hand.'

a. **When I bring a sword upon a land**: This establishes the context for all that Ezekiel wrote regarding the **watchman**. As spoken before in Ezekiel chapter 3:16-27, the image of the watchman has the context of warning of God's approaching judgment. Ezekiel's role as a **watchman** was connected to **when he sees the sword coming upon the land**.

i. There are many who consider themselves watchmen to the people of God today. They watch carefully and look for signs of error or apostasy. There is always a place for those to do what Ezekiel was called to do as a watchman – to discern that God's judgment was coming soon and to warn **the people**. Yet many who consider themselves modern "watchmen" focus on the examination of supposed error more than the proclamation of God's truth. This is a distortion of Ezekiel's calling as a **watchman**.

ii. Another way this modern office of watchman may distort the Biblical idea is by untruthful or unfair examination of others in search of error or apostasy. If a watchman alerts people to dangers but does not give an honest and fair report, then he will not be believed when he warns of a genuine danger.

b. **If he blows the trumpet and warns the people**: When the judgment of God came upon the land and especially to correct God's people, the **watchman** had a sacred responsibility to warn the people. If he did, then if any did not heed the warning, his **blood** was **upon himself**. This was a great assurance to Ezekiel and Jeremiah because they warned many but few listened.

c. **He who takes warning will save his life**: When the judgment of God comes upon the land, the only preservation is in hearing the **warning** of the watchman and responding properly.

d. **If the watchman sees the sword coming and does not blow the trumpet**: If the watchman did not warn the people about God's judgment, then the **blood** of those who perished would be held against the watchman.

2. (7-9) Ezekiel the watchman.

"So you, son of man: I have made you a watchman for the house of Israel; therefore you shall hear a word from My mouth and warn them for Me. When I say to the wicked, 'O wicked *man*, you shall surely die!' and you do not speak to warn the wicked from his way, that wicked *man* shall die in his iniquity; but his blood I will require at your hand. Nevertheless if you warn the wicked to turn from his way, and he does not turn from his way, he shall die in his iniquity; but you have delivered your soul.

a. **I have made you a watchman for the house of Israel; therefore you shall hear a word from My mouth and warn them for Me**: The watchman did not gain his knowledge by studying the armies of the Babylonian empire, or by looking at the false prophets among God's people at that time. Ezekiel heard from God that judgment was coming soon, and had to announce it.

b. **O wicked man, you shall surely die**: This was the main message of Ezekiel (and Jeremiah), though in general they brought the message to Jerusalem and to the kingdom of Israel more than to specific individuals.

c. **If you warn the wicked to turn from his way, and he does not turn from his way**: If the watchman faithfully delivered his message, then the response of the one he warned was the responsibility of the one who heard it. It could be said to the watchman, **you have delivered your soul**.

B. The fairness of God's judgments.

1. (10-11) God's judgment is fair because He takes no special pleasure in it.

"Therefore you, O son of man, say to the house of Israel: 'Thus you say, "If our transgressions and our sins *lie* upon us, and we pine away in them, how can we then live?"' Say to them: '*As* I live,' says the Lord God, 'I have no pleasure in the death of the wicked, but that the wicked turn from his way and live. Turn, turn from your evil ways! For why should you die, O house of Israel?'

a. **If our transgressions and our sins lie upon us, and we pine away in them, how can we then live?** This was an accusing question raised against the fairness of God's judgment. The idea was that God was happy to make His judgment so severe that it left no room for His people to repent.

b. **I have no pleasure in the death of the wicked, but that the wicked turn from his way and live**: God responded to the accusing question of His people by declaring a basic principle about His nature and dealings with humanity. God takes no special **pleasure in the death of the wicked**. God's heart is for people to repent, to **turn from** their **way and live**. God is *not* sadistic and cruel, making repentance impossible because He loves to see humanity suffer.

i. The fact that God does not take **pleasure in the death of the wicked** does not mean that it will not happen. God's general desire for all humanity is that they would repent, turn to Him and be saved; yet He will not spare the requirements of justice and holiness for those who refuse to **turn** to Him.

ii. It is especially important to understand these statements in their context; that Ezekiel spoke this regarding the judgment to come upon Judah and Jerusalem in *this life*, and not in first reference to eternal judgment. Nevertheless, since this principle is so rooted in God's character, it applies to God's eternal judgments. God is not "happy" when people choose hell; His general desire for all humanity is that they would repent, turn to Him and be saved.

c. **Turn, turn from your evil ways**: This communicates the desire, even the **pleasure** of God. The Lord's longing is that men and women would choose life (Deuteronomy 30:19) and not death. God wanted **Israel** to live and not **die**. The question, **why should you die, O house of Israel?** means that they didn't *have* to perish in the coming judgment.

2. (12-16) The principle of the changed life.

"Therefore you, O son of man, say to the children of your people: 'The righteousness of the righteous man shall not deliver him in the day of

his transgression; as for the wickedness of the wicked, he shall not fall because of it in the day that he turns from his wickedness; nor shall the righteous be able to live because of *his righteousness* in the day that he sins.' When I say to the righteous *that* he shall surely live, but he trusts in his own righteousness and commits iniquity, none of his righteous works shall be remembered; but because of the iniquity that he has committed, he shall die. Again, when I say to the wicked, 'You shall surely die,' if he turns from his sin and does what is lawful and right, *if* the wicked restores the pledge, gives back what he has stolen, and walks in the statutes of life without committing iniquity, he shall surely live; he shall not die. None of his sins which he has committed shall be remembered against him; he has done what is lawful and right; he shall surely live.

a. **The righteousness of the righteous man shall not deliver him in the day of his transgression**: God told Ezekiel to speak to another accusing objection from the people of God. This was an accusation based on fatalism, which basically said: *the good are good and the bad are bad and nothing can be done about it.* To answer that objection, God reminded them all that every **righteous man** could end up with a life dominated by **his transgression**. His prior righteousness would not rescue him on the day of God's judgment.

b. **As for the wickedness of the wicked, he shall not fall because of it in the day that he turns from his wickedness**: On the same principle, someone who lived a prior life of **wickedness** was not pre-ordained to continue that way. They could turn and be spared in the season of God's judgment.

c. **When I say to the righteous that he shall surely live, but he trusts in his own righteousness**: No one is so righteous that they cannot fall into great error and danger if they were to trust in their **own righteousness** instead of God and His mercy. To do so may mean to have all of one's **righteous works** account for nothing before God, and **he shall die**. The same principle worked in reverse for the **wicked**. In both cases, if God pronounced "**he shall surely live**" to the righteous or "**you shall surely die**" to the wicked, neither was an irrevocable or irreversible pronouncement.

d. **If the wicked restores the pledge, gives back what he has stolen**: Again, the point is clear. God does not want us to regard human destiny as fatalistically determined by a person's past, either for good or evil.

3. (17-20) Unfairness found with Israel, not God.

"Yet the children of your people say, 'The way of the LORD is not fair.' But it is their way which is not fair! When the righteous turns from his

righteousness and commits iniquity, he shall die because of it. But when the wicked turns from his wickedness and does what is lawful and right, he shall live because of it. Yet you say, 'The way of the LORD is not fair.' O house of Israel, I will judge every one of you according to his own ways."

a. **The way of the LORD is not fair**: This was another accusation against God and His prophets. When Ezekiel and others announced God's coming judgment, some responded by questioning the fairness of it.

b. **But it is their way which is not fair**: God boldly replied to their accusation. God was entirely fair; it was the **children of your people** who unfairly looked to fate or the past to determine a person's destiny.

c. **When the righteous turns from his righteousness…when the wicked turns from his wickedness**: Yet, as in the previous verses, God declared that man is not fatalistically bound to his past, whether his past was **righteous** or was **wicked**.

d. **I will judge every one of you according to his own ways**: This was God's standard of judgment, and it was (and is) entirely fair. It was fair under the old covenant, which was greatly based on works. It is also (in another sense) fair under the new covenant, where a person's faith is proved to be real by their works (James 2:14-17).

C. The messenger from Jerusalem.

1. (21) The messenger arrives.

And it came to pass in the twelfth year of our captivity, in the tenth *month,* on the fifth *day* of the month, *that* one who had escaped from Jerusalem came to me and said, "The city has been captured!"

a. **In the twelfth year of our captivity**: This was seven years after the first prophecies of the Book of Ezekiel (Ezekiel 1:2-3).

b. **The city has been captured**: The messenger told of what Ezekiel had long predicted, that Jerusalem would be utterly overwhelmed by the armies of Babylon. This was a sad and tragic vindication of the prophet.

2. (22-24) The arrogant proclamation of the few Jewish survivors remaining in Judea.

Now the hand of the LORD had been upon me the evening before the man came who had escaped. And He had opened my mouth; so when he came to me in the morning, my mouth was opened, and I was no longer mute. Then the word of the LORD came to me, saying: "Son of man, they who inhabit those ruins in the land of Israel are saying, 'Abraham was

only one, and he inherited the land. But we *are* many; the land has been given to us as a possession.'

a. **He opened my mouth**: God had given Ezekiel a sense of a significant revelation to come (**the hand of the LORD had been upon me the evening before**) but had made the prophet **mute** until the messenger came.

b. **Abraham was only one, and he inherited the land. But we are many; the land has been given to us as a possession**: These were the thoughts and words of the small remnant that remained behind in Jerusalem and Judea. Here we learn that they thought *they* would inherit the land and rebuild a new Israel and Jerusalem. But God had promised that this would come from returning exiles, not those who remained in the land.

i. Jeremiah described these remaining few and the tragic events connected with them in Jeremiah 40-44.

3. (25-26) God's answer to the surviving remnant.

"**Therefore say to them, 'Thus says the Lord GOD: "You eat *meat* with blood, you lift up your eyes toward your idols, and shed blood. Should you then possess the land? You rely on your sword, you commit abominations, and you defile one another's wives. Should you then possess the land?"'**

a. **You eat meat with blood, you lift up your eyes toward your idols, and shed blood**: These few survivors who somehow evaded death and exile were not godly, covenant-keeping men. They did not observe God's dietary laws, they did not worship Yahweh alone, and they were violent.

b. **Should you then possess the land?** God repeated this question twice to emphasize that they *would not* **possess the land**. God's promise to restore Israel and Jerusalem would be accomplished, but not through ungodly men like these.

4. (27-29) God's promise of judgment on the few survivors.

"**Say thus to them, 'Thus says the Lord GOD: "*As* I live, surely those who *are* in the ruins shall fall by the sword, and the one who *is* in the open field I will give to the beasts to be devoured, and those who *are* in the strongholds and caves shall die of the pestilence. For I will make the land most desolate, her arrogant strength shall cease, and the mountains of Israel shall be so desolate that no one will pass through. Then they shall know that I *am* the LORD, when I have made the land most desolate because of all their abominations which they have committed."'**

a. **Those who are in the ruins shall fall by the sword**: The survivors did not truly escape God's judgment; it was only delayed it for a short time.

The same judgments of **the sword, the beasts**, and **pestilence** would strike them in time. Jeremiah 40-44 proved this to be true.

b. **I will make the land most desolate**: The arrogant dreams of the few survivors would come to nothing. God would further His work of making the **land most desolate** despite their **arrogant strength**.

c. **Then they shall know that I am the** LORD: Jerusalem had just fallen, and an almost unimaginable calamity came upon the people. Yet God promised a *further* desolation to come, and it would come because of their terrible idolatry (**because of all their abominations which they have committed**).

5. (30-33) The people were pleased to hear Ezekiel but did not truly listen.

"As for you, son of man, the children of your people are talking about you beside the walls and in the doors of the houses; and they speak to one another, everyone saying to his brother, 'Please come and hear what the word is that comes from the LORD.**' So they come to you as people do, they sit before you** *as* **My people, and they hear your words, but they do not do them; for with their mouth they show much love,** *but* **their hearts pursue their** *own* **gain. Indeed you** *are* **to them as a very lovely song of one who has a pleasant voice and can play well on an instrument; for they hear your words, but they do not do them. And when this comes to pass—surely it will come—then they will know that a prophet has been among them."**

a. **The children of your people are talking about you**: God wanted Ezekiel to know that his message was getting out to the people. Even if they did not obey what God told them to do, they did talk about him and regard what he said as **the word that comes from the** LORD.

b. **They hear your words, but they do not do them**: In a superficial sense Ezekiel was popular as a prophet. People talked about his prophetic words and gave lip-service and the words being from God. Yet it was a very superficial sense; they heard, but they did not really listen or **do them**.

c. **With their mouth they show much love, but their hearts pursue their own gain**: People *said* good and kind things about Ezekiel's preaching, but it made no difference in their hearts or lives. They still lived for **their own gain** and not the honor and holiness of God.

d. **You are to them as a very lovely song**: They liked to listen to Ezekiel as anyone likes to listen to a good singer (**a pleasant voice**) and well-played music (**play well on an instrument**). They enjoyed the prophet's "music" but did not respond to his message with truth, faith and action.

e. **Then they will know that a prophet has been among them**: Ezekiel had already been proved a true prophet because Jerusalem had been captured (Ezekiel 33:21). Yet as his prophecies continued to be fulfilled and woe came to those who did not receive them with faith and action, at the very least the people would **know** that Ezekiel was indeed a true **prophet**, and should never be regarded as an entertainer or mere inspirational speaker.

Ezekiel 34 – Of Shepherds and Sheep

A. God's word to the shepherds of His people.

1. (1-2) The accusation against the unfaithful shepherds of Israel.

And the word of the LORD came to me, saying, "Son of man, prophesy against the shepherds of Israel, prophesy and say to them, 'Thus says the Lord GOD to the shepherds: "Woe to the shepherds of Israel who feed themselves! Should not the shepherds feed the flocks?

a. **Prophesy against the shepherds of Israel**: The idea of the *shepherd* in the ancient Near East often meant a king or a prince. Joshua is an example of a civil leader called a shepherd (Numbers 27:17), as well as King David (2 Samuel 5:2). Here the idea includes that, but also includes the idea of those who are *spiritual* leaders among God's people. Jeremiah is an example of a spiritual leader who was called a shepherd (Jeremiah 17:16).

i. The New Testament will later make this idea perfectly clear. When Peter wrote, *Shepherd the flock of God which is among you, serving as overseers, not by compulsion but willingly, not for dishonest gain but eagerly* (1 Peter 5:2), he meant spiritual shepherds. Peter wrote this keeping in mind that Jesus is always the ultimate Shepherd among God's people (1 Peter 2:25).

ii. The idea of the LORD and His Messiah as the perfect Shepherd of God's people goes all the way back to Genesis 49:24, and is of course reflected in passages such as Psalm 23.

iii. "The 'shepherd' as an image of political rulers goes back to the Sumerian royal tradition (4th millennium B.C.E.). The motif became widespread throughout the ancient Near East." (Vawter and Hoppe)

b. **Woe to the shepherds of Israel who feed themselves**: Regarding both civil and spiritual leaders, God rebuked and warned those **shepherds** who were concerned about feeding themselves, and not their flock. The obvious question was asked: **Should not the shepherds feed the flocks?** Godly shepherds must serve more for the benefit of the flock than their own benefit.

i. "This may be acceptable in real life, where shepherds are justifiably motivated by self-interest, but when the image is used metaphorically of humans tending humans, the shepherd holds office for the sake of the ruled." (Block)

ii. In His great teaching on the Good Shepherd in John 10, Jesus explained this principle. *The good shepherd gives His life for the sheep* (John 10:11). Peter later wrote of this same idea (1 Peter 5:2). Faithful shepherds care for the flock, sometimes at significant self-sacrifice.

2. (3-4) The greed of the unfaithful shepherds of Israel.

You eat the fat and clothe yourselves with the wool; you slaughter the fatlings, *but* you do not feed the flock. The weak you have not strengthened, nor have you healed those who were sick, nor bound up the broken, nor brought back what was driven away, nor sought what was lost; but with force and cruelty you have ruled them.

a. **You eat the fat and clothe yourselves with the wool**: The unfaithful leaders of Israel (both civil and spiritual) exploited their flocks without caring for them in return (**but you do not feed the flock**). It wasn't wrong for the shepherd to make his living from the flock, but it was wrong to do it in a way that neglected love for the flock and the needs of the sheep.

i. The New Testament clearly teaches that those who serve God's people have the right to be supported by those they serve (1 Corinthians 9:7-14, 1 Timothy 5:17-18). Yet that is a right that can and should be set aside when it is better for the kingdom of God to do so (Acts 20:33-35).

ii. Yet Ezekiel's principle is *always* valid. If the shepherd does receive his livelihood from the sheep, *he must appropriately care for the sheep* with his heart and work. If he does not feed and care for the sheep, he is an unfaithful and unworthy shepherd.

iii. "The bill of particulars was presented in verse 3, with the forms of the verbs in the Hebrew original indicating that the faithless shepherds were continually doing these acts. The emphasis was that the shepherds had but one objective in mind, namely, their own enjoyment and pleasure." (Feinberg)

iv. "Ezekiel's figure assumes the forceful removal of wool, making it look like the sheep are left naked before the elements." (Block)

b. **You do not feed the flock**: As this idea is developed in the Scriptures, we understand that the main way that a godly shepherd feeds God's sheep is by faithfully teaching God's word to them (Isaiah 55:1-2, Jeremiah 3:15, John 21:15-17, 1 Corinthians 3:2, Hebrews 5:12-14, 1 Peter 2:2). We are *nourished in the words of faith* (1 Timothy 4:6). Every word of God is like bread to us (Matthew 4:4).

c. **The weak you have not strengthened, nor have you healed those who were sick**: The unfaithful shepherd does not care for the evident needs among God's people. Perhaps there will always be some hidden problems in the flock, but what is revealed must be cared for.

d. **Strengthened…healed…bound up…brought back…sought**: These words describe the actions of the faithful, godly shepherd. Many of these ideas are included in the concepts of *equipping* and *edifying* described in Ephesians 4:11-12. The variety of terms suggests that the godly shepherd will have something of the wisdom of a good doctor, able to diagnose the condition of the sheep.

- Where there is weakness, he looks for the sheep to **strengthened**.

- Where there is illness, he looks for the sheep to be **healed**.

- Where there are wounds or brokenness, he looks for them to be **bound up**.

- Where the sheep are disobedient, he looks for them to be **brought back**.

- Where the sheep are lost, he wants for them to be **sought**.

   i. "No person is fit for the office of a shepherd, who does not *well understand* the *diseases* to which sheep are incident, and the *mode of cure*. And is any man fit for the *pastoral office*, or to be a shepherd of souls, who is not well acquainted with the *disease of sin* in all its *varieties*, and the *remedy* for this disease, and the proper mode of administering it, in those various cases? He who does not know Jesus Christ as his *own Saviour*, never can recommend him to others. He who is not saved, will not save." (Clarke)

e. **But with force and cruelty you have ruled them**: Instead of the care, wisdom, and compassion that a faithful shepherd should have, these unfaithful shepherds used **force and cruelty**. This was their shameful crime and one reason they were objects of God's rebuke and approaching judgment.

   i. Jesus specifically spoke out against this kind of leadership in Matthew 20:25-28. He said that this kind of leadership was characteristic of the ungodly, and should not mark leaders among God's people. Jesus certainly does not lead with **force and cruelty**.

ii. Leaders must make difficult choices and those choices will more than occasionally displease people. Ezekiel (or Jesus) never meant that faithful shepherds will please everyone. Yet it means that when difficult choices are made, they will be made and carried out with love and compassion. Godly shepherds will not lead with **force**, coercion, manipulation, threats, anger, or other forms of **cruelty**. This will be true of both their public leadership (such as with a congregation) *and* private leadership (such as with a staff or leadership team).

iii. Adam Clarke spoke of his own day, the early 1800s: "God, in this country, *unpriested* a whole hierarchy who fed not the flock, but *ruled them with force and cruelty*; and he raised up a new set of shepherds better qualified, both by sound doctrine and learning, to feed the flock. Let these be faithful, lest God cause *them to cease*, and raise up other feeders."

3. (5-6) The result of the work of the unfaithful shepherds.

So they were scattered because *there was* no shepherd; and they became food for all the beasts of the field when they were scattered. My sheep wandered through all the mountains, and on every high hill; yes, My flock was scattered over the whole face of the earth, and no one was seeking or searching *for them*."

a. **So they were scattered because there was no shepherd**: In both the civil and spiritual realms, when sheep have unfaithful shepherds sometimes they think the answer is *no shepherds*. They think that almost any kind of leadership among God's people is unnecessary and that the flock can lead itself. Ezekiel specifically spoke against this kind of thinking. When there **was no shepherd**, it was no better for the sheep.

b. **They became food for all the beasts of the field**: This was the result of the scattering. *Some of God's flock* **became food for all the beasts of the field**. The unfaithful shepherds soured the sheep on the principle of leadership among God's people, and the flock ended up suffering greatly because of it.

c. **My sheep... My flock**: For emphasis, God twice stated that *the flock belongs to Him*. It's always dangerous when civil or spiritual leaders begin to think that God's people belong to them, that they in any sense *own* them. Peter repeated this idea in 1 Peter 5:2-3.

i. "But *my flock* is more than an expression of ownership; it is a term of endearment." (Block)

ii. Godly shepherds should never use the phrase "my church" in any way other than indicating the church *entrusted to them*, the congregation *they serve* and are part of. "My church" should never be used in a possessive sense; the church always belongs to Jesus Himself (Matthew 16:18).

d. **No one was seeking or searching for them**: There is a sense of sadness in these words, sadness over the fact that there are so few godly shepherds. Even if the number of faithful shepherds is large by itself, it seems to be never enough to meet the need or adequately care for God's flock.

i. "In short, the shepherds were both unfaithful and unconcerned." (Smith)

4. (7-10) God promises to hold the unfaithful shepherds to account.

'**Therefore, you shepherds, hear the word of the LORD: "***As* **I live," says the Lord GOD, "surely because My flock became a prey, and My flock became food for every beast of the field, because** *there was* **no shepherd, nor did My shepherds search for My flock, but the shepherds fed themselves and did not feed My flock"— therefore, O shepherds, hear the word of the LORD! Thus says the Lord GOD: "Behold, I** *am* **against the shepherds, and I will require My flock at their hand; I will cause them to cease feeding the sheep, and the shepherds shall feed themselves no more; for I will deliver My flock from their mouths, that they may no longer be food for them."**

a. **Therefore, you shepherds**: God saw the unfaithful shepherds and would not be silent about their sins. These shepherds did not seem able to correct themselves, so God would correct them.

i. **As I live**: "The threat contained therein was certain to come to pass for it was sealed with a divine oath." (Smith)

b. **Because My flock became a prey**: If the shepherds stopped paying attention to the flock and stopped caring about them, God did not stop. He noticed when His own **flock became a prey**, and He saw when His **shepherds** failed to **search for** the lost sheep.

c. **The shepherds fed themselves and did not feed My flock**: Not only did the shepherds neglect the flock so they **became a prey**, but *they themselves* **fed** on the flock. They were more like the beasts that ate the sheep than true shepherds who should care for them.

d. **I am against the shepherds, and I will require My flock at their hand**: God solemnly promised to hold the unfaithful, ungodly shepherds to account. In the eyes of the flock, they may seem to go unpunished; God promised to deal with them.

- God would do it by removing them from their position (**cause them to cease feeding the sheep**).

- God would do it stopping their abuse of the flock (**the shepherds shall feed themselves no more**).

- God would do it by removing His flock from them (**I will deliver My flock from their mouths**).

    i. **I am against the shepherds**: "They have provoked me to displeasure to be their enemy, and I will appear and act so. They are enemies to my sheep, yet pretended to be shepherds, I will be an open enemy to them." (Poole)

    ii. **I will require**: "It expresses the legal disposition of calling an evildoer to account, in this case holding the criminal shepherds accountable for the fate of the flock." (Block)

5. (11-16) God promises to do the work that the unfaithful shepherds would not do.

'For thus says the Lord GOD: "Indeed I Myself will search for My sheep and seek them out. As a shepherd seeks out his flock on the day he is among his scattered sheep, so will I seek out My sheep and deliver them from all the places where they were scattered on a cloudy and dark day. And I will bring them out from the peoples and gather them from the countries, and will bring them to their own land; I will feed them on the mountains of Israel, in the valleys and in all the inhabited places of the country. I will feed them in good pasture, and their fold shall be on the high mountains of Israel. There they shall lie down in a good fold and feed in rich pasture on the mountains of Israel. I will feed My flock, and I will make them lie down," says the Lord GOD. "I will seek what was lost and bring back what was driven away, bind up the broken and strengthen what was sick; but I will destroy the fat and the strong, and feed them in judgment."

    a. **I Myself will search for My sheep and seek them out**: Out of love for His sheep, God promised to do the work that the unfaithful shepherds would not do. The LORD would deal with the ungodly shepherds (Ezekiel 34:7-10), but He would also **seek** out the lost sheep neglected by the bad shepherds.

        i. **Indeed I Myself**: "The construction is emphatical in the Hebrew and well expressed here; I, the Owner, the Lover, the Maker, the great Shepherd, even I." (Poole)

        ii. "The picture of the shepherd searching out the wanderer, in verse 12, is a remarkable foreshadowing of the parable of the lost sheep (Luke

15:4ff.), which our Lord doubtless based on this passage in Ezekiel." (Taylor)

iii. There is a subtle but clear testimony here to the deity of Jesus Christ. Without doubt, Ezekiel 34 presents *Yahweh* as the good and perfect shepherd of Israel. Without ambiguity, Jesus took that title to Himself (most clearly in John 10:1-18), demonstrating that He is God.

iv. **I will seek out**: "Who is this that says, 'I will'? When a man says, 'I will,' it is often braggart impudence; but when God says, 'I will' and 'you shall,' such words are expressive alike of sovereign determination and irresistible power." (Spurgeon)

b. **He is among his scattered sheep**: God promised to come down among His own **scattered sheep** to seek them and care for them. In the greatest sense, this was wonderfully fulfilled in the work of Jesus Christ.

i. **On a cloudy and dark day**: "The reference to *a day of clouds and thick darkness* (12, RSV) has eschatological overtones (cf. Ps. 97:2; Joel 2:2; Zeph. 1:15) and suggests that this deliverance is to be the day of the Lord for Israel, that is to say, the day when the Lord acts in salvation and judgment to usher in a new age of his righteous rule on earth." (Taylor)

c. **I will bring them out from the peoples and gather them from the countries**: As promised in other places (Ezekiel 11:17, 36:24), God made promises associated with the New Covenant. These promises had a partial fulfillment in the return from exile but still await their true and perfect fulfillment.

i. "In beautiful and unforgettable words Ezekiel predicted a literal return and restoration of the people of Israel to their own land. Notice it will be a regathering from worldwide exile and dispersion." (Feinberg)

ii. "In Ezekiel's time, the Lord brought His people back from Babylon; but the picture here is certainly much broader than that, for the Lord spoke about 'countries.'" (Wiersbe)

d. **I will bring them to their own land**: God promised to restore Israel **to their own land**. While there had always been the presence of a Jewish remnant in the land of Israel, this began to be fulfilled in a remarkable and significant way in the Zionist movement starting in the late 1800s. The establishment of the State of Israel in 1948 was an important milestone in the fulfillment of this promise, though we would say that it is yet to be completely fulfilled.

i. "It is both unnecessary and impossible to spiritualize these promises. If the scattering were literal, and no one is foolhardy as to deny this, then the regathering must be equally so." (Feinberg)

e. **I will feed them in good pasture**: The restoration God promised to Israel was not only geographical but also *spiritual*. The restoration of the land is much further along in its fulfillment than the spiritual restoration of Israel.

i. **They shall lie down in a good fold**: "When the Lord reveals to you that he has loved you with an everlasting love, is not that a good place to lie down in? When he tells you that having so loved you, he will never cast you away, is not that a good place to lie down in? When he tells you that your warfare is accomplished, and that your sin is pardoned, is not that a good place to lie down in?" (Spurgeon)

f. **I will feed My flock... I will seek... bring back... bind up the broken... strengthen**: What the unfaithful shepherds of Ezekiel 34:3-4 failed to do, God would ultimately do Himself. This doesn't exclude the use of men and women in this work, but means that God will make sure that it happens.

i. "This message certainly must have brought hope to the exiles as they realized the Lord has not forsaken them but would care for them as a shepherd for his sheep." (Wiersbe)

ii. "It illustrates as clearly as anything can do the tender, loving qualities of the God of the Old Testament, and strikes a death-blow at those who try to drive a wedge between Yahweh, God of Israel, and the God and Father of our Lord Jesus Christ." (Taylor)

iii. Alexander on the words of Jesus in John 10: "It certainly appears that he had Ezekiel 34 in mind. He was declaring to those discerning Jews that he was the true and righteous Shepherd of whom Ezekiel spoke—the Messiah. He would lay down his life for the sheep, not exploit them."

g. **I will destroy the fat and the strong, and feed them in judgment**: God promised to judge the proud among the sheep, those who were **fat and strong**, but not fed of the LORD. There would be a cleansing of judgment among God's people, as described in the following verses.

i. **Feed them in judgment**: "It is an irony; I will feed them, but with wormwood and gall, my sore but just judgments and displeasure." (Poole)

B. God's word to His flock, His own people.

1. (17-19) Don't trample the pasture and foul the water.

'And *as for* you, O My flock, thus says the Lord GOD: "Behold, I shall judge between sheep and sheep, between rams and goats. *Is it* too little for you to have eaten up the good pasture, that you must tread down with your feet the residue of your pasture—and to have drunk of the clear waters, that you must foul the residue with your feet? And *as for* My flock, they eat what you have trampled with your feet, and they drink what you have fouled with your feet."

a. **As for you, O My flock**: In Ezekiel 34:1-16 Yahweh gave a severe rebuke to the unfaithful shepherds of Israel. Now God spoke to the **flock**. The sins of the shepherds *did not excuse* the sins of the flock. They had their own accountability to God.

> i. Modern western culture often divides the world into two categories: *oppressors* and *victims*. Great attention is given to the sins and crimes of the oppressors, and often rightly so. Yet we err when we think there are never circumstances when one thought to be a victim can also have responsibility for their own sins and failings before God.

b. **I shall judge between sheep and sheep, between rams and goats**: God recognized that *all sheep are not the same*, and He reserved the right to make such distinctions. When considering sheep abused by a shepherd, it may be that one sheep has no responsibility, another sheep has some responsibility, and a third sheep has great responsibility. These distinctions may be difficult for us to make, but God can and does make them perfectly.

> i. "Some think Ezekiel turns here from the kings to lesser officials who had mistreated their fellow countrymen. God will judge between one class (the weak and the helpless) and another (the strong and the oppressive)." (Feinberg)

> ii. "The flock will in fact be purified, not only of its bad leadership but also of its bad members." (Taylor)

> iii. "Don't read into 'rams and he-goats' (v. 17) the New Testament image of 'sheep and goats' as found in Matthew 25:31–46, because in Bible times, it was customary for shepherds to have both sheep and goats in the flocks." (Wiersbe)

c. **Is it too little for you to have eaten up the good pasture, that you must tread down with your feet the residue of your pasture**: God's charge against these erring sheep was not that they ate up their own **good pasture** (indicating they had food enough). The charge against them was that they **tread down** the already eaten pasture, ruining it for the future. They did not care for their own pasture but trampled it down.

i. In acting as if the pasture belonged to *them*, these renegade sheep spoiled it for others. This shows that damage can be done to the flock not only by the shepherd, but also by sheep who are not considerate of other sheep, and who treat the pasture as if it were theirs to do with as they pleased.

ii. "They had abused their positions of strength and 'bullied' the other sheep, driving them away… there was no place for such irresponsible behavior among leaders." (Alexander)

d. **To have drunk of the clear waters, that you must foul the residue with your feet**: They not only spoiled the pasture for the other sheep, they also fouled the clear waters. Again, they treated the **clear waters** as if they were their own and therefore spoiled the waters for the other sheep.

e. **They eat what you have trampled with your feet, and they drink what you have fouled with your feet**: This was the misery of God's flock. They had to live in an unpleasant, unsustainable pasture because other sheep had abused it. They had to drink muddied waters because of the inconsiderate actions of renegade sheep among God's flock.

i. **They eat what you have trampled**: "The poor, misled, and muzzled people are glad to eat such as they can catch. They are fed with traditions, legendary fables, indulgences, vowed pilgrimages, penances." (Trapp)

2. (20-24) God will protect His flock against renegade sheep.

'Therefore thus says the Lord GOD to them: "Behold, I Myself will judge between the fat and the lean sheep. Because you have pushed with side and shoulder, butted all the weak ones with your horns, and scattered them abroad, therefore I will save My flock, and they shall no longer be a prey; and I will judge between sheep and sheep. I will establish one shepherd over them, and he shall feed them—My servant David. He shall feed them and be their shepherd. And I, the LORD, will be their God, and My servant David a prince among them; I, the LORD, have spoken.

a. **I Myself will judge between the fat and the lean sheep**: God promised to judge these renegade sheep, who in some way flattered themselves by thinking they were the "better ones" of the flock. They thought of themselves as the **fat**, mature, healthy sheep. God noted that the way they threw their weight around (**you pushed with side and shoulder, butted the weak ones**) actually abused the other sheep and made them leave the pasture (**scattered them abroad**).

i. It is a story told in many churches. Those who consider themselves to be mature, knowledgeable believers cause great trouble. In Ezekiel's picture, they are the fat sheep that spoil the pasture and the waters for the other sheep. Their disruptions to the peace of God's flock spoil the food for other sheep and even make them scatter.

ii. "It is not only the leaders who are at fault, but within the flock there are those who are concerned only with their own interests, and not content with this, are deliberately spoiling life for others." (Wright)

iii. **Pushed… butted**: "It would be interesting to know whether Ezekiel had any specific examples of oppression in mind as he uttered these words. The shoddy treatment of the Hebrew slaves during the siege of Jerusalem was certainly an apt example of the truth of his allegations (Jeremiah 34:8–11)." (Taylor)

b. **Therefore I will save My flock, and they shall no longer be a prey; and I will judge between sheep and sheep**: God promised to rescue His precious flock, not only from the unfaithful shepherds (Ezekiel 34:1-16) but also from the renegade sheep. Ironically, just as with the unfaithful shepherds, the renegade sheep made other sheep **a prey**. They scattered them out of their pasture where they were picked off by hungry beasts. Therefore, God promised to **judge between sheep and sheep**.

c. **I will establish one shepherd over them**: God now once again returned to the new covenant phrasing and perspective. He had in mind the ultimate, perfect gathering of Israel as part of the new covenant promises when He would even set **David** over them as **their shepherd**.

i. "What started out as an oracle of judgment ends as an oracle of salvation that speaks directly about Judah's future." (Vawter and Hoppe)

ii. "The full realization of the prediction of verse 22 must be in the future in Messiah's reign. How much is to be accomplished in Messiah's kingdom! Is it any wonder that the godly in Israel have always looked with longing and faith to that hour of blessed consummation?" (Feinberg)

d. **I, the LORD, will be their God, and My servant David a prince among them**: This plain promise is most appropriately seen *not* as a strange and imprecise reference to Jesus the Messiah, but as part of the several promises that King David will once again rule over Israel in the Millennial Kingdom (Isaiah 55:3-4, Jeremiah 30:8-9, Ezekiel 37:25, Hosea 3:5).

i. Most commentators believe that this reference to **David** is really a reference to the Messiah, the Son of David, fulfilled in Jesus Christ.

They would say the same of the many other passages (noted above) which speak of David's future rule over Israel. Yet we can simply observe that if God did not intend David, He would not have said it. There is nothing in these texts themselves that *demand* that it is the Messiah and not David.

ii. **My servant David a prince**: In this particular passage, David is not even described as a *king*, but in a lesser office – **prince**. The idea is that this is when Jesus Messiah is King over all the earth, and David rules Israel as a **prince** under Him.

iii. "In Ezekiel 34:24 the prophet does not call him 'king' (*melek*) but 'prince' (*nasi*).... He will not be a typical ancient Near Eastern monarch, but God's 'servant' who presides over the kingdom that God rules. This David as God's servant has a certain latitude in the fulfillment of his responsibilities." (Vawter and Hoppe)

iv. "Significantly for our discussion, David's divine election had earlier been described as a call from the 'pasture' (*naweh*), from following the flock, to be 'ruler' (*nagid*) of Yahweh's people Israel." (Block)

v. **A prince among them**: "The prophet emphasizes the ruler's identification with the people by noting that he will be not only 'prince over Israel' (v. 23; cf. 19:1, etc.) but 'prince in their midst.'" (Block)

3. (25-30) God's promise to bring blessing and security to His flock.

"I will make a covenant of peace with them, and cause wild beasts to cease from the land; and they will dwell safely in the wilderness and sleep in the woods. I will make them and the places all around My hill a blessing; and I will cause showers to come down in their season; there shall be showers of blessing. Then the trees of the field shall yield their fruit, and the earth shall yield her increase. They shall be safe in their land; and they shall know that I *am* the LORD, when I have broken the bands of their yoke and delivered them from the hand of those who enslaved them. And they shall no longer be a prey for the nations, nor shall beasts of the land devour them; but they shall dwell safely, and no one shall make *them* afraid. I will raise up for them a garden of renown, and they shall no longer be consumed with hunger in the land, nor bear the shame of the Gentiles anymore. Thus they shall know that I, the LORD their God, *am* with them, and they, the house of Israel, *are* My people," says the Lord GOD.'"

a. **I will make a covenant of peace with them**: Again, all this points towards the new covenant, especially in its perfection and culmination in the Millennial Kingdom. The promises of peace in the millennium are also found in passages such as Isaiah 2:4 and Jeremiah 23:5-6.

> i. **A covenant of peace**: "The description offers one of the fullest explications of the Hebrew notion of *shalom*. The term obviously signifies much more than the absence of hostility or tension. It speaks of wholeness, harmony, fulfillment, humans at peace with their environment and with God." (Block)

> ii. "The original is emphatic: *vecharatti lahem berith* shalom, *'And I will cut with them the peace covenant;' that is, a covenant sacrifice*, procuring and establishing peace between God and man, and between man and his fellows." (Clarke)

b. **They will dwell safely in the wilderness and sleep in the woods**: That this points to the Millennial Kingdom is also indicated by the promises of the transformation of the ecological order (**cause wild beasts to cease from the land… there shall be showers of blessing**) as is promised in other passages about the millennium (Isaiah 11:1-10, Isaiah 65:20-25).

> i. "The context is the consummation of the present age and the opening of the new age. The scattered flock have been gathered to their own land in an eschatological act of deliverance, not without its element of judgment. United and purified, they now enter upon the supernatural golden age of peace and prosperity." (Taylor)

> ii. "*The showers in their season* refer to the former rains, which break the summer drought in late October and November, and the latter rain (*gesem*), which soaks the ground between December and March. On their regularity and copiousness depended the fertility of the whole land of Palestine." (Taylor)

> iii. **There shall be showers of blessing**: "The refreshings of the Spirit are often compared to a shower (see Isaiah 44:3). The literal is the primary concept with the corollary of spiritual elements. It is interesting to compare with the 'showers of blessing' the mention of 'the times of refreshing' of Acts 3:19-20. The curse will be lifted from the earth." (Feinberg)

c. **They shall dwell safely, and no one shall make them afraid**: God promised that in the completion and perfection of the new covenant, Israel would be restored and set **safely** in the land (as also in Jeremiah 23:6 and 30:8-9). God would provide all their needs, and **they shall no longer be consumed with hunger in the land.**

i. **Garden of renown**: "The meaning must be that God will provide for his people plantations which will bring them renown among the nations by reason of their abundant produce." (Taylor)

ii. "The abundant fertility of the land, however, is paralleled in other golden-age prophecies, such as Hosea 2:22; Joel 3:18; Amos 9:13f.; Zechariah 8:12, all of which see God's future blessings in terms of agricultural prosperity." (Taylor)

iii. **No longer a prey for the nations**: "They are still that today, but God says, 'I will,' and when He says that, He *is* going to do it, my friend." (McGee)

d. **Thus they shall know that I, the LORD their God, am with them**: God would use this preservation and exaltation of Israel to reveal and glorify Himself. He would take the **shame of the Gentiles** forever away from Israel, and bring glory to Himself.

i. "I think we do not attach sufficient importance to the restoration of the Jews. We do not think enough of it. But certainly, if there is anything promised in the Bible it is this. I imagine that you cannot read the Bible without seeing clearly that there is to be an actual restoration of the children of Israel." (Spurgeon)

4. (31) God's assurance to His flock.

"You are My flock, the flock of My pasture; you *are* men, *and* I *am* your God," says the Lord GOD.

a. **You are...the flock of My pasture**: This gave great assurance, even to the erring shepherds and renegade sheep. As long as they were within Yahweh's **pasture**, they need only respond to the Chief Shepherd's correction and instruction.

b. **You are men, and I am your God**: This wonderful reminder assured Israel that even though they were like sheep, they were much more than sheep. They were **men**, made in the image of God and capable of so much more than sheep. They needed to recognize their place as creatures (**men**) and God's place as Creator (**I am your God**). This was both their glory and their responsibility before God.

i. Ezekiel's phrasing here (**you are men, and I am your God**) acknowledged the great divide between humanity and deity. In Ezekiel's day that divide had not yet been completely bridged by the Messiah, Jesus Christ, both God and man.

Ezekiel 35 – Jehovah Shammah; the LORD is There

A. The announcement of God's judgment against Edom, Mount Seir.

1. (1-3a) God brings a word to Ezekiel against Mount Seir.

Moreover the word of the LORD came to me, saying, "Son of man, set your face against Mount Seir and prophesy against it, and say to it, 'Thus says the Lord GOD:

a. **Set your face against Mount Seir**: On the eastern side of the Jordan River, **Mount Seir** was a center of the Edomites, the descendants of Jacob's brother Esau. This was a word **against** the Edomites. Ezekiel had already spoken a short word against Edom (Ezekiel 25:12-14).

i. "Edom had sought to block Israel's first entrance into the Promised Land (Numbers 20:14–21; 24:15–19)." (Alexander)

ii. Alexander noted a long history of conflict between the Edomites and the kings of Israel (and Judah), during the reigns of:

- Saul (1 Samuel 14:47).
- Solomon (1 Kings 11:14–22).
- Jehoshaphat (2 Chronicles 20:1–23).
- Jehoram (2 Kings 8:21).
- Ahaz (2 Chronicles 28:17).

iii. "The 8th-century prophet Amos inveighed against Edom for stifling natural brotherly compassion and pursuing Israel with the sword (Amos 1:11–12), and Isaiah viewed the nation as the archenemy of Israel (Isaiah 34; cf. 63:1–6)." (Block)

b. **And prophesy against it**: The theme of this general section of Ezekiel brings encouragement and hope to Israel and promises of future restoration. Part of that hope was the assurance that God would deal with some of their enemies and rivals, such as ancient Edom.

338

i. Perhaps Ezekiel put this prophecy here to answer the question, "How can we be restored if there are enemies like Edom who hate us so deeply and wish to take advantage of our desolation?"

2. (3b-4) The announcement of judgment.

"Behold, O Mount Seir, I *am* against you;
I will stretch out My hand against you,
And make you most desolate;
I shall lay your cities waste,
And you shall be desolate.
Then you shall know that I *am* the LORD.

a. **I am against you; I will stretch out My hand against you**: For the fourth time in three verses, the word **against** is repeated. Like the solemn repetition of a drumbeat, Edom heard the terrible news that Yahweh, the covenant God of Israel, was **against** them.

b. **I shall lay your cities waste**: God promised to bring destruction and desolation to the cities of Edom. He would do it in a way that revealed Himself to them (**then you shall know that I am the LORD**).

B. The reasons for God's judgment against Edom.

1. (5-9) Because of their ancient hatred.

"Because you have had an ancient hatred, and have shed *the blood of* the children of Israel by the power of the sword at the time of their calamity, *when* their iniquity *came to an* end, therefore, *as* I live," says the Lord GOD, "I will prepare you for blood, and blood shall pursue you; since you have not hated blood, therefore blood shall pursue you. Thus I will make Mount Seir most desolate, and cut off from it the one who leaves and the one who returns. And I will fill its mountains with the slain; on your hills and in your valleys and in all your ravines those who are slain by the sword shall fall. I will make you perpetually desolate, and your cities shall be uninhabited; then you shall know that I *am* the LORD.

a. **Because you have had an ancient hatred**: God's first stated reason for judgment against Edom was their **ancient hatred** of Israel. *God* may long remember a society's sins and one day judge them (as in 1 Samuel 15:1-3). But this is not the place of *man*. For us, God does not want us to hold on to any **ancient hatred** against peoples, races, or nations.

i. "The Edomites were the descendants of *Esau*; the Israelites, the descendants of *Jacob*. Both these were brothers; and between them there was contention even in the womb, and they lived generally in a state of enmity. Their descendants kept up the ancient feud: but the Edomites were implacable; they had not only a *rooted* but *perpetual enmity* to the Israelites, harassing and distressing them by all possible means." (Clarke)

ii. "Edom could not escape the application of the Abrahamic covenant, which explains the strong language and the irrevocable judgment on her. When a nation gives itself over to perpetual hatred of Israel, then there is no other alternative than perpetual desolation from God." (Feinberg)

b. **And have shed the blood of the children of Israel**: Edom gave expression to their **ancient hatred** by joining with armies set against Israel and by taking advantage of Israel **at the time of their calamity**.

i. **Have shed the blood**: "The victims are not merely Judeans who may have fallen to Edomite soldiers participating in Nebuchadrezzar's campaign; the bloodguilt was incurred by searching out and slaughtering fugitives." (Block)

ii. "Psalm 137:7 and Lamentations 4:21–22 imply that Edom gladly aided the Babylonian invasion of Judah in 589–586 b.c. Obadiah 10–14 also denounces Edom for her betrayal of Israel in time of need." (Alexander)

iii. **At the time of their calamity**: "To afflict the afflicted is cruel. This is scarcely of man, bad as he is. He must be possessed by the *malignant spirit* of the *devil*, when he wounds the wounded, insults over the miseries of the afflicted, and seeks opportunities to add affliction to those who are already under the rod of God." (Clarke)

c. **I will prepare for you blood**: Since Edom was responsible for the shedding the blood of Israel, God promised, "**Therefore blood shall pursue you**." The punishment would fit their crime. Of the mountains of Edom, God said He would **fill its mountains with the slain**.

i. "The four occurrences of blood (Hebrew, *dam*) in verse 6 constitute a play on the name of Edom (red)." (Feinberg)

ii. "These were murderous actions. Where the blood of Abel had cried out to Yahweh to avenge Cain's murder (Genesis 4:10), here the blood of Edom's victims takes on a life of its own, like a near kinsman relentlessly pursuing the criminal and demanding full retribution." (Block)

iii. **On your hills and in your valleys and in all your ravines**: "The height of indignity in the Orient was not to be properly buried. The slain of Edom would be found in the mountains, hills, valleys and watercourses, all without benefit of burial." (Feinberg)

d. **Your cities shall be uninhabited**: The judgment would be so severe that many Edomite cities would become empty and **perpetually desolate**.

i. "The main cities were Petra and Teman, which now lie in ruins. The prediction has been literally fulfilled." (Feinberg)

ii. "Edom's sin was perpetual hatred, and Edom's punishment shall be perpetual desolations. Edomites would never return into friendship with the Israelites, but still hate, and molest, and waste them; now for just recompence Edom's cities shall be wasted, and never return to their former glory." (Poole)

2. (10-13) Because of their jealousy.

"Because you have said, 'These two nations and these two countries shall be mine, and we will possess them,' although the LORD was there, therefore, *as* I live," says the Lord GOD, "I will do according to your anger and according to the envy which you showed in your hatred against them; and I will make Myself known among them when I judge you. Then you shall know that I *am* the LORD. I have heard all your blasphemies which you have spoken against the mountains of Israel, saying, 'They are desolate; they are given to us to consume.' Thus with your mouth you have boasted against Me and multiplied your words against Me; I have heard *them.*"

a. **These two nations and these two countries shall be mine**: When the Babylonian armies came against Judah and Jerusalem, the Edomites believed that they could use Israel's crisis to enlarge their own dominion. Instead of helping troubled Israel or at least sympathizing with them, for selfish gain they took advantage of Israel's crisis.

i. Some think the **two countries** are Edom and Judah, and others think they are Judah and Israel. The sense is the same in both; Edom wanted the land of Judah and Israel and thought they might take it when the Assyrians exiled Israel out of the land and when the Babylonians depopulated Judah.

ii. "The fall of Jerusalem made it possible for Edom to exact its revenge on Judah by appropriating a portion of its territory. This is precisely what Edom did by expanding into the Negeb." (Vawter and Hoppe)

iii. "The Edomites, shut away in their mountain fastnesses, must often have cast greedy eyes at the more fertile lands to the north-west of them. But their only chance of success lay in Judah's weakness, and this they attempted to exploit." (Taylor)

iv. "Archeological evidence for Edomite encroachment into Judean territory is available from several sources. Arad Letter 24 refers to the pressure of the Edomites at this southern military outpost even before the fall of Jerusalem. An Edomite seal, whose nationality is established by the name Qaus, discovered at Aroer, 12 miles southeast of Beer-sheba, suggests Edomite presence at this place a short time later." (Block)

b. **Although the LORD was there**: The Edomites wanted the land of Judah (and Israel), and thought that since the Babylonians had taken the Jews out of the land, it was theirs for the taking. They forgot the great truth that even though the Jews were temporarily exiled out of the land, **the LORD was there**. He would guard and preserve *His* land against them.

i. Even when God abandoned the temple regarding the special sense of His presence and glory (Ezekiel 11:23), Yahweh *had not* abandoned the land. It was still His land and He still had a sacred purpose for it.

ii. "With their typical ancient Near Eastern perspective they assumed that a land whose population had been deported and whose cities lay in ruins must have been abandoned by its god." (Block)

iii. "It is interesting to note that, even in the hour of Judah's judgment, God is still regarded as being there in the land and is shown to identify himself with his people." (Taylor)

iv. "From this one incident we gather that whatever may be the machinations and devices of the enemies of God's people, though there be nothing else to thwart them, there is this as an effectual barrier – the saints are God's heritage, and the Lord is there, to guard and hold his own." (Spurgeon)

v. "If Edom forget that the Lord is there, that forgetfulness does not change the fact. That land was, and is, sacred for carrying out a Divine purpose, for the world, and through Israel; and God has never abandoned it. He is still there; and whosoever may covet it cannot hold it, for He will dispossess them." (Morgan)

vi. "When all conflicts shall be ended, when the scattered shall be gathered, when the tabernacle of the Lord shall be among them; then this which is Zion's bulwark to-day, shall be her everlasting glory. JEHOVAH-SHAMMAH – 'The Lord is there.'" (Spurgeon)

vii. "How often do our foes plot against us, supposing that we shall fall an easy prey, and that they can divide the spoils without let. But God is there." (Meyer)

c. **I will do according to your anger and according to the envy**: God promised to answer the **anger** of Edom and their **envy** against Israel. Their **anger** and **envy** were evident in their **hatred against them**.

i. Ezekiel 35 speaks powerfully to any people or nation who sets themselves against Israel:

- With anger and envy (Ezekiel 35:11).
- With an ancient hatred (Ezekiel 35:5).
- With a desire to take their land (Ezekiel 35:10).
- With rejoicing in Israel's bloodshed (Ezekiel 35:6).
- By taking advantage of Israel's troubles and increasing them (Ezekiel 35:5).
- By acting as if God Himself was not present in the land of Israel (Ezekiel 35:10).
- By speaking against and blaspheming the God of Israel (Ezekiel 35:12).

ii. When *any* nation or people sets themselves against Israel and God's purpose in such a way, they can expect perpetual desolation (Ezekiel 35:9). This is especially tragic when, as in the case of Edom and Israel, *they should be brothers*. This is a powerful, accurate, and sad picture of many in the Arab and Palestinian world against the Jewish people and Israel today.

d. **With your mouth you have boasted against Me**: In hoping to take advantage of troubled Israel and even to **consume** them, Edom insulted the God of Israel. They **boasted against** Yahweh and spoke **multiplied** words against Him. God **heard** those words and promised to hold Edom accountable for them.

i. We see the connection between the words Edom spoke **against** God (Ezekiel 35:12-13) and the judgment God had determined *against* Edom (Ezekiel 35:1-3).

ii. "The arrogant insults hurled at the people of Judah were tantamount to blasphemies against the Lord, which he had heard." (Taylor)

iii. **I have heard them**: "I have heard your words, you shall feel my sword." (Poole)

3. (14-15) The joy of the earth when Edom is judged.

'Thus says the Lord God: "The whole earth will rejoice when I make you desolate. As you rejoiced because the inheritance of the house of Israel was desolate, so I will do to you; you shall be desolate, O Mount

Seir, as well as all of Edom—all of it! Then they shall know that I *am* **the** LORD."'**

a. **The whole earth will rejoice when I make you desolate**: Because Edom **rejoiced** in Israel's desolation, so God would bring desolation to Edom – and the world would be happy about it. God's judgments are true; the punishments fit the crime.

i. "In their arrogance, Edom rejoiced over the fall of Israel; but one day, the whole earth would rejoice over the fall of Edom!" (Wiersbe)

ii. "As thou wast sick of the devil's disease, rejoicing at other men's harms; so, by a strange turn of things, others shall rejoice at thy just destruction, and revel in thy ruins: and at the last day especially, when thou shalt be awarded thy portion with the devil and his angels." (Trapp)

b. **Then they shall know that I am the** LORD: God would reveal Himself to Israel and to a watching world through His judgments upon Edom.

Ezekiel 36 – A New Covenant for Israel's Land and People

A. A promise to renew the land of Israel.

1. (1-5) A prophecy to the mountains of Israel.

"And you, son of man, prophesy to the mountains of Israel, and say, 'O mountains of Israel, hear the word of the LORD! Thus says the Lord GOD: "Because the enemy has said of you, 'Aha! The ancient heights have become our possession,'"' therefore prophesy, and say, 'Thus says the Lord GOD: "Because they made *you* desolate and swallowed you up on every side, so that you became the possession of the rest of the nations, and you are taken up by the lips of talkers and slandered by the people"— therefore, O mountains of Israel, hear the word of the Lord GOD! Thus says the Lord GOD to the mountains, the hills, the rivers, the valleys, the desolate wastes, and the cities that have been forsaken, which became plunder and mockery to the rest of the nations all around— therefore thus says the Lord GOD: "Surely I have spoken in My burning jealousy against the rest of the nations and against all Edom, who gave My land to themselves as a possession, with wholehearted joy *and* spiteful minds, in order to plunder its open country.""

a. **Prophesy to the mountains of Israel**: As before Ezekiel prophesied to the *Mount Seir* (Ezekiel 35:1-2), so now he prophesied to the **mountains of Israel**. What he said impacts the people, but the focus is on the land itself.

b. **The ancient heights have become our possession**: This was the taunt; the claim of **the enemy** of Israel. They thought that because the Jewish people were taken away in exile that the land could be theirs.

i. **Swallowed you up**: "The enemy intended to swallow the people of God, the verb meaning literally to pant or snuff up, a figure from the panting of wild beasts, as a wild beast ravenously smells after prey to devour it." (Feinberg)

ii. **Slandered**: "Used elsewhere of the 'bad report' about his brothers that Joseph brought to his father (Genesis 37:2), of slanderous stories of plots against the righteous (Proverbs 10:18; 25:10; Psalm 31:13; Jeremiah 20:10), and of unfavorable (and faithless) reports resulting from an investigation (Numbers 13:32; 14:36–37)." (Block)

c. **Thus says the Lord GOD to the mountains, the hills, the rivers, the valleys, the desolate wastes, and the cities**: The clear emphasis in this section is on the *land* of Israel. There is certainly a connection with and an impact upon the people, but God's enduring interest in the *land* of Israel is emphasized.

d. **I have spoken in My burning jealousy against the rest of the nations and against all Edom, who gave to themselves as a possession**: God spoke a solemn and powerful word **against** Edom and all the nations who sought to take the land of Israel to themselves. They set themselves against God's purpose and will, when they, with **spiteful minds** hoped to **plunder** the country of Israel.

i. **Burning jealousy**: "Jealousy is hot as hell; [Song of Solomon 8:6] it is implacable, [Proverbs 6:34-35] and very vindictive." (Trapp)

2. (6-12) The land of Israel restored from her shame.

"Therefore prophesy concerning the land of Israel, and say to the mountains, the hills, the rivers, and the valleys, 'Thus says the Lord GOD: "Behold, I have spoken in My jealousy and My fury, because you have borne the shame of the nations." Therefore thus says the Lord GOD: "I have raised My hand in an oath that surely the nations that *are* around you shall bear their own shame. But you, O mountains of Israel, you shall shoot forth your branches and yield your fruit to My people Israel, for they are about to come. For indeed I *am* for you, and I will turn to you, and you shall be tilled and sown. I will multiply men upon you, all the house of Israel, all of it; and the cities shall be inhabited and the ruins rebuilt. I will multiply upon you man and beast; and they shall increase and bear young; I will make you inhabited as in former times, and do better *for you* than at your beginnings. Then you shall know that I *am* the LORD. Yes, I will cause men to walk on you, My people Israel; they shall take possession of you, and you shall be their inheritance; no more shall you bereave them *of children.*"

a. **Say to the mountains, the hills, the rivers, and the valleys**: God continued His word directed to the *land* of Israel. Some feel uncomfortable with these prophetic passages that so clearly focus on Israel's *future* in her promised land. They feel such promises contradict the principle that God is Lord over all the earth.

> i. Taylor spoke well to this concern: "To those who feel that this is altogether too materialistic a concept of God and too constricting for the God of the whole earth, the enlightened Israelite would probably answer that it is no more unreasonable than that the God of all time should declare one day in seven as his own and that the God of all nature should claim a tenth of its produce for himself. Authority over the whole is witnessed to by the surrender of the part."

b. **You have borne the shame of the nations**: God looked with compassion and care upon Israel, under so much attack, conquest, and hatred from **the nations of the world**. What was true in Ezekiel's day has remained true through the centuries and up to the present day.

> i. "The land has borne the insults of the nations long enough, and Yahweh's own passion has been ignited. He will have the last word." (Block)

c. **The nations that are around you shall bear their own shame**: In a solemn **oath**, God promised that He would vindicate Israel and the **shame** the nations hoped to place upon Israel would come upon Israel's enemies.

> i. **The nations that are around you**: "Moabites, Ammonites, and Idumeans shall be repaid in their own coin; I will, as sure as I am God, as sure as I can, so surely make them a taunt, a proverb, and a curse among men." (Poole)

d. **O mountains of Israel, you shall shoot forth your branches and yield your fruit**: God promised to deal with Israel's enemies, but He also promised to uniquely and powerfully bless the land of Israel. There would come a divine ecological and agricultural renewal to the land of Israel.

> i. According to Israeli government statistics and reports, though only 20% of Israel's land is suitable for farming, since the establishment of the modern state of Israel in 1948 they have more than tripled the amount of land used for farming and production has increased *sixteen times*. What used to be an agricultural wasteland is now a model for the world, and Israel produces 95% of its own food requirements and has a large agricultural export industry. We can regard these impressive developments as a mere beginning of the much greater fruitfulness promised in the fullness of God's plan for Israel and her land.

> ii. "The present great reforestation projects in the State of Israel, amazing as they are, are only harbingers of the reality to come." (Feinberg)

iii. **My people Israel**: "What a welcome sound it should have been for Ezekiel's audience to hear Yahweh referring to Israel endearingly as *ammi*, 'my people,' once again." (Block)

e. **Indeed I am for you, and I will turn to you, and you shall be tilled and sown**: God specifically promised that He was and is **for** the *land of Israel*, not only the Jewish people. He promised blessing and renewal *to the land*, saying it would be **tilled and sown**.

i. "By a clever and unique wordplay, the hostile orientation formula *hineni alekem*, usually 'I am against you,' is transformed into a declaration of commitment: *I am on your side*." (Block)

ii. There is a wonderful spiritual application from this literal promise. God can restore that which is dead and unfruitful. "Do you think that you will never be glad again; that shadow will always lie athwart your path; and that desolation shall hold undisputed empire? It shall not be so. O desolate mountains, ye shall shoot forth your branches, and yield fruit; and it is near to come." (Meyer)

f. **I will multiply men upon you**: The blessed and renewed land would receive many more people, both from birth and immigration. **The cities shall be inhabited and the ruins rebuilt**.

i. "The phrase *they will increase and be fruitful* is an obvious echo of the divine blessing of beasts in Genesis 1:22 and humans in Genesis 1:28 as well as Genesis 9:1, 7." (Block)

ii. In 1867 the American writer Mark Twain visited the land of Israel and was amazed at how small a city Jerusalem was: "A fast walker could go outside the walls of Jerusalem and walk entirely around the city in an hour. I do not know how else to make one understand how small it is" (*The Innocents Abroad*). The population and vitality of modern Israel indicate at the very least the beginning of the fulfillment of this promise.

g. **And do better for you than at your beginning**: God promised not only to *restore* Israel but to bless them *beyond* previous times. This promise is focused on the land but certainly connected to the Jewish people as well.

h. **No more shall you bereave them of children**: As explained in the following verses, God would make the land of Israel a *blessing* to the Jewish people once again. In the worst days of the people, it seemed that the land was against them and actually took their dear children away. Such a curse would be reversed.

3. (13-15) The nations will see and tell of the blessedness of the land of Israel.

'Thus says the Lord GOD: "Because they say to you, 'You devour men and bereave your nation *of children,*' therefore you shall devour men no more, nor bereave your nation anymore," says the Lord GOD. Nor will I let you hear the taunts of the nations anymore, nor bear the reproach of the peoples anymore, nor shall you cause your nation to stumble anymore," says the Lord GOD.'"

a. **You devour men and bereave your nation**: This is what men *formerly* said of the land of Israel. It was a desolate and seemingly forsaken land. In many ways, this described the land of Israel from the Roman conquests of the first and second centuries until the Zionist movement starting in the 19th century. Scarcity, disease, and barrenness marked that land.

i. **You devour men**: The figure of speech uses the words spoken by the unfaithful spies in Numbers – that it was *a land that devours its inhabitants* (Numbers 13:32).

ii. "In a sense the land of promise was a bereaver of the nation, for it was subject, through the chastisements of God, to droughts (Jeremiah 14:1; Amos 4:7), to blasting and mildew (Amos 4:9), locust (Joel 1), and famine (Haggai 1:10-11; 2:17)." (Feinberg)

iii. In 1867 the American author Mark Twain toured the land of Israel and described it as a "desolate country whose soil is rich enough, but is given over wholly to weeds—a silent mournful expanse.... A desolation.... We never saw a human being on the whole route.... hardly a tree or shrub anywhere.... Even the olive tree and the cactus, those fast friends of a worthless soil, had almost deserted the country." (*The Innocents Abroad*)

iv. Spurgeon said in an 1864 sermon, "These words were addressed to the mountains of Palestine. Albeit that they are now waste and barren, they are yet to be as fruitful and luxuriant as in the days of Israel's grandeur."

b. **You shall devour men no more, nor bereave your nation anymore**: God promised to ecologically transform the land of Israel, making it a hospitable land of plenty once again. Today this can be seen; God working through the effort and ingenuity of the Israeli people, as well as through supernatural blessing.

c. **Nor will I let you hear the taunts of the nations anymore**: The work God would do for the land of Israel would be greater than ecological. He would also raise Israel's status in the eyes of other nations, and give them a place of great security.

B. A promise of a new covenant, to renew the people of Israel.

1. (16-19) God's judgment upon a disobedient Israel.

Moreover the word of the LORD came to me, saying: "Son of man, when the house of Israel dwelt in their own land, they defiled it by their own ways and deeds; to Me their way was like the uncleanness of a woman in her customary impurity. Therefore I poured out My fury on them for the blood they had shed on the land, and for their idols *with which* they had defiled it. So I scattered them among the nations, and they were dispersed throughout the countries; I judged them according to their ways and their deeds.

a. **They defiled it by their own ways and deeds**: Far back at the beginning of Israel's history as a nation, God promised that their disobedience would bring a curse upon their land. In their disobedient **ways and deeds** it could be said that Israel **defiled** their own land.

i. "Had they continued faithful to me, they had never been removed from it: but they polluted it with their crimes; and I abhorred the land on that account, and gave both them and it up to the destroyers." (Clarke)

ii. **Like the uncleanness of a woman**: "The prophet was not making moral judgments about women or human potential for good. Ezekiel was trying to convince the exiles that his message of restoration was worth listening to. Apparently his fellow exiles needed convincing." (Vawter and Hoppe)

b. **Therefore I poured out My fury on them for the blood they had shed on the land, and for their idols**: Among the many sins of His people, God judged them for their crimes against one another (**blood they had shed**) and their crimes against God and His honor (**their idols**).

i. "When the prophet spoke of blood poured out, he was probably referring to murders, judicial violence and even child sacrifice in the worship of idols (see Ezekiel 16:36; 23:37)." (Feinberg)

c. **So I scattered them among the nations**: God long before, at the beginning of Israel's history as a nation, promised that He would punish them with exile if they were to persist in their disobedience and rejection of Him. This eventually happened, and God **judged them according to their ways and their deeds**.

i. "In disciplining Israel in this manner, the Lord risked his own reputation in the world... when God scattered Israel among the nations, they perceived that Israel's God was weak; thereby the name of the Lord was profaned among them." (Alexander)

2. (20-23) God's concern for His own holy name.

When they came to the nations, wherever they went, they profaned My holy name—when they said of them, 'These *are* the people of the LORD, *and* yet they have gone out of His land.' But I had concern for My holy name, which the house of Israel had profaned among the nations wherever they went. "Therefore say to the house of Israel, 'Thus says the Lord GOD: "I do not do *this* for your sake, O house of Israel, but for My holy name's sake, which you have profaned among the nations wherever you went. And I will sanctify My great name, which has been profaned among the nations, which you have profaned in their midst; and the nations shall know that I *am* the LORD," says the Lord GOD, "when I am hallowed in you before their eyes.

a. **When they came to the nations, wherever they went, they profaned My holy name**: When the Jewish people were exiled out of their land, they did not necessarily glorify God in those foreign places. The mere fact of their exile (**yet they have gone out of His land**) could be seen as God's rejection of His people.

i. "The assertion that the Israelites have desecrated the name of Yahweh wherever they have gone might have led Ezekiel's audience to expect another wave of judgment." (Block)

b. **But I had concern for My holy name**: God's promises of restoration to Israel were not only for the sake of Israel but even more so for His **holy name**. Israel **profaned** His name **among the nations**, yet God promised to **sanctify** His own name and reputation.

i. "He wants his name to be great, so that the nations may regard him not as an ineffective tribal god, but as the Lord of the whole earth. And Israel is to be the channel through which this vindication is going to be achieved." (Taylor)

c. **When I am hallowed in you before their eyes**: When God was once again honored as holy among the people of Israel, it would reveal Yahweh to the nations (**the nations shall know that I am the LORD**).

i. "When the nations see Israel's return to its land, they will draw only one conclusion: Israel's national deity has acted to save the people. By restoring Israel to its land, God could uphold God's own dignity before the rest of the world." (Vawter and Hoppe)

ii. This is a promise to Israel but has some relevance to all who relate to God through the new covenant. "The church also finds it a difficult role to accept, but in an age when God's power is all too often discredited by reason of his people's failures, the church needs to be prepared to

be treated harshly for the sake of God's greater glory in the world."
(Taylor)

3. (24) A promise to gather scattered Israel.

**For I will take you from among the nations, gather you out of all
countries, and bring you into your own land.**

a. **For I will take you from among the nations**: When Ezekiel first gave
this prophecy, Israel was practically desolate and her people were exiled.
God promised to not only bring back His people from the Babylonian
captivity, but a greater and more complete gathering to come.

i. "This does not relate to the restoration from Babylon merely. The
Jews are at this day scattered in all *Heathen, Mohammedan,* and
Christian countries. From these they are to be gathered, and brought to
repossess their own land." (Clarke)

b. **And bring you into your own land**: God promised to restore Israel to
their **own land**. As with Ezekiel 11:16-17, this was a remarkable promise
to make to *post-exile* Israel. This promise to **gather** Israel is a common
feature of the promises of the new covenant God will make with Israel and
invite the Gentile world to embrace. (as in Deuteronomy 30:1-6, Jeremiah
23:3, Jeremiah 32:37, and Ezekiel 11:16-17).

i. **Into your own land**: "God didn't give them the land because of
their righteousness (Deuteronomy 9:6), and He won't restore the land
because of anything good they have done. God in His grace gives us
what we don't deserve." (Wiersbe)

ii. Throughout the Bible, God reveals His plan of redemption through
a series of covenants. After the extended story of the fall and ruin of
humanity in Genesis 1-11, the story of the covenants begins.

• The Abrahamic Covenant promised to Abraham and his
covenant descendants a *land,* a *nation,* and a *blessing* to extend to
all nations (Genesis 12:1-3).

• The Mosaic or Sinai Covenant gave Israel the *law,* the *sacrifices,*
and the *choice* of blessing or curse (Exodus 19).

• The Davidic Covenant that promised an *everlasting dynasty,* a
perfect ruler, and the *Promised Messiah* (2 Samuel 7).

• The New Covenant, where God's plan of redemption through
the covenants was completed and perfected. Over the span of
Old Testament passages that announce the new covenant (such
as Deuteronomy 30:1-6, Jeremiah 23:1-8, Jeremiah 31:31-34,
Jeremiah 32:37-41, Ezekiel 11:16-20, Ezekiel 36:16-28, Ezekiel

37:11-14, and 37:21-28), we see the promises of a *gathered Israel,* of *cleansing and spiritual transformation,* of a *new and real relationship with God,* and the *reign of the Messiah.*

iii. "Therefore, the new covenant replaced the Mosaic covenant by adding those things that made it better, but not by eliminating the good, righteous, and godly Mosaic stipulations that described how to live a godly life." (Alexander)

4. (25) A promise to cleanse filthy Israel.

Then I will sprinkle clean water on you, and you shall be clean; I will cleanse you from all your filthiness and from all your idols.

a. **Then I will sprinkle clean water on you**: The new covenant promises a spiritual cleansing of God's people, a cleansing made possible by the death of Jesus when the new covenant was instituted.

i. "Its symbolism is derived from ritual washings with water which were intended to remove ceremonial defilement (cf. Exodus 30:17–21; Leviticus 14:52; Numbers 19:17–19)." (Taylor)

b. **I will cleanse you from all your filthiness and from all your idols**: The sin and corruption mentioned previously in Ezekiel 36:17-18 would be cleansed by God's work through the new covenant. This would not be the mere *covering* of sin as accomplished by the imperfect sacrifices of the Old Testament, but a true *cleansing* of sin by the finished work of Jesus Christ on the cross.

i. This reference to cleansing by the **clean water** of the new covenant is the likely connection Jesus had in mind when He spoke of being *born of water* in John 3:5. As Paul would later write of the believer, *you were washed* (1 Corinthians 6:11).

ii. "It is likely that Christ was calling the attention of Nicodemus to this passage when He spoke in John 3:5 of the new birth through water and the Spirit; the Ezekiel promise was about to be fulfilled." (Wright)

iii. **From all your filthiness** is a large promise. "From all your actual filthiness, as well as from all your original filthiness, will I cleanse you. From all your secret filthiness, and from all your public filthiness; from everything that was wrong in the family; from everything that was wrong in the business; from everything that was wrong in your own heart — 'From all your filthiness will I cleanse you.'" (Spurgeon)

5. (26-27) A promise to spiritually renew Israel.

I will give you a new heart and put a new spirit within you; I will take the heart of stone out of your flesh and give you a heart of flesh. I will

put My Spirit within you and cause you to walk in My statutes, and you will keep My judgments and do *them.*

a. **I will give you a new heart and put a new spirit within you**: This is the spiritual transformation promised in the new covenant. Instead of the law working from the outside in, God promised a new heart to work from the inside out.

> i. "Israel will experience a real 'change of heart' and will become, by God's gracious initiative, the kind of people that they have in the past so signally failed to be." (Taylor)

> ii. "True religion begins, then, with the heart, and the heart is the ruling power of manhood. You may enlighten a man's understanding and you have done much, but as long as his heart is wrong, the enlightenment of the understanding only enables him to sin with a greater weight of responsibility resting upon him." (Spurgeon)

b. **A new heart and put a new spirit**: Jesus referred to this great work of spiritual transformation through the new covenant when He spoke of being *born again* in John 3. Paul spoke of it when he wrote of believers being new creations in Jesus Christ (2 Corinthians 5:17).

c. **I will take the heart of stone out of your flesh and give you a heart of flesh**: God promised a new nature in the new covenant. In that covenant men and women are made new, with a new nature patterned after the nature of Jesus Himself (Ephesians 4:21-24).

> i. "In the ancient world the heart was the center for volition and the intellectual catalyst for feeling and action. A 'heart of stone' implied inflexibility and willfulness, while a 'heart of flesh' meant submission and compliance." (Vawter and Hoppe)

> ii. **The heart of stone**: "Stubborn, senseless, untractable heart, that receives no kindly impressions from the word, providences, or Spirit of God in its ordinary operations and influences, that hardens itself in a day of provocation, that is hardened by the deceitfulness of sin." (Poole)

> iii. **A heart of flesh**: "One that can *feel*, and that can *enjoy*; that can feel *love to God* and to *all men*, and be a proper habitation for the living God." (Clarke)

d. **I will put My Spirit within you**: Another aspect of the new covenant is the promise of the indwelling Holy Spirit. Under the new covenant, the Spirit dwells in every believer (Romans 8:9), and is promised to fill the believer with special presence and power (Acts 1:5 and 1:8).

i. "Jeremiah [Jeremiah 31:33] and Ezekiel obviously have the same covenant renewal in mind, but what Jeremiah attributes to the divine Torah, Ezekiel ascribes to the infusion of the divine *ruah*." (Block)

ii. "An incarnate God is a mystery, – the Word was made flesh and dwelt among us; but, here is another mystery, God dwells in every son of God. God dwelleth in us, and we in him." (Spurgeon)

iii. "The Holy Spirit cannot dwell in the old heart; it is a filthy place, devoid of all good, and full of enmity to God. His very first operation upon our nature is to pull down the old house and build himself a new one, that he may be able to inhabit us consistently with his holy spiritual nature." (Spurgeon)

e. **Cause you to walk in My statutes**: The spiritual transformation and indwelling Holy Spirit would help the believer to obey God's law. Obedience would be more of a matter of *being* what God has *already made* the believer as a new man or woman in Jesus Christ, filled with God's own Holy Spirit.

6. (28-30) A promise to bless the land and her agriculture.

Then you shall dwell in the land that I gave to your fathers; you shall be My people, and I will be your God. I will deliver you from all your uncleannesses. I will call for the grain and multiply it, and bring no famine upon you. And I will multiply the fruit of your trees and the increase of your fields, so that you need never again bear the reproach of famine among the nations.

a. **Then you shall dwell in the land that I gave to your fathers**: The promises of **land** and gathering to the land are part of the very fabric of the new covenant. It is a plain and serious error to subtract these promises from the new covenant itself.

i. "The return mentioned in this passage does not refer to the return to Canaan under Zerubbabel but to a final and complete restoration under the Messiah in the end times. The details of Israel's reestablishment on her land set forth above simply did not occur in the returns under Zerubbabel, Ezra, and Nehemiah." (Alexander)

b. **You shall be My people, and I will be your God**: This phrase speaks of a restored and true relationship between God and His people. The cleansing and transformative work of the new covenant would make a depth and strength of relationship possible for all God's people that only a select few knew before.

c. **I will deliver you from all your uncleannesses**: Though the people of God were stained by multiple **uncleannesses**, God's provision through the Messiah's sacrifice, and the new covenant instituted by that sacrifice, would truly cleanse God's people. With new hearts, they would see their **uncleannesses** as things to be delivered from.

i. "No article of our creed is so much opposed by Satan, as that of the forgiveness of sin by Christ's merits, which is the very life and soul of a Church. All the former articles of the creed are perfected in this, and all the following articles are effects thereof: hold it fast, therefore." (Trapp)

d. **I will call for the grain and multiply it**: As was promised earlier in the chapter, God would send a revival of agricultural abundance upon the land of Israel (Ezekiel 36:6-12).

i. "Supernatural fertility of the land is one of the accompaniments of the kingdom (see v. 35; 47:1-12; Isaiah 35:1-2; 55:13; Zechariah 8:12)." (Feinberg)

7. (31-32) Israel's response in light of their unworthiness for these promises.

Then you will remember your evil ways and your deeds that *were* not good; and you will loathe yourselves in your own sight, for your iniquities and your abominations. Not for your sake do I do *this*," says the Lord God, "let it be known to you. Be ashamed and confounded for your own ways, O house of Israel!"

a. **Then you will remember your evil ways**: The outpouring of grace received from the new covenant would not make God's people indifferent towards sin, even towards past sins. They would **loathe** themselves over their **iniquities and abominations**. The inner transformation promised in Ezekiel 36:26-27 would give them a sensitive conscience toward sin, both past and present.

i. "When some people remember their sins, they enjoy them again in the dirty depths of their imagination. This is evidence that they really haven't judged them and repented. When true children of God remember their past disobedience, they're ashamed of themselves and abhor themselves because of what they have done to the Lord, themselves, and others." (Wiersbe)

ii. "Augustine was famous, saith another for two of his works: his Retractions, which are the confessions of his errors; and his Confessions, which are the retractions of his life." (Trapp)

b. **Not for your sake do I do this**: Yahweh repeated the idea from Ezekiel 36:22-23. This outpouring of grace and restoration would be more for the glory and reputation of Yahweh than for Israel.

i. "Very impressive is the prophet's insistence upon the fact that this is to be done, not for the sake of Israel, but for the sake of the Name of God." (Morgan)

8. (33-36) A promise to restore the desolate places.

'Thus says the Lord GOD: "On the day that I cleanse you from all your iniquities, I will also enable *you* to dwell in the cities, and the ruins shall be rebuilt. The desolate land shall be tilled instead of lying desolate in the sight of all who pass by. So they will say, 'This land that was desolate has become like the garden of Eden; and the wasted, desolate, and ruined cities *are now* fortified *and* inhabited.' Then the nations which are left all around you shall know that I, the LORD, have rebuilt the ruined places *and* planted what was desolate. I, the LORD, have spoken *it*, and I will do *it*."

a. **On the day that I cleanse you from all your iniquities, I will also enable you to dwell in the cities**: Once again, a key component of the new covenant promises is the gathering of Israel back to their land, and the blessing upon the land. The **desolate land** would be **tilled** again and made fruitful.

i. "There had been a day when the Lord refused to be inquired of by His disobedient people (Ezekiel 14:3; 20:3), but now the Lord would be accessible for their turning to Him in genuine repentance and would grant their requests." (Feinberg)

ii. The repeated promises of the restoration of national and geographical Israel as part of the new covenant show us something important and often neglected. There is no doubt that the work of Jesus on the cross and His victory at the resurrection inaugurated the new covenant (Luke 22:20). Yet, there is a real sense in which the new covenant *is not yet complete* until these promised blessings upon Israel are fulfilled. We may say that the glorious return of Jesus, and the millennial kingdom He then establishes, will complete all the promises of the new covenant.

b. **The nations which are left all around you shall know that I, the LORD, have rebuilt the ruined places**: God's work in Israel and through the new covenant would be a powerful testimony to a watching world. The full work of the new covenant would proclaim the greatness of Yahweh.

i. "The results of the restoration would be their repentance and the return of all that prosperity which through sin they had forfeited, and, consequently, a renewal of their witness to the nations round about of truth concerning Jehovah." (Morgan)

ii. "Let her [the Church] also remember that her gifts and calling are not for her sake, but for the honour of the Name; that, being sanctified in her, God may make Himself known to the nations." (Morgan)

iii. "God has yet to defend His name in this earth. There are a great many people who ridicule the church today and the people who are in it. They blaspheme God because of it. God is going to justify Himself in this earth, and He is going to sanctify His name down here." (McGee)

c. **I, the LORD, have spoken it, and will do it**: To remove all doubt and to assure the trust of His people, Yahweh gave a solemn oath regarding these promises. One disregards or diminishes these promises in opposition to God's solemn oath.

i. "How these prophetic promises will be fulfilled remains an open question. Nevertheless, to reduce these oracles to symbolic language and to restrict their fulfillment to the NT church is to annul the hope that the prophet was attempting to restore." (Block)

9. (37-38) A promise to restore a relationship with God.

'**Thus says the Lord GOD: "I will also let the house of Israel inquire of Me to do this for them: I will increase their men like a flock. Like a flock** *offered as* **holy** *sacrifices,* **like the flock at Jerusalem on its feast days, so shall the ruined cities be filled with flocks of men. Then they shall know that I** *am* **the LORD."'"**

a. **I will also let the house of Israel inquire of Me**: The restored and deepened relationship in light of the new covenant would mean a new dynamic of prayer for Israel. They could take the privilege that Hebrews 4:16 says belongs to every believer under the new covenant: to boldly come to the throne of grace to find help in time of need.

i. "Though I have repeated so often my promise to return them, to rebuild, to multiply them, yet they shall know it is their duty to entreat it, to wait on me, and then I will give a merciful answer and do it. Thus Daniel prayed, when he knew the return was sure and near." (Poole)

b. **I will increase their men like a flock**: Though a miraculous population increase was previously promised (as in Ezekiel 36:10-11), here Ezekiel presents its accomplishment as an answer to prayer (**inquire of Me**). This shows us that the increase of a flock is connected to prayer, and that God wants us to pray for what He has promised.

i. "I trust we all feel the missionary spirit; we all long to see the kingdom of the Lord come, and to see the converts in Zion multiplied. But God has appended to the granting of our desire that we should pray for it: we must plead and enquire, or else the increase will be withheld." (Spurgeon)

ii. **A flock offered as holy sacrifices**: "Literally 'flock of holy things' and evidently refers to animals intended for sacrifice. Just as these filled Jerusalem in their thousands (cf. 2 Chronicles 35:7), so the rebuilt cities of Israel would be filled with throngs of men." (Taylor)

iii. "The sacrificial simile would have come easily to Ezekiel the priest. It is tempting to wonder whether he thought beyond the mere numerical similarity to the picture of a people who were ready to be offered, like the sheep, as living sacrifices in the service of God." (Taylor)

c. **So shall the ruined cities be filled with flocks of men**: The restoration of people, life and vitality to Israel is an important part of the new covenant. The new covenant is not only a work of spiritual restoration, it also promises the restoration of Israel in terms of both population and land.

i. The image of **flocks of men** speaks not only of the *large number* of the increase, but also of something more. "There is this additional beauty about the promise, that the sheep which were brought to Jerusalem on the solemn feasts were not only numerous, but they were the best sheep in the land, because no animal could be offered to God if it had any blemish." (Spurgeon)

Ezekiel 37 – Life to Dry Bones and Unity to God's People

A. A dead nation restored to life.

1. (1-3) The valley of bones.

The hand of the LORD came upon me and brought me out in the Spirit of the LORD, and set me down in the midst of the valley; and it *was* full of bones. Then He caused me to pass by them all around, and behold, *there were* very many in the open valley; and indeed *they were* very dry. And He said to me, "Son of man, can these bones live?" So I answered, "O Lord GOD, You know."

a. **The hand of the LORD came upon me**: Ezekiel's remarkable prophetic experience is not specifically called a *vision*, but that seems to be the sense of the phrase, **brought me out in the Spirit of the LORD**. We regard what follows as something Ezekiel saw as a vision, not with his physical sense of sight.

i. "The mention of the hand of the Lord indicates prophetic ecstasy and inspiration. Ezekiel was brought out in the Spirit of the Lord, that is, in vision, and set down in the valley." (Feinberg)

b. **In the midst of the valley; and it was full of bones**: Ezekiel saw a large expanse, a **valley**. This was truly *Death Valley*; the floor of the valley was so dense with human **bones** that it was described as **full of bones**. Ezekiel saw them **all around**, noticing **there were very many in the open valley**.

i. "The *valley* is the same word as the 'plain' in Ezekiel 3:22 (Heb. *biqa*), and probably the same location is intended." (Taylor)

ii. The people represented by these **bones** were not only dead; they were also disgraced. In the thinking of ancient Israel (and the ancient Near East), an unburied corpse with exposed remains was a shocking disgrace to the dead. These **bones** were obviously denied proper burial.

iii. "The bones lay on the surface of the valley, like the remains of corpses denied a proper burial and left for scavenging buzzards. As an Israelite and especially as a priest, Ezekiel knew how important was the proper treatment of human corpses." (Block)

iv. "The vision may have been prompted by the actual memory of seeing the Israelite dead strewn outside Jerusalem or scattered along the desert road that led Ezekiel and his companions into exile." (Taylor)

c. **Indeed they were very dry**: Apart from their presence in a living body, bones are dead. **Dry** bones are not only dead; they have been long dead. Bones are what remain when life has passed. If something never had life, it would not leave bones. Yet when something has been dead so long, we give up hope it will ever live again.

d. **Can these bones live?** One might hope that a recently dead corpse might somehow resuscitate. No one hopes that scattered, detached **bones** might **live**. Admirably, Ezekiel responded to God's question with the only hope that could be found, saying "**O Lord GOD, You know.**"

- Ezekiel had no hope in the bones, but he did have hope in God.
- Ezekiel did not presume to know what God wanted to do with the bones.
- Ezekiel was confident that God *did* know.

2. (4-6) Speaking life to dead bones.

Again He said to me, "Prophesy to these bones, and say to them, 'O dry bones, hear the word of the LORD! Thus says the Lord GOD to these bones: "Surely I will cause breath to enter into you, and you shall live. I will put sinews on you and bring flesh upon you, cover you with skin and put breath in you; and you shall live. Then you shall know that I *am* the LORD.""

a. **Prophesy to these bones**: In the previous verse, Ezekiel deliberately left the matter with God, to His power and wisdom. In turn, God gave the prophet something to do. God commanded him to speak, to **prophesy** to the dry, dead **bones**. By all outward observation this was a vain and foolish act.

i. Many years later the Apostle Paul acknowledged that the message of the cross – God's rescue for lost humanity in the person and work of Jesus, especially His sacrifice at the cross – was *foolishness to those who are perishing* (1 Corinthians 1:18).

ii. "If we want revivals, we must revive our reverence for the Word of God. If we want conversions, we must put more of God's Word into our sermons; even if we paraphrase it into our own words, it must still be his Word upon which we place our reliance, for the only power which will bless men lies in that." (Spurgeon)

b. **O dry bones, hear the word of the LORD**: Ezekiel could only preach this message full of faith in God. Yet if he was confident that he spoke **the word of the LORD**, he knew God's word had supernatural power.

c. **Surely I will cause breath to enter into you, and you shall live**: God promised to fill the dry bones with **breath**. He promised to **bring flesh** upon those bones and cover them **with skin**. God would make the once dead and dry bones **live**.

i. This was a work of revival; restoring life to something that at one time had life. This was not the creation of life from nothing; it was the restoration of life to something that had been long dead.

ii. This was *God's declaration*. The bones could never create life within themselves. As the **word of the LORD** was proclaimed over them, they received God's promise of life.

iii. The life would be marked by **breath** living once again in these bones. This has a double sense because the ancient Hebrew words for **breath** and *spirit* are the same. This was a granting of God's Spirit (as previously promised in Ezekiel 36:27) *and* the restoration of life-giving breath.

iv. "At its root *ruah* denotes the sense of 'air in motion', i.e. wind or breath. This can extend from a gentle breeze to a stormy wind, or from a breath that is breathed to a raging passion. It comes to mean both man's spirit, or disposition, and also emotional qualities like vigour, courage, impatience and ecstasy. It covers not only man's vital breath, given to him at birth and leaving his body in his dying gasp, but also the Spirit of God who imparts that breath. Such is the rich variety of the word used here by Ezekiel." (Taylor)

v. "The resurrection that follows does not refer directly to individual resurrection from death. It is symbolic of the recreation and revitalizing of the nation as a whole, as the interpretation shows." (Wright)

3. (7-8) Dead bones assemble together.

So I prophesied as I was commanded; and as I prophesied, there was a noise, and suddenly a rattling; and the bones came together, bone to bone. Indeed, as I looked, the sinews and the flesh came upon them, and the skin covered them over; but *there was* no breath in them.

a. **So I prophesied as I was commanded**: If Ezekiel had any doubts, he put them away and did what God **commanded**. To human perception this proclamation of the word of God was foolish, yet Ezekiel obeyed.

b. **The bones came together, bone to bone**: As Ezekiel **prophesied**, there was first a **noise** among the bones, a **rattling**. As he continued, the bones began to assemble themselves into skeletons.

> i. The text does not specifically say, but it can be assumed that the bones assembled themselves *properly*, as skeletons and not as weird combinations of bones. When God restores, He puts things together in the right way.

> ii. **A rattling**: "Since, apart from the Spirit, we are powerless, we must value greatly every movement of his power. Notice, in this account of the vision in the valley, how the prophet draws attention to the fact of the shaking and the noises, and the coming of the sinews and the flesh, even before there was any sign of life. I think that, if we want the Spirit of God to bless us, we must be on the watch to notice everything he does." (Spurgeon)

c. **The sinews and flesh came upon them**: After the bones were assembled, muscles and tissue came upon the bones. The bones were full of activity, yet still did not yet have the **breath** of life in them. The reviving of the dry bones clearly happened in stages.

- Stirring of the bones.
- Assembly of the bones.
- Sinews and flesh upon the bones.
- Skin upon the tissues covering the bones.
- Awaiting the breath of God.

> i. "The sequence involving bones, sinews, flesh, and skin reflects an understanding of anatomy available to anyone who had witnessed the slaughter of an animal; it also reverses the decomposition process." (Block)

> ii. "The body is the soul's sheath, [Daniel 7:15] the soul's suit. The upper garment is the skin, the inner the flesh; the inmost of all, bones and sinews." (Trapp)

> iii. "So here were men in skin, with flesh, sinews, bones; but, like Adam before inspired with the breath of life, the spirit of life was yet wanting." (Poole)

iv. "There is no teaching in the Scriptures that the resurrection of anyone from physical death will take place in stages, such as is stated here for the dried bones of the people of Israel." (Feinberg)

4. (9-10) The second prophecy to the bones brings life and strength.

Also He said to me, "Prophesy to the breath, prophesy, son of man, and say to the breath, 'Thus says the Lord God: "Come from the four winds, O breath, and breathe on these slain, that they may live."'" So I prophesied as He commanded me, and breath came into them, and they lived, and stood upon their feet, an exceedingly great army.

a. **Prophesy to the breath**: The previous verse left the valley full of revived, activated bodies that yet lacked breath. Now Ezekiel was told to call upon the **breath** (spirit, wind), praying the breath/spirit would come **on these slain, that they may live**.

b. **Come from the four winds, O breath**: In this vision, Ezekiel had already proclaimed God's word to the dead and dry bones, and had seen a remarkable work done. Yet it was not enough; there also needed to be a work *by the Holy Spirit*. Ezekiel was commanded to pray – to boldly **prophesy to the** Spirit – calling on the Spirit to come upon those on whom the word of God had worked.

i. "The second action was tantamount to praying, as Ezekiel besought the Spirit of God to effect the miracle of re-creation, to breathe into man's nostrils the breath of life (cf. Genesis 2:7). This time the effect was devastating. What preaching by itself failed to achieve, prayer made a reality." (Taylor)

ii. "First, the prophet prophesies to the bones – here is preaching; and next, he prophesies to the four winds – here is praying. The preaching has its share in the work, but it is the praying which achieves the result, for after he had prophesied to the four winds, and not before, the bones began to live." (Spurgeon)

iii. "When you have done your best, and have failed of the highest results, prophesy to the Spirit; cry to the four winds, because He may come in the icy north wind of tribulation, or the warm west wind of prosperity; but speak with the certain assurance of, 'Thus saith the Lord God: Come!'" (Meyer)

c. **So I prophesied as He commanded me**: Perhaps this was, humanly speaking, an easier message for Ezekiel to preach. He had the encouragement of seeing the beginning of a supernatural work with the activation of the dry bones. Now he **prophesied** and prayed for the work to be completed.

d. **Breath came into them**: After Ezekiel's faithful proclamation of God's message, the work of reviving the dry bones was completed. The **breath** of God came into the reanimated bodies, and they **stood upon their feet**.

i. "There is no hope for humanity in man. But these dry bones can live. By the Word, and the Spirit of God, men can be reborn; and at last healed of their separations, and united under one King." (Morgan)

ii. "Decayed Churches can most certainly be revived by the preaching of the Word, accompanied by the coming of the heavenly 'breath' from the four winds. O Lord, send us such revivals now, for many of thy Churches need them." (Spurgeon)

e. **An exceedingly great army**: The bones were not revived to become a group of spectators or to live for their own comfort. They became an **army**, and an **exceedingly great** one. They lived to act under the orders of the one who gave them life.

i. **Exceedingly great army**: "So the Hebrew, or Army of strong, courageous, and well-ordered soldiers. The phrase in the Hebrew is very full; a power, or great host, very, very great. Thus they rise, that the prophet and we might know how safe they would be in themselves, and how terrible to their enemies." (Poole)

ii. With all word and no spirit, we can be an army of the dead – assembled, solid, but without the true breath of life.

5. (11-14) God explains the vision to Ezekiel.

Then He said to me, "Son of man, these bones are the whole house of Israel. They indeed say, 'Our bones are dry, our hope is lost, and we ourselves are cut off!' Therefore prophesy and say to them, 'Thus says the Lord God: "Behold, O My people, I will open your graves and cause you to come up from your graves, and bring you into the land of Israel. Then you shall know that I *am* the Lord, when I have opened your graves, O My people, and brought you up from your graves. I will put My Spirit in you, and you shall live, and I will place you in your own land. Then you shall know that I, the Lord, have spoken *it* and performed *it*," says the Lord.'"

a. **These bones are the whole house of Israel**: We might have supposed that Ezekiel understood that the **bones** in his vision represented his people. Yet, it might have surprised him when God revealed they represented **the whole house of Israel**, not only those from the kingdom of Judah. The restoration would include those from the northern kingdom of Israel that fell to the Assyrians some 150 years earlier.

b. **Our bones are dry, our hope is lost, and we ourselves are cut off**: The house of Israel had reason to say this, both those from the south and the north. Their only **hope** for life and restoration was in God.

> i. **Our hope is lost**: "They were the words of despondency, born of the realisation of the desolation produced by the Divine Reprobation. It was an accurate description." (Morgan)

c. **I will open your graves and cause you to come up**: The same message is communicated through a slightly different picture. Instead of the bones being exposed, here they are buried in **graves**. The effect is the same; life is brought to that which was dead.

> i. "Cynics in Ezekiel's audience might have assumed a sinister motive, perhaps to rob the tombs or to desecrate the remains, both common practices in the ancient Near East. But now Yahweh poses as a tomb robber like no other. The treasure he is after is the bodies of his people, whom he will raise from the grave." (Block)

d. **Bring you into the land of Israel**: As promised many times in other places (such as Ezekiel 36:24 and 36:28), this revival of Israel also included their restoration to the land.

> i. "The meaning of our text, as opened up by the context, is most evidently, if words mean anything, first, that there shall be a political restoration of the Jews to their own land and to their own nationality; and then, secondly, there is in the text, and in the context, a most plain declaration, that there shall be a spiritual restoration, a conversion in fact, of the tribes of Israel." (Spurgeon in 1884)

e. **Then you shall know that I am the LORD**: God would powerfully reveal Himself to Israel through this great work of revival and restoration to the land.

f. **I will put My Spirit in you, and you shall live**: The breath in the revived bones was more than the breath of human life; it was the **Spirit** of the living God. This is another way of expressing the great promise found in the previous chapter (Ezekiel 36:27).

> i. Undeniably, Ezekiel 37:1-14 is about God's promised restoration of Israel. It is a restoration so wide and so deep that any fair examination of Israel's history must confess that it has not yet happened. This means that it is yet to be fulfilled, and will be fulfilled as part of God's plan for Israel in the very last days.

> ii. At the same time, this chapter teaches many principles of how God works in revival, and how God's servants should think and act relevant

to such a mighty reviving work. If we put the modern servant of God in Ezekiel's place, we can make the following observations.

- God's servant must know that the bones are dead and dry.

- God's servant must walk among the dead.

- God's servant must proclaim God's word.

- God's servant must have almost a foolish confidence in God's Word.

- God's servant must understand that the Spirit works in a process.

- God's servant must recognize that the work of the Holy Spirit is essential.

- God's servant must boldly pray for the Spirit to move.

- God's servant must speak in the power of faith.

- God's servant must notice every evidence of the Spirit's work.

- God's servant must look for God's people to be revived into an army of service.

- God's servant must not say that hope is lost.

B. One kingdom under one king.

1. (15-17) Two sticks become one stick.

Again the word of the LORD came to me, saying, "As for you, son of man, take a stick for yourself and write on it: 'For Judah and for the children of Israel, his companions.' Then take another stick and write on it, 'For Joseph, the stick of Ephraim, and *for* all the house of Israel, his companions.' Then join them one to another for yourself into one stick, and they will become one in your hand.

a. **Take a stick for yourself and write on it**: At God's instruction, Ezekiel took two sticks. On one was writing identifying it with **Judah** and on the other was writing identifying it with **Ephraim** (that is, **Israel**). The sticks represented the kingdom of the northern ten tribes (**Israel**) and the kingdom of the southern two tribes (**Judah**).

i. In Ezekiel's day the northern kingdom had been conquered and destroyed for some 150 years. Yet God still considered them a people, even though they were scattered among the nations.

ii. "Incidentally, these same scriptures show the folly of the Anglo-Israel delusion with its position of ten lost tribes…. The prophets all recognized the northern tribes as still in existence and knew of no such error as 'lost' tribes (cf. Isaiah 43:5-7, 'every one'; Isaiah 49:5-6; Jeremiah 3:12-15)." (Feinberg)

b. **Joseph, the stick of Ephraim**: The tribe of Ephraim was the largest and most influential tribe of the northern kingdom. Several times in the Old Testament the northern kingdom was called **Ephraim**.

> i. "Joseph was the father of Ephraim and Manasseh, the two dominant tribes in the northern kingdom. Of these two, Ephraim, the younger son, dominated northern politics from the beginning." (Block)

> ii. "Jeroboam, the first king of the ten tribes, was an *Ephraimite. Joseph* represents the ten tribes in general; they were in the hand of *Ephraim*, that is, *under the government of Jeroboam*." (Clarke)

c. **Join them one to another**: Either in appearance or in reality, Ezekiel was to join the two sticks together so they would **become one in your hand**.

> i. "His clenched fist will thus grasp the place where the two sticks meet, and it will appear as if he is holding one long stick in the middle." (Taylor)

> ii. "Certainly no basis exists in this text for the strange Mormon teaching that the sticks refer to two scrolls. According to the convoluted interpretation of this cult, Ezekiel was prophesying that one day the Book of Mormon (the stick or scroll of Ephraim) would be joined to the Bible (the stick or scroll of Judah) to form the complete revelation of God." (Smith)

2. (18-20) The meaning of the joined sticks.

"And when the children of your people speak to you, saying, 'Will you not show us what you *mean* by these?'— say to them, 'Thus says the Lord God: "Surely I will take the stick of Joseph, which *is* in the hand of Ephraim, and the tribes of Israel, his companions; and I will join them with it, with the stick of Judah, and make them one stick, and they will be one in My hand."' And the sticks on which you write will be in your hand before their eyes.

a. **Will you not show us what you mean by these?** Ezekiel's audience among the exiles were somewhat mystified by this acted-out prophecy. Perhaps they wondered what God would have to do with the northern kingdom (**Joseph** and **Ephraim**) some 150 years after their seeming extinction.

b. **Make them one stick, and they will be one in My hand**: Generally, the meaning was plain. When God ultimately restored the tribes of Israel, He would restore them all. That which was previously divided in the days of Rehoboam (1 Kings 12-14) would be restored as one.

> i. "Taking away the deadly feud that hath so long time been between them, breaking down the partition wall, &c. I will once more bring them all under one king, and make them of one mind." (Trapp)

> ii. "Especially significant for the Israelites was Yahweh's unequivocal declaration that all the descendants of Jacob were heirs of the covenant. Against the grain of centuries of history and deep-seated prejudices, Yahweh extends his grace to the whole house of Israel—not only Judah but Joseph and his confederates as well." (Block)

3. (21-23) The promise to gather, unify, and restore Israel.

"Then say to them, 'Thus says the Lord God: "Surely I will take the children of Israel from among the nations, wherever they have gone, and will gather them from every side and bring them into their own land; and I will make them one nation in the land, on the mountains of Israel; and one king shall be king over them all; they shall no longer be two nations, nor shall they ever be divided into two kingdoms again. They shall not defile themselves anymore with their idols, nor with their detestable things, nor with any of their transgressions; but I will deliver them from all their dwelling places in which they have sinned, and will cleanse them. Then they shall be My people, and I will be their God.

a. **Gather them from every side and bring them into their own land**: The restoration after the Babylonian exile was only a shadow of this promise. This was a promise to bring the Jewish people **from among the nations**, from a scattering much broader than the Babylonian captivity.

b. **I will make them one nation in the land**: This looked forward to a restoration much greater than what happened in the days of Ezra, Zerubbabel, and Nehemiah. God would bring the Jewish people *as a whole* back into the land.

c. **In the land, on the mountains of Israel**: This phrasing emphasizes that God made this promise regarding the *literal land* of Israel.

d. **They shall no longer be two nations**: Gathered together under **one king**, they would be established in the literal land of Israel under a literal king.

> i. Vawter and Hoppe acknowledge that this has not yet been fulfilled in history: "Despite the prophet's words and various attempts, the divisions between north and south remained. In the NT period, these divisions were clear enough in the animosity between Jew and Samaritan."

ii. "Whether it's the Children of Israel or the saints in the church today, the Lord wants His people to be united. 'Behold, how good and how pleasant it is for brethren to dwell together in unity' (Psalm 133:1). Paul appealed to the believers in Corinth to cultivate unity in the church (1 Corinthians 1:10), and he exhorted the Ephesian believers to 'make every effort to keep the unity of the Spirit through the bond of peace' (Ephesians 4:3, NIV)." (Wiersbe)

e. **They shall not defile themselves with their idols**: These promises are typical of passages that speak of the new covenant. The promises of purity (**shall not defile**), of cleansing (**will cleanse them**), and relationship (**they shall be My people, and I will be their God**) are often characteristic of the new covenant.

i. Among other things, this shows that the unity promised here is a unity of purity and devotion to *one king*. It is not the unity of compromise and lack of standards.

ii. "Provoked by their defiling and abominable acts, Yahweh had abandoned his people. Now that he has purified them, he may return and normalize the covenant relationship with them." (Block)

4. (24-28) David, king over the restored Israel.

"David My servant *shall be* king over them, and they shall all have one shepherd; they shall also walk in My judgments and observe My statutes, and do them. Then they shall dwell in the land that I have given to Jacob My servant, where your fathers dwelt; and they shall dwell there, they, their children, and their children's children, forever; and My servant David *shall be* their prince forever. Moreover I will make a covenant of peace with them, and it shall be an everlasting covenant with them; I will establish them and multiply them, and I will set My sanctuary in their midst forevermore. My tabernacle also shall be with them; indeed I will be their God, and they shall be My people. The nations also will know that I, the LORD, sanctify Israel, when My sanctuary is in their midst forevermore.""

a. **David My servant shall be king over them**: In Ezekiel 37:22 God said that there would be one king over the restored and unified Israel. Here we learn that the one king is David (as previously stated in Ezekiel 34:23-25).

b. **They shall dwell in the land that I have given to Jacob My servant**: The clear, repetitive nature of these promises of a specific, literal land cause wonder at the attempts to spiritualize such promises and deny that God has no future plan for ethnic Israel in their ancestral land.

i. "Jacob means here the *twelve tribes*; and the *land given to them* was the whole land of *Palestine*; consequently, the promise states that, when they return, they are to possess the whole of the *Promised Land*." (Clarke)

c. **My servant David shall be their prince forever**: This plain promise is most appropriately seen *not* as a strange and imprecise reference to Jesus the Messiah, but as part of the several promises that King David will once again rule over Israel in the Millennial Kingdom (Isaiah 55:3-4, Jeremiah 30:8-9, Hosea 3:5).

i. Most commentators believe that this reference to **David** is really a reference to the Messiah, the Son of David, fulfilled in Jesus Christ. They would say the same of the many other passages (noted above) which speak of David's future rule over Israel. Yet we can simply observe that if God did not intend David, He would not have said it. There is nothing in these texts themselves that demand that it is the Messiah and *not* David.

d. **I will make a covenant of peace with them, and it shall be an everlasting covenant with them**: God here seems to describe the new covenant as both a **covenant of peace** (as in Ezekiel 34:25 and Isaiah 54:10) and an **everlasting covenant** (as in Ezekiel 16:60, Isaiah 55:3, and Hebrews 13:20). It is the covenant that brings true *shalom*, and the covenant that never ends.

i. "This shalom represents much more than merely the absence of war. It denotes a state of harmony and equilibrium among all participants in the divine-human-territorial relationships." (Block)

e. **I will establish them and multiply them**: These promises are characteristic of the new covenant (as in Ezekiel 36:10-11). God's ultimate restoration of Israel would be on a large scale, not a small scale.

i. **The nations also will know**: "Then all nations would see that it was the Lord who made Israel holy. She would be set apart from all nations as God's special possession. No other nation would have the Lord dwelling in its sanctuary uniquely in its midst as would Israel." (Alexander)

f. **I will set My sanctuary in their midst forevermore**: The promise of this **sanctuary** will be described in great detail in Ezekiel chapters 40 through 48. To Ezekiel and the Babylonian exiles, no restoration could be complete without some kind of temple.

i. "The restoration of the temple is thus far more than simply a matter of repairing war-damage. It is God's way of demonstrating that he is not dead and that Israel are still his people." (Taylor)

ii. "The restoration of the sanctuary is the climax of all that this prophet had to say." (Smith)

Ezekiel 38 – The Defeat of Gog and Defense of Israel

A. Yahweh draws Gog to attack Israel.

1. (1-3) God against Gog of the land of Magog.

Now the word of the LORD came to me, saying, "Son of man, set your face against Gog, of the land of Magog, the prince of Rosh, Meshech, and Tubal, and prophesy against him, and say, 'Thus says the Lord GOD: "Behold, I *am* against you, O Gog, the prince of Rosh, Meshech, and Tubal.

a. **Set your face against Gog, of the land of Magog**: In this general context of God's restoration of Israel, here Ezekiel prophesied against **Gog** (a ruler) and **Magog** (the place of Gog). Here Gog is noted as **the prince of Rosh, Meshech, and Tubal**.

i. Identifying Gog and the battle described in this chapter has interested interpreters and students of Bible prophecy since ancient times. It is a difficult problem without an entirely clear solution, for several reasons.

- There is no other Old Testament description of or connection with **Gog** (apart from 1 Chronicles 5:4, which seems to have no relevance to this passage). Gog seems to be a wholly new and strange enemy of Israel.

- **Magog** is mentioned as a descendant of Japheth in Genesis 10:2 (and 1 Chronicles 1:5) but is never presented as a threat or enemy of Israel in any Old Testament passage.

- The phrase **prince of Rosh** has also been translated as *chief prince*, with the idea that the word **rosh** describes the greatness of the prince, not a place where the prince rules (**Rosh**). Translators and interpreters do not agree if it should be **prince of Rosh** or *chief prince*.

- If **Rosh** is understood as a name of a people or place, it has no other connection or reference in the Old Testament. There are many who think that **Rosh** speaks of *Russia* or the *Russians*, but the only direct evidence of this is the similar sound of the names.

- **Meshech** and **Tubal** were peoples to the north of Israel, somewhere near the Black Sea and the Caspian Sea. These were peoples nowhere else noted in the Old Testament for any threat or animosity against Israel.

- Though the names **Meshech** and **Tubal** have a similar sound to the Russian cities of *Moscow* and *Tobolsk*, similar sounding names alone are not enough to make a certain connection with Russia and her cities.

ii. "Notice also that none of these enemies are the old ones with which we are familiar as hostile to Israel. It is a new confederacy and antagonism." (Morgan)

iii. Several older commentators (such as Matthew Poole, John Trapp, and Adam Clarke) identified **Gog** with Antiochus IV Epiphanes, the great persecutor of the Jewish people in the period between the Old and New Testaments. This is an extremely unlikely conclusion.

iv. Others see **Gog** as a king who lived more than a hundred years before Ezekiel's time (*Gyges*, the king of Lydia). This is also an unlikely conclusion.

v. **The land of Magog**: "Magog, a Japhetic descendant (Genesis 10:2) in the table of nations, is identified by Josephus (Antiquities I, 123 [vi. 1]) as the land of the Scythians, a mountainous region around the Black and Caspian seas. This position is generally accepted." (Alexander)

vi. Feinberg on **Rosh**: "Byzantine and Arabic writers mentioned a people called Rus inhabiting the country of Taurus and reckoned among the Scythians. There have been many writers who connected the name Rosh with the Russians, but this is not generally accepted today."

vii. "It's tempting to identify Rosh with Russia and therefore Meschech with Moscow and Tubal with Tobolsk, both cities in Russia; but we would have a hard time defending this on linguistic grounds. This doesn't rule out the participation of modern Russia, since it is located in the north (vv. 6, 15; 39:2), but neither does it demand it." (Wiersbe)

viii. **Meshech and Tubal**: "The biblical and extrabiblical data, though sparse, would imply that Meshech and Tubal refer to geographical areas or countries in eastern modern Turkey, southwest of Russia and northwest of Iran." (Alexander)

ix. John Trapp is an example of speculative guessing regarding the identity of the people mentioned here. Trapp wrote that **Meshech** represented the Muslims and **Tubal** the Roman Catholics. "These two are thus conjoined to show, as some think, that Turks and Popelings shall at length join their forces to root out the true religion, and that, while they are tumultuating and endeavouring the Church's downfall, Christ shall come upon them and confound them."

b. **Behold, I am against you, O Gog, the prince of Rosh**: Though the similar sounding name does not certainly identify **Rosh** with Russia, that identification matches what we do know about Gog and Rosh. We know they are a new, previously unnamed enemy (unlike Babylonia or Assyria or Egypt), that this ruler Gog rules over more than one people (including **Meshech and Tubal**), and that Gog's territory is found in the far north in respect to Israel (Ezekiel 38:15).

i. "Unlike the Egyptians, Assyrians, and Babylonians, with whom Judah had frequent contact, the peoples in the distant north were shrouded in mystery. The reports of these mysterious people groups that filtered down spoke of wild peoples, brutal and barbaric. This combination of mystery and brutality made Gog and his confederates perfect symbols of the archetypal enemy, rising against God and his people." (Block)

ii. Feinberg wrote in summary of Ezekiel 38 and 39: "They tell, if interpreted literally, of a coming northern confederacy of nations about the Black and Caspian seas with Persia and North Africa, who will invade the promised land after Israel's restoration to it."

2. (4-6) God promises to turn and pull Gog to attack Israel.

I will turn you around, put hooks into your jaws, and lead you out, with all your army, horses, and horsemen, all splendidly clothed, a great company *with* bucklers and shields, all of them handling swords. Persia, Ethiopia, and Libya are with them, all of them *with* shield and helmet; Gomer and all its troops; the house of Togarmah *from* the far north and all its troops—many people *are* with you.

a. **I will turn you around, put hooks into your jaws, and lead you out**: God promised to bring Gog **with all** his **army** against Israel. Whatever Gog's *own* motivations for attack and invasion might be, there would be an overriding Divine purpose in this.

i. Those who see Gog as a leader of Russia have offered many ideas as to why Russia would invade Israel (a desire for a warm water port, a desire to intervene in the Middle East for the sake of oil, a desire for Dead Sea minerals). At the time of this writing, there is an active Russian military involvement in Syria, in support of a Syrian government that has at times been hostile to Israel.

ii. The reader may weigh such possibilities for himself or herself, with the understanding that political and military circumstances constantly change. Yet despite whatever human motivation may be present, the ultimate reason is that God said He would *compel* Gog to come against Israel.

b. **With all your army, horses, and horsemen, all splendidly clothed**: Ezekiel described the army with the terms that made sense to him and were relevant to most of human history. This was a large, fast, well-equipped army, ready for conquest.

i. "Here the prophet saw the final manifestation of antagonism to Jehovah and His people. He saw it gathering itself in terrific force, the mightiest alliance that had ever acted against Israel." (Morgan)

ii. "These verses create the impression that Gog is an imperial power with vast military resources." (Block)

iii. "Some have found great difficulty in the references to armor, buckler, shield, sword and helmet, but even in our day of advanced weapons of warfare it is interesting *to* learn that in some parts of the world conflict is going on with primitive weapons. (And how else could an ancient writer have described warfare? He knew nothing of planes and guns.) It is our concern only to understand what the commonsense interpretation of the passage indicates." (Feinberg)

c. **Persia, Ethiopia, and Libya are with them**: Coming from the far north (Ezekiel 38:15), Gog also had allies to the west (**Persia**), to the south (**Ethiopia**) and to the east (**Libya**) of Israel.

d. **Gomer and all its troops; the house of Togarmah from the far north**: Most regard **Gomer** as a people from Cappadocia, in modern Turkey. The **house of Togarmah** is often regarded as the Armenian people to the north of Israel.

i. "Gomer (probably the ancient Cimmerians) and Beth Togarmah (possibly the ancient Til-garimmu southeast of the Black Sea)." (Alexander)

ii. "Gomer identified a wild tribe living in the fog-bound region north of the Black Sea, perhaps as far west as the Crimean Peninsula." (Block)

iii. The mention of specific nations communicates at least two impressions.

- The nations allied with Gog and Magog will come from every direction against Israel.

- The number of listed nations allied with Gog and Magog is seven, perhaps indicating a completeness or fullness in the opposition.

3. (7-9) Magog's armies come into the land of Israel.

"Prepare yourself and be ready, you and all your companies that are gathered about you; and be a guard for them. After many days you will be visited. In the latter years you will come into the land of those brought back from the sword *and* gathered from many people on the mountains of Israel, which had long been desolate; they were brought out of the nations, and now all of them dwell safely. You will ascend, coming like a storm, covering the land like a cloud, you and all your troops and many peoples with you."

a. **Prepare yourself and be ready**: Since Gog would come with great armies against Israel, they must **prepare** and **be ready**. Because they came drawn by God (Ezekiel 38:4) and would serve His purpose, they must **prepare** and **be ready**.

i. "Yahweh appears to be charging Gog to assume leadership over the vast forces allied with him by serving as their guardian, in keeping with his role as their leader." (Block)

b. **After many days… In the latter years**: This prophecy of Gog and Magog would not be fulfilled soon, but would be fulfilled in the very last days. They would come against Israel after they had been **brought back from the sword and gathered from many people** in fulfillment of previous prophecies.

i. "The phrase *miyamim rabbim* ('after many days,' v.8) was normally used to express an indefinite time period—a long time. It was however, used sometimes to reach as far as the end times (cf. Jeremiah 32:14, Daniel 8:26, Hosea 3:4)." (Alexander)

ii. "The attack will eventually come *in the latter years* (8), a clear eschatological indication." (Taylor)

c. **Now all of them dwell safely**: Gog would come against Israel when they enjoyed security in their land.

d. **You will ascend, coming like a storm**: The armies of Gog would come against Israel as a great destructive power, something like a plague.

i. "It is clearly stated that all these hordes will issue from the far north of the promised land and will be numerous indeed. If ever an invasion could succeed because of superior numbers, this will be it. But the entire story has not been told." (Feinberg)

ii. **Like a storm**: "This storm is violent, with confused, tumultuous noises, and with devastation, as the word implieth; and come as a cloud, that is, as dark, as large, and as inevitable, and which continueth the violent waving storm." (Poole)

4. (10-13) Gog's evil plan.

'Thus says the Lord God: "On that day it shall come to pass *that* thoughts will arise in your mind, and you will make an evil plan: You will say, 'I will go up against a land of unwalled villages; I will go to a peaceful people, who dwell safely, all of them dwelling without walls, and having neither bars nor gates'— to take plunder and to take booty, to stretch out your hand against the waste places *that are again* inhabited, and against a people gathered from the nations, who have acquired livestock and goods, who dwell in the midst of the land. Sheba, Dedan, the merchants of Tarshish, and all their young lions will say to you, 'Have you come to take plunder? Have you gathered your army to take booty, to carry away silver and gold, to take away livestock and goods, to take great plunder?'"'

a. **You will make an evil plan**: God deliberately pulled Gog and his allies to come against Israel (Ezekiel 38:4). At the same time, Gog was prompted by his own **evil plan**, by the **thoughts** in his own **mind**. Yahweh did not drag an *unwilling* Gog to come against Israel.

b. **I will go up against a land of unwalled villages**: The first evil thought Gog had against Israel was to attack them because they seemed defenseless as they were gathered back into the land. The second was **to take plunder and to take booty**; to attack Israel out of economic interest. Gathered back to the land in prosperity, there was **plunder** to seize.

i. "Gog calculated that the attack against the people of God would be relatively easy and extremely profitable." (Smith)

ii. "Let this be clearly noted. The invasion of Gog and his allies was an invasion not of a land desolated, but of the land in which the people of God were seen dwelling in peace and prosperity." (Morgan)

c. **In the midst of the land**: "An interesting phrase is employed to define the place where God's people will be dwelling. It is called the middle (literally, the navel) of the earth, as explained in 5:5. The land of Israel is in the center of the earth as far as God's purposes for the world are concerned (cf. Deuteronomy 32:8)." (Feinberg)

> i. "'The center of the earth' is Jerusalem, which this text conceives as being more than a political capital or religious center. It is the very basis of the world's historical order." (Vawter and Hoppe)

> ii. "Rabbinic literature states: 'As the navel is set in the centre of the human body, so is the land of Israel the navel of the world...situated in the centre of the world, and Jerusalem in the centre of the land of Israel, and the sanctuary in the centre of Jerusalem, and the holy place in the centre of the sanctuary, and the ark in the centre of the holy place, and the foundation stone before the holy place, because from it the world was founded.'" (Feinberg)

d. **Sheba, Dedan, the merchants of Tarshish**: The trading peoples of the world looked upon Gog's intent with interest. They could also perhaps benefit from Gog's conquest and plunder of Israel.

> i. "Sheba and Dedan were Arab peoples. Tarshish has been identified with Great Britain, but not on good grounds. It may be either Spain or Sardinia, for there was a [place known as] Tartessus in both areas." (Feinberg)

> ii. "Gog's enterprise has roused the greed of other nations to join in the plunder, or to traffic in the stolen goods. They are typical of those who will not initiate wrong-doing, but are eager to cash in on the proceeds of it." (Taylor)

> iii. "The young lions of Tarshish are taken to mean either strong leaders and princes or greedy rulers of these commercial communities." (Feinberg)

5. (14-17) Gog will come upon God's people Israel.

"Therefore, son of man, prophesy and say to Gog, 'Thus says the Lord God: "On that day when My people Israel dwell safely, will you not know *it?* **Then you will come from your place out of the far north, you and many peoples with you, all of them riding on horses, a great company and a mighty army. You will come up against My people Israel like a cloud, to cover the land. It will be in the latter days that I will bring you against My land, so that the nations may know Me, when I am hallowed in you, O Gog, before their eyes." Thus says the Lord God: "Are** *you* **he of whom I have spoken in former days by My servants the prophets of Israel, who prophesied for years in those days that I would bring you against them?**

a. **You will come from your place out of the far north, you and many peoples with you**: At the appointed time, Gog and those allied with him would come against Israel. Certainly, this includes the seven nations or peoples mentioned in Ezekiel 38:3-6 and likely means more not specifically mentioned.

b. **All of them riding on horses, a great company**: Ezekiel described the attack with the only images of swift military attack that made sense to Ezekiel, the people of his day, and most of human history. They would come **like a cloud**, a massive and unstoppable storm.

c. **It will be in the latter days**: Once again, Ezekiel emphasized that this attack against Israel would happen in the last days of human history as we presently know it. God would bring it to pass then to glorify Himself among the nations (**so that the nations may know Me, when I am hallowed in you**).

i. The emphasis on this dramatic battle **in the latter days** has led many to wonder and speculate when Gog and his allies would attack Israel. Admittedly, some regard Ezekiel 38 and 39 as nothing more than a prophetic parable that says, "God will protect His people." Such a casual approach to these chapters seems to lack serious regard for the text and its meaning.

ii. "The time element was distinctly stated as 'in the latter years,' which is equivalent to 'the latter days' of verse 16. No student of prophecy can afford to overlook this phrase in the Old Testament or its parallel in the New Testament." (Feinberg)

iii. Though there is much we do not know about Gog's attack against Israel, there is collectively much we do know.

- A leader from the north (Gog), who was not an ancient enemy of Israel, will lead a confederation of nations against Israel (Ezekiel 38:1-6).

- He will be motived by his own evil plans *and* pulled by God (Ezekiel 38:10).

- It will happen in the latter days, distant from Ezekiel's time (Ezekiel 38:8).

- The allied nations will come from every point on the compass, including Persia (modern Iran), and peoples from the lands of modern Turkey, Libya, Ethiopia, and perhaps Armenia and Germany (Ezekiel 38:1-6).

- Gog and his allies will come as a massive, swift, and well-equipped army (Ezekiel 38:4-6).

- Gog will come against Israel when they are gathered back to their land (Ezekiel 38:8, 12).

- Gog will come against Israel when they enjoy considerable safety (Ezekiel 38:8).

- Gog will come against Israel when they are prosperous (Ezekiel 38:12-13).

- Other nations will watch and wonder how they might benefit themselves from Gog's conquest of Israel (Ezekiel 38:12-13).

- Yahweh will defend Israel and defeat Gog, and thereby glorify Himself among the nations (Ezekiel 38:16).

- This victory will fulfill the prophetic expectation of several previous prophets of Israel (Ezekiel 38:17).

iv. Collectively, these markers help us suppose when in God's future prophetic plan this battle may happen. Yet, the information is not complete enough for much certainty among several options.

- This battle may happen before the beginning of the last seven-year period of human government, before the glorious return of Jesus Christ. It may in some way usher in the dominance of the final world leader and his government.

- This battle may happen in the middle of the last seven-year period of human government before the glorious return of Jesus Christ. It may mark the promised hostility against Israel and the Jewish people and their promised protection by God.

- This battle may happen at the end of the last seven-year period of human government before the glorious return of Jesus Christ. There is a connection between Revelation 19:17-18 and Ezekiel 39:17-20.

- This battle may happen as referenced by Revelation 20:7-9. Not all Christians agree on the specific concepts of God's plan for the future, but some of those who see the establishment of a physical, material kingdom of Jesus over this earth for 1,000 years think that the Gog invasion happens at the end of that 1,000 years, as Revelation 20:7-9 mentions Gog and Magog.

v. Each one of these scenarios has its own objections and problems, and this may be a case where the specific fulfillment of the prophecy is not truly understood until its fulfillment.

d. **Are you he of whom I have spoken in former days by My servants the prophets**: This rhetorical question with the assumed answer of "yes" means that this attack and God's action in it was prophesied by previously appointed messengers in Israel.

i. "In any case we must somehow link this chapter with Joel 3 and Zechariah 14, which also describe a great attack on Jerusalem, during which the Lord appears to overthrow the enemy." (Wright)

ii. "Notice that twice it is stated (Ezekiel 38:17; 39:8) that former prophets foretold this invasion (Psalm 2:1-3; Isaiah 29:1-8; Joel 2:20; 3:9-21; Zechariah 12:1 ff.; 14:2-3)." (Feinberg)

B. The promise of judgment against Gog.

1. (18-20) God's fury against Gog in a great earthquake.

"And it will come to pass at the same time, when Gog comes against the land of Israel," says the Lord God, "*that* My fury will show in My face. For in My jealousy *and* in the fire of My wrath I have spoken: 'Surely in that day there shall be a great earthquake in the land of Israel, so that the fish of the sea, the birds of the heavens, the beasts of the field, all creeping things that creep on the earth, and all men who *are* on the face of the earth shall shake at My presence. The mountains shall be thrown down, the steep places shall fall, and every wall shall fall to the ground.'

a. **When Gog comes against the land of Israel…My fury will show in My face**: Yahweh vowed that though Gog thought Israel would be an easy conquest (Ezekiel 38:11), His own **fury** would rise against Gog and his allies.

i. **Fury will show in My face**: "The reaction to the audacity and effrontery of the invasion of Gog and his forces was stated in bold terms and a vivid anthropomorphism (see Psalm 18:8). The picture is of the breath which an angered man inhales and exhales through his nose. God's patience would be exhausted with the repeated attempts of Israel's enemies to annihilate her." (Feinberg)

b. **Surely in that day there shall be a great earthquake in the land of Israel**: One way that God would defend Israel and come against Gog was to send a **great earthquake**. It isn't immediately apparent how this **earthquake** would harm only the hostile attacking armies, but that is apparently the case.

c. **All men who are on the face of the earth shall shake at My presence**: The **great earthquake** would humble man and bring glory to God. As

mountains and **every wall** fell, they would know it was the hand of the Lord at work.

2. (21-23) God's judgment against Gog.

I will call for a sword against Gog throughout all My mountains," says the Lord GOD. "Every man's sword will be against his brother. And I will bring him to judgment with pestilence and bloodshed; I will rain down on him, on his troops, and on the many peoples who *are* with him, flooding rain, great hailstones, fire, and brimstone. Thus I will magnify Myself and sanctify Myself, and I will be known in the eyes of many nations. Then they shall know that I *am* the LORD.'"

a. **I will call for a sword against Gog**: Because Gog was arrogant enough to invade God's own land (**My mountains**) God would come against Gog and his allies with military power. One way it would come would be as the allied nations began to attack one another (**every man's sword will be against his brother**).

> i. "Gog's armies and the nations following him would become so confused that they would slay one another in suicidal strife (cf. Judges 7:22; 1 Samuel 14:20; Haggai 2:22; Zechariah 14:13), while the Lord supernaturally destroyed them." (Alexander)

b. **I will bring him to judgment with pestilence and bloodshed**: Yahweh would also send disease and death against the attacking armies. This would be a demonstration of His justice.

c. **Flooding rain, great hailstones, fire, and brimstone**: The instruments of previous judgments would all be sent against Gog and his allies.

> i. "I slew others, Sennacherib's army, by pestilence, probably this was the angel's sword; others, as Ammon, Moab, Mount Seir, with blood by their own swords; the Amorites with hailstones, Sodom and Gomorrah with fire and brimstone, the old world with an overflowing flood. Each single was dreadful, but all meet in the destruction of Gog to make it most terrible." (Poole)

> ii. "The invaders are destroyed by earthquake (cf. Zechariah 14:4-5), by violent distrust of one another (Zechariah 14:13), by pestilence (Zechariah 14:12), and by torrential rain and fire from heaven (Revelation 20:9)." (Wright)

d. **I will magnify Myself and sanctify Myself**: This overwhelming and obviously divine defeat of Gog and her allies would testify to the whole world of God's character and power.

Ezekiel 39 – The Disposal of Gog and the Cleansing of Israel

A. Recounting of the attack and defeat described in Ezekiel 38.

1. (1-2) Yahweh directs Gog to attack Israel.

"And you, son of man, prophesy against Gog, and say, 'Thus says the Lord GOD: "Behold, I *am* against you, O Gog, the prince of Rosh, Meshech, and Tubal; and I will turn you around and lead you on, bringing you up from the far north, and bring you against the mountains of Israel.

a. **Prophesy against Gog**: In Hebrew literature, it was common to give an account and then to repeat it to give emphasis and a few additional details. Ezekiel 39:1-8 is a summary of what was described in Ezekiel 38.

i. "The overthrow of Gog and his forces is here retold in different language and in fuller detail. This is typical of Hebrew poetry and of the kind of semi-poetical writing which is used in these oracles. It is fond of repetition and delights to revert to previous statements and enlarge on them, even though the result is to destroy all sense of consecutive arrangement." (Taylor)

b. **I am against you, O Gog, the prince of Rosh, Meshech, and Tubal**: The words of Ezekiel 38:1-2 are repeated. **Gog** speaks of a person, a ruler (**the prince**). **Rosh** either describes one place where Gog rules, or completes the phrase *chief prince*. **Meshech** and **Tubal** are other places under the domain of Gog.

c. **Bringing you up from the far north**: Coming with his allied nations, Gog comes from the north to attack the land of Israel. He does this not only from his own evil plans (Ezekiel 38:10), but ultimately because God promised to **turn** him and **lead** him, to **bring** him against Israel.

2. (3-5) Gog defeated.

Then I will knock the bow out of your left hand, and cause the arrows to fall out of your right hand. You shall fall upon the mountains of Israel, you and all your troops and the peoples who *are* with you; I will give you to birds of prey of every sort and *to* the beasts of the field to be devoured. You shall fall on the open field; for I have spoken," says the Lord God.

a. **I will knock the bow out of your left hand**: Ezekiel described warfare as he knew it. A skilled archer was effective in battle, but not with the **bow** knocked from the hand and **arrows** dropped to the ground. Gog's military effort against Israel would fail.

i. "The *bow* is held by the *left hand*; the *arrow* is pulled and discharged by the *right*." (Clarke)

b. **You shall fall upon the mountains of Israel**: Gog – either himself personally or the army that was the extension of his power – would die in Israel in their unsuccessful attack.

c. **I will give you to birds of prey of every sort and to the beasts of the field**: Gog and his armies would not only be dead but disgraced as their unburied corpses littered the field of battle.

i. "It will be seen that the serious and fatal weakness of the enemies of Israel will be their reliance on numbers, and their confidence that Israel's weakness means their strength and ultimate victory. They fail, as always, to take God into account." (Feinberg)

3. (6-8) Magog itself attacked, and God's name glorified.

"And I will send fire on Magog and on those who live in security in the coastlands. Then they shall know that I *am* the Lord. So I will make My holy name known in the midst of My people Israel, and I will not let *them* profane My holy name anymore. Then the nations shall know that I *am* the Lord, the Holy One in Israel. Surely it is coming, and it shall be done," says the Lord God. "This *is* the day of which I have spoken.

a. **I will send fire on Magog**: Either as part of the battle or soon afterward, God promised to send **fire** against Gog's land (**Magog**). Gog brought the battle to Israel, but God would bring the battle to him.

b. **And on those who live in security in the coastlands**: The same **fire** that came upon Magog would also come against **the coastlands**. The term does not refer to a distinct place, but to unspecified and distant **coastlands** or islands.

i. Some have thought to connect **coastlands** to the United States or other modern nations. There is no foundation for this other than speculation and mystery at the fact that many modern nations (such as the United States) seem to be unmentioned in Biblical prophecy.

ii. "The isles referred to are the coastland and islands of the Mediterranean. Though the judgment on the enemies will occur in Israel, the catastrophe will extend far out to the ends of the earth to accomplish the purpose of God." (Feinberg)

c. **So I will make My holy name known in the midst of My people Israel**: God would use this remarkable victory over Gog and his allies, this miraculous defense of Israel, to bring His people to a restored relationship and to holiness. The result that **I will not let them profane My holy name anymore** means that though Israel was gathered to the land and lived in relative safety and prosperity, a true relationship with Yahweh had not yet been restored. It would be after this battle.

i. **My holy name**: "The Gog debacle will demonstrate once and for all the holiness of Yahweh, not as a theological abstraction but in action, as he stands to defend his people against the universal conspiracy of evil." (Block)

d. **Then the nations shall know that I am the LORD**: Through this, God would reveal Himself not only to Israel but also to all of the watching world. God would glorify Himself through His defense of Israel and defeat of Gog.

e. **Surely it is coming, and it shall be done**: God solemnly affirmed Ezekiel's prophecy. The great victory over Gog would fulfill what God had **spoken** before (as also in Ezekiel 38:17).

B. Gog in defeat.

1. (9-10) Defeated Gog plundered by Israel.

"Then those who dwell in the cities of Israel will go out and set on fire and burn the weapons, both the shields and bucklers, the bows and arrows, the javelins and spears; and they will make fires with them for seven years. They will not take wood from the field nor cut down *any* from the forests, because they will make fires with the weapons; and they will plunder those who plundered them, and pillage those who pillaged them," says the Lord GOD.

a. **Those who dwell in the cities of Israel will go out and set on fire and burn the weapons**: Israel will destroy all the military equipment (described with seven terms) brought by Gog and his allies. Protected by Yahweh, they would no longer need the weapons themselves.

i. "These are not the weapons of a modern army, but Ezekiel used language the people could understand." (Wiersbe)

ii. "Usually weapons left by a defeated enemy would be added to the victor's cache of arms. After all, there would be other battles to fight. The war against Gog was to be no ordinary war. It will be the final battle, whose conclusion will make armaments obsolete." (Vawter and Hoppe)

b. **For seven years**: This speaks of the vast amount of military equipment brought by Gog and her allies and left behind on the field of battle. There would be so much that they could use their fuel for **seven years**.

c. **They will plunder those who plundered them**: What the evil Gog and his allies intended for Israel would fall upon the defeated attackers themselves.

i. "The plunderers will be plundered and the robbers will be robbed. What the enemy will intend for Israel (Ezekiel 38:12) will be visited upon them, another vivid example of the law of recompense in kind." (Feinberg)

2. (11-16) Defeated Gog buried by Israel.

"It will come to pass in that day *that* I will give Gog a burial place there in Israel, the valley of those who pass by east of the sea; and it will obstruct travelers, because there they will bury Gog and all his multitude. Therefore they will call *it* the Valley of Hamon Gog. For seven months the house of Israel will be burying them, in order to cleanse the land. Indeed all the people of the land will be burying, and they will gain renown for it on the day that I am glorified," says the Lord GOD. "They will set apart men regularly employed, with the help of a search party, to pass through the land and bury those bodies remaining on the ground, in order to cleanse it. At the end of seven months they will make a search. The search party will pass through the land; and *when anyone sees a man's bone, he shall set up a marker by it, till the buriers have buried it in the Valley of Hamon Gog. *The* name of *the* city *will* also *be* Hamonah. Thus they shall cleanse the land."'

a. **In that day I will give Gog a burial place there in Israel**: Yahweh promised to give a proper **burial** to the slain soldiers of Gog and his allies. This could be regarded as a compassionate act, but it was more probably to **cleanse the land**. The unburied bodies of the slain defiled Israel (or any land), and God's renewed people would be concerned to **cleanse the land**.

i. **A burial place**: "It is the site of mass burial. A common burial ground was suggested by the awkwardly singular form of *meqom sam geber* (lit. 'a place where there is a grave')." (Block)

b. **It will obstruct travelers**: The number of bodies would be so great that it would seem to fill the valley where they were buried, making it impassable by **travelers**.

c. **They will set apart men regularly employed, with the help of a search party**: The effort to find and bury the remains of Gog's army would be organized and thorough, **in order to cleanse** the land. The effort would take a total of **seven months**.

i. "Their work will take seven months, so immense were Gog's forces and so complete was God's victory. The Israelites contribute nothing to this victory; they merely clean up the battlefield." (Vawter and Hoppe)

d. **Till the buriers have buried it in the Valley of Hamon Gog**: The valley of burial would become known as *Gog Valley*.

i. "So great will be the carnage that Gog will give his name to the valley, which will receive a new name commemorating God's victory over Israel's adversaries." (Feinberg)

ii. **Hamonah**: "It's likely that the city called Hamonah ('horde,' referring to the 'horde' of soldiers slain) will be established as a headquarters for this mopping-up operation." (Wiersbe)

3. (17-20) Defeated Gog as a grotesque sacrificial feast.

"And as for you, son of man, thus says the Lord God, 'Speak to every sort of bird and to every beast of the field:

"Assemble yourselves and come;
Gather together from all sides to My sacrificial meal
Which I am sacrificing for you,
A great sacrificial meal on the mountains of Israel,
That you may eat flesh and drink blood.
You shall eat the flesh of the mighty,
Drink the blood of the princes of the earth,
Of rams and lambs,
Of goats and bulls,
All of them fatlings of Bashan.
You shall eat fat till you are full,
And drink blood till you are drunk,
At My sacrificial meal
Which I am sacrificing for you.
You shall be filled at My table

With horses and riders,
With mighty men
And with all the men of war," says the Lord God.

a. **Speak to every sort of bird and to every beast of the field**: The section dealing directly with Gog and his allies ends with this strange and grotesque picture of **bird** and **beast** scavengers feasting upon the corpses of the defeated enemy.

b. **Gather together from all sides to My sacrificial meal**: The strange and powerful picture is further developed. As it was customary to often eat a ceremonial meal with an animal sacrifice, God considered this meal for **bird** and **beast** something of a **sacrificial meal**. The armies of Gog were like **rams and lambs** offered in sacrifice.

i. "After destroying the invading army of Gog, Yahweh adds a horrid indignity to the fate of the fallen warriors. Their corpses will be a sacrificial meal that birds and animals will consume. It is a stunning reversal. Instead of human beings consuming the animals of sacrifice, it is the animals who consume the human beings sacrificed for Yahweh's honor." (Vawter and Hoppe)

ii. In Revelation John linked this sacrificial feast with the aftermath of the battle of Armageddon (Revelation 19:17-21). He also linked the invasion of Gog and Yahweh's defense of His people to a battle at the end of Jesus' 1,000-year reign (Revelation 20:7-9). Because John links aspects of Ezekiel 38-39 to two chronologically separated events, it is likely that he uses Ezekiel 38-39 as *examples* of these future events rather than the events actually fulfilling the prophecies of Ezekiel 38-39.

c. **You shall eat fat till you are full**: There would be so many corpses of the defeated enemy that it would be more than the birds and beasts could eat.

i. **My table**: "The sacrificial feast mentioned in verse 19 is referred to as 'my table' because it is the Lord who will hold the feast. It is a vivid figure to bring out the idea of vast carnage, deserved judgment and irrevocable doom." (Feinberg)

ii. "The metaphor is drawn from what all Israelites picture. Very few of us in England have ever seen an abattoir, or slaughter-house, or watched the ritual slaughter of animals, so it would be useless to use them as an illustration of blood pouring everywhere. But every Israelite had watched the blood flowing at the sacrifices. This was not pointless slaughter, since most sacrifices were eaten by the worshippers after they had been offered. They provided the fairly infrequent occasions when the average man had a meat meal. But here the quantities of blood that flowed at the sacrifices are used pictorially of the death of those who have campaigned against God." (Wright)

C. Yahweh's exaltation among the nations.

1. (21-24) God vindicated among the Gentiles.

"I will set My glory among the nations; all the nations shall see My judgment which I have executed, and My hand which I have laid on them. So the house of Israel shall know that I *am* the LORD their God from that day forward. The Gentiles shall know that the house of Israel went into captivity for their iniquity; because they were unfaithful to Me, therefore I hid My face from them. I gave them into the hand of their enemies, and they all fell by the sword. According to their uncleanness and according to their transgressions I have dealt with them, and hidden My face from them.'"

a. **I will set My glory among the nations**: The amazing restoration described generally in Ezekiel 34 through 39 was focused on Israel, but never limited to them. God's intention was also to **set** His **glory among the nations**. He would do this through the execution of His **judgment**.

b. **The house of Israel shall know that I am the LORD their God from that day forward**: This restoration would bring Israel permanently into a new relationship with God. This looks to the ultimate restoration described by Paul in Romans 11:26, when *all Israel will be saved*.

c. **The Gentiles shall know that the house of Israel went into captivity for their iniquity**: The nations would know that Israel's suffering was never because God was unable to help them. They would see that Yahweh was not a weak god or mere local deity. They would know that Yahweh Himself directed ancient Israel's suffering. The calamity came upon **the house of Israel** because of their sin and unfaithfulness. That was why Yahweh **hid** His **face from them**.

i. "The sottish heathen thought meanly of the God of Israel, and reckoned they came into captivity because the people of some greater god had by the power of their god prevailed against Israel's God and his people; but by this overthrow given to Gog, they shall see it was not impotence in Israel's God, but iniquity in Israel's people, that brought them into captivity." (Poole)

2. (25-29) God in fellowship with His restored people.

"Therefore thus says the Lord GOD: 'Now I will bring back the captives of Jacob, and have mercy on the whole house of Israel; and I will be

jealous for My holy name— after they have borne their shame, and all their unfaithfulness in which they were unfaithful to Me, when they dwelt safely in their *own* land and no one made *them* afraid. When I have brought them back from the peoples and gathered them out of their enemies' lands, and I am hallowed in them in the sight of many nations, then they shall know that I *am* the LORD their God, who sent them into captivity among the nations, but also brought them back to their land, and left none of them captive any longer. And I will not hide My face from them anymore; for I shall have poured out My Spirit on the house of Israel,' says the Lord GOD."

a. **Now I will bring back the captives of Jacob**: Ezekiel first spoke these words to the Jewish exiles in Babylon, who especially after the fall of Jerusalem and Judah wondered if God would ever restore Israel. These promises were precious to them, and were given a minor and imperfect fulfillment in the return from captivity under Ezra and Zerubbabel. The greater and complete restoration still waits, as the New Testament recognizes (Romans 11:26).

> i. "We must never overlook the literal significance of this promise. All Israel, insists the apostle of the Gentiles, who never lost his love for his own people, shall be saved. The blindness which has happened to them is only till the fullness of the Gentile contingent to the one Church has been brought in." (Meyer)

b. **After they have borne their shame, and all their unfaithfulness**: Israel's restoration would come in a spirit of repentance. They would see all that God did for them and it would humble them in light of His generous love. They would see and admit that it was their own sins that sent them into captivity and suffering.

> i. "He observes the response of the house of Israel to the new outpouring of divine mercy. Far from being a source of pride at having been selected as the objects of divine compassion, the experience of grace will lead to a recognition of their own unworthiness." (Block)

> ii. "In that day of restoration, dwelling securely in their land, they would still bear their shame, that is to say, repentance for past failure would be profound, even in the day of restoration. By that attitude of mind Jehovah would be sanctified among them in the sight of the nations, but they would have the infinite healing of His unveiled face, and the abiding energy of His outpoured Spirit." (Morgan)

> iii. **Left none of them captive any longer**: "Ezekiel's declaration that not a single individual will be left behind when Yahweh restores his people is without parallel in the OT. Yahweh's restoration is not only

total, however; it is permanent. He promises never again to hide his face from his people." (Block)

c. **I will not hide My face from them anymore**: The completion of this work would be a true standing in God's grace. With God's Spirit **poured out** upon Israel, they would have a relationship with God based on the work and merits of the Messiah, not their own work and merits.

i. "The imagery envisioned here is that Israel will prosper only when God's face is toward Israel. When God is absent from Israel disaster results. No doubt Ezekiel borrows this imagery from the blessing of Aaron in Numbers 6:25-26." (Vawter and Hoppe)

ii. "It was sin that caused God to hide his face, and now grace shall be given to keep them out of sin, and to engage them to constant obedience, that God may rejoice over them to do them good in this their latter end." (Poole)

iii. **I shall have poured out My Spirit on the house of Israel**: "Finally, Ezekiel 36:27 is reiterated with the powerful statement, put in the prophetic perfect tense, that *I have poured out my spirit upon the house of Israel* (RV). To put this in the future (as RSV) weakens the dramatic force of this assertion. True, God had not yet done this in reality; but it was such an assured word that it could be spoken by Ezekiel as if it were an accomplished fact." (Taylor)

Ezekiel 40 – Measuring the Courts of the New Temple

A. The vision of the new temple.

1. (1-2) Ezekiel is taken to Jerusalem in a vision.

In the twenty-fifth year of our captivity, at the beginning of the year, on the tenth *day* of the month, in the fourteenth year after the city was captured, on the very same day the hand of the LORD was upon me; and He took me there. In the visions of God He took me into the land of Israel and set me on a very high mountain; on it toward the south *was* something like the structure of a city.

a. **In the twenty-fifth year of our captivity**: This final, great vision of Ezekiel is recorded in chapters 40 through 48. It is almost the last prophecy dated, and many years after the fall of Jerusalem (**the fourteenth year after the city was captured**).

i. "These visions were given to the prophet some twelve years after the latest of those already considered except the brief one concerning the overcoming of Tyre by Nebuchadnezzar (Ezekiel 29:17-20), which was incorporated with the burdens of the nations." (Morgan)

ii. "If the preceding salvation oracles are to be dated shortly after the fall of the city (cf. Ezekiel 33:21–22), more than a decade separates this prophetic experience from the preceding oracles." (Block)

b. **The beginning of the year, on the tenth day of the month**: It is not clear if Ezekiel intended the civil or the religious calendar of Israel. If it was the religious calendar, then it was the day on Israel's calendar when they were to begin preparation for the Passover (10 Nisan).

i. "Whether they actually observed the Passover or not in exile, surely they would be contemplating Israel's redemption out of Egypt and the creation of their nation. This vision, then, would be an encouragement that the Lord would complete his purposes for the nation in the messianic kingdom." (Alexander)

c. **The hand of the LORD was upon me**: Ezekiel insisted the source of this extended prophecy was God. Yahweh was the source of the minute and sometimes strange detail of this prophecy.

d. **In the visions of God He took me into the land of Israel and set me on a very high mountain**: We are not told the name of the **mountain**, but from the description that follows we gather that Ezekiel could, in his vision, see Jerusalem.

i. Significantly, the last time Ezekiel visited Jerusalem in a vision was far back in Ezekiel 8-11. In that vision, he saw the temple profaned by God's people and the glory of God departing from the temple. What Ezekiel saw in the previous vision was *real*. It was presented in a condensed and dramatic form but described real sins and desecrations of the people. The departure of God's glory from the temple was spiritual, yet *real*.

ii. In this visionary visit to Jerusalem at the end of his ministry, what Ezekiel the prophet saw was real. He saw an actual temple and the glory of God restored in a real and powerful way. These were **visions of God**, but described real things.

iii. Ezekiel went in a vision, but to a *real land*. "Why the prophet's destination should be identified as *eres yisa'el*, 'the land of Israel,' [used elsewhere only in 27:17 and 47:18] rather than Ezekiel's generally preferred *admat yisra'el* is not clear. Whether intentional or not, it orients the reader toward the territorial interests that will characterize later chapters." (Block)

iv. **A very high mountain**: "Mount *Moriah*, the mount on which Solomon's temple was built, 2 Chronicles 3:1." (Clarke)

e. **Something like the structure of a city**: The vision of the temple unfolding in the following chapters really was **something…like a city**. It was large and surrounded by massive walls just like an ancient city.

i. **Like the structure of a city**: "So the temple seemed to him, for its many courts, walls, towers, gates." (Trapp)

2. (3) The man with the measuring rod.

He took me there, and behold, *there was* a man whose appearance *was* like the appearance of bronze. He had a line of flax and a measuring rod in his hand, and he stood in the gateway.

a. **There was a man whose appearance was like the appearance of bronze**: As Yahweh led Ezekiel to Jerusalem, He also appointed a guide for the prophet. This **man** was likely an angelic being, indicated by his radiant appearance (**bronze**). Some regard him as the angel of the LORD, but this is not specifically stated.

> i. "Like *bright polished brass*, which strongly reflected the rays of light. Probably he had what we would term a *nimbus* or *glory* round his head. This was either an *angel*; or, as some think, a personal appearance of our blessed Lord." (Clarke)

b. **He had a line of flax and a measuring rod**: The angelic being had two instruments for measuring. One was some kind of rope or string, and the other was a solid **rod**.

c. **He stood in the gateway**: The supernatural guide was waiting for Ezekiel.

3. (4) The man with the measuring rod speaks to Ezekiel.

And the man said to me, "Son of man, look with your eyes and hear with your ears, and fix your mind on everything I show you; for you *were* brought here so that I might show *them* to you. Declare to the house of Israel everything you see."

a. **Look with your eyes and hear with your ears, and fix your mind on everything**: The radiant man told Ezekiel to focus his senses, paying close attention. If the description of the temple that follows was merely spiritual or symbolic, there would be no need to so carefully note the details.

> i. "Ezekiel is to concentrate on what the guide is about to show him. After all, he is not simply a tourist visiting an historical site, or even a worshiper on a pilgrimage to a shrine. He is a mediator of divine revelation." (Block)

b. **Declare to the house of Israel everything you see**: The audience for this vision was primarily **the house of Israel**. It was most relevant to them as part of God's promised future restoration. *What* Ezekiel saw, as recorded in Ezekiel chapters 40 through 48, has been the subject of much dispute, and is something of a dividing line for Biblical interpreters.

> i. In his commentary, John B. Taylor listed four different interpretive approaches to these chapters:

> > • *Literal prophetic*: Ezekiel 40-48 describes a temple that he expected would be built by the returning exiles in their restoration to the land. For example, Adam Clarke believed that Ezekiel simply gave the plan of Solomon's temple from memory,

and set it here as an encouragement to the exiles that they would in fact be restored to Jerusalem and the temple would be rebuilt.

- *Symbolic Christian*: Ezekiel 40-48 symbolically describes the Christian church. Smith described this perspective: "The best approach is to see these chapters as illustrative of spiritual truths. The main points thus symbolized in these chapters are these: God would provide for his people a Temple, a priesthood and a worship system related to, but different from, that which they had formerly known. A united people, including Gentiles, would occupy the inheritance which God had promised to their forefathers."

- *Dispensationalist*: Ezekiel 40-48 describes a temple of features of a coming millennial age. This future temple belongs not so much to the eternal age (as in Revelation 21:22) but to the period of a literal thousand-year reign of Jesus over this earth. Especially for the Jewish people in the millennium, Ezekiel's temple will bring to remembrance and memorialize God's gracious work for Israel and the rich types and ceremonies that looked forward to the perfect work of the Messiah, Jesus Christ. This view "declares that the prediction speaks of the restoration and establishment of the people of Israel in their own land in the last days of their national history, their conversion to the Lord through faith in their long-rejected Messiah, and the manifest presence and glory of the Lord in their midst." (Feinberg)

- *Apocalyptic*: Ezekiel 40-48 present symbolic and fantastic images of a coming age, connected to images and ideas popular in the pagan world of that day. "Chapters 40–48 replace the conventional prophecies of chapters 33–37 with imagery that is primarily mythic. The prophet chooses to speak about Jerusalem's future by recasting imagery deriving from the ancient Near Eastern mythic motif of the 'cosmic mountain.'" (Vawter and Hoppe)

ii. This commentary will examine these chapters primarily under the *dispensationalist* framework. The reader must decide whether to favor a more literal approach or a more figurative and spiritual approach. Though there are things to be said for and against each approach, in the author's opinion the best approach is to regard this temple as real, yet to be fulfilled in a future phase of God's unfolding plan of the ages.

- The fundamental weakness of the *literal prophetic* approach is that it was not fulfilled. The temple rebuilt in the days of Ezra and Zerubbabel did not answer to this description. "It does not correspond to the one that was built after the return, nor to Herod's Temple." (Wright)

- The fundamental weakness of the *symbolic* approach is that the entire tone of Ezekiel's record points to this temple as something real, not spiritualized. Significantly, the radiant being did not say much to Ezekiel, probably only calling out the measurements. There was no explanation of or pointing towards a symbolic interpretation of the temple, only a detailed tour and specific dimensions. The message is that this temple is *real*, not metaphorical. It is visionary and prophetic, yet real. This symbolic view was "favored by the church Fathers and the Reformers. They saw in these chapters Christ and the spiritual endowments of the church in the Christian era. This is entirely too subjective and would mean nothing for either Ezekiel or his contemporaries." (Feinberg) Alexander adds, "The figurative or 'spiritualizing' interpretative approach does not seem to solve any of the problems of Ezekiel 40–48; it tends to create new ones. When the interpreter abandons a normal grammatical-historical hermeneutic because the passage does not seem to make sense taken that way and opts for an interpretative procedure by which he can allegorize, symbolize, or 'spiritualize,' the interpretations become subjective. Different aspects of a passage mean whatever the interpreter desires."

- The fundamental weakness of the *apocalyptic* approach is that this text lacks many of the generally understood aspects of apocalyptic literature.

iii. The idea that this temple and various aspects regarding it should be understood as fulfilled in a future phase of God's unfolding plan of the ages has its own problems. Perhaps the plainest and commonly made objection is that since Jesus made a perfect and final sacrifice (Hebrews 9:28, 10:10 and other similar passages) it is unthinkable that God would establish or sanction any kind of sacrificial system or ceremony. There are several ways to answer this objection.

- We would *never* think that the Old Covenant system of sacrifice and ritual would be restored for believers as a ground of their approach to God or their righteousness (Galatians 3:23-25 and Colossians 2:16-17).

- We would *never* think that animal sacrifice could atone for or take away sin, something accomplished only by what Jesus did on the cross (as in Hebrews 9:11-15 and 10:1-14, 10:18). Yet it must be recognized that animal sacrifices *never* took away sin; they only looked forward to the perfect sacrifice God would provide through the Messiah, fulfilled at the cross of Jesus.

- God *does* sanction memorials and ceremonial remembrance of the work of Jesus on the cross. "Just as the Old Testament sacrifices could have value in pointing forward to the death of Christ, why may they not have equal value in pointing back to the death of Christ as an accomplished fact? The celebration of the Lord's Supper through the Christian centuries has added not one infinitesimal particle to the efficacy of the work of Christ on the cross, but who will dare to deny that it has value for the believer, since it is enjoined upon us as a memorial?" (Feinberg)

- Jesus specifically said that He would observe the Lord's Supper in the age to come (Luke 22:18). There will be active, even ceremonial remembrance of the sacrificial work of Jesus in the age to come. It is reasonable to think it could also include the temple services and sacrifices described here. "If the Lord's Table is a memorial and the sacrifices of the Ezekiel system are memorials, the two should not in any way conflict with each other but should be able to coexist." (Alexander)

- Apparently the first Christians (including the Apostle Paul) were more comfortable with *some kind* of participation with temple services and rituals than we might think. Paul's participation with and sponsorship of Christians fulfilling vows at the temple seemingly connected with *some* kind of sacrifice speaks to this (Acts 21:23-24, 21:26-27).

- "Even in our day we see the spiritual value and great avenue of worship for church believers as they celebrate the Passover service.... It does not enter their minds that they are saved by the observance of this service; but the celebration is an extremely instructive, vivid picture lesson of the death of the Lamb of God." (Alexander)

iv. In many ways, the description of Ezekiel's temple is presented in a way appropriate for a period *after* the finished work of Jesus Christ. Though there is a literal temple and animal sacrifice, many other features of the Old Testament order as given through Moses are *not* mentioned.

- There is no mention of Pentecost, though other feasts are mentioned: Passover and the Feast of Unleavened Bread (Ezekiel

45:21-24), Tabernacles (Ezekiel 45:25), and Firstfruits (Ezekiel 44:30). Pentecost is not mentioned because it was fulfilled in the church (Acts 2).

- There is no mention of a veil because since the work of Jesus such a separation is no longer necessary.

- There is no mention of the ark of the covenant because the work of Jesus at the cross fulfilled the place of atonement and propitiation.

- There is no mention of a high priest because Jesus is the high priest.

- There is no mention of a king because Jesus is the king of kings.

- There is no mention of silver and gold, because in a millennial age those things do not have the same value.

v. "Ezekiel isn't the only prophet who said there would be a holy temple during the Kingdom Age. You find a kingdom temple and kingdom worship mentioned in Isaiah 2:1–5, 60:7, 13; Jeremiah 33:18; Joel 3:18; Micah 4:2; Haggai 2:7–9; and Zechariah 6:12–15, 14:16, 20–21. Ezekiel 37:24–28 records God's promise to His people that He would put His sanctuary among them. 'My tabernacle also shall be with them; indeed, I will be their God, and they shall be My people.'" (Wiersbe)

vi. "It seems, therefore, that Ezekiel 40–48 may be primarily describing the millennial temple, its regulations for worship, and the tribal allotments. The Millennium is only a beginning, sort of a microcosm, of the eternal state and a transition into it. Consequently, to observe reflections of Ezekiel 40–48 in the picture of the eternal state revealed in Revelation 21–22 should be expected and should not surprise the reader." (Alexander)

vii. "The temple will be a place of learning for both Jews and Gentiles (Isaiah 2:1–3), and no doubt the worshipers will study the Old Testament law and learn more about Jesus. They will study the New Testament as well and see the deeper significance of the sacrifices and the feasts." (Wiersbe)

c. **Everything you see**: What follows is a tour of the temple complex, led by this radiant man and recorded by Ezekiel. The tour is filled with measurements and descriptions. The details of Ezekiel's vision only become manageable with diagrams, which are readily available from a variety of searchable sources.

i. "The competent opinion of architects who have studied the plan given here is that all these dimensions could be drawn to scale to produce a beautiful sanctuary of the Lord." (Feinberg)

ii. "Appreciating the prophet's excitement about what he saw is difficult for modern readers, who see the temple as nothing more than a building. For Ezekiel and his readers, the temple was *the* mode of God's presence in the world." (Vawter and Hoppe)

iii. "Ezekiel's experience might be likened to a young couple who go frequently to the site of their future dream home. They step off the dimensions of the home, perhaps sketch in the dust its configuration. They relish every moment of the anticipation. In their minds they can visualize that home in all its grandeur." (Smith)

B. The outer court of the new temple.

1. (5) The wall outside the temple.

Now there was a wall all around the outside of the temple. In the man's hand was a measuring rod six cubits *long, each being a* cubit and a handbreadth; and he measured the width of the wall structure, one rod; and the height, one rod.

a. **There was a wall all around the outside of the temple**: This wall around the temple compound is what helped to make the whole scene look something like a city (as in Ezekiel 40:2).

b. **In the man's hand was a measuring rod six cubits long, each being a cubit and a handbreadth**: Here Ezekiel defined the approximate size of the measures. The **cubit** was what was sometimes known as the *long cubit*, about 20.5 inches (52 centimeters) long. A **rod** was six of these measures, about 10 feet 3 inches (3.12 meters).

i. "He is given a shining heavenly guide, who carries a measuring rod of about 10 feet 4 inches. (The so-called 'long cubit' of v. 5 was 20.679 inches, as opposed to the ordinary cubit of about 17.5 inches.)" (Wright)

ii. "Ezekiel is using the long cubit for all his measurements, i.e. approximately 20½ ins, as against the customary cubit of 17½ ins. The angel's measuring-rod would thus be about 10 feet 3 inches long." (Taylor)

c. **He measured the width of the wall structure**: The surrounding walls were therefore about ten feet (3.12 meters) tall and wide. We note that **he measured**; the radiant being did the measuring work and told Ezekiel the results.

i. **He measured**: Ezekiel didn't measure the temple and its courts, because they don't belong to him. Through His representative, *God* measures the temple and its courts. They belong to Him.

ii. "To measure property is symbolic of claiming it for yourself." (Wiersbe)

iii. **In the man's hand**: "The prophet is called to see and hear, but the standard is not put into his hand." (Poole)

2. (6-10) The eastern gateway.

Then he went to the gateway which faced east; and he went up its stairs and measured the threshold of the gateway, *which was* one rod wide, and the other threshold *was* one rod wide. Each gate chamber *was* one rod long and one rod wide; between the gate chambers *was a space of* five cubits; and the threshold of the gateway by the vestibule of the inside gate *was* one rod. He also measured the vestibule of the inside gate, one rod. Then he measured the vestibule of the gateway, eight cubits; and the gateposts, two cubits. The vestibule of the gate *was* on the inside. In the eastern gateway *were* three gate chambers on one side and three on the other; the three *were* all the same size; also the gateposts were of the same size on this side and that side.

a. **Then he went to the gateway which faced east**: Ezekiel's tour of the temple started on the east side of the temple grounds. It was the eastern gate which directly led to the entrance of the temple, so this was a logical place to begin.

i. "It is significant that the entrance into the temple is from the east, since it was toward the east that God left the temple according to Ezekiel 11:23." (Vawter and Hoppe)

b. **Threshold of the gateway... gate chamber**: The gate was actually something of a tower, with rooms and compartments known as **gate chambers**. For a better representation of the size and dimensions, one may consult diagrams which are readily available from a variety of searchable sources.

i. **Gate chambers**: "These chambers were for the priests and Levites to lodge in during their ministration, according to their courses in the temple, where they kept watch continually night and day. The whole was framed in very great harmony and just proportions." (Poole)

ii. "In verse 10 reference was made again to the eastward gate, which was in some ways the most important of all, for through it the glory of God would return to the sanctuary (chap. 43)." (Feinberg)

3. (11-16) The entrance to the eastern gateway.

He measured the width of the entrance to the gateway, ten cubits; *and* **the length of the gate, thirteen cubits.** *There was* **a space in front of the gate chambers, one cubit** *on this side* **and one cubit on that side; the gate chambers** *were* **six cubits on this side and six cubits on that side. Then he measured the gateway from the roof of** *one* **gate chamber to the roof of the other; the width** *was* **twenty-five cubits, as door faces door. He measured the gateposts, sixty cubits high, and the court all around the gateway** *extended* **to the gatepost.** *From* **the front of the entrance gate to the front of the vestibule of the inner gate** *was* **fifty cubits.** *There were* **beveled window** *frames* **in the gate chambers and in their intervening archways on the inside of the gateway all around, and likewise in the vestibules.** *There were* **windows all around on the inside. And on each gatepost** *were* **palm trees.**

a. **He measured the width of the entrance to the gateway**: Again, this describes something more than an entrance to the temple area. This was a building in itself, of substantial size and with chambers and rooms of its own.

i. "In antiquity, gates to cities or to important buildings were elaborate structures in their own right. They had small rooms that opened on the passageway. Some had a vestibule on the outside that provided a transition space between the outside world and the structure that one was entering." (Vawter and Hoppe)

ii. **As door faces door**: "The phrase, *from door to door*, suggests that a door led from each of the side rooms on to the outer court, a reasonable probability to allow the Levitical door-keepers to get to their stations to control the crowds who would throng through the gateways at festival time." (Taylor)

b. **He measured the gateposts, sixty cubits high**: The tower-like structure of the eastern gate (and the other gates) was some 100 feet (31.5 meters) tall.

i. "We cannot find a spiritual significance in every measurement, but we note the symmetry of the temple and its precincts." (Wright)

c. **Beveled window frames…on each gatepost were palm trees**: Ezekiel described the structure in some detail, including decorative features.

i. "All the terminology is not clear in the Hebrew language since some words are used only in this context. Therefore, the exact meaning of each item and the corresponding relationship of each dimension cannot always be certain." (Alexander)

ii. **Palm trees**: "Engraven with curious art for beauty, and whose upper branches spreading themselves along under the arches seemed to bear up the arches." (Poole)

4. (17-19) The pavement of the outer court.

Then he brought me into the outer court; and *there were* chambers and a pavement made all around the court; thirty chambers faced the pavement. The pavement was by the side of the gateways, corresponding to the length of the gateways; *this was* the lower pavement. Then he measured the width from the front of the lower gateway to the front of the inner court exterior, one hundred cubits toward the east and the north.

a. **He brought me into the outer court**: Having entered through the eastern gate, now Ezekiel saw the **outer court**. There was a **lower pavement**, meaning that there were at least two levels to the outer court.

b. **One hundred cubits toward the east and the north**: The outer court was a generous expanse of space.

5. (20-23) The northern gateway.

On the outer court was also a gateway facing north, and he measured its length and its width. Its gate chambers, three on this side and three on that side, its gateposts and its archways, had the same measurements as the first gate; its length *was* fifty cubits and its width twenty-five cubits. Its windows and those of its archways, and also its palm trees, *had* the same measurements as the gateway facing east; it was ascended by seven steps, and its archway *was* in front of it. A gate of the inner court was opposite the northern gateway, just as the eastern *gateway;* and he measured from gateway to gateway, one hundred cubits.

a. **On the outer court was also a gateway facing north**: Coming from the east, Ezekiel's guide directed him to the right toward the northern gateway. **It had the same measurements as the first gate.**

b. **He measured gateway to gateway, one hundred cubits**: Again, the general dimensions point to a large temple area.

6. (24-27) The southern gateway.

After that he brought me toward the south, and there a gateway was facing south; and he measured its gateposts and archways according to these same measurements. *There were* windows in it and in its archways all around like those windows; its length *was* fifty cubits and its width twenty-five cubits. Seven steps led up to it, and its archway *was* in front of them; and it had palm trees on its gateposts, one on this side and

one on that side. *There was* also a gateway on the inner court, facing south; and he measured from gateway to gateway toward the south, one hundred cubits.

a. **He brought me toward the south**: Ezekiel's guide then directed him across the court to the southern gate. As the guide **measured**, it had the **same measurements** as the east and the southern gates. There was no gate on the western side since the temple was situated closer to the western wall.

b. **Its archway was in front of them; and it had palm trees on the gateposts**: As before, Ezekiel noted not only the dimensions but some of the details of the design.

C. The inner court of the new temple.

1. (28-37) The gateways of the inner court.

Then he brought me to the inner court through the southern gateway; he measured the southern gateway according to these same measurements. Also its gate chambers, its gateposts, and its archways *were* according to these same measurements; *there were* windows in it and in its archways all around; *it was* fifty cubits long and twenty-five cubits wide. *There were* archways all around, twenty-five cubits long and five cubits wide. Its archways faced the outer court, palm trees *were* on its gateposts, and going up to it *were* eight steps.

And he brought me into the inner court facing east; he measured the gateway according to these same measurements. Also its gate chambers, its gateposts, and its archways *were* according to these same measurements; and *there were* windows in it and in its archways all around; *it was* fifty cubits long and twenty-five cubits wide. Its archways faced the outer court, and palm trees *were* on its gateposts on this side and on that side; and going up to it *were* eight steps.

Then he brought me to the north gateway and measured *it* according to these same measurements— also its gate chambers, its gateposts, and its archways. It had windows all around; its length *was* fifty cubits and its width twenty-five cubits. Its gateposts faced the outer court, palm trees *were* on its gateposts on this side and on that side, and going up to it *were* eight steps.

a. **He brought me to the inner court**: In his vision and directed by his guide, Ezekiel came to the **inner court** of the temple structure. There is no mention made of a specific court of the Gentiles or court of the women.

b. **There were archways all around...going up to it were eight steps**: Accessible from the south, east, and north, the inner court was raised **eight steps** above the outer court. As before, **palm trees were on its gateposts**.

2. (38-43) The chamber for sacrifices.

There was **a chamber and its entrance by the gateposts of the gateway, where they washed the burnt offering. In the vestibule of the gateway** *were* **two tables on this side and two tables on that side, on which to slay the burnt offering, the sin offering, and the trespass offering. At the outer side of the vestibule, as one goes up to the entrance of the northern gateway,** *were* **two tables; and on the other side of the vestibule of the gateway** *were* **two tables. Four tables** *were* **on this side and four tables on that side, by the side of the gateway, eight tables on which they slaughtered** *the sacrifices.* ***There were*** **also four tables of hewn stone for the burnt offering, one cubit and a half long, one cubit and a half wide, and one cubit high; on these they laid the instruments with which they slaughtered the burnt offering and the sacrifice. Inside** *were* **hooks, a handbreadth wide, fastened all around; and the flesh of the sacrifices** *was* **on the tables.**

a. **There was a chamber and its entrance by the gateposts**: Coming into the inner court, there were rooms holding **tables** for the preparation and performance of sacrifices. Specifically mentioned are the **burnt offering**, the **sin offering**, and the **trespass offering**.

i. It is not necessary that the emphasis of each of these offerings be for the atonement of sin. Though they sometimes had that association, they also were used with the emphasis of *complete consecration* and *purification*.

- "The ritual of the burnt offering involved the total consumption of the offering by fire; no portion was ever eaten by humans." (Block)

- "Purification offerings functioned only to decontaminate sacred objects and places (cf. Ezekiel 43:19–27)." (Block)

- Guilt offering: "In principle the offering is perceived as restitution, reparation, for sullying a sacred object or person." (Block)

ii. "The sin and guilt offerings, therefore, reminded the Israelite that he was sinful and that he needed the Messiah's innocent blood, typified in the animal, to cleanse him of his sin and to bring forgiveness from God." (Alexander)

b. **The flesh of the sacrifice was on the tables**: Coming from a priestly background, this would be of special interest to Ezekiel. For many Bible students and teachers, the presence of such **sacrifices** makes it unthinkable that this could describe a literal temple with literal sacrifices, sanctioned and established by God after the finished work of Jesus Christ on the cross at Calvary.

i. Yet, as noted before, these may be fairly regarded as *memorials* pointing back to the work of Jesus. Animal sacrifices were *never* actually effective for the cleansing of sin, only as representations and shadows of the future reality fulfilled by Jesus the Messiah in His crucifixion. Even so, the literal presence of these sacrifices does not mean that they should or could be regarded as effective for the cleansing of sin. Much as the bread and the cup of the Lord's Table is a powerful spiritual representation and memorial of Jesus' work on the cross, these sacrifices can be regarded in a similar way.

ii. "Just as the Lord's Supper now detracts not one iota from the glory of the work of Calvary, but rather has been a constant memorial of it for over nineteen hundred years, so the sacrifices of the millennial age will be powerless to diminish the worth of the Saviour's death on Calvary, but will rather be a continuous memorial of it for a thousand years." (Feinberg)

iii. "The use of animal sacrifices in the millennial temple no more minimizes or negates the finished work of Christ than these sacrifices did before Jesus died. It appears that the sacrifices will be offered in a memorial sense and as expressions of love and devotion to the Lord (Isaiah 56:5–7; 60:7). They will also bring people together for fellowship and feasting to the glory of the Lord." (Wiersbe)

iv. "It is important to observe that millennial sacrifices are discussed elsewhere in the OT prophets (Isaiah 56:5–7; 60:7, 13; 66:20–23; Jeremiah 33:15–22; Zechariah 14:16–21). The concept is not unique to Ezekiel." (Alexander)

v. "Since Israel did not receive their Messiah in His first coming, they have never celebrated a memorial of His redeeming work. Need we begrudge them this in the light of the fact that the Scriptures are so clear that God has appointed the sacrifices for that age, and surely for their commemorative value?" (Feinberg)

vi. **Hooks**: "Learned conjectures here, as in many other places, perplex more than explain. Hooks, on which the slaughtered sacrifice might be hanged, while they prepared it further, were needful, and the word imports such iron hooks." (Poole)

3. (44-46) The chambers for the singers and the priests.

Outside the inner gate *were* **the chambers for the singers in the inner court, one facing south at the side of the northern gateway, and the other facing north at the side of the southern gateway. Then he said to me, "This chamber which faces south** *is* **for the priests who have charge of the temple. The chamber which faces north** *is* **for the priests who have charge of the altar; these** *are* **the sons of Zadok, from the sons of Levi, who come near the Lord to minister to Him."**

a. **The chambers for the singers in the inner court**: In Ezekiel's temple, the priests (or Levites) served not only in the administration of sacrifice but also in the leading of music for worship and praise of God.

b. **Priests who have charge of the temple**: In addition to the **singers**, there were also those who guarded and looked over the temple and its administration.

i. **Charge of the temple**: "While scholars commonly assume that cultic service is involved, this is probably incorrect. The verb *samar* is primarily a military term, 'to keep, to guard, to watch,' from which derives *mismeret*, which refers fundamentally to military guard duty." (Block)

c. **Priests who have charge of the altar**: A third category of workers were those who conducted sacrifice. **These are the sons of Zadok**, descended from that high priest, who served the people but whose chief job was to **come near to the Lord to minister to Him**.

i. **Zadok**: "The high priest, who was put in by Solomon's depriving of Abiathar, in whose race the high priesthood continued." (Poole)

ii. "The name Zadok means 'righteous,' and in his book, the Prophet Ezekiel emphasizes separation and holiness." (Wiersbe)

4. (47-49) Measuring the inner court and its passage.

And he measured the court, one hundred cubits long and one hundred cubits wide, foursquare. The altar *was* **in front of the temple. Then he brought me to the vestibule of the temple and measured the doorposts of the vestibule, five cubits on this side and five cubits on that side; and the width of the gateway was three cubits on this side and three cubits on that side. The length of the vestibule** *was* **twenty cubits, and the width eleven cubits; and by the steps which led up to it** *there were* **pillars by the doorposts, one on this side and another on that side.**

a. **The altar was in front of the temple**: Though there was no mention of the laver for washing or some of the other features of the previous temples, there was an **altar** to accommodate the sacrifices.

b. **Then he brought me to the vestibule of the temple**: Ezekiel's guide then **brought** him to the temple building itself. It also had specific measurements and dimensions, the description of which would be unnecessary and even meaningless in a purely spiritual or symbolic temple.

i. "Ezekiel continued to set forth detail after detail, making it increasingly difficult to interpret the whole in a figurative manner, in which case the abundance of minute details is worthless and meaningless." (Feinberg)

c. **Pillars by the doorposts, one on this side and another on that side**: These two **pillars** remind us of the two pillars in Solomon's temple named *Jachin* and *Boaz* (1 Kings 7:21).

Ezekiel 41 – Measuring the New Temple

A. The temple in general.

1. (1-4) The dimensions of the sanctuary.

Then he brought me into the sanctuary and measured the doorposts, six cubits wide on one side and six cubits wide on the other side—the width of the tabernacle. The width of the entryway *was* ten cubits, and the side walls of the entrance *were* five cubits on this side and five cubits on the other side; and he measured its length, forty cubits, and its width, twenty cubits.

Also he went inside and measured the doorposts, two cubits; and the entrance, six cubits *high;* and the width of the entrance, seven cubits. He measured the length, twenty cubits; and the width, twenty cubits, beyond the sanctuary; and he said to me, "This *is* the Most Holy *Place.*"

a. **Then he brought me into the sanctuary**: Because Ezekiel was a priest himself, he could go into the **sanctuary** – the holy place – with his radiant guide. It was a real room with actual spatial dimensions.

b. **He went inside**: Ezekiel did *not* follow his radiant guide into **the Most Holy Place**. Ezekiel was a priest, but not the high priest, who alone had access into the holy of holies. Again, this was a real room with actual, measurable dimensions.

2. (5-11) The walls of the temple with their chambers.

Next, he measured the wall of the temple, six cubits. The width of each side chamber all around the temple *was* four cubits on every side. The side chambers *were* in three stories, one above the other, thirty chambers in each story; they rested on ledges which *were* for the side chambers all around, that they might be supported, but not fastened to the wall of the temple. As one went up from story to story, the side chambers became wider all around, because their supporting ledges in the wall of the temple ascended like steps; therefore the width of the structure

increased as one went up *from* the lowest *story* to the highest by way of the middle one. I also saw an elevation all around the temple; it was the foundation of the side chambers, a full rod, *that is,* six cubits *high.* The thickness of the outer wall of the side chambers *was* five cubits, and so also the remaining terrace by the place of the side chambers of the temple. And between *it and* the *wall* chambers was a width of twenty cubits all around the temple on every side. The doors of the side chambers opened on the terrace, one door toward the north and another toward the south; and the width of the terrace *was* five cubits all around.

a. **The side chambers were in three stories**: As part of the temple building, there was an arrangement of rooms and **chambers**, and these were on three different levels.

i. "The description of the side rooms (5-11) is difficult to follow. They were probably used to store gifts and tithes and various temple vessels (cf. Nehemiah 13.5,9,12)." (Wright)

b. **The thickness of the outer wall of the side chambers was five cubits**: The walls of the temple building were thick and secure. Ezekiel did not see a spiritual building, but a carefully engineered and strongly built structure.

i. "The massiveness of the walls is remarkable; both inside and outside walls are thicker than the width of the rooms." (Block)

3. (12) The building to the west of the temple.

The building that faced the separating courtyard at its western end *was* seventy cubits wide; the wall of the building *was* five cubits thick all around, and its length ninety cubits.

a. **The building that faced the separating courtyard at its western end**: The western side of the temple complex had no gate, and this building stood **at its western end**.

b. **The wall of the building was five cubits thick**: This was a substantial building with real, measurable dimensions.

B. Features of the temple.

1. (13-17) The temple building as a whole.

So he measured the temple, one hundred cubits long; and the separating courtyard with the building and its walls *was* one hundred cubits long; also the width of the eastern face of the temple, including the separating courtyard, *was* one hundred cubits. He measured the length of the building behind it, facing the separating courtyard, with its galleries on the one side and on the other side, one hundred cubits, as well as

the inner temple and the porches of the court, their doorposts and the beveled window frames. And the galleries all around their three stories opposite the threshold were paneled with wood from the ground to the windows—the windows were covered— from the space above the door, even to the inner room, as well as outside, and on every wall all around, inside and outside, by measure.

a. **He measured the temple, one hundred cubits long**: The temple building itself was 172 feet (52.5 meters) long.

b. **Their doorposts and the beveled window frames**: Ezekiel and his guide noticed not only the dimensions but also the design details of the temple.

2. (18-20) Designs on the temple building.

And *it was* made with cherubim and palm trees, a palm tree between cherub and cherub. *Each* cherub had two faces, so that the face of a man *was* toward a palm tree on one side, and the face of a young lion toward a palm tree on the other side; thus *it was* made throughout the temple all around. From the floor to the space above the door, and on the wall of the sanctuary, cherubim and palm trees *were* carved.

a. **It was made with cherubim and palm trees**: The design of **palm trees** has been frequently noted before in Ezekiel's temple, and was also featured in Solomon's temple (1 Kings 6:29-35). The design of **cherubim** was prominent in both the previous tabernacle and temple (Exodus 25:18-22 and 26:1; 1 Kings 6:23-35).

i. "In these figures aspirations of life and prosperity (palm) and security (cherubim) coalesce. In Israelite thought, the divine resident of this house was the source of both." (Block)

b. **Each cherub had two faces...the face of a man...and the face of a young lion**: We learn from Ezekiel 10:14 (and Revelation 4:7) that cherubim have four faces. Here, two of the four faces are noted and depicted in the design.

i. "It is interesting to notice the two types of life represented by the two faces of the cherubim, one being a man and the other a young lion. Interpreted by the earlier symbolism of the prophecy, this suggested perfect realisation of created life, and its perfect exercise in kingly dominion." (Morgan)

3. (21-22) The table before the LORD.

The doorposts of the temple *were* square, *as was* the front of the sanctuary; their appearance was similar. The altar *was* of wood, three cubits high, and its length two cubits. Its corners, its length, and its sides *were* of wood; and he said to me, "This *is* the table that *is* before the LORD."

a. **The altar was of wood**: This does not seem to be the same altar mentioned previously in Ezekiel 40:47. This altar is too small for animal sacrifice with a height of just over 5 feet (about 1.5 meters) and a length of less than 3.5 feet (about 1 meter). Made of wood and normally covered with metal, this is likely the altar of incense that stood inside the temple building. It was a representation of the prayers of God's people.

i. "The altar of verse 22 was not the altar of sacrifice, nor the table of shewbread, but the altar of incense before the Lord (see Exodus 30:1-3; I Kings 7:48). It has been suggested that it was an altarlike table (cf. Ezekiel 44:16)." (Feinberg)

b. **This is the table that is before the LORD**: Standing in the holy place, just outside of the most holy place, this altar of incense could be said to stand **before the LORD**. It was also true because of its use, representing prayers that come before God.

4. (23-26) The doors of the temple.

The temple and the sanctuary had two doors. The doors had two panels *apiece,* **two folding panels: two** *panels* **for one door and two panels for the other** *door.* **Cherubim and palm trees** *were* **carved on the doors of the temple just as they** *were* **carved on the walls. A wooden canopy** *was* **on the front of the vestibule outside.** *There were* **beveled window** *frames* **and palm trees on one side and on the other, on the sides of the vestibule—also on the side chambers of the temple and on the canopies.**

a. **The doors had two panels**: The doors were of some sort of **folding** construction, having two **panels** presumably hinged in some way.

i. John Trapp's comment on these **doors** shows the subjective and speculative nature of spiritualizing Ezekiel's temple. He thought the doors spoke of the Lord's Supper and baptism: "Understand hereby the means of grace, and ministers dispensing the same, whereby souls are brought home to Christ."

b. **A wooden canopy was on the front**: Once more, the detailed nature of this description only makes sense if Ezekiel described a literal, material temple that will one day stand in Jerusalem.

Ezekiel 42 – Chambers for the Priests

A. Rooms for the priests.

1. (1-9) Upper and lower chambers.

Then he brought me out into the outer court, by the way toward the north; and he brought me into the chamber which *was* opposite the separating courtyard, and which *was* opposite the building toward the north. Facing the length, *which was* one hundred cubits (the width was fifty cubits), was the north door. Opposite the inner court of twenty *cubits,* and opposite the pavement of the outer court, *was* gallery against gallery in three *stories.* In front of the chambers, toward the inside, *was* a walk ten cubits wide, at a distance of one cubit; and their doors faced north. Now the upper chambers *were* shorter, because the galleries took away *space* from them more than from the lower and middle stories of the building. For they *were* in three *stories* and did not have pillars like the pillars of the courts; therefore *the upper level* was shortened more than the lower and middle levels from the ground up. And a wall which *was* outside ran parallel to the chambers, at the front of the chambers, toward the outer court; its length *was* fifty cubits. The length of the chambers toward the outer court *was* fifty cubits, whereas that facing the temple *was* one hundred cubits. At the lower chambers *was* the entrance on the east side, as one goes into them from the outer court.

a. **He brought me out into the outer court**: Ezekiel's radiant guide (Ezekiel 40:3) took him away from the temple building back to the **outer court**. There they noted **gallery against gallery in three stories**. These held **chambers** or rooms.

b. **They were in three stories and did not have pillars like the pillars of the courts**: Once more we see a remarkable description of detail that is appropriate of a real, material temple.

2. (10-12) Access to the chambers.

Also *there were* chambers in the thickness of the wall of the court toward the east, opposite the separating courtyard and opposite the building. *There was* a walk in front of them also, and their appearance *was* like the chambers which *were* toward the north; they *were* as long and as wide as the others, and all their exits and entrances *were* according to plan. And corresponding to the doors of the chambers that *were* facing south, as one enters them, *there was* a door in front of the walk, the way directly in front of the wall toward the east.

a. **There were chambers in the thickness of the wall**: Many of the walls in these structures were rather thick, and it made sense to make rooms or **chambers** in the walls themselves.

b. **All their exits and entrances were according to plan**: There was nothing about this structure that was haphazard. All of it was **according to plan**.

3. (13-14) Holy chambers to the north and south.

Then he said to me, "The north chambers *and* the south chambers, which *are* opposite the separating courtyard, *are* the holy chambers where the priests who approach the LORD shall eat the most holy offerings. There they shall lay the most holy offerings—the grain offering, the sin offering, and the trespass offering—for the place *is* holy. When the priests enter them, they shall not go out of the holy *chamber* into the outer court; but there they shall leave their garments in which they minister, for they *are* holy. They shall put on other garments; then they may approach *that* which *is* for the people."

a. **The holy chambers where the priests who approach the Lord shall eat the most holy offerings**: Since many of the sacrifices included a sacrificial or ceremonial meal shared by the priests and sometimes those bringing the offering, provision was made for a place to **eat the most holy offerings**. This was a meal of *fellowship* between God and man.

i. **The priests** had the right to eat of certain offerings. "Ministers must eat as well as others; they are not of the chameleon kind – cannot live upon the air; and the Lord Christ 'hath ordained that,' as 'they which waited at the altar were partakers of the altar,' 'so also should they that preach the gospel live of the gospel,' [1 Corinthians 9:13-14]." (Trapp)

ii. **The grain offering**: "The *grain offering* (*minha*) represented a gift or tribute to deity, consisting of grain or flour. Either the offering could be burned up entirely on an altar or portions of it could be reserved for the priests." (Block)

b. **There they shall lay the most holy offerings**: When **grain** and animals were brought for sacrifice, they could be stored in these chambers.

i. "Such storage space housed ritual equipment, votive gifts, and the revenue taken in by the temple. Since revenue was not in money but in kind, enormous space was required for sacks of grain, amphorae of oil, and the kegs of wine, not to mention other kinds of goods that found their way into the priests' hands." (Block)

c. **There they shall leave their garments in which they minister:** The storage chambers were also for the **holy** clothing worn by the priests as they served. When their duties were completed, they were to **put on other garments** to go out among **the people**.

i. "The priests must wear special clothes when they are functioning as priests in the temple (verse 14). God and man are separate, and until the time of Christ only a privileged class could serve in the temple. The clothes spoke of separation to God from the dirt and dust of ordinary life." (Wright)

B. Outer dimensions of the new temple.

1. (15-19) The measure on each side.

Now when he had finished measuring the inner temple, he brought me out through the gateway that faces toward the east, and measured it all around. He measured the east side with the measuring rod, five hundred rods by the measuring rod all around. He measured the north side, five hundred rods by the measuring rod all around. He measured the south side, five hundred rods by the measuring rod. He came around to the west side *and* measured five hundred rods by the measuring rod.

a. **He measured the east side with the measuring rod:** After the general tour through the temple complex, the radiant guide finished with an overall perspective of the temple complex. It had the same measurements on each side.

b. **Five hundred rods by the measuring rod all around:** This is a large area, much larger than the present temple mount. Some believe that the measurement should be 500 cubits instead of 500 rods, but there is small support for this approach. It is better understood that this reflects the transformed geography of Jerusalem and the land of Israel in the millennial age.

i. "This wall was found to form a square of five hundred reeds which equals about 3,062,500 square yards (42:15–20)." (Smith) This is a space:

- Almost 1 square mile (about 2.56 square kilometers).
- About 633 acres (about 256 hectares).

ii. "The entire area was much too large for Mount Moriah where Solomon's and Zerubbabel's temples stood. The scheme requires a great change in the topography of the land which will occur as indicated in Zechariah 14:9-11, the very time which Ezekiel had in view." (Feinberg)

iii. "Some argue that an area five hundred rods square would be too large and not fit the topography well. But such an argument is not persuasive when Zechariah and other prophets demonstrate that the whole Palestinian topography will undergo geographical modifications at the beginning of the Millennium. No good reason appears to reject the term 'rod' in these verses." (Alexander)

iv. "It will not have a court of the Gentiles with the all-important separating wall (Ephesians 2:14) nor will it have a separate court of the women. In the millennial temple, our Lord's desire will be fulfilled that His house be a house of prayer for men and women of all nations (Mark 11:17; Isaiah 56:7; Jeremiah 7:11)." (Wiersbe)

2. (20) The purpose of the wall.

He measured it on the four sides; it had a wall all around, five hundred *cubits* long and five hundred wide, to separate the holy areas from the common.

a. **Five hundred... long and five hundred wide**: The reader will observe that the word *cubits* in Ezekiel 42:20 is in italics, indicating that it is not in the Hebrew manuscript but that the translators added it. The reference to **five hundred** better connects with the five hundred rods mentioned in the previous verses.

b. **To separate the holy areas from the common**: The purpose of the wall around the temple compound was to communicate the principle of God's holiness, as separated from that which is **common**.

i. "Verse 20 concludes with a note explaining the function of the outside walls. They are not constructed to keep enemy forces out, if by these forces one means human foes of Israel, but to protect the sanctity of the sacred area from the pollution of common touch and to prevent the contagion of holiness from touching the people." (Block)

Ezekiel 43 – God's Glory Comes to Ezekiel's Temple

A. The glory of God comes to Ezekiel's temple.

1. (1-2) The glory of the LORD comes through the eastern gate.

Afterward he brought me to the gate, the gate that faces toward the east. And behold, the glory of the God of Israel came from the way of the east. His voice *was* like the sound of many waters; and the earth shone with His glory.

a. **The gate that faces toward the east**: This was where Ezekiel's visionary tour of the temple began (Ezekiel 40:6). Also, many years before, in a vision Ezekiel saw the glory of God *depart* from the temple, and it left through the east gate (Ezekiel 11:23).

i. "Although Yahweh could have entered the temple area through the northern or southern gate, the choice of the east gate is deliberate, leading in a straight line along the central spine of concentrated sacrality to the holy of holies." (Block)

b. **The glory of the God of Israel came from the way of the east**: From the same direction Ezekiel saw God's glory depart (Ezekiel 11:23), so now in his vision he saw it come to this new temple.

i. Without **the glory of the God of Israel**, Ezekiel's temple was nothing more than a building. *With* the **glory** of God, it was a sacred place, a habitation for God and the radiance of His presence.

ii. It is hard to *define* the glory of God; we could call it the radiant outshining of His character and presence. The Bible says that God's glory radiates throughout all His creation (Psalm 19:1-4). Yet there is also the concept of the visible, tangible glory of God – the *shekinah* – and this is scattered about the Old Testament. In many cases it is described as a cloud.

- This is the cloud that stood by Israel in the wilderness (Exodus 13:21-22).

- This is the cloud of glory that God spoke to Israel from (Exodus 16:10).

- This is the cloud from which God met with Moses and others (Exodus 19:9, 24:15-18, Numbers 11:25, 12:5, 16:42).

- This is the cloud that stood by the door of the Tabernacle (Exodus 33:9-10).

- This is the cloud from which God appeared to the High Priest in the Holy Place inside the veil (Leviticus 16:2).

- This is the cloud of Ezekiel's vision, filling the temple of God with the brightness of His glory (Ezekiel 10:4).

- This is the cloud of glory that overshadowed Mary when she conceived Jesus by the power of the Holy Spirit (Luke 1:35).

- This is the cloud present at the transfiguration of Jesus (Luke 9:34-35).

- This is the cloud of glory that received Jesus into heaven at His ascension (Acts 1:9).

- This is the cloud that will display the glory of Jesus Christ when He returns in triumph to this earth (Luke 21:27, Revelation 1:7).

c. **His voice *was* like the sound of many waters; and the earth shone with His glory**: As Ezekiel experienced in his vision, the glory of God had an aspect that could be *heard* and *seen*. It sounded like the awesome and inspiring sound of a great waterfall (**the sound of many waters**). It looked massive and radiant (**the earth shone**).

> i. "The voice of Jehovah was as the sound of many waters, but in speaking to Ezekiel it became the voice of a man, and declared that Jehovah had taken up His abode in the house, that He would dwell in the midst of Israel forever, and that she should no more defile His holy name." (Morgan)

2. (3-5) Ezekiel's understanding of and reaction to God's glory.

It was **like the appearance of the vision which I saw—like the vision which I saw when I came to destroy the city. The visions *were* like the vision which I saw by the River Chebar; and I fell on my face. And the glory of the LORD came into the temple by way of the gate which faces toward the east. The Spirit lifted me up and brought me into the inner court; and behold, the glory of the LORD filled the temple.**

a. **It was like the appearance of the vision which I saw**: Ezekiel recognized this as the same display of glory he saw in a *negative* sense in Ezekiel 10 and 11 by **the River Chebar**. Then the glory of God came in judgment, **to destroy the city**.

i. Since we are not given details, we don't know if Ezekiel saw merely a radiant cloud of God's glory, or the elaborate throne-chariot of Ezekiel 1 and 8-11, complete with a series of wheels and active cherubim. Yet, Ezekiel knew that *it was the same glory* of God on display.

ii. **To destroy the city**: The specific verse referred to seems to be Ezekiel 9:8: *Ah, Lord GOD! Will You destroy all the remnant of Israel in pouring out Your fury on Jerusalem?*

b. **I fell on my face**: Though Ezekiel had seen this vision of the glory of God twice before (in Ezekiel 1 and Ezekiel 10-11), it was in no way a familiar or comfortable sight. In holy reverence to God, he **fell** on his **face**. The sense is that Ezekiel didn't *choose* to do this; it was a natural response. He had done the same before (Ezekiel 1:28; 3:23; 9:8, and 11:13).

i. **Fell on my face**: "In reverence to his majesty, in admiration of his mercy, and in the sense of mine own unworthiness. The nearer any one cometh to God, the lower he falleth in his own eyes." (Trapp)

c. **The glory of the LORD came into the temple**: The sense is that this happened fairly swiftly; there was no delay or hovering. When the glory of God left the temple, there was the sense of hovering, as if reluctant to depart (Ezekiel 10:18-19). God fills with His glory readily and only withdraws reluctantly.

i. "When Moses dedicated the tabernacle (Exodus 40) and Solomon the temple (2 Chronicles 5:11–14), the glory of God moved in, signifying that the Lord had accepted their worship and approved of their work." (Wiersbe)

ii. "The Shekinah glory is never mentioned in connection with the restoration (Zerubbabel's) temple, so that temple cannot be the fulfillment of what is predicted here." (Feinberg)

d. **Behold, the glory of the LORD filled the temple**: The **Spirit** brought Ezekiel to see the **glory** fill the temple, and the prophet's repetition indicates a sense of wonder. It was as if Ezekiel said, *His glory really does fill the temple!*

i. "Now that the temple had been described, it was necessary to signify that the building was accepted by God." (Feinberg)

3. (6-9) God's claim to the temple and to Israel.

Then I heard *Him* speaking to me from the temple, while a man stood beside me. And He said to me, "Son of man, *this is* the place of My throne and the place of the soles of My feet, where I will dwell in the midst of the children of Israel forever. No more shall the house of Israel defile My holy name, they nor their kings, by their harlotry or with the carcasses of their kings on their high places. When they set their threshold by My threshold, and their doorpost by My doorpost, with a wall between them and Me, they defiled My holy name by the abominations which they committed; therefore I have consumed them in My anger. Now let them put their harlotry and the carcasses of their kings far away from Me, and I will dwell in their midst forever.

a. **Then I heard Him speaking to me from the temple**: The voice of Yahweh Himself spoke from the temple, showing that the glory of God was the active representation of His presence. Where the glory was, God was; and where God is, He speaks.

b. **While a man stood beside me**: This was, presumably, the radiant man who was Ezekiel's tour guide through the temple (Ezekiel 40:3-4); likely an angelic being. This is the last mention of the radiant man.

i. "Nothing more is said about him. He disappears mysteriously from view, leaving the prophet to concentrate on the message he is about to receive from the newly arrived divine king, who now begins to speak." (Block)

c. **This is the place of My throne… where I will dwell in the midst of the children of Israel forever**: Yahweh proclaimed that He had come back to the temple to *reign*. It was His **throne**, where He would stand (**the place of the soles of My feet**), and where He would abide. This shows not only God's abiding, even eternal relationship with Israel as a covenant people, but also shows God's regard for *that land*. This will be especially evident in the millennial kingdom, the general context of Ezekiel 40-48.

i. **And He said to me, "Son of Man"**: This address "is not only typically Ezekielian; this is precisely how Yahweh's first speech to Ezekiel had been introduced in 2:1." (Block)

ii. "The words here are an echo of Solomon's prayer in 1 Kings 8:12, 13, 27." (Taylor)

iii. **Where I will dwell in the midst of the children of Israel forever**: "The word *forever* made this declaration more far-reaching than anything which was spoken concerning the Tabernacle of Moses or the Temple of Solomon (43:7a)." (Smith)

d. **No more shall the house of Israel defile My holy name**: This day of a renewed temple, God's glory, and promise of near dwelling would also be a day of holiness for Israel. Their sinful practices of the past (such as idolatry on the **high places**) would continue no more.

> i. In Ezekiel's temple there is no dividing line between Jew and Gentile or men and women; the dividing line is between what is holy and what is profane (or common).

> ii. "This passage reminds us that people who frequent 'holy places' ought to be 'holy people.' The Jewish remnant that returned to their land to rebuild the temple would need to take this message to heart, and we need to take it to heart today." (Wiersbe)

> iii. "Since this was to be in the fullest sense the residence of the Lord, there had to be absolutely nothing that would defile. They would follow the pollution of idolatry no longer. The modern mind has no concept of the depths of degradation and filth to which the idolatry of that day led, unless one has read somewhat widely in extrabiblical sources." (Feinberg)

> iv. **With the carcasses of their kings**: "Either the dead bodies of their deceased kings, buried too near the temple, less likely; or by the sacrificing of men to their idols, to Moloch; or idols are here called carcasses, as dead, stinking, loathsome things in the sight of God." (Poole)

> v. "It appears that God was displeased with their *bringing their kings so near his temple*. David was buried in the *city of David*, which was on *Mount Zion*, near to the temple; and so were almost all the kings of Judah; but God requires that the place of his temple and its vicinity shall be kept unpolluted; and when they *put away* all kinds of defilement, then will he *dwell among them*." (Clarke)

e. **When they set their threshold by My threshold... they defiled My holy name**: When Israel thought of themselves living *near* or *beside* God, they did not honor and obey Him fully. God's true desire was to **dwell in their midst forever**, and to do so as part of a new covenant transformation of Israel.

> i. We note God's solemn promise: **I will dwell in their midst forever**. The plain and clear meaning of these words challenges all who believe God is forever finished with Israel as Israel.

4. (10-12) God's purpose for the detailed description of Ezekiel's temple.

"Son of man, describe the temple to the house of Israel, that they may be ashamed of their iniquities; and let them measure the pattern. And

if they are ashamed of all that they have done, make known to them the design of the temple and its arrangement, its exits and its entrances, its entire design and all its ordinances, all its forms and all its laws. Write *it* down in their sight, so that they may keep its whole design and all its ordinances, and perform them. This *is* the law of the temple: The whole area surrounding the mountaintop *is* most holy. Behold, this *is* the law of the temple.

a. **Describe the temple to the house of Israel, that they may be ashamed of their iniquities**: This states at least one of the reasons God gave this vision to Ezekiel. Through his description of the promised **temple**, down to the **measure** of its **pattern**, Israel would see how great the restoring love and grace of God was toward them. It would make them **ashamed of their iniquities**.

i. "The vision of the glory of the House was given in order to produce shame in the hearts of the people for those evil ways which had robbed them of their glory." (Morgan)

b. **Make known to them the design of the temple and its arrangement**: Again, the very detail of the description was an assurance to Israel that *this was real*. Their restoration would be *real*. This made it important for Ezekiel to **write it down in their sight**.

i. The greater message for Ezekiel and the exile community was, *God isn't finished with you yet. He will gather, rebuild, restore, and bring His glory.* Yet this message wasn't communicated with fairy tales and wild stories, but with the prophetic declaration of real things that would *surely* happen.

c. **This is the law of the temple**: A foundational principle of Ezekiel's temple was *holiness*. The **law of the temple** (said twice for emphasis) was **the whole area surrounding the mountaintop is most holy**. The presence of God's glory abided in holiness.

i. Block titled the section of Ezekiel 43:12 through to the end of Ezekiel 46 as *The New Torah*. He translated the opening line of Ezekiel 43:12 as, *this is the Torah of the temple.* "Whereas most translations understand the word legally, and render *torah* as 'law,' the noun is derived from the Hiphil form of 'to teach, instruct.' Accordingly, 'instruction' is more precise etymologically. Ezekiel reflects long-standing Israelite tradition in associating 'instruction' with the priests (Ezekiel 7:26), particularly instruction in cultic and ceremonial matters." (Block)

B. The altar of burnt offerings.

1. (13-17) The measurements of the altar.

"These are the measurements of the altar in cubits (the *cubit is* one cubit and a handbreadth): the base one cubit high and one cubit wide, with a rim all around its edge of one span. This *is* the height of the altar: from the base on the ground to the lower ledge, two cubits; the width of the ledge, one cubit; from the smaller ledge to the larger ledge, four cubits; and the width of the ledge, *one* cubit. The altar hearth *is* four cubits high, with four horns extending upward from the hearth. The altar hearth *is* twelve cubits long, twelve wide, square at its four corners; the ledge, fourteen *cubits* long and fourteen wide on its four sides, with a rim of half a cubit around it; its base, one cubit all around; and its steps face toward the east."

a. **These are the measurements of the altar**: After the description of God's glory and the promise of His abiding presence, Ezekiel went back to describing the place of sacrifice. Like every true altar of Yahweh, this **altar** points to the cross, and the finished work of Jesus Messiah upon the cross.

i. "Now that God has returned to the temple (Ezekiel 43:1–12), it is necessary for the prophet to provide ordinances that will regulate the temple's use. The center of the temple complex is the altar, so the prophet begins with it." (Vawter and Hoppe)

ii. "It is not surprising that He starts with the altar of burnt-offering in the centre of the inner court (13, cf. 40.47). We too can approach God only through the blood shed on the altar of the cross." (Wright)

iii. Some have tried to explain the design of Ezekiel's altar by linking it to Babylonian altars. We can't explain every detail of Ezekiel's design, but as Block noted it was much more like Solomon's altar than anything Babylonian: "The details of Ezekiel's altar reflect either firsthand familiarity with the preexilic altar, or an ancient document or tradition describing it."

iv. We must always remember that in all of Ezekiel's temple and altar section, *there is no command to build*. Ezekiel only described what was. If this temple and altar are to be built and used (in the millennial period, as the author believes), then it will be *God's* doing and not man's.

b. **The cubit is one cubit and a handbreadth**: This was the same unit previously used to measure the temple (Ezekiel 40:5). It was about 20.5 inches (52 centimeters) long.

i. As with the description of Ezekiel's temple, one may consult many of the visual diagrams and representations for a sense of the dimensions and structure.

c. **This is the height of the altar**: The dimensions show that the altar was large and that it was *real*. It had real, actual spatial dimensions. It was also tall, with estimates of its height from 20 feet (Wright) to 12 feet (Vawter and Hoppe).

i. **Horns**: "They were regarded as of the utmost sanctity and the sacrificial blood was smeared upon them (Exodus 29:12; Ezekiel 43:20); they were also regarded as places of refuge (cf. 1 Kings 1:50ff.; 2:28ff.)." (Taylor)

ii. Adam Clarke on two phrases in Ezekiel 43:15, **the altar hearth**: *haharel*, 'the mount of God.' **From the hearth**: "*umihaariel*, 'and from the lion of God.' Perhaps the first was a name given to the *altar* when *elevated* to the honour of God, and on which the victims were offered to him, and the second, the *lion of God*, may mean the *hearth*, which might have been thus called, because it *devoured* and consumed the burnt-offerings, as a lion does his prey."

d. **Its steps face toward the east**: This was a hint that Ezekiel understood that when Israel was finally and fully restored to the land, and Yahweh's covenant promises to them fulfilled in their Messiah, the Mosaic law would in some sense be set aside. In the law of Moses, it was specifically commanded that there be *no steps* leading to the altar (Exodus 20:26).

i. **Toward the east**: "As in the tabernacle and the temple of Solomon, the priests would always face west in their ministering (unlike the idolaters who faced the sun and worshiped it, Ezekiel 8:16)." (Feinberg)

2. (18-27) The consecration ceremony for the altar.

And He said to me, "Son of man, thus says the Lord God: 'These *are* the ordinances for the altar on the day when it is made, for sacrificing burnt offerings on it, and for sprinkling blood on it. You shall give a young bull for a sin offering to the priests, the Levites, who are of the seed of Zadok, who approach Me to minister to Me,' says the Lord God. You shall take some of its blood and put *it* on the four horns of the altar, on the four corners of the ledge, and on the rim around it; thus you shall cleanse it and make atonement for it. Then you shall also take the bull of the sin offering, and burn it in the appointed place of the temple, outside the sanctuary. On the second day you shall offer a kid of the goats without blemish for a sin offering; and they shall cleanse the altar, as they cleansed *it* with the bull. When you have finished cleansing *it*, you shall offer a young bull without blemish, and a ram from the flock without blemish. When you offer them before the Lord, the priests shall throw salt on them, and they will offer them up *as* a burnt offering to the Lord. Every day for seven days you shall prepare a goat *for* a sin

offering; they shall also prepare a young bull and a ram from the flock, both without blemish. Seven days they shall make atonement for the altar and purify it, and so consecrate *it.* When these days are over it shall be, on the eighth day and thereafter, that the priests shall offer your burnt offerings and your peace offerings on the altar; and I will accept you,' says the Lord GOD."

a. **These are the ordinances for the altar on the day when it is made**: Through Ezekiel and his vision, God instructed Israel how they should consecrate the altar for this temple to come.

i. The ceremony is presented as if it were Ezekiel himself who would perform it, the same as in Exodus 29, which was written as if Moses would perform the purification ceremony. As a priest, Ezekiel was qualified to represent the one who would, many years in the future, perform this purification ceremony for the altar.

ii. "Basic to the action described here is the aim of setting the altar apart for its holy function and cleansing it from every taint of the secular, a process which takes a full seven days." (Alexander)

b. **You shall give a young bull for a sin offering to the priests**: A series of sacrifices over **seven days** consecrated the altar, and it would then begin its normal service **on the eighth day and thereafter**.

i. As noted before (in Ezekiel 40), these may be fairly regarded as *memorials* pointing back to the work of Jesus. Animal sacrifices were *never* actually effective for the cleansing of sin, only as representations and shadows of the future reality fulfilled by Jesus the Messiah in His crucifixion. Even so, the literal presence of these sacrifices does not mean that they should or could be regarded as effective for the cleansing of sin. Much as the bread and the cup of the Lord's Table is a powerful spiritual representation and memorial of Jesus' work on the cross, these sacrifices can be regarded in a similar way.

ii. "The offerings presented thereon were meant to be memorials, much as the Lord's Supper is no efficacious sacrifice but a memorial of a blessedly adequate and all-sufficient sacrifice for all time. Thus, whereas the sacrifices of the Old Testament economy were prospective, these are retrospective." (Feinberg)

iii. "Old Testament believers weren't forgiven because animals died, but because they put their faith in the Lord (Hebrews 11; Psalm 51:16–17; Habakkuk 2:4). Therefore, the use of animal sacrifices in the millennial temple no more minimizes or negates the finished work of Christ than these sacrifices did before Jesus died. It appears that the sacrifices will be offered in a memorial sense and as expressions of love and devotion to the Lord (Isaiah 56:5–7; 60:7). They will also bring people together for fellowship and feasting to the glory of the Lord." (Wiersbe)

iv. **Of the seed of Zadok**: "Non-Zadokites were debarred from priestly office on account of their past idolatrous associations with rural shrines (44:10) and were allowed only to act as temple servants." (Alexander)

v. **The priests shall throw salt on them**: "The preservative qualities of salt apparently rendered it a perfect symbol of the permanence of covenant relationship. The addition of salt to the ritual served as a reminder to Ezekiel and the priests of Yahweh's commitment to his people." (Block)

vi. **And I will accept you**: "Through the Levitical offerings the sacrifices of Israel and they themselves as well were accepted by the Lord. Thus Ezekiel is not presenting a new administrative principle with God, for acceptance with God is on the basis of sacrifice." (Feinberg)

Ezekiel 44 – The Prince and the Priests

A. The east gate and the prince.

1. (1-2) The shut east gate.

Then He brought me back to the outer gate of the sanctuary which faces toward the east, but it *was* shut. And the LORD said to me, "This gate shall be shut; it shall not be opened, and no man shall enter by it, because the LORD God of Israel has entered by it; therefore it shall be shut.

a. **Then He brought me back**: It seems at this point Ezekiel was led by Yahweh Himself, and not the radiant man of Ezekiel 40:3. Some believe the radiant man was the angel of the LORD, Yahweh Himself.

i. John Trapp drew this spiritual application from Ezekiel 44:1: "Christ must be followed, though he seem to lead us in and out, backward and forward, as if we were treading a maze."

b. **To the outer gate of the sanctuary which faces toward the east**: This was where Ezekiel's tour of the temple compound began (Ezekiel 40:6).

i. **This gate shall be shut**: "This verse has been adduced by the Roman Catholics to prove the *perpetual virginity* of the mother of our Lord; and it may be allowed to be as much to the purpose as any other that has been brought to prove this very precarious point, on which no stress should ever be laid by any man. Mary was a virgin when she brought forth Jesus." (Clarke)

c. **It was shut**: For emphasis, the idea is repeated three times in this verse. The gate was **shut** and **no man shall enter by it**. The reason it was shut was **because the LORD God of Israel has entered by it**. It was a gate especially reserved for God Himself. It was separated for God's use alone.

i. "Once Yahweh has made his grand entrance into his temple, however, no one else may enter here. Priests must enter the inner court to perform their services, but not even they may follow in Yahweh's steps." (Block)

ii. "The closure of the gate then is not a menacing symbol but an encouraging one... Since Yahweh entered the temple through this gate, it is unseemly that others should use it. Since God will never leave the temple again, the gate will remain closed." (Vawter and Hoppe)

iii. On the temple mount in Jerusalem today, the eastern gate is completely closed, filled in with stone blocks. Yet this is not the fulfillment of Ezekiel 44:1-2; the gate mentioned here belongs to a temple compound yet to come.

iv. "This gate is not the 'golden gate' located in the old city of Jerusalem today, because the dimensions of the two temple areas are vastly different. The structures of the current 'temple area' will not exist in the millennial period." (Alexander)

2. (3) The privilege of the prince.

As for the prince, *because* he *is* the prince, he may sit in it to eat bread before the LORD; he shall enter by way of the vestibule of the gateway, and go out the same way."

a. **As for the prince**: Ezekiel wrote of a ruler, a **prince**, who would have special privilege regarding the gate. This ruler is likely David, whose future rule over Israel is mentioned several times in Ezekiel (Ezekiel 34:23-25 and 37:25) and elsewhere (Isaiah 55:3-4, Jeremiah 30:8-9, Hosea 3:5). In Ezekiel 37:25 it is specifically written that David would be **prince** over Israel.

   i. The identity of **the prince** is a matter of much discussion among Bible commentators and teachers. A few take it to be Jesus the Messiah, and some that he is a civil leader or a high priest.

   ii. The fact that **the prince** must offer a sin offering (Ezekiel 45:22) and has sons (Ezekiel 46:16) means it is unlikely that **the prince** is Jesus Messiah.

b. **He may sit in it to eat bread before the LORD**: This gives us more indication that the **prince** is not the Messiah, who is also Yahweh Himself. Yet this **prince** has special access to the gate complex. The gate itself is not open to him, but he may sit in its chambers and **vestibule** there in fellowship with the LORD.

   i. "The prince, Messiah's representative in a special sense, will then have the privilege of sitting in the very gate where the Lord Himself will have entered. He will perform certain religious acts in the presence of the Lord." (Feinberg)

B. Those admitted to the temple.

1. (4-5) Marking who may enter the house of the LORD.

Also He brought me by way of the north gate to the front of the temple; so I looked, and behold, the glory of the LORD filled the house of the LORD; and I fell on my face. And the LORD said to me, "Son of man, mark well, see with your eyes and hear with your ears, all that I say to you concerning all the ordinances of the house of the LORD and all its laws. Mark well who may enter the house and all who go out from the sanctuary.

a. **He brought me by way of the north gate to the front of the temple**: Because the east gate was shut, Ezekiel was **brought** to the right and came through the **north gate**.

b. **Behold, the glory of the LORD filled the house of the LORD**: The glory Ezekiel saw fill the temple in Ezekiel 43:1-4 remained there. As promised, it would be His dwelling place forever (Ezekiel 43:7). Ezekiel's reaction was as before; he **fell on** his **face** (Ezekiel 43:3).

i. "Remarkably, not a word is said about the high priest or the most sacred space of all—the holy of holies, the throne room of Yahweh himself." (Block)

c. **Mark well who may enter the house and all who go out from the sanctuary**: God wanted Ezekiel to carefully note those allowed and those excluded from the temple. A similar kind of distinction is described as relevant to the eternal state (Revelation 21.7-8 and 22:14-15).

2. (6-9) Those excluded from the temple.

"Now say to the rebellious, to the house of Israel, 'Thus says the Lord GOD: "O house of Israel, let Us have no more of all your abominations. When you brought in foreigners, uncircumcised in heart and uncircumcised in flesh, to be in My sanctuary to defile it—My house—and when you offered My food, the fat and the blood, then they broke My covenant because of all your abominations. And you have not kept charge of My holy things, but you have set *others* to keep charge of My sanctuary for you." Thus says the Lord GOD: "No foreigner, uncircumcised in heart or uncircumcised in flesh, shall enter My sanctuary, including any foreigner who *is* among the children of Israel.

a. **Let Us have no more of your abominations**: God spoke to the people of Ezekiel's own day, to the **rebellious** in the **house of Israel**. In light of the glory to come one day to the temple described by Ezekiel, Israel owed Yahweh their complete allegiance and the complete rejection of idolatry (**abominations**).

> i. "The future Temple would be restricted to those who had complied with the initiatory commands of the Lord and who had surrendered their hearts to him." (Smith)

b. **When you brought in foreigners, uncircumcised in heart and uncircumcised in flesh**: In the past, they were disobedient by bringing in **foreigners** – those who had *not* accepted the covenant God made with Israel – and allowed them to serve in the temple.

> i. "Under no circumstances should aliens or the uncircumcised in the heart or flesh serve in the sanctuary of Jehovah. This had been the sin of the past, and must not be repeated." (Morgan)

> ii. "It is clear from vs. 5-8 that in the last days of Solomon's Temple the priests had allowed anyone, even uncovenanted pagans, to act as priests and temple servants. Either they had been lazy or busy with their own affairs, and had hired others to do their work; or they had taken bribes from pagans who wanted to serve in the Temple, perhaps for the offerings that they were able to take home and resell." (Wright)

c. **You have not kept charge of My holy things**: Israel did not care for the holy things God entrusted to them in His law, the temple, and their associated rituals. They let the ungodly **keep charge of My sanctuary**.

d. **No foreigner, uncircumcised in heart or uncircumcised in flesh, shall enter My sanctuary**: Because of Israel's past sin in allowing those out of covenant with God to have leadership and participation in the temple, God promised that in His future temple there would be a true separation and those not in covenant could not even **enter** His **sanctuary**.

> i. "The religions of the ancient Near East frequently used foreign captives as temple servants to aid the priests. The Lord's rebuke of Israel in these verses reflected ancient Israel's adoption of this practice." (Alexander)

> ii. Matthew Poole thought of these as mere *visitors* to the temple. "None of these, or such like, shall on any colour of pretence be brought into my sanctuary. Perhaps Solomon showed Sheba's queen too much, we are sure Hezekiah showed the ambassadors too much, yet we read not that either of them showed the sanctuary."

C. The laws of the priests.

1. (10-14) The Levites who were far from God.

"And the Levites who went far from Me, when Israel went astray, who strayed away from Me after their idols, they shall bear their iniquity. Yet they shall be ministers in My sanctuary, *as* gatekeepers of the house and ministers of the house; they shall slay the burnt offering and the sacrifice for the people, and they shall stand before them to minister to them. Because they ministered to them before their idols and caused the house of Israel to fall into iniquity, therefore I have raised My hand in an oath against them," says the Lord GOD, "that they shall bear their iniquity. And they shall not come near Me to minister to Me as priest, nor come near any of My holy things, nor into the Most Holy *Place;* but they shall bear their shame and their abominations which they have committed. Nevertheless I will make them keep charge of the temple, for all its work, and for all that has to be done in it.

a. **The Levites who went far from Me**: God now spoke to the **Levites**, those who **strayed** from Yahweh along with the rest of Israel, going **after their idols**. This was true of the Levites of Ezekiel's day, now in their exile.

i. **The Levites**: "They were specially appointed for tabernacle service, their duties including maintenance of the tabernacle, carrying the ark of the covenant, and restricted cultic service. According to Numbers 3–4 the last duty included assisting the priests in their temple service." (Block)

b. **Yet they shall be ministers in My sanctuary**: God promised a future restoration of the Levites who previously went astray. In the restoration of Ezekiel's temple, they would be **gatekeepers** and servants (**ministers**) of the temple.

i. "Though lapsed, they shall not be altogether discarded, partly for the honour of the priesthood, but principally for the encouragement of such as, having fallen by infirmity, rise again by repentance." (Trapp)

c. **They shall bear their iniquity**: Repeated twice, this phrase emphasizes that God held the Levites accountable for their sin and idolatry, and God would discipline them because of it.

i. **I have raised My hand in an oath against them**: "Sworn against them, that they shall suffer for this their iniquity. This lifting up the hand is the form of an oath, Exodus 6:8 Deuteronomy 32:40 Ezekiel 20:5." (Poole)

d. **They shall not come near to Me to minister to Me as priest**: In Ezekiel's future temple the Levites would not be allowed to perform sacrifices as priests. They would be allowed to perform the previously mentioned functions. This would be part of their discipline for previous idolatry, as they would **bear their shame and their abominations which they have committed**.

> i. "Far from causing the Levites to gloat with pride over their assignment, this act of divine grace will precipitate a sense of shame and intense unworthiness over their restoration within the cult of Yahweh." (Block)

> ii. This fact of the Levites being disciplined for their prior sin during the time of Ezekiel's temple demonstrates that this does not belong to the eternal realm, but to the millennial period.

e. **Nevertheless I will make them keep charge of the temple**: For emphasis, God repeated the principle. The Levites would not be excluded from all service relevant to the temple, only the work of priestly sacrifice.

> i. "Yet mercy is not lacking, for they will not be excluded from all types of priestly ministry. It is only that they will lose the dignity of the higher services of the priesthood, such as were performed in the holy place or the first compartment of the tabernacle and temple." (Feinberg)

> ii. "These were menial tasks. Nevertheless, they were tasks which had to be done and the ordinary people were not permitted to do them, so we must beware of denigrating the duties of the Levites in Ezekiel's temple. They have their counterparts today in all aspects of church life and doubtless then, as now, many reckoned it a privilege to be attending on the people of God in the more mundane details of their religion. After all, they were doing their duties by divine appointment." (Taylor)

2. (15-16) The priests and their ministry to the Lord.

"But the priests, the Levites, the sons of Zadok, who kept charge of My sanctuary when the children of Israel went astray from Me, they shall come near Me to minister to Me; and they shall stand before Me to offer to Me the fat and the blood," says the Lord God. "They shall enter My sanctuary, and they shall come near My table to minister to Me, and they shall keep My charge.

a. **But the priests, the Levites, the sons of Zadok**: Here God spoke to the **sons of Zadok**. The **sons of Zadok** were of the tribe of Levi (**the Levites**) and were of the family of Aaron (**the priests**). Zadok received the right to the priesthood in the days of Solomon (1 Kings 2:35). They were not like the other Levites in general, being noted for their faithfulness (**who kept charge of My sanctuary when the children of Israel went astray from Me**).

i. "The new priesthood is confined to the line of Zadok, who was a descendant of Eleazar, the third son of Aaron. Representatives of this line had evidently stood firm." (Wright)

ii. "Zadok was the son of Ahitub of the line of Eleazar (2 Samuel 8:17; 1 Chronicles 6:7-8). He was faithful to David during the insurrection of Absalom (2 Samuel 15:24 ff.), and anointed Solomon as king after the abortive attempt of Adonijah to seize the throne (1 Kings 1:32 ff.)." (Feinberg)

b. **They shall come near Me to minister to Me**: With great emphasis, God declared that the ministry of the priests was fundamentally to *God Himself.* This is noted in the phrases, **near Me to minister to Me… before Me to offer to Me… to minister to Me**.

i. Seen in light of the new covenant, there is a spiritual application of this. Every believer is a priest unto God (1 Peter 2:5 and 2:9; Revelation 1:6 and 5:10). This charge to the sons of Zadok emphasizes the principle that believers in general (and God's servants in particular) have their first service *to God Himself.* We do serve one another and a needy world for the glory of Jesus, but God first says to us, **they shall come near to Me to minister to Me.**

3. (17-19) The clothing of the priests.

And it shall be, whenever they enter the gates of the inner court, that they shall put on linen garments; no wool shall come upon them while they minister within the gates of the inner court or within the house. They shall have linen turbans on their heads and linen trousers on their bodies; they shall not clothe themselves with *anything that causes* sweat. When they go out to the outer court, to the *outer* court to the people, they shall take off their garments in which they have ministered, leave them in the holy chambers, and put on other garments; and in their holy garments they shall not sanctify the people.

a. **Whenever they enter the gates of the inner court, that they shall put on linen garments**: When the sons of Zadok came to perform their priestly service, they were to do it in the **linen garments** and **linen turbans** and **linen trousers** prescribed for the priests. The purpose of the linen was so they would **not clothe themselves with anything that causes sweat**. God wanted His priests (ancient and modern, literal and spiritual) to serve Him in the peace and rest of the Spirit, not the **sweat** of human effort apart from God.

i. "The linen not only depicted purity by its whiteness, but its coolness kept the priests from perspiring and thereby becoming unclean." (Alexander)

b. **They shall take off their garments**: When their service was over, they were to leave their special priestly "uniforms" behind at the temple.

i. **They shall not sanctify the people**: "To 'sanctify the people,' in this text, is to persuade them that they are sanctified by the touch or sight of the priestly vestments. The monks at this day make the silly people believe that they cannot be damned when they die if they be buried in a Franciscan's cowl." (Trapp)

4. (20-22) The outward displays of holiness for the priests.

"They shall neither shave their heads, nor let their hair grow long, but they shall keep their hair well trimmed. No priest shall drink wine when he enters the inner court. They shall not take as wife a widow or a divorced woman, but take virgins of the descendants of the house of Israel, or widows of priests.

a. **They shall keep their hair well trimmed**: Their hair was not to be shaved, but their hair was not to be **long**. They were to avoid extremes in either way.

i. "Like scarred skin, both the shaved head and long, unkempt hair were considered signs of disfigurement (cf. Lev. 19:27). If the sacrificial animals were to be without defect or blemish, how much more those functionaries who stand before the holy God in service?" (Block)

ii. **Nor let their hair grow long**: "Priding themselves in it, as Absalom, giving ill example by such excess. Shall only poll their heads; when the hair is grown somewhat, they shall trim, cut the ends of their hair, and keep it in moderate size." (Poole)

iii. "As women's: some heathen priests nourished their hair to a great length. A shag-haired minister is an ugly sight: bushes of vanity become not such, of any men." (Trapp)

b. **No priest shall drink wine**: They will not be under the influence of even the relatively mild wine of that day.

i. "They must be in full control of their faculties so as to offer intelligent worship to God, not using drink (or drugs?) to release their inhibitions (cf. Proverbs 31:4-5)." (Wright)

ii. "The prohibition concerning drinking wine is in agreement with Leviticus 10:9. What disastrous results such imbibing can have is clear from the tragedy of Nadab and Abihu…. The zeal of the priests, moreover, is to be holy and true, not induced by outward carnal stimulants." (Feinberg)

c. **They shall not take as wife a widow or divorced woman**: The sons of Zadok in the days of Ezekiel's temple must also observe the marriage regulations relevant to the priests of Israel.

5. (23) The teaching and leading work of the priests.

"And they shall teach My people *the difference* between the holy and the unholy, and cause them to discern between the unclean and the clean. In controversy they shall stand as judges, *and* judge it according to My judgments. They shall keep My laws and My statutes in all My appointed meetings, and they shall hallow My Sabbaths.

a. **They shall teach My people the difference between the holy and the unholy**: This was one of the fundamental duties of the priests of Israel. They were by both instruction and example to teach Israel the difference **between the unclean and the clean**.

i. "This verse conflates Leviticus 10:10-11, which first highlights the necessity of the priest to make these same distinctions, and then speaks of the priest's responsibility to teach (*hora*) Israel all the statutes (*huqqim*) that Yahweh had communicated to Moses." (Block)

b. **In controversy they shall stand as judges**: The priests of ancient Israel could also serve as judges or mediators. This was because they were supposed to be well versed in the **laws** and **statutes** of God, and able to apply them in given situations.

i. "The judicial role of the religious functionaries in Israel has a long history. Deuteronomy 33:10 perceives this role as a natural corollary to the Levites' teaching responsibilities." (Block)

c. **They shall keep My laws and My statutes**: The priests were also called to live lives of obedience to God. This was to be true of their **appointed meetings** for worship, teaching, and sacrifice and also of God's appointed **Sabbaths**.

6. (25-27) The defilement of the priests.

"They shall not defile *themselves* by coming near a dead person. Only for father or mother, for son or daughter, for brother or unmarried sister may they defile themselves. After he is cleansed, they shall count seven days for him. And on the day that he goes to the sanctuary to minister in the sanctuary, he must offer his sin offering in the inner court," says the Lord God.

a. **They shall not defile themselves by coming near a dead person**: As was true of the priests commanded by Moses, so it is to be of the priests in the time of Ezekiel's temple. They are to avoid dead bodies and carcasses. Theirs will be a ministry of *life*, not death.

i. "There would be individuals entering the Millennium with natural bodies from the tribulation period. These, of course, would ultimately die physically, though physical life would be much longer during the Millennium (cf. Isaiah 65:20)." (Alexander)

ii. "Since death is viewed in Scripture as Levitically defiling, bringing to remembrance most forcefully the sin of Adam which introduced death into the human family, priests will have to be careful in their contact with the dead." (Feinberg)

iii. "The Jews tell us that he who comes within four cubits of the dead is defiled; and the law, though it determine not at what distance such are defiled, it doth determine that they are unclean till evening by touch or coming near the carcass of any but man, and the defilement by coming near a dead man lasted seven days." (Poole)

b. **He must offer his sin offering**: If the priest must have contact with a dead body (as in the case of a close relative), then he will have to follow the prescribed sacrifice for cleansing upon resuming priestly service.

7. (28-31) The inheritance and provision for the priests.

"It shall be, in regard to their inheritance, *that* I *am* their inheritance. You shall give them no possession in Israel, for I *am* their possession. They shall eat the grain offering, the sin offering, and the trespass offering; every dedicated thing in Israel shall be theirs. The best of all firstfruits of any kind, and every sacrifice of any kind from all your sacrifices, shall be the priest's; also you shall give to the priest the first of your ground meal, to cause a blessing to rest on your house. The priests shall not eat anything, bird or beast, that died naturally or was torn *by wild beasts*.

a. **I am their inheritance**: This principle was true in the days when the priesthood was established by Moses, and would also be true in the days of Ezekiel's temple. They would have no true inheritance in the land of Israel; Yahweh Himself would be **their inheritance**.

i. "Like the Old Testament priests, the kingdom priests will not have an inheritance of land but will have the Lord as their inheritance and be able to live from the temple offerings." (Wiersbe)

ii. By spiritual analogy, we can relate this to our inheritance in God. "We possess God as the flower the sunlight; as a babe the mother. All

His resources are placed at our disposal… All the resources which have been placed at His disposal in His ascension and eternal reign are gifts which He holds for men." (Meyer)

b. **They shall eat the grain offering, the sin offering, and the trespass offering**: Though they would not have the same land inheritance as the other tribes of Israel, God promised to provide for His priests. One way they would be provided for was to receive a part of what came to the temple as offerings. Portions of the **sacrifices** and the **firstfruits** will be given **to the priest**.

i. "The priests earn their living by doing the special work that God has given them, and their income comes from the offerings (28-30). God still calls some to what we call wholetime service, and in giving for their support we are giving to God, as were the people who brought their offerings to the Temple." (Wright)

c. **To cause a blessing to rest on your house**: God promised that even in the period of the millennial temple to come, there would be blessing upon those who gave to God's work. The blessing would not only be financial, but it would **rest on your house**.

i. "Tithe and be rich. See Malachi 3:10." (Trapp)

d. **The priest shall not eat anything, bird or beast, that died naturally or was torn by wild beasts**: Things that died naturally or were killed in some kind of accident must not be food for the priests. This would violate the principle of not touching dead bodies (Ezekiel 44:25), but also be an expression of their trust that God would provide. They will not have to scavenge for food as some animals might.

Ezekiel 45 – Regarding the Priests of Ezekiel's Temple

A. The land for the priests.

1. (1-5) The portion for the Levites.

"Moreover, when you divide the land by lot into inheritance, you shall set apart a district for the LORD, a holy section of the land; its length *shall be* twenty-five thousand *cubits,* and the width ten thousand. It *shall be* holy throughout its territory all around. Of this there shall be a square plot for the sanctuary, five hundred by five hundred *rods,* with fifty cubits around it for an open space. So this is the district you shall measure: twenty-five thousand *cubits* long and ten thousand wide; in it shall be the sanctuary, the Most Holy *Place.* It shall be a holy *section* of the land, belonging to the priests, the ministers of the sanctuary, who come near to minister to the LORD; it shall be a place for their houses and a holy place for the sanctuary. *An area* twenty-five thousand *cubits* long and ten thousand wide shall belong to the Levites, the ministers of the temple; they shall have twenty chambers as a possession.

a. **You shall set apart a district for the LORD:** There will be a real distribution of land in the time of Ezekiel's temple. As part of the distribution among the tribes of Israel, there would be a special **district for the LORD,** to be **a holy section of the land.** It would be a large area of land. **Length** means from east to west, and **width** from north to south.

i. **You shall set apart:** "Although Yahweh identifies the land to be set aside for himself, the use of the second person implies the involvement of the Israelites in the process." (Block)

ii. "The division of the land among the various tribes is the subject of Ezekiel 47–48. Here the text deals with only one part of the land: the location of the temple and the holy city. This land belongs directly to the Lord, while the rest of the land is the inheritance of the tribes." (Vawter and Hoppe)

iii. "The student of Ezekiel's prophecy is struck again and again with the mass of details and particulars that characterize the last nine chapters of the book. This is the strongest and most irrefutable argument against taking these chapters in an allegorical or symbolical or spiritualizing sense." (Feinberg)

b. **Of this there shall be a square plot for the sanctuary**: The temple (and Jerusalem) will be in the special district for Yahweh.

c. **Belonging to the priests, the ministers of the sanctuary**: The district will be directly managed and governed by the previously mentioned priests, also with areas to **belong to the Levites**.

i. "The land belonging to God directly is approximately 166 square kilometers (64 square miles). Three parts comprise this area. The northernmost portion comprising some 65 square kilometers (25 square miles) belonged to the Levites. Next came a strip of the same size that was available to the priests. It also was the site of the sanctuary. The last strip, which was about 34 square kilometers (13 square miles), was for the city itself. The land to the east and west of this sacral land was for the prince. The rest of the land of Israel belonged to the tribes." (Vawter and Hoppe)

ii. John B. Taylor has one of the better maps or diagrams of the allotment of the sacred portion of land described in Ezekiel 45:1-8.

iii. "During the old dispensation, the Levites were allowed to own land but were scattered throughout Israel so they could minister to the people (Joshua 21). Genesis 49:5–7; 34:25–31 suggests that this scattering was also a form of discipline." (Wiersbe)

2. (6) The portion for the whole house of Israel.

"You shall appoint as the property of the city *an area* five thousand *cubits* wide and twenty-five thousand long, adjacent to the district of the holy *section;* it shall belong to the whole house of Israel.

a. **Appoint as the property of the city**: The city of Jerusalem will have an appointed portion.

b. **It shall belong to the whole house of Israel**: The city of Jerusalem itself will be the heritage of all Israel, not any one particular tribe.

3. (7-8) The portion of the prince.

"The prince shall have *a section* on one side and the other of the holy district and the city's property; and bordering on the holy district and

the city's property, extending westward on the west side and eastward on the east side, the length *shall be* side by side with one of the *tribal* portions, from the west border to the east border. The land shall be his possession in Israel; and My princes shall no more oppress My people, but they shall give *the rest of* the land to the house of Israel, according to their tribes."

a. **The prince shall have a section on one side**: The prince previously mentioned in Ezekiel 44:1-3 will have his own appointed portion of land.

b. **My princes shall no longer oppress My people**: The period of time connected to Ezekiel's temple will be a time of righteousness and just rulership among God's leaders.

i. "The princes of Israel abandon the sins which their privileged position of influence makes possible and give their attention to their real duty, the promotion of righteousness in the land." (Taylor)

ii. "The most notable case is found in 1 Kings 21 where Ahab confiscated the vineyard of Naboth (cf. also Numbers 36:7-9; Isaiah 5:8; Hosea 5:10, ASV; Micah 2:1-2). No one will be deprived of his rightful possession in that era of righteousness and justice under Messiah's benevolent reign." (Feinberg)

B. The offerings of the temple priests.

1. (9-12) A call for justice and fairness.

'Thus says the Lord GOD: "Enough, O princes of Israel! Remove violence and plundering, execute justice and righteousness, and stop dispossessing My people," says the Lord GOD. "You shall have honest scales, an honest ephah, and an honest bath. The ephah and the bath shall be of the same measure, so that the bath contains one-tenth of a homer, and the ephah one-tenth of a homer; their measure shall be according to the homer. The shekel *shall be* twenty gerahs; twenty shekels, twenty-five shekels, *and* fifteen shekels shall be your mina.

a. **Enough, O princes of Israel**: In the previous lines God spoke of the coming righteous age connected to Ezekiel's temple, and said it would be a time when *princes shall no more oppress* the people of God (Ezekiel 45:8). That vision of a future righteousness could inspire the leaders (**princes**) of Ezekiel's day to **remove violence and plundering, execute justice and righteousness, and stop dispossessing** God's people in their own day.

b. **You shall have honest scales**: God cares greatly about simple honestly and integrity among men. **Scales** and every **measure** should be righteous and fair.

i. "The ephah was the dry measure equal to about eight or nine gallons or one bushel, divided into sixths for calculation purposes. The bath was a liquid measure equal to about nine gallons or ninety-one pints, divided into tenths. A hin was the sixth part of a bath." (Feinberg)

ii. **Honest scales**: "Leviticus 19:35-36, Proverbs 11:1; Proverbs 16:11; Proverbs 20:10; Proverbs 20:23, Micah 6:10-11." (Trapp)

2. (13-17) The offering of the prince.

"This *is* the offering which you shall offer: you shall give one-sixth of an ephah from a homer of wheat, and one-sixth of an ephah from a homer of barley. The ordinance concerning oil, the bath of oil, *is* one-tenth of a bath from a kor. A kor *is* a homer or ten baths, for ten baths *are* a homer. And one lamb shall be given from a flock of two hundred, from the rich pastures of Israel. These shall be for grain offerings, burnt offerings, and peace offerings, to make atonement for them," says the Lord GOD. "All the people of the land shall give this offering for the prince in Israel. Then it shall be the prince's part *to give* burnt offerings, grain offerings, and drink offerings, at the feasts, the New Moons, the Sabbaths, and at all the appointed seasons of the house of Israel. He shall prepare the sin offering, the grain offering, the burnt offering, and the peace offerings to make atonement for the house of Israel."

a. **This is the offering which you shall offer**: God listed a variety of things to be used for offering at Ezekiel's temple. They included items for grain offerings (**wheat, barley,** and **oil**) and for animal sacrifice (**lamb**).

i. "The people have a responsibility for contributing to the maintenance of the public worship of God. Ezekiel also assumes that one of the prince's duties is to administer the contributions made by the people." (Vawter and Hoppe)

ii. **To make atonement**: "These rituals of atonement were commemorative of the complete and finished work of Christ for sin through the sacrifice of himself. They were in no way efficacious. They were picture-lessons and reminders to the people of their Messiah's marvelous saving work. What praise and worship they would give to the Lord for his gracious provision for sin as they viewed these sacrificial reminders in worship (cf. Revelation 5:7–14)!" (Alexander)

b. **All the people of the land shall give this offering to the prince in Israel**: God's appointed leader (likely David, according to Ezekiel 34:23-25, 37:25; Isaiah 55:3-4; Jeremiah 30:8-9; Hosea 3:5) would receive these offerings of the people so that he could offer them to the LORD on their behalf.

3. (18-20) Atonement for sins done in ignorance.

'**Thus says the Lord God: "In the first** *month,* **on the first** *day* **of the month, you shall take a young bull without blemish and cleanse the sanctuary. The priest shall take some of the blood of the sin offering and put** *it* **on the doorposts of the temple, on the four corners of the ledge of the altar, and on the gateposts of the gate of the inner court. And so you shall do on the seventh** *day* **of the month for everyone who has sinned unintentionally or in ignorance. Thus you shall make atonement for the temple.**

a. **You shall take a young bull without blemish and cleanse the sanctuary**: Ezekiel described the cleansing sacrifices for the temple.

i. "There is nothing of this in the Mosaic law; it seems to have been a new ceremony. An annual purification of the sanctuary may be intended." (Clarke)

ii. "Even the temple needs to be 'cleansed' once a year (Ezekiel 45:18-19, cf. Hebrews 9:23) because its ministers are human and sinful, and even though they have kept from deliberate sin, there is much that contaminates (verse 20, cf. Psalm 19:12)." (Wright)

b. **So you shall do on the seventh day of the month for everyone who has sinned unintentionally or in ignorance**: These will be the memorial sacrifices to recognize the ongoing need for cleansing and the separation between the holy and the profane.

i. "Twice a year the sacred ceremony of cleansing the sanctuary was to be performed, on the first day of the first month, and on the first day of the seventh month." (Morgan)

ii. "There is no special Day of Atonement in the Millennium. That special day had its full fruition in the special day of efficacious atonement provided by Christ on the cross." (Alexander)

iii. **Unintentionally or in ignorance**: The King James translates this the *erring* and the *simple*. "There was to be special thought of the erring and simple; for these two characters a special offering was made. Perhaps the erring were too hardened and the simple too obtuse to bring an offering for themselves; but they were not forgotten... Whenever we draw around the altar of God, whether in the home or church, we should remember the erring and simple." (Meyer)

4. (21-25) The Passover offering.

"In the first *month,* **on the fourteenth day of the month, you shall observe the Passover, a feast of seven days; unleavened bread shall be**

eaten. And on that day the prince shall prepare for himself and for all the people of the land a bull *for* a sin offering. On the seven days of the feast he shall prepare a burnt offering to the Lord, seven bulls and seven rams without blemish, daily for seven days, and a kid of the goats daily *for* a sin offering. And he shall prepare a grain offering of one ephah for each bull and one ephah for each ram, together with a hin of oil for each ephah. "In the seventh *month,* on the fifteenth day of the month, at the feast, he shall do likewise for seven days, according to the sin offering, the burnt offering, the grain offering, and the oil."

a. **You shall observe the Passover**: Among the feasts celebrated at Ezekiel's future temple will be **Passover**. God's redemption of Israel from Egypt and His greater redemption through the work of Jesus on the cross will always be remembered.

b. **A feast of seven days; unleavened bread shall be eaten**: The feast of **unleavened bread** was connected with Passover and will also be celebrated.

Ezekiel 46 – Worship at Ezekiel's Future Temple

A. Worship at the temple.

1. (1-8) The prince and the offerings.

'**Thus says the Lord GOD: "The gateway of the inner court that faces toward the east shall be shut the six working days; but on the Sabbath it shall be opened, and on the day of the New Moon it shall be opened. The prince shall enter by way of the vestibule of the gateway from the outside, and stand by the gatepost. The priests shall prepare his burnt offering and his peace offerings. He shall worship at the threshold of the gate. Then he shall go out, but the gate shall not be shut until evening. Likewise the people of the land shall worship at the entrance to this gateway before the LORD on the Sabbaths and the New Moons. The burnt offering that the prince offers to the LORD on the Sabbath day** *shall be* **six lambs without blemish, and a ram without blemish; and the grain offering** *shall be one* **ephah for a ram, and the grain offering for the lambs, as much as he wants to give, as well as a hin of oil with every ephah. On the day of the New Moon** *it shall be* **a young bull without blemish, six lambs, and a ram; they shall be without blemish. He shall prepare a grain offering of an ephah for a bull, an ephah for a ram, as much as he wants to give for the lambs, and a hin of oil with every ephah. When the prince enters, he shall go in by way of the vestibule of the gateway, and go out the same way.**

a. **The gateway of the inner court that faces toward the east shall be shut six working days; but on the Sabbath it shall be opened**: At Ezekiel's future temple, the gateway to the inner court will only be opened on the **Sabbath** and special **New Moon** festivals.

i. **On the Sabbath**: "That the people may see Christ in the glass of the ceremonies, and call upon his name. We under the gospel have a clearer light and free access, on Lord's days especially, and other times of holy meetings." (Trapp)

ii. "The emphasis here is unmistakably on the Sabbath and the new moon, which alone should indicate the Jewish setting of the passage, and that we are not here on Christian or New Testament ground." (Feinberg)

iii. **And stand by the gatepost**: "The prince is to stand by the post of the gate, that is, the jamb between the vestibule and the series of guard recesses, since the inner gates were mirror images of the outer. This vantage point enables him, as guardian and patron of the cult, to observe the cultic activity of the priests." (Block)

iv. **New Moon**: "Since Israel's calendar was a lunar one, the new moon had significance for them where it has not for us. Moreover, the feasts were reckoned in relation to the phases of the moon." (Feinberg)

b. **The priests shall prepare his burnt offerings and his peace offerings**: Special offerings directed by **the prince** will be regularly offered in connection with the Sabbath.

i. "Notice here that legalizers and seventh-day observance advocates always fail to realize that the Sabbath consisted in more than just abstinence from labor on the seventh day of the week, important as that was for the commandment, but included also specific sacrifices to be offered by an authorized priest in a designated place of God's choosing. It is folly and worse to take one part of the observance and wholly discard or disregard another." (Feinberg)

c. **Likewise the people of the land shall worship at the entrance to this gateway**: Just as in previous expressions of the temple in Jerusalem, Ezekiel's temple will be a place of worship for all **the people of the land**, not only the priests.

d. **The burnt offering that the prince offers to the LORD**: Ezekiel described some of the specific sacrifices and offerings the **prince** will commission the priests to perform on his behalf and on behalf of the people.

i. "It remains only to state that the burnt offering for the Sabbath will be enlarged considerably over that of the Mosaic law (cf. v. 4 with Numbers 28:9)." (Feinberg)

2. (9-11) Feast days and festivals.

"But when the people of the land come before the LORD on the appointed feast days, whoever enters by way of the north gate to worship shall go out by way of the south gate; and whoever enters by way of the south

gate shall go out by way of the north gate. He shall not return by way of the gate through which he came, but shall go out through the opposite gate. The prince shall then be in their midst. When they go in, he shall go in; and when they go out, he shall go out. At the festivals and the appointed feast days the grain offering shall be an ephah for a bull, an ephah for a ram, as much as he wants to give for the lambs, and a hin of oil with every ephah.

a. **Whoever enters by way of the north gate to worship shall go out by way of the south gate**: There will be an established flow of traffic for **the people of the land** as they come to worship at Ezekiel's future temple.

i. "Ezekiel's vision of hundreds of thousands of people thronging the temple courts 'before Yahweh' on the prescribed festival days would have been a logistical nightmare, which this ordinance sought to manage." (Block)

b. **The prince shall be in their midst**: God's appointed ruler for Israel in the millennium will be a leader truly *among* the people. He will be **in their midst. When they go in, he shall go in; and when they go out, he shall go out.**

i. "The prince will not isolate himself from the people on the feast days but be a part of the crowd." (Wiersbe)

ii. In this prince, Meyer saw an illustration of the work of Jesus for His people. "He never puts His sheep forth without going before them. He never thrusts us into the fight without preceding us. If we have to take the way of the Cross, we may always count on seeing Him go first, though we follow Him amazed."

3. (12) The prince and the east gate.

"Now when the prince makes a voluntary burnt offering or voluntary peace offering to the LORD, the gate that faces toward the east shall then be opened for him; and he shall prepare his burnt offering and his peace offerings as he did on the Sabbath day. Then he shall go out, and after he goes out the gate shall be shut.

a. **The gate that faces toward the east shall then be opened for him**: At special **voluntary burnt offerings or voluntary peace offerings**, God's appointed leader for Israel in the millennium will use the **east** gate.

i. "If the prince desired to make a freewill offering of a burnt offering of consecration or a fellowship offering of thanksgiving, the east gate was to be opened specially for this act of worship and then closed when he finished." (Alexander)

b. **Then he shall go out, and after he goes out the gate shall be shut**: Each specific detail gives more and more evidence that this is meant for some *literal* fulfillment. The details are meaningless in a merely spiritualized fulfillment. We may not be able to understand what each individual detail means or how it will be fulfilled, but we can trust that it will be.

i. John Trapp saw in this verse a ground for week-day Bible studies: "Here is warrant for our week day lectures, a voluntary service well accepted; provided that afterwards one shut the gate, and men return to their honest labours."

4. (13-15) The daily burnt offerings.

"You shall daily make a burnt offering to the LORD of a lamb of the first year without blemish; you shall prepare it every morning. And you shall prepare a grain offering with it every morning, a sixth of an ephah, and a third of a hin of oil to moisten the fine flour. This grain offering is a perpetual ordinance, to be made regularly to the LORD. Thus they shall prepare the lamb, the grain offering, and the oil, *as* a regular burnt offering every morning."

a. **You shall daily make a burnt offering to the LORD**: In Ezekiel's future temple, there will be daily offerings to remember and memorialize the perfect work of Jesus' sacrifice at the cross.

i. "In this day of restoration, the ceremonial offerings are observed, with this difference, that until Christ came they were prophetic and anticipatory, whereas now they are memorial." (Morgan)

b. **A perpetual ordinance, to be made regularly to the LORD**: The custom of the daily offering will continue through the entire period of the future millennium.

i. "This verse is a ratifying of all prescribed in Ezekiel 46:13-14. These three verses direct the daily sacrifice; and because they mention only the morning sacrifice and one lamb, some think that here less is required than in Numbers 28:3-4; but they forget that there is a parity of reason for the evening sacrifice, and that this is included. They were to do in the evening oblation as they did in the morning." (Poole)

B. Inheritance and offerings.

1. (16-18) Inheritance given to sons and to servants.

'Thus says the Lord GOD: "If the prince gives a gift *of some* of his inheritance to any of his sons, it shall belong to his sons; it is their possession by inheritance. But if he gives a gift of some of his inheritance to one of his servants, it shall be his until the year of liberty, after which

it shall return to the prince. But his inheritance shall belong to his sons; it shall become theirs. Moreover the prince shall not take any of the people's inheritance by evicting them from their property; he shall provide an inheritance for his sons from his own property, so that none of My people may be scattered from his property.""

a. **If the prince gives a gift of some of his inheritance to any of his sons, it shall belong to his sons; it is their possession by inheritance**: In the millennial period associated with Ezekiel's temple, the appointed **prince** will be able to grant an **inheritance** to his sons. Yet if he were to give **some of his inheritance to one of his servants**, it would be a gift until the year of jubilee (**the year of liberty**).

i. **To any of his sons**: "The prince will be a married man and will have sons who can inherit his land (Ezekiel 46:16–18)." (Wiersbe)

ii. **The year of liberty**: "That is, to the year of *jubilee*, called the *year of liberty*, because there was then a general release. All servants had their liberty, and all alienated estates returned to their former owners." (Clarke)

b. **The prince shall not take any of the people's inheritance by evicting them from their property**: God's appointed **prince** will not abuse or oppress the people. Israel will receive righteous leadership throughout the millennial period.

i. "The prophet did not want royal property to grow at the expense of ordinary citizens. Ezekiel specifically forbids the prince from giving the property of citizens to his family and friends. If the prince wishes to make a gift of land to anyone, that land must come from his own holdings." (Vawter and Hoppe)

2. (19-20) The place offerings were prepared.

Now he brought me through the entrance, which *was* at the side of the gate, into the holy chambers of the priests which face toward the north; and there a place *was* situated at their extreme western end. And he said to me, "This *is* the place where the priests shall boil the trespass offering and the sin offering, *and* where they shall bake the grain offering, so that they do not bring *them* out into the outer court to sanctify the people."

a. **Now he brought me through the entrance**: It isn't entirely clear who **brought** Ezekiel to the temple entrance. Perhaps it was the radiant man of Ezekiel 40:1-3.

b. **This is the place where the priests shall boil the trespass offering**: Ezekiel was led to the place where the sacrifices will be prepared.

3. (21-24) The kitchens of the temple.

Then he brought me out into the outer court and caused me to pass by the four corners of the court; and in fact, in every corner of the court *there was another* court. In the four corners of the court *were* enclosed courts, forty *cubits* long and thirty wide; all four corners *were* the same size. *There was* a row *of building stones* all around in them, all around the four of them; and cooking hearths were made under the rows of stones all around. And he said to me, "These *are* the kitchens where the ministers of the temple shall boil the sacrifices of the people."

a. **In every corner of the court there was another court**: The layout of what Ezekiel saw may be difficult to picture, but the clear sense is of generous space for all the business of the temple.

b. **These are the kitchens**: There were specific places for the preparation of the sacrificial meals associated with the **sacrifices of the people**. The sacrificial meals were an important part of the offerings made, an act of fellowship not only among men, but also symbolically between God and man.

i. "Although only the northern kitchen is reported, the symmetry of the overall structure suggests that a counterpart also existed on the south side." (Block)

ii. "This feature of Israelite worship shows how concretely the people expressed their belief that God has made provision for the most basic of bodily needs: the need for food. It also symbolizes the union between God and Israel. The worship that went on in the temple was not confined to word and gesture. It included the eating and the experience of fellowship that comes from sharing a meal." (Vawter and Hoppe)

iii. "So the temple was a place for sacrificing, cooking and eating, as well as for prayer and so-called 'spiritual' activities. The Christian church has been the poorer when it has drawn a firm dividing line between spiritual life and social activities. In Ezekiel's temple, at any rate, there was envisaged a healthy fusion of the two elements, and this was typical of much in Old Testament worship." (Taylor)

Ezekiel 47 – The River of Life

A. The river from the temple.

1. (1-2) The river's source: the temple.

Then he brought me back to the door of the temple; and there was water, flowing from under the threshold of the temple toward the east, for the front of the temple faced east; the water was flowing from under the right side of the temple, south of the altar. He brought me out by way of the north gate, and led me around on the outside to the outer gateway that faces east; and there was water, running out on the right side.

a. **There was water, flowing from under the threshold of the temple**: Led back to the **door of the temple** (presumably by the radiant man of Ezekiel 40:3), Ezekiel saw something that never existed in the temple before: a river **flowing** directly from the temple.

i. "Ezekiel uses this imagery to affirm that the new temple, like the old, will be a font of blessing for Israel." (Vawter and Hoppe)

ii. Significantly, the river does not come from a king's palace or a government building. It doesn't come from a marketplace, a place of business, or an athletic arena. It comes from God's house.

b. **There was water, running out on the right side**: In all of its recorded history, Jerusalem never had such a river. There were streams and springs, but never a rich, mighty river, and never one flowing from this part of the city. In the semi-arid geography of Israel a river like this was both a blessing and a miracle. It brought life, growth, vitality, refreshment, hope, and security.

i. "Blessing, fertility and water are almost interchangeable ideas in the Old Testament" (Taylor). We think of the beauty of Psalm 46:4: *There is a river whose streams shall make glad the city of God.*

ii. "Jerusalem is the only great city of the ancient world that wasn't located on a river, and in the east, a dependable water supply is essential for life and for defense. During the Kingdom Age, Jerusalem shall have a river such as no other nation ever had." (Wiersbe)

iii. **Running out on the right side**: "The waters seem to have been at first *in small quantity*; for the words imply that they *oozed* or *dropped out*. They were at first so small that they came, *drop by drop*; but they increased." (Clarke)

iv. "We have reminders that flowing streams are parables of the flowing life of God (e.g. Psalm 42:1; Jeremiah 2:13; John 4:10-15)." (Wright)

v. Trapp gave a typical spiritualized explanation of this river: "The gospel of grace, and the gifts of the Holy Ghost thereby conveyed into the hearts of believers, and poured out upon the world by the death of Christ."

vi. Though such a river has symbolic meaning, we should not miss the plain promises of such a river in the coming kingdom of the Messiah.

- *A fountain shall flow from the house of the LORD* (Joel 3:18).
- *And in that day it shall be – that living waters shall flow from Jerusalem* (Zechariah 14:8).

vii. John mentioned a *similar* river relevant to the eternal state in Revelation, but it isn't the same as this river. "The variance between Ezekiel's account of this river and that of John in the Revelation centers on the river's source. God is the source of both rivers; but Ezekiel saw the river issuing from the temple, whereas John saw the river coming from the throne of God and of the Lamb (a temple not existing according to Revelation 21:22)." (Alexander)

2. (3-5) The river's increasing depth.

And when the man went out to the east with the line in his hand, he measured one thousand cubits, and he brought me through the waters; the water *came up to my* ankles. Again he measured one thousand and brought me through the waters; the water *came up to my* knees. Again he measured one thousand and brought me through; the water *came up to my* waist. Again he measured one thousand, *and it was* a river that I could not cross; for the water was too deep, water in which one must swim, a river that could not be crossed. He said to me, "Son of man, have you seen *this?*" Then he brought me and returned me to the bank of the river.

a. **When the man went out to the east with the line in his hand**: Ezekiel's unnamed guide followed the course of the river as it flowed **out to the east**. He followed the river **one thousand cubits** (about one-third of a mile or one-half a kilometer) from some point, perhaps its origin from the temple.

b. **He brought me through the waters**: Together with the unnamed guide, Ezekiel went into and **through the waters**. The river was not something for Ezekiel to simply look at or think about; it was something for him to enter into.

c. **The water came up to my ankles**: At the measured distance (**one thousand cubits**), the river was as deep as Ezekiel's ankles. It wasn't very deep, but Ezekiel was in it as much as he could be, experiencing all the depth the river had at that point.

i. The phrase, **the water came up to my ankles**, is literally *water of ankles*. Taylor relates how this led to a bad translation and bad theology: "So strange did this phrase seem to the lxx translator that he virtually transliterated it and made 'water of remission,' with the result that many early Christian commentators applied this symbolism to the waters of baptism. A warning to both translators and interpreters!"

d. **Again he measured one thousand and brought me through the waters**: Ezekiel's guide continued eastward with the flow of the river, and he **brought** Ezekiel with him along the way. This continued for four measures of **one thousand** cubits in total.

e. **The water came up to my knees... up to my waist**: As Ezekiel continued, the river became deeper at each measuring point. Starting at ankle depth, then up to his **knees**, then his **waist**. At each point along the way, Ezekiel was in the river as deep as he could be. He didn't artificially sink himself into the river, but his experience matched the actual depth of the river.

i. This rapid increase in depth – from a small trickle of a stream to ankle depth, to knee depth, to waist depth, all in the course of about a mile (or 1.5 kilometers) – is *miraculous*. We read nothing of other streams leading into this; it is a miraculous and abundant provision.

ii. "Why was it necessary to bring Ezekiel through the waters in vision? The purpose was to reveal to him both the size and depth of the river. The trickle (the literal of 'ran out' of v. 2 is 'trickled forth') had become a veritable river during the measuring activity of the man in the vision." (Feinberg)

f. **It was a river that I could not cross; for the water was too deep**: The rapid increase of the river's depth and power showed what a mighty river this was. It soon came to the point where the water was over Ezekiel's head, and all he could do was **swim**.

i. Fundamentally, this shows us the miraculous nature of a real river in a real Messianic kingdom to come. Yet by spiritual analogy, there is a powerful picture of increasing progress and depth in our spiritual life. It illustrates a progression from ankles, to knees, to waist, to depths where one can no longer touch the ground and must swim. God's people read this and feel a call to *go deeper*. They shouldn't stop until they are *swimming*, carried along by God's currents and comfortable in that place.

ii. "We need the ankle-depths of walking to be exchanged for the knee-depths of praying; and these for the loin-depths of perfect purity; and these for the length, depth, breadth, and height of the love of Christ." (Meyer)

iii. Spurgeon saw a spiritual analogy between the life of faith and swimming. We start out "floating in faith," somewhat passively, just keeping our head up out of the water. We then progress to swimming by faith. "How blessedly our friend Mr. Mueller of Bristol swims! What a master swimmer he is! He has had his feet off the bottom many years and as he swims he draws along behind him some 2,000 orphan children, whom, by God's grace, he is saving from the floods of sin and bringing, we trust, safe to shore." (Spurgeon)

iv. Many commentators and preachers through the centuries have seen the increasing depth of this river to be an illustration of the great depths of God's word. "Scriptures have their shallows wherein the lamb may wade, like as they have their profundities wherein the elephant himself may swim. Augustine condemned the Holy Scriptures at first, as neither eloquent nor deep enough for the elevation of his wit. But afterwards, when he was both a better and a wiser man, he saw his own shallowness, and admired the never enough adored depth of God's holy oracles." (Trapp)

g. **He brought me and returned me to the bank of the river**: When it was clear that the water was too deep for Ezekiel and he **could not cross** it, then his guide brought him out of the river and back to the **bank**. He asked Ezekiel to carefully think about what he saw and experienced (**have you seen this?**).

3. (6-12) The power of the river.

When I returned, there, along the bank of the river, *were* very many trees on one side and the other. Then he said to me: "This water flows

toward the eastern region, goes down into the valley, and enters the sea. *When it* reaches the sea, *its* waters are healed. And it shall be *that* every living thing that moves, wherever the rivers go, will live. There will be a very great multitude of fish, because these waters go there; for they will be healed, and everything will live wherever the river goes. It shall be *that* fishermen will stand by it from En Gedi to En Eglaim; they will be *places* for spreading their nets. Their fish will be of the same kinds as the fish of the Great Sea, exceedingly many. But its swamps and marshes will not be healed; they will be given over to salt. Along the bank of the river, on this side and that, will grow all *kinds of* trees used for food; their leaves will not wither, and their fruit will not fail. They will bear fruit every month, because their water flows from the sanctuary. Their fruit will be for food, and their leaves for medicine."

a. **Many trees on one side and the other**: Once out of the river Ezekiel noticed the **many trees**. They grew along both sides of the river.

i. "The deepest valley rift in the world is the Arabah in the Holy Land. The waters of the river will flow east through the Arabah into the Dead Sea." (Feinberg)

b. **When it reaches the sea, its waters are healed**: Ezekiel's guide described the miraculous properties of this river. As the river flowed out from Jerusalem then down into the Dead Sea, those lifeless waters were **healed**. There would be a **very great multitude of fish** in that strange body of water that previously held no life. This can and will be fulfilled both literally in a coming kingdom age and is also a fitting symbol of God's present work through the gospel.

i. There is also an obvious but possibly overlooked point here: God cares about the environment and promises to restore and heal it. Despite the many who worship the creation instead of the Creator, God Himself cares about His creation. His salvation and work of redemption extend to the environment.

ii. "Its waters are miraculously *healed, rapa* normally refers to the healing of a diseased body, but in this case the miracle involves neutralizing the baneful chemicals in the water, so it becomes fresh." (Block)

iii. Jesus may very well have had this image of Ezekiel in mind (or a similar one) when He spoke of rivers of living water (John 7:37-38). There is a valid spiritual application of this wonderful image, *and* a literal fulfillment to come.

iv. Yet many commentators unfortunately feel comfortable ignoring any future literal fulfillment of this and see it only as a visionary parable.

"This sea is the wide world dead in sins and trespasses. [Ephesians 2:1] These fishers are Christ's apostles and ministers, who are called fishers of men, [Matthew 4:19] and their preaching compared to fishing." (Trapp)

c. **Its swamps and marshes will not be healed; they will be given over to salt**: There will remain certain areas near the former Dead Sea that will keep their old characteristics. Perhaps this is so that the useful minerals gained from the Dead Sea would still be available from these places.

i. "The preservation of some pockets of saltiness is intentional, recognizing the economic benefit of the minerals found in and around the Dead Sea. *Salt* (*melah*) is not only a valuable seasoning and preserving agent; the word functions generically for a wide range of chemicals extracted from the sea." (Block)

ii. As an example of an overly-spiritualized approach to this passage, consider how Clarke thought of the **swamps** and **marshes** of verse 11: "A description applicable to the Roman Catholic Church, that is both schismatic and heretic from the Church of Jesus Christ, which is built on the *foundation of the prophets and apostles, Jesus himself being the chief corner stone*; for the Church of Rome, leaving this foundation, is now built on the foundation of councils and traditions, and lying miracles; the popes in their succession being its only corner stones."

d. **Will grow all kinds of trees used for food**: Along the sides of the river, there were remarkable fruit trees with **leaves** that **will not wither** and **fruit** that will never **fail**. In some unknown way, **their leaves** will be used **for medicine**.

i. Matthew Poole had an unfounded and interesting speculation: "These trees most likely were palmetto trees, whence the balm that healeth, the fruit that feedeth, and juice that refresheth, and allays our thirst."

B. The borders of the land.

1. (13-14) The promise of the land, and two portions for Joseph.

Thus says the Lord GOD: "These *are* the borders by which you shall divide the land as an inheritance among the twelve tribes of Israel. Joseph *shall have two* portions. You shall inherit it equally with one another; for I raised My hand in an oath to give it to your fathers, and this land shall fall to you as your inheritance.

a. **These are the borders by which you shall divide the land**: This emphasizes that this was not a symbolic or spiritual land, God gave specific

borders to mark it. There will be real land that will be given to the real **twelve tribes of Israel**.

i. These are all **twelve tribes**. "Although the nation had been divided politically for nearly four hundred years, as in the case of all his prophetic colleagues Ezekiel's vision of Israel's future is based on the tradition of a united nation consisting of twelve tribes of Israel descended from Jacob's twelve sons." (Block)

ii. "The boundaries are substantially those originally given to Moses in Numbers 34:1-15. In Numbers the southern boundary is given first; here the reckoning is from the north." (Feinberg)

b. **Joseph shall have two portions**: As was with the division of the land under Joshua, the two sons of Joseph (Ephraim and Manasseh) would each have their portion.

c. **I raised My hand in an oath to give it to your fathers, and this land shall fall to you**: Again, God emphasized that this was a real land that would continue and fulfill the promises of a real land to Israel's patriarchs. God made these promises to:

- Abraham in Genesis 13:15 and 15:18.
- Isaac in Genesis 26:3.
- Jacob in Genesis 28:13.

i. This granting of the land in the millennial kingdom will be an extension and a fulfillment of those long ago and often repeated promises.

2. (15-20) The borders of the land on every side.

"This *shall be* **the border of the land on the north: from the Great Sea,** *by* **the road to Hethlon, as one goes to Zedad, Hamath, Berothah, Sibraim (which** *is* **between the border of Damascus and the border of Hamath), to Hazar Hatticon (which** *is* **on the border of Hauran). Thus the boundary shall be from the Sea to Hazar Enan, the border of Damascus; and as for the north, northward, it is the border of Hamath.** *This is* **the north side.**

"On the east side you shall mark out the border from between Hauran and Damascus, and between Gilead and the land of Israel, along the Jordan, and along the eastern side of the sea. *This is* **the east side.**

"The south side, toward the South, *shall be* **from Tamar to the waters of Meribah by Kadesh, along the brook to the Great Sea.** *This is* **the south side, toward the South.**

"The west side *shall be* the Great Sea, from the *southern* boundary until one comes to a point opposite Hamath. This *is* the west side.

a. **This shall be the border of the land**: Using landmarks on the north, east, south, and west, God described the borders of Israel in the period of Ezekiel's temple, a period regarded as the millennial reign of Jesus Messiah.

i. "This is the area which God swore to give to the nation (14, cf. Genesis 15:18-21; Numbers 34:1-12), and which was ruled by Solomon (1 Kings 4:24)." (Wright)

ii. In his commentary, Daniel Block has a very good map. As he envisions it, if these borders were put upon a modern map it would include all of Lebanon and a good portion of Syria (including Damascus). It would *not* include modern Jordan or Egypt, and *not* extend southward to modern Eilat.

iii. "Only twice in Israel's history did the political borders of Israel extend as far north as Lebo-hamath: under David and under Jeroboam II (2 Kings 14:25)." (Block)

b. **From the Great Sea, by the road to Hethlon**: Many landmarks are listed, but we believe that since the geography of this part of the world will be significantly transformed right before this period begins, it is impossible to exactly establish what these places will mark in the coming age. In *general*, we can say that it is an area somewhat larger than the land Israel occupied in the Old Testament.

i. The description shows that this is *not* the eternal state. "The western boundary was the Great Sea (v.20; cf. Numbers 34:6). In contrast the land of God's people in the eternal state will have no sea since the sea will no longer exist (Revelation 21:1)." (Alexander)

3. (21-23) The command to divide the land.

"Thus you shall divide this land among yourselves according to the tribes of Israel. It shall be that you will divide it by lot as an inheritance for yourselves, and for the strangers who dwell among you and who bear children among you. They shall be to you as native-born among the children of Israel; they shall have an inheritance with you among the tribes of Israel. And it shall be *that* in whatever tribe the stranger dwells, there you shall give *him* his inheritance," says the Lord God.

a. **Thus you shall divide this land**: The repeated commands to **divide** the land indicate that this is a real land, not a spiritual representation. The best way to understand this is that this division of the land is yet to come, but will come in a kingdom period when the world is ruled in a direct way by Jesus Messiah.

i. **You will divide it by lot**: The general allotments of land were assigned to each tribe. Within each tribal allotment, particular portions of land would be assigned to families **by lot**.

b. **And for the strangers who dwell among you**: The land God promised to Israel in this kingdom period would not be for Israelites alone. There would be people from other lands and ethnic groups (**strangers**) living there also. By God's command, these were to be treated **as native-born among the children of Israel**. They would even have **inheritance** rights.

i. "The Pentateuch prescribes humane treatment for the aliens living in Israel (cf. Exodus 22:21; 23:9; Leviticus 19:10, 33–34; 23:22; Deuteronomy 14:29; 24:14–15, 17–22). Such treatment is a moral obligation that derives from Israel's experience as aliens in Egypt. Ezekiel goes far beyond the Torah's legislation." (Vawter and Hoppe)

ii. "It is based on the principle that if these men choose to accept the standards, the religion and the way of life within Israel as a permanency, i.e. as proselytes who settle and have children there (verse 22), then they are entitled to the same treatment as native Israelites." (Taylor)

Ezekiel 48 – "The LORD is There"

A. The division of the land.

1. (1-8) The seven northern tribes.

"Now these *are* the names of the tribes: From the northern border along the road to Hethlon at the entrance of Hamath, to Hazar Enan, the border of Damascus northward, in the direction of Hamath, *there shall be* one *section for* Dan from its east to its west side; by the border of Dan, from the east side to the west, one *section for* Asher; by the border of Asher, from the east side to the west, one *section for* Naphtali; by the border of Naphtali, from the east side to the west, one *section for* Manasseh; by the border of Manasseh, from the east side to the west, one *section for* Ephraim; by the border of Ephraim, from the east side to the west, one *section for* Reuben; by the border of Reuben, from the east side to the west, one *section for* Judah; by the border of Judah, from the east side to the west, shall be the district which you shall set apart, twenty-five thousand *cubits* in width, and *in* length the same as one of the *other* portions, from the east side to the west, with the sanctuary in the center.

a. **These are the names of the tribes**: Here God listed the seven tribes of Israel that will have a share of the northern portion of land in the coming kingdom period. For a visual representation, the reader is recommended to consult commentaries or other searchable maps and diagrams.

b. **There shall be one section for Dan**: It seems that the land was apportioned from north to south in bands or layers. One notable difference is that there is no land occupied on the east side of the Jordan River where the three Transjordan tribes (Reuben, Gad, and half of Manasseh) formerly had land.

i. **For Dan**: Curiously, Dan is omitted in a listing of the tribes regarding the 144,000 in Revelation 7. Many think it was because Dan was the first tribe to embrace idolatry (Genesis 49:16-17 and Judges 17-18). Now, as a demonstration of God's great grace, not only is **Dan** included, they are listed *first*.

ii. **For Judah**: "It is immediately evident that Judah and Benjamin, the tribes which remained faithful to the Davidic dynasty, will be honored by proximity to the center of the millennial kingdom." (Feinberg)

2. (9-12) The district of the LORD.

"The district that you shall set apart for the LORD shall be twenty-five thousand *cubits* in length and ten thousand in width. To these—to the priests—the holy district shall belong: on the north twenty-five thousand *cubits in length*, on the west ten thousand in width, on the east ten thousand in width, and on the south twenty-five thousand in length. The sanctuary of the LORD shall be in the center. *It shall be* **for the priests of the sons of Zadok, who are sanctified, who have kept My charge, who did not go astray when the children of Israel went astray, as the Levites went astray. And** *this* **district of land that is set apart shall be to them a thing most holy by the border of the Levites.**

a. **The district that you shall set apart for the LORD**: As previously described in Ezekiel 45:1-6, this is an area that *Israel* will **set apart for the LORD**. It contains the temple described in Ezekiel 40-43, with **the sanctuary of the LORD** in **the center**.

b. **It shall be for the priests**: This will be a district set aside for the LORD, that He in turn provides for His priests.

3. (13-14) The area for the Levites.

"Opposite the border of the priests, the Levites *shall have an area* **twenty-five thousand** *cubits* **in length and ten thousand in width; its entire length** *shall be* **twenty-five thousand and its width ten thousand. And they shall not sell or exchange any of it; they may not alienate this best** *part* **of the land, for** *it is* **holy to the LORD.**

a. **The Levites shall have an area**: Bordering the area of the priests will be land God has set aside for the Levites, who would serve at the temple to support and assist the work of the priests.

b. **It is holy to the LORD**: The land will remain God's set-apart possession; therefore the Levites will not be permitted to **sell or exchange any of it**.

4. (15-20) The land apportioned for the city.

"The five thousand *cubits* **in width that remain, along the edge of the twenty-five thousand, shall be for general use by the city, for dwellings and common-land; and the city shall be in the center. These** *shall be* **its**

measurements: the north side four thousand five hundred *cubits*, the south side four thousand five hundred, the east side four thousand five hundred, and the west side four thousand five hundred. The common-land of the city shall be: to the north two hundred and fifty *cubits*, to the south two hundred and fifty, to the east two hundred and fifty, and to the west two hundred and fifty. The rest of the length, alongside the district of the holy *section, shall be* ten thousand *cubits* to the east and ten thousand to the west. It shall be adjacent to the district of the holy *section*, and its produce shall be food for the workers of the city. The workers of the city, from all the tribes of Israel, shall cultivate it. The entire district *shall be* twenty-five thousand *cubits* by twenty-five thousand *cubits*, foursquare. You shall set apart the holy district with the property of the city.

a. **Shall be for general use by the city**: Here God apportioned land for Jerusalem in the kingdom period. It included land **for dwellings and common-land**.

i. "The city is about a mile and a half square (16), with an open space on each side (17), and land for cultivation to the east and west (18,19)." (Wright)

ii. "Notice once again the great minuteness of detail. This is more than strange, it is inexplicable, if all the statements are to be taken symbolically. As far as we are aware, no such abundance of details occurs anywhere else in Scripture outside the instructions for the construction of the tabernacle and its priestly service, which no orthodox expositor feels called upon to interpret other than with strict literalness. Then it is only consistent to do the same here." (Feinberg)

b. **Its produce shall be food for the workers of the city**: There would be land for farms and gardens bringing **food** to the people and workers of the city.

5. (21-22) The portion for the prince.

"The rest *shall belong* to the prince, on one side and on the other of the holy district and of the city's property, next to the twenty-five thousand *cubits* of the *holy* district as far as the eastern border, and westward next to the twenty-five thousand as far as the western border, adjacent to the *tribal* portions; *it shall belong* to the prince. It shall be the holy district, and the sanctuary of the temple *shall be* in the center. Moreover, apart from the possession of the Levites and the possession of the city *which are* in the midst of what *belongs* to the prince, *the area* between the border of Judah and the border of Benjamin shall belong to the prince.

a. **The rest shall belong to the prince**: As previously described in Ezekiel 45:7-8, there will be land set aside for the Messiah's appointed ruler, **the prince**.

b. **The area between the border of Judah and the border of Benjamin shall belong to the prince**: There will be additional lands that would be given to the prince.

6. (23-29) The five southern tribes.

"As for the rest of the tribes, from the east side to the west, Benjamin *shall have* **one** *section;* **by the border of Benjamin, from the east side to the west, Simeon** *shall have* **one** *section;* **by the border of Simeon, from the east side to the west, Issachar** *shall have* **one** *section;* **by the border of Issachar, from the east side to the west, Zebulun** *shall have* **one** *section;* **by the border of Zebulun, from the east side to the west, Gad** *shall have* **one** *section;* **by the border of Gad, on the south side, toward the South, the border shall be from Tamar** *to* **the waters of Meribah** *by* **Kadesh, along the brook to the Great Sea. This** *is* **the land which you shall divide by lot as an inheritance among the tribes of Israel, and these** *are* **their portions," says the Lord G**OD**.**

a. **As for the rest of the tribes**: After listing the land allotments for the seven tribes north of the LORD's district (Ezekiel 48:1-8), now the list continues with the land allotments for the tribes to the south of the LORD's district.

b. **This is the land which you shall divide by lot as an inheritance**: Each of the tribes would be restored to the land and none of them will be forgotten before God.

B. The city: Yahweh Shammah.

1. (30-34) The gates of the city.

"These *are* **the exits of the city. On the north side, measuring four thousand five hundred** *cubits* **(the gates of the city** *shall be* **named after the tribes of Israel), the three gates northward: one gate for Reuben, one gate for Judah, and one gate for Levi; on the east side, four thousand five hundred** *cubits***, three gates: one gate for Joseph, one gate for Benjamin, and one gate for Dan; on the south side, measuring four thousand five hundred** *cubits***, three gates: one gate for Simeon, one gate for Issachar, and one gate for Zebulun; on the west side, four thousand five hundred** *cubits* **with their three gates: one gate for Gad, one gate for Asher, and one gate for Naphtali.**

a. **These are the gates of the city**: The city – Jerusalem in the Messiah's kingdom to come – will have memorial gates for each tribe.

i. "The image of a city with twelve gates distributed equally among the four sides and named after the twelve tribes of Israel is strikingly unconventional. City walls were usually designed intentionally with only one gate." (Block)

ii. The twelve gates "beautifully symbolizes at the same time in visible form the unity and harmony in the nation so long divided. All the ancient rivalries, contentions and jealousies will be gone, and blessed unity will prevail." (Feinberg)

iii. All this is suggestive of, but not the same as, the eternal state as described in Revelation 21:12-14. "The whole passage leads us to compare Revelation 21, with its description of a new heaven and a new earth and the vision of the new Jerusalem coming down out of heaven from God. It too had twelve gates, named after the twelve tribes of Israel, but it also had twelve foundations inscribed with the names of the twelve apostles of the Lamb." (Taylor)

b. **One gate for Joseph**: This list of the tribes follows the pattern of the 12 direct sons of Jacob/Israel. Joseph is one tribe, not two.

2. (35) The name of the city.

All the way around *shall be* **eighteen thousand** *cubits;* **and the name of the city from** *that* **day** *shall be:* **THE LORD IS THERE."**

a. **All the way around shall be eighteen thousand cubits**: Once more, an actual measurement gives a literal and not a symbolic sense.

i. "This will be a 'kingdom Jerusalem,' a new city for the new nation and the new era." (Wiersbe)

ii. "The measurement of 18,000 reeds calls for a circumference somewhat less than six miles. Jerusalem in Josephus' day (first century, A.D.) was about four miles." (Feinberg)

b. **THE LORD IS THERE**: Throughout the larger section of Ezekiel 40-48, the name of the city of Jerusalem is never specifically mentioned. Here we discover why; God will give the city a new name. It will be known as *Yahweh Shammah*, "Yahweh is There." In that day, the overwhelming character and idea of Jerusalem would be that *God was there*.

i. Ezekiel experienced the horror of seeing the glory of God departing from the temple in a vision (Ezekiel 11). Then he saw it return (Ezekiel 43:5). Now, in the new name for the city, he received the assurance that God would *remain*.

ii. "We bethink us of the truth that there is to be a millennial age — a time of glory, and peace, and joy, and truth, and righteousness. But what is to be the glory of it? Why this, 'Jehovah-shammah, the Lord is there!'" (Spurgeon)

iii. The principle will carry on into the eternal state. *And I heard a loud voice from heaven saying, Behold, the tabernacle of God is with men, and He will dwell with them, and they shall be His people. God Himself will be with them and be their God.* (Revelation 21:3)

iv. Wiersbe explains: "This is one of seven compound names of Jehovah found in the Old Testament."

- Jehovah Jireh—'the LORD will provide' (Genesis 22:13–14).
- Jehovah Rapha—'the LORD who heals' (Exodus 15:26).
- Jehovah Shalom—'the LORD our peace' (Judges 6:24).
- Jehovah Tsidkenu—'the LORD our righteousness' (Jeremiah 23:6).
- Jehovah Shammah—'the LORD is present' (Ezekiel 48:35).
- Jehovah Nissi—'the LORD our banner' (Exodus 17:8–15).
- Jehovah Ra'ah—'the LORD our shepherd' (Psalm 23:1).

v. "The name tells of complete satisfaction; that of God, and that of man. God is at rest among His people, His original purpose realised. Man is seen at rest in God, his true destiny reached." (Morgan)

Bibliography

Alexander, Ralph H. *The Expositor's Bible Commentary, Volume 6 "Ezekiel"* (Grand Rapids, Michigan: Zondervan,1986)

Block, Daniel I. *The Book of Ezekiel, Chapters 1-24* (Grand Rapids, Michigan: Eerdmans, 1997)

Block, Daniel I. *The Book of Ezekiel, Chapters 25-48* (Grand Rapids, Michigan: Eerdmans, 1997)

Clarke, Adam *The Holy Bible, Containing the Old and New Testaments, with A Commentary and Critical Notes, Volume IV – Isaiah to Malachi* (New York: Eaton and Mains, 1827?)

Feinberg, Charles L. *The Prophecy of Ezekiel.* (Chicago, Illinois: Moody Press, 1969)

Keil, Carl Friedrich and Delitzsch, Franz *Commentary on the Old Testament, Volume 9* (Peabody, Massachusetts: Hendrickson, 1996).

McGee, J. Vernon *Ezekiel* (Nashville, Tennessee: Thomas Nelson, 1991)

Meyer, F.B. *Our Daily Homily* (Westwood, New Jersey: Revell, 1966)

Morgan, G. Campbell *Searchlights from the Word* (New York: Revell, 1926)

Morgan, G. Campbell *An Exposition of the Whole Bible* (Old Tappan, New Jersey: Revell, 1959)

Poole, Matthew *A Commentary on the Holy Bible, Volume 2* (London: The Banner of Truth Trust, 1968)

Smith, James E. *The Major Prophets* (Joplin, Missouri: College Press, 1995)

Spurgeon, Charles Haddon *The New Park Street Pulpit, Volumes 1-6* and *The Metropolitan Tabernacle Pulpit, Volumes 7-63* (Pasadena, Texas: Pilgrim Publications, 1990)

Taylor, John B. *Ezekiel, an Introduction and Commentary* (Nottingham, England: Inter-Varsity Press, 1969)

Vawter, Bruce and Hoppe, Leslie J. *A New Heart – A Commentary on the Book of Ezekiel* (Grand Rapids, Michigan: Eerdmans, 1991)

Wiersbe, Warren W. *Be Reverent* (Colorado Springs, Colorado: Victor, 1990)

Wright, Reverent J. Stafford "Ezekiel" *Daily Bible Commentary, Psalms-Malachi* (London: Scripture Union, 1973)

Author's Remarks

As the years pass, I love the work of studying, learning, and teaching the Bible more than ever. I'm so grateful that God is faithful to meet me in His Word.

Once again, I am tremendously grateful to Alison Turner for her proofreading and editorial suggestions, especially with a challenging manuscript. Alison, thank you so much!

Thanks to Brian Procedo for the cover design and the graphics work.

Most especially, thanks to my wife Inga-Lill. She is my loved and valued partner in life and in service to God and His people.

David Guzik

David Guzik's Bible commentary is regularly used and trusted by many thousands who want to know the Bible better. Pastors, teachers, class leaders, and everyday Christians find his commentary helpful for their own understanding and explanation of the Bible. David and his wife Inga-Lill live in Santa Barbara, California.

You can email David at
david@enduringword.com

For more resources by David Guzik,
go to www.enduringword.com

CPSIA information can be obtained
at www.ICGtesting.com
Printed in the USA
LVHW021617230322
714168LV00001B/15